THE BRITISH EMPIRE

THE BRITISH EMPIRE
ITS STRUCTURE AND SPIRIT
1497–1953

by

ERIC A. WALKER

FELLOW OF ST. JOHN'S COLLEGE AND EMERITUS VERE HARMSWORTH PROFESSOR
OF IMPERIAL AND NAVAL HISTORY IN THE UNIVERSITY OF CAMBRIDGE

Second and Extended Edition

BOWES & BOWES

First edition published by the Oxford University Press February 1943
Second Impression   April 1944
Third Impression November 1944
Fourth Impression   1946
Second and extended edition published by Bowes & Bowes
Publishers Ltd. Cambridge 1953

Printed in Great Britain for BOWES & BOWES, LIMITED
by A. R. MOWBRAY & Co. LIMITED in the City of Oxford

CONTENTS

A MAP SHOWING THE POLITICAL DIVISIONS OF THE WORLD
IS TO BE FOUND AT THE END OF THE TEXT

INTRODUCTION

IN essaying to describe the spirit and structure of the British Empire I have traced the history of the Empire from the beginning, the whole three hundred and fifty years of it. But the proportion I have kept will show that I have not attempted to write a systematic politico-economic, and still less a constitutional, history. Four-fifths of the book deals with the period since 1833, fully two-fifths with that since 1914, and this not because the story of the earlier days lacks interest and importance, but because the spirit and structure that we know have been shaped most directly for us by the events of these more recent years. Nor have I treated the Empire in the manner of the anatomist who cuts up the body and finds the spirit fled. Bearing in mind that the first meaning of 'structure' is 'the way in which a thing holds together', I have tried to see always the complex and living whole in which each part acts upon the rest.

Many tribes and nations have made their contributions to the spirit of the Empire, but it is the peoples of Great Britain—the English, Welsh and Scots, reinforced presently by those Irish who held most firmly to the traditions of their English, Welsh and Scottish forbears—who have played the chief part throughout in the making and maintenance of the British Empire. These peoples have been always the common factor; it is their spirit which has informed the Empire, a spirit sprung from a love of personal freedom, a leaning towards tolerance that has been inculcated by the abiding necessity of coming to terms with one another in their own islands, a respect for tradition and prescriptive right, and, arising from that respect, a readiness, more marked perhaps among the conservative English than the others, to make do with whatever lies nearest to hand rather than to have recourse to theory and invention. And since it is peoples of these same stocks who have played the chief part in the making and maintenance of the United States, I have had much to say of that Republic, which, sprung from the thirteen colonies that broke away from the First British Empire in 1783, has latterly joined hands with the Second British Empire to defend all that the English-speaking peoples have in common everywhere.

The vigorous and adaptable British spirit has created a decentralised empire of unexampled size, dispersion and variety. This empire represents that spirit's share in the direction and control of the outpouring of men, goods and ideas from Western Europe, which began tentatively in the fifteenth century and gathered strength in the sixteenth as centralised governments in alliance with mercantile capital overcame the mediaeval Church and feudalism, and decked ocean-going ships superseded the ancient galleys of more sheltered waters. It is, and always has been, a commercial empire, an empire of the sea-ways.

Roughly speaking, for nearly a century and three-quarters after the founding of its first settlements beyond the Atlantic the colonial half of the Empire lay to the westward of Great Britain and the commercial half to the eastward. Even before the loss of the principal American colonies in 1783, however, the balance of imperial interest had begun to swing towards the east, and during the next fifty years or so the British built up an Indian Empire on the ruins of that of the Great Moguls, possessed themselves of stepping-stones on the way to Asia, and laid the foundations of Australia and New Zealand. The long Victorian Age saw, first, the consolidation of the Indian Empire and the peopling of great colonies of settlement in North America, South Africa and Australasia, and then, with the speeding-up of the Industrial Revolution and the consequent competition of other colonising Powers, the acquisition of vast protectorates and protected states for the most part in tropical Africa, South-East Asia and the Pacific. The addition of mandated and trusteeship territories does not alter the fact that it is this Victorian Empire that the British have since been seeking to adapt to rapidly changing circumstances.

At the outbreak of the Axis War in 1939 the British Empire covered nearly one quarter of the land surface of the globe and claimed the allegiance of some 550,000,000 souls, about one quarter of the human race. But 'British' had long been a word of ever-widening meaning. Less than 15 per cent of these British subjects and British protected persons were Europeans, let alone men of British stock, and of them two-thirds were concentrated in the British Isles and a further one-sixth just across the Atlantic in Canada. In contrast close upon four-fifths of the inhabitants of the Empire were Asians, the vast majority of them Indians.

The scattered territories of the Empire border as a rule upon oceans or great seas, for the British, setting out from a group of islands, have had to work their way into other lands from the coasts and, whenever they have found themselves landlocked in their progress, have always tried to get down to the friendly sea. These territories fall into seven main groups, four of which look out upon the Atlantic Ocean, the Mediterranean of the modern world. First are the British Isles themselves; secondly, the chain of islands and mainland enclaves that runs down the eastern shores of the Americas from Newfoundland by way of the West Indies to the Falkland Islands and, behind these, the continental mass of Canada whose western limits are set by the Pacific Ocean; thirdly, the West African dependencies whose fortunes were once so closely linked with those of the Americas by the slave trade; fourthly, the Union of South Africa with its mandated territory of South-West Africa. The fifth group is the broad belt of tropical territories that runs northward from the Union's frontiers right through Central and East Africa to the Red Sea. There it makes contact with the sixth group. This group lies scattered along the length of the Mediterranean Sea and Indian Ocean from Gibraltar to Singapore, centring upon the solid bulk of India. Lastly, Australia, New Zealand and the Pacific islands reach out, as it were, north-westward towards Singapore and north-eastward towards the Panama canal and the great English-speaking communities of North America.

The uniform colouring of the Empire on the political map of the world has long been misleading, for, if red be the cartographer's badge of empire in the old sense, it has tended to keep alive the idea that all these brave dots and patches represent 'possessions' of the peoples of the United Kingdom. Nothing could be further from the truth. The sovereign Dominions of Canada, Australia, New Zealand and South Africa have for many years past been freely associated on equal terms with the United Kingdom and one another in the British Commonwealth of Nations. Pakistan and Ceylon also are now Dominions, India a Republic though still within the Commonwealth, and Southern Rhodesia a self-governing colony. The territories under all these Governments make up the British Commonwealth. They cover far more than half the area of the Empire and contain the vast majority of its inhabitants.

On the other hand the Crown colonies, protectorates, mandated and trusteeship territories can fairly be coloured red, for they constitute a truly dependent colonial empire covering more than a quarter of the whole area and containing close upon 17 per cent of the Empire's peoples. Even so this dependent empire includes vassal sultanates under varying degrees of imperial control, many territories whose legislatures contain unofficial nominee or elective elements, and some territories which enjoy a close approximation to self-government. This Colonial Empire can in no wise be regarded as an 'imperial estate' that is to be developed for the benefit of the Mother Country. The British Government draws no tribute from it; by long custom the revenue raised in each territory is spent in that territory; the British taxpayer is accustomed to going to the rescue of those in difficulties, and has latterly begun to spend considerable sums on the social and economic advancement of all of them.

It may be that this strange Empire is even now breaking up with the passing of the world conditions under which it arose, leaving nothing better to take its place. If that be so, its disappearance will be a disaster for mankind hardly relieved by the fact that its history would doubtless survive as the record of a great human achievement. But need it be so? Already there are signs that this Empire, which has displayed remarkable vitality and flexibility in the past, may hope to continue, changed indeed but still recognisably 'the Empire', and to contribute all that has hitherto made its maintenance worth while to the making of an even wider and more beneficent system of world government. In any event an understanding of its spirit and structure is essential to the proper ordering of the post-war world.

Eric A. Walker

St. John's College, Cambridge

August, 1953

THE BRITISH EMPIRE

I

THE FIRST BRITISH EMPIRE

THE English Crown was early in the field as a patron of exploration, but the expansion of the English began comparatively late. As far back as 1497, shortly after Columbus had discovered America for Spain and while da Gama was carrying the flag of Portugal to India by way of the Cape of Good Hope, Henry VII sent the Venetian, John Cabot, to find him a way to the gold and spices of the East Indies and was rewarded by the discovery of the Newfoundland codbanks. But the English made no successful transoceanic colony for more than a hundred years thereafter. The England of Henry VII and his immediate successors was in no state to undertake costly and sustained ventures overseas. It was in the main a primary producer whose commerce was still partly in the hands of privileged Germans, a thinly-peopled country off the coast of a by no means densely populated continent, entangled in France and flanked by restive Wales, hostile Scotland and resentful Ireland. Hence, while the Portuguese were building up a widespread empire in Africa, Brazil and the East Indies, and the Spaniards another even more imposing in the Americas and the Philippines, the English must deal with their neighbours as best they might and weather a religious, social and economic revolution. It was only towards the close of the sixteenth century that they could turn their thoughts seriously to distant trade and colonisation.

Even so, for long years their main colonising effort was directed towards Ireland. Ever since the middle of the twelfth century, when Norman adventurers pushed their way in under papal patronage, English kings had wavered between treating Ireland as a subordinate principality and a field for settlement. Usually they had been content to maintain an unruly colony centring upon Dublin with a Parliament almost as old as England's own, and from time to time had tried to enforce there a policy of segregation that has its modern counterpart in southern Africa. Inside the Pale there was an essentially feudal English society, for all that the settlers tended to become Irish in their ways and sentiments; outside the Pale were the tribes, 'the wild Irish'; along the fluctuating frontier tribesmen and colonists behaved towards one another as their kind have always tended to behave. From about 1560, however, the English reinforced presently by the Scots began to plant Ireland more comprehensively, an undertaking which they pressed ruthlessly when Catholic Spain tried to use Catholic Ireland, as so many would-be invaders have tried since, as a base from which to attack Protestant England. In 1609, after fierce fighting, a colony of Englishmen and Scots was settled in Ulster, the most notable and permanent of all the plantations in the island; but already, two years since, after repeated failures, the English had made a still more fruitful plantation beyond the Atlantic in Virginia, and were now contemplating another in 'the still-vex'd Bermoothes' on the road from England to the Old Dominion. So it went on throughout the seventeenth century, side by side with the 'colonisation' of the waste spaces of England and Wales themselves. Twelve of the Old Thirteen mainland colonies and many others in the West Indies had been founded before the battle of the Boyne in 1690 cleared the ground for the final plantation of Ireland.

There were good reasons for this westward outpouring of the British. The England of James I was very different from that of Henry VII. During the intervening hundred years the Tudors had set up strong rule and, remembering their Welsh blood, had incorporated Wales in the English shire and parliamentary system on equal terms. The Channel Islands remained, but the loss of Calais had relieved the English of the last of their Continental commitments; shortly thereafter the ancient enemy beyond the Border had begun to swing away from 'the auld alliance' with France and had now given a king to the three monarchies of the British Isles; the Irish had been subdued for the time being, and the long Elizabethan naval war with Philip's Spain was recently ended. In short, Englishmen were free at last to exploit the fact that their country lay no longer on the outer edge of the *orbis terrarum* but at the main cross-roads where the trade and war routes of the great new world met those of western and central Europe.

The English also had the necessary equipment. During the past century they had varied their economy and broken free from foreign economic control. They still exported herrings, as they had long done, and a diminishing quantity of wool; but stout broadcloth was not the only manufacture they were now sending abroad, and they had found a gold-mine in Cabot's codbanks. They were also masters of their own finance and commerce. Thomas Gresham had founded the Royal Exchange early in Elizabeth's reign, and near the end of it, thirty years later, the Queen had expelled the Hansa merchants from their concession at the Steelyard where Cannon Street station now stands. Moreover, building on foundations laid by the fifteenth-century Merchant Venturers in the Low Countries, Scandinavia and the Baltic states, English merchants had gained concessions of their own in foreign parts under royal charter. Those charters permitted the holders of them or their agents to leave the realm and take certain commodities with them, promised them support against interlopers or 'free traders' of their own nationality, and gave official countenance to acts against subjects of foreign Princes which would otherwise have ranked as sheer piracy, but left them to make arrangements with the rulers of their prospective spheres of influence for the exercising of the powers thus entrusted to them. Such was the Muscovy Company which had traded with Russia by way of Archangel since 1554, the Levant Company of 1581, more than one experimental venture on the African coast, and, most famous and long-lived of all, the East India Company of 1600.

Side by side with this increasing commercial activity had gone the growth of the Royal Navy and mercantile marine. During the fifteenth century the Italians and Portuguese had done much to improve the making of maps and the building and handling of the decked sailing ships which alone could face the ocean rollers. Since then the English, finding a nursery of seamen in the Newfoundland fisheries, had done much more and in the early years of James's reign, with their advancing knowledge of mathematics, were making good maps for themselves and building merchant vessels of 1,100 tons or so. Merchant ships, of course, went armed and English sovereigns still relied on the merchantmen to supplement the royal ships; but the distinction between men-of-war and merchantmen was becoming more and more marked. Elizabeth's shipwrights had evolved the *Revenge* class of battleship which formed the solid core of the fleet that destroyed the Spanish Armada, and now their successors were building for James the *Prince Royal* of

1,200 tons. Meanwhile Spain had ceased to be an insuperable barrier to English expansion. The winds of Heaven and the guns of her enemies had robbed her of three more armadas since 1588; the Dutch shattered the last of them in Gibraltar Bay in the very year of the founding of Virginia.

Further, Englishmen had good and sufficient motives for venturing beyond the oceans. Hostility to Spain counted for much in the founding of Virginia, the first of the Old Thirteen Colonies, to the northward of the Spanish Caribbean possessions; it was still an argument for founding Georgia, the last of them, on the borders of Spanish Florida more than a century later. Nor is it enough to dismiss as verbiage Charles I's explanation that colonies had been founded 'not only with desire of inlarging the Territories of our Empire, But chiefly out of a pious and religious affection and desire of propagating the Gospell'. The argument from prestige rings true, as it does still in our day, but so does the appeal to missionary effort. After all, the best of the Spaniards had tried to live up to like professions for a hundred years past; the Dutch East India Company, a worldly-minded association if ever there was one, could honestly look forward to spreading the light of the Reformed doctrines; earnest Englishmen, whose divines were labouring to make 'one more exact Translation of the holy Scriptures into the *English Tongue*' while the first ships were sailing for Virginia, could support colonising ventures in the expectation that salvation would thus be brought to 'the damned sauvages'. It is easy to sneer at 'English hypocrisy' or 'philanthropy and five per cent', as did the contemporary critic who wrote that

> *'Their gain shall be the knowledge of our Faith,*
> *And ours such riches as the country hath',*

but holders of the contact theory will not deny that such men were right in believing that the English way of life would impress itself upon the weaker peoples of the New World, and cynics should recall that they belonged to a generation which still believed that a man's religion was the most important and most communicable thing he had about him.

Another social motive also played its part in the early days. The economic upheaval that had followed the seizure of the Church lands, the swing over from agriculture to sheep-farming, and the influx of American gold and silver had upset prices and produced great wealth in England and deep poverty for the first time in ugly juxtaposition. Men firmly believed that England and Wales, a quarter of whose lands still lay waste, were over-populated. They looked to colonisation, not for the last time, to draw off the surplus population, relieve unemployment, and check crime and disorder. The Elizabethan Poor Law and the foundation of Ulster and Virginia belong to the same decade.

But when all is said and done the dominant motive was the pursuit of wealth and the comfort and power that go therewith. Raleigh could seek for El Dorado in his golden city of Manoa long after Virginia had been founded, and forty years later still Prince Rupert could hope to find a mountain of gold at the sources of the Gambia river. In default of gold English adventurers would be content with gems and spices, and, though they soon gave up the search for the North-East Passage to the Indies, were seeking diligently for the North-West Passage sixty years after Frobisher's failure in 1576 and hoping that one of Virginia's estuaries might yet prove to be the entry to a northern Straits of Magellan. But they were also prepared to colonise for the sake of more prosaic trade. They wanted to settle all sorts and conditions of Englishmen overseas where they could bring up their families. According to the mercantilist ideas of the time, these colonies were to furnish markets for English manufacturers, make it worth while to build big merchant ships armed and armable, contribute to the prosperity of Englishmen on either side of the Atlantic, swell the customs revenues, open up fishing grounds free from the monopolistic Dutch, and give this Greater England the timber, tar, hemp, iron and copper for her ships, the potash and pearl ash essential for her basic cloth industry, and the luxuries which had become necessities to her wealthier classes, for all of which she was now dependent on the favour of foreign governments in the Baltic, the Netherlands or the Mediterranean. Hence it was that England's early colonising effort was directed chiefly towards temperate regions of the North American mainland where these things might be found, and hence it was that King James, personal prejudice apart, waxed furious when the Virginians took to growing tobacco.

Commerce and colonisation, 'trade and plantations', were thus two sides of the same thing and were naturally supervised by a single committee of the Privy Council. The actual business of settlement was sometimes done by a proprietor or group of proprietors who might hope to find a return in quit rents, the judicious sale of offices and so forth. More usually it was done by companies, modelled on the contemporary trading companies, whose charters empowered them to issue land titles and to govern Englishmen, still liegemen of the King for all that they had left England. Virginia was founded by a company in 1607, and then Bermuda. In 1620, one year after a Dutch trader had landed the first cargo of Negro slaves in Virginia, the Pilgrim Fathers stepped ashore in New England under the aegis of a company. Thus were sown the dragon's teeth from which armed men sprang in the mid-nineteenth century. The real impetus to the New England settlements was, however, given by yet another company which in 1629 founded Massachusetts, the parent of Rhode Island and Connecticut. For a long time these colonies marked the northern limit of recognised English expansion, for Newfoundland was treated officially as a mere shelter for fishermen during the season, and in 1632 Charles I restored to France Quebec and the foothold in Acadie (Nova Scotia) which had been won by English adventurers and colonists. Meanwhile, between 1624 and 1632, Barbados and the Leeward Islands of St. Kitts, Nevis, Antigua and Montserrat had been occupied, and Catholic and proprietary Maryland planted between Puritan New England and Anglican Virginia. Long before the outbreak of the English Civil War ten years later West Indian adventurers were established on the coasts of Yucatan and Honduras.

In other continents the English confined themselves to trading ventures. The Guinea Company, refraining from the trade in slaves, set up factories in 1631 on the Gold Coast and near Sierra Leone in rivalry with the Dutch at Goree and the French on the Senegal, while the East India Company, with which the Guinea Company was associated, followed the example of its more powerful Dutch competitor by fixing its headquarters in Java, at Bantam. Finding no vent there for broadcloth in exchange for spices, it opened stations around Surat on the west coast of India as the respectful client of the Great Mogul, there to buy the cotton goods that were acceptable to the Javanese and English publics alike. So John Company resolutely sought profit 'at sea and in quiet trade', untroubled as yet by the traders' nightmare of empire; indeed in 1620 it refused to accept from two of its captains the annexation of Table Bay, the obvious halfway house between the Channel and the Straits of Sunda. This prize it left to be taken by the Dutch thirty years later; meanwhile, after the massacre of some of its employees by the Dutch at Amboyna in 1623, it withdrew from all its island posts except Bantam. By the time the Civil War had broken out at home the Company was established at the three pivotal points on the mainland from which it was destined to advance to the mastery of India; at Surat, the predecessor of Bombay in the west, at Fort St. George near Madras in the south-east, and in the north-east near Calcutta on the river Hooghly.

Such were the English foundations on which the First British Empire was to rise majestic in three continents during the long century that lay between the end of the Civil War in 1649 and the close of the Seven Years War in 1763.

The triumph of the Parliament's arms was the prelude to marked changes in the structure and spirit of the growing English Empire. Dominant Commonwealth interests swung away from the North American mainland to the West Indies and the West Coast of Africa which was so closely connected with the Caribbean by winds, ocean currents and the slave trade. A group of London merchants, furnished with a parliamentary charter, ousted the royalist Guinea Company and tried to revive John Hawkins's half-forgotten speculation of a hundred years back by organising an English slave trade, while Cromwell invited the Puritan New Englanders to migrate to Jamaica, which he had taken from the Spaniards, and thus make room for English 'malignants' and such Irishmen as had not yet found a place in 'Hell or Connaught'. Both plans miscarried; the London merchants were too much harried by foreigners and Prince Rupert's privateers to carry out their scheme, while the New Englanders declined to move and thus postponed the Irish invasion of North America to a later day. Much greater success attended the deportation overseas of criminals and political prisoners, the emigration of royalists to the West Indies and Virginia, and the exodus of malcontents from Bermuda to the Bahamas.

The Restored Monarchy interested itself in North America as well as the Caribbean and West Africa. During the twenty-five years that passed between the Restoration and the day when Charles II lay 'an unconscionable time a-dying' six more mainland colonies were planted or annexed: North and South Carolina, New Amsterdam taken from the Dutch and renamed New York, Delaware, New Jersey and Pennsylvania, while a seventh, New

B

Hampshire, was carved out of the flank of over-mighty Massachusetts. Twelve of the Old Thirteen Colonies had thus come into being, and, in 1670, Prince Rupert had helped to found the Hudson's Bay Company, last of the great old chartered companies, to engross the fur trade northward of French Quebec. The Royal Adventurers, with Rupert in the van once more, displaced the Parliament's men on the West Coast and successfully launched the English slave trade from their headquarters at Cape Coast Castle and branch establishments at Accra, Anamabo and Dixcove on the Gold Coast, and at Fort James on the Gambia river. Bankrupted in 1672 the Adventurers handed over to the Royal African Company.

The new company, rejoicing in a charter for a thousand years, carried on the ill work in competition with Dutchmen, Danes, Brandenburgers, and even Courlanders. It found a good market beyond the Atlantic. Even before Cromwell had taken Jamaica in 1655, small-holders and their European servants had been withdrawing from the English Antilles to more tolerable regions farther north, and capitalists had begun to work the abandoned lands with gangs of white indentured labourers or Negro slaves. The islands, valued already as bases for privateers in this heyday of the buccaneers or as entrepôts for illicit traffic with the Spanish colonies, were becoming valued still more highly as producers of sugar. One proof of their growing economic importance was the extension to them of colonial self-government as it was understood in those days. The older settlements in Barbados, Bermuda, Nevis and St. Kitt's had received representative institutions similar to those of the mainland colonies long before the Civil War, and now between 1664 and 1672 like privileges were granted to Jamaica, the Bahamas, Antigua and Montserrat. The two last were, moreover, grouped with St. Kitt's and Nevis under a Captain-General, and in 1689 these four Leeward Islands were given an elective federal legislature with its seat at St. Kitt's.

So the English sugar islands prospered, and the first great triangle of English oceanic commerce took shape: from England to the West African coast with trade goods, thence to the West Indies with slaves, and so home with rum and molasses. Early in the eighteenth century the second triangle was marked out: from Great Britain to North America with English manufactures and continental goods; from the mainland to the West Indies with timber, dried fish and farm produce; from the West Indies again home. The common angle of both triangles was in the Caribbean, the common factors molasses and rum. By 1730 the West Indian interest was strong in the Parliament that had by this time overshadowed the Crown.

The Royal African Company was not so fortunate as its West Indian customers, for the Revolution of 1688 exposed the mono-polistic Elizabethan and Stuart companies to attack. Membership of the Muscovy Company was thrown open on payment of a small fee; in 1697 the Royal Africans were deprived of their monopoly but were still held responsible for the maintenance of their forts and the safeguarding of the commerce on the West Coast that had thus been opened to all English subjects. It is true that the British slave trade received a great impetus in 1713 when France, in accord-ance with the Treaty of Utrecht, handed over the coveted Asiento which gave its new British holders the right to import a limited quantity of slaves and other goods into the Spanish colonies. Neither the Asiento, however, nor permission to levy export duties on the West African trade effectively helped the Company, and the government subsidy which it received from 1729 onwards was too small to save it. With its affairs in Chancery and its secre-tary in gaol it made way in 1750 for a modestly subsidised Company of British Merchants which represented the great slave-trading interests of London, Bristol and Liverpool; of Liverpool particu-larly, which by this time was outstripping its more ancient rivals as the headquarters of the British slave trade. Lancashire men were making fortunes by selling black men in the Americas long before the Industrial Revolution enabled their grandsons to make fortunes still greater by spinning slave-grown American cotton.

Meanwhile the East India Company had slowly gathered strength in the background, in spite of unpopularity at home, terrible mortality among its servants in the East, and French and Dutch hostility everywhere. It acquired St. Helena in 1659 as a useful posting-house for its homeward bound fleets, and a year or two later received the island of Bombay, part of the dowry of Charles II's Portuguese Queen, which soon superseded Surat as its west coast centre. In 1683 it gave up its old Javanese station at Bantam and went instead to Bencoolen in neighbouring Sumatra; then, since confusion was spreading in India as the Mogul Empire broke down, it frankly fortified Madras, occupied and fortified Calcutta to defend its rapidly expanding Bengal trade, and began to exercise jurisdiction over Indians and Europeans alike within the narrow confines of its concessions. It, too, fared ill after the Glorious Revolution, for, though its charter was renewed, a rival company was allowed to compete with it for trade and official favour to the perplexity of the Mogul and the great profit of some of his subordinates. At last, however, the two rivals joined forces during the War of the Spanish Succession, and John Company thus enlarged went forward as one of the minor territorial powers of India.

Defending this expanding trade and colonisation, and in large measure paid for by them, was the growing power of the Royal Navy. Charles I had begun to build his ship-money fleet after thirty years of neglect; the Commonwealth, heir to his unfinished work, ran the government deeply into debt to finance a great navy, and found in Robert Blake a commander who could withstand the superior power of the Dutch Republic and even show the English flag for the first time in the Mediterranean. The Restored monarchy carried on the Commonwealth tradition as far as its jealous parliaments would allow, for Charles II and James, his brother and Lord High Admiral, loved the tall ships that were to be 'a safeguard unto our most gracious Sovereign Lord, and his Dominions, and a security for such as pass on the seas upon their lawful occasions'. Charles differentiated the Navy from the Army by organising its officers as a professional class, and from the Mercantile Marine by giving up the old practice of commandeering merchant ships, which had proved themselves unable to remain in the line during the recent Dutch war, but reserving withal the right to impress their crews for the royal service. His fleet fought two more stubborn wars with the Dutch, which ended on the whole in England's favour, and maintained its country's position as a Mediterranean power during the twenty years that Charles garrisoned Tangier, which had come to him with Catherine of Braganza.

Lack of money compelled Charles to abandon Tangier in 1684. Meanwhile Louis XIV was busy transforming Richelieu's Toulon into a strong naval base and outbuilding the combined fleets of Holland and England. Hence the two Maritime Powers were in grave peril in 1689 when William of Orange, ruler of both, challenged Louis' France. The victories of Barfleur and La Hogue, however, turned the tide and gave William time to overhaul the English Navy. He could afford to do so, for mercantile capital was piling up fast in the hands of Englishmen. Jews had been leaving the Netherlands for the island security of England since Cromwell's day, and, now that England had her Bank, a currency reformed by Sir Isaac Newton and a national debt, London was fast supplanting Amsterdam as the financial centre of Western Europe. England was able to take the offensive at sea on the outbreak of the War of the Spanish Succession, and found herself the leading naval power at the end of it. The French, Spanish and friendly Dutch fleets were broken or decayed; captured Spanish Gibraltar and Minorca, supplemented by the use of the Tagus estuary allowed her by her 'most ancient ally' of Portugal, made her a Mediterranean power; France's recognition of her exclusive sovereignty over Newfoundland and the Hudson's Bay Territories, together with the cession of Acadie now renamed Nova Scotia, gave her a dominating position in North America.

Strong in the recent Anglo-Scottish Union which had made their island 'Great Britain', the British steadily strengthened their hold beyond the seas. During Walpole's long and peaceful administration they appointed justices of the peace to reside among the scarcely recognised settlers in Newfoundland and an admiral as visiting Governor [1728]; they planted Georgia, last of the Old Thirteen Colonies, between Florida and South Carolina as a frontier guard against Spaniards and Indians and a receptacle for the unfortunate; presently their East India Company and its sepoys began to follow their French rivals into the mazes of South Indian dynastic politics. Thus it was that Great Britain had to fight in three continents as well as on the high seas when, in 1740, she entered the War of the Austrian Succession with her depleted Navy. That struggle, ending in stalemate, was followed by the plantation of neglected Nova Scotia with British and American settlers round the port of Halifax. Then, during the Seven Years War which came so swiftly in 1756, after the customary bad start which lost her Minorca 'for the duration', Britain's fleets swept the seas and enabled her armies to drive the Bourbons before them in the Americas and Asia. She not only recovered Minorca under the terms of the Treaty of Paris, but acquired French Canada and Louisiana as far westward as the Mississippi, Spanish Florida, the French West Indian islands of Tobago, Grenada and Dominica, and French Senegal. Her East India Company moreover was dominant in the parts around Madras, and, thanks to Clive's victory at Plassey, master of the huge province of Bengal; in short, now that the French Company has been disarmed, it was the only European Power of importance in India, a major Power rivalled only by the Mahratta Confederacy in the west, Hyderabad in the centre and Mysore in the south.

The First British Empire stood at the peak of its fortunes in 1763 on the morrow of the Seven Years War, broad-based upon trade, finance and manufacture, free settlement, indentured labour and slavery; exulting in the freedom of the seas, cherishing the rule of law and the birthright of free-born Englishmen everywhere to speak their minds and manage their own affairs. Twenty years later its western half, the colonial as distinct from the commercial half, lay in ruins.

The causes of that swift disaster lay far back in the origins and nature of the colonies of settlement. These had never been easy to govern if only because of distance and the composite character of their societies. The British settlers, who formed the majority, represented all the nations of the British Isles, and the rest came from many parts of western Europe. They represented moreover all grades of society. The early expectation that the colonies would draw off the down-and-outs had on the whole been disappointed. Poor folk had been despatched overseas from time to time by public or private charity; others of many ranks had been sent out as indentured servants, expelled vagrants, political offenders or plain criminals; others again had been kidnapped, for 'spiriting' was one of the minor industries of Bristol well into the eighteenth century. But no colonial empire was ever built on the failures and misfits of society. The bulk of the emigrants throughout had been of the ambitious sort seeking to better themselves, or less enterprising folk going to join their friends, or the adventurous taking ship 'for to admire and for to see, for to observe this world so wide'.

Emigration westward had never been large by modern standards, but at three or four periods it had been considerable for the time and of a significant kind. Republican-minded Puritans poured across to New England during the Reign of Thorough between 1629 and 1640, and again when the oppressive Clarendon Code came into force after the Restoration; resentful Royalists trooped across to the West Indies, and in smaller numbers to the southern mainland colonies, during the Civil War and the Commonwealth. These men set their rival marks on Massachusetts and Virginia, the future centres of resistance to George III and his Parliaments. Presently frontiersmen from the Irish Pale, finding their occupation gone after William of Orange had subjugated all Ireland, went west to fight Indians, and a generation later were joined by Lowland Scots with a similar training who had been put out of business by England's final conquest of the Highlands. Far more important than these border toughs were the Protestant Irishmen who were driven across the Atlantic from about 1720 onwards under pressure of the land laws and the ruination of Ireland's industries by the hardening British laws of trade. These men, ancestors of America's 'Scotch-Irish', were the living links between the simultaneous American and Irish revolutions that wrecked the First British Empire.

The shooting stage was reached in North America by way of a deadlock in both departments of the Old Colonial System: the constitutional and the economic.

The constitutional difficulty arose from the uneven development of the parliamentary system in different parts of the Empire. When Virginia was being founded, England herself had merely representative institutions and not what later generations have learned to call responsible government. The King exercised real power; ministers were still his servants responsible to him and removable only by his will, their own good sense or lack of courage, or by decapitation following the cumbrous and perhaps unduly expensive parliamentary processes of impeachment and bill of attainder. On the other hand King and ministers must go to the Houses for most of the legislation and money they needed for the governance of the realm. Scotland stood outside the English Empire in haughty penury, her ancient single-chamber Parliament of the three Estates overshadowed by the Lords of the Articles, a committee of its own, and from time to time also by the Kirk Assembly. Ireland, nominally a separate kingdom, had a bicameral Parliament almost as ancient as England's own; but under Poyning's Laws of 1494, which had been enacted mainly to protect the colonists of the Pale from their Lord Deputy and a docile legislature, that Parliament was forbidden to meet or discuss bills without leave of the King in Council, and might see the King apply English statutes to Ireland over its head.

As for the transatlantic colonies, everyone agreed that Englishmen took their birthrights with them wherever they might go, and one of the chiefest of these was the right to demand of the King redress of grievance, through their elected or nominated representatives, before the granting of taxes to supplement the royal revenues. It followed that if Englishmen at home exercised this right at Westminster, Englishmen overseas must have similar facilities in their own colonies; hence, just as Englishmen in the Irish Pale had been given their own Parliament long ago, so almost from the first the practice arose of setting up in each American colony representative institutions modelled not so much upon the English Parliament as upon the governmental machinery of the chartered trading companies. There was a Governor appointed either by the Crown or the Proprietors or, in one or two cases in New England, the colonists themselves in terms of their treasured charters; a Council for executive, legislative and judicial work, nominated as a rule by the Governor on behalf of the Proprietors or the Crown, but in one or two cases elected directly or indirectly by the colonists; always there was an elective Assembly. By the middle of the eighteenth century nine of the thirteen mainland colonies were Crown colonies, that is, their Governors were appointed by the King, while two others were still proprietary and two chartered; but whatever their status the general situation was the same in nearly all of them and in the West Indian islands also. The relations of executive and legislature were what they had been in James I's time; the Governor was responsible in nearly every case to an overseas superior, the Councillors were responsible to him, and both must turn for legislation and revenue to a jealous Assembly which, as time went on, was usually elected in a more democratic manner than in Old England.

The inevitable happened in all parts of the Empire, though in different degrees. The struggle in England between King and Parliament for control of ministers and the purse strings led to the Civil War, the execution of one King and the flight of another, an unwelcome union with Scotland, a still more unwelcome Hanoverian Succession, and a long Whig ascendancy which established much of the cabinet and two-party system. True, nothing but the collapse of the First British Empire was to force George III to accept the younger Pitt and the full principles of cabinet responsibility; but even George, in his efforts to rule as Patriot King, had been obliged to rely on influencing the Houses to which power had long since passed.

Meanwhile colonies had frequently objected to sending appeals to the distant Privy Council; their Assemblies were as a rule loath to vote money for defence, and distinctly averse to providing permanent salaries for Governors, councillors or judges; Assembly committees encroached where they could on the sphere of the executive. But though quarrels on these heads never reached a solution, neither did they reach such a pitch of desperation as at home. This Empire of many legislatures and, in the last resort, one executive centring upon London rubbed along tolerably well for several generations, and bequeathed in essentials its institutions and colonial division of powers to the state and federal governments of the United States. Disaster only came when the British Parliament tried to play the part of an overriding imperial legislature to half a continent and the adjacent islands in which the modern Dominion mind was already well developed; that is, a growing nationalism combined with warm traditional loyalty to His Majesty and deep suspicion of both Houses at Westminster.

It had all been clear and simple in the early days; colonies, like trade, were the King's business and not Parliament's. That was the principle embodied in the old colonial charters. It was this principle which had moved royalist Ireland and Barbados to repudiate the claim of the Long Parliament that colonies belonged to the people of England, inspired Catholic Maryland and Barbados again to claim for themselves, and therefore by implication for other colonies, full legislative rights within their own borders and freedom from all taxation for revenue other than that voted by their Assemblies, and encouraged Puritan Massachusetts to behave like a scarcely crowned republic throughout the middle decades of the seventeenth century. It need occasion no surprise that on the morrow of the Seven Years War chartered Rhode Island and Connecticut should have regarded themselves as 'two Republicks . . . the Allies of Great Britain and not her subjects', or that Benjamin Franklin and Alexander Hamilton, echoing the words of James I and Charles I themselves, should have maintained that their allegiance was due to the King alone, since 'America is no part of the dominion of Great Britain, but of the King's Dominions'.

The economic organisation of the Old Empire was closer knit than the political framework. It was defined mainly in the Navigation Acts. The principles of these laws of trade were much older than the overseas Empire, for as early as the reign of Richard II it had been laid down that English trade ought to be in English hands and carried in English ships. Be that as it may, the fostering

of commerce, industry and agriculture for the benefit of Englishmen
everywhere was the duty of the King; it followed therefore that
colonists took with them the expectation of royal aid and liability
to royal restraints in these matters. No serious attempt was made to
regulate imperial trade during the pre-Civil War period; but the
scene changed when power passed to the Rump of the Commons
backed by the growing financial power of London. The Navigation
Ordinance of 1651, the first of the comprehensive laws of trade,
was a navigation law pure and simple aimed at the carrying trade
and herring monopoly of the Dutch. Henceforward trade within
the English Empire was to be reserved for English, including of
course colonial, ships with mainly English crews, while none but
English or Irish ships were to bring herrings into England or
Ireland.

The Restoration Parliaments went much further. They undertook to regulate imperial trade and industry more or less on the
French and Dutch lines which exiled Royalists and acquisitive
men of the Commonwealth had learned to envy and admire. It
amounted to this: enumerated articles must come from the colonies
to England before going to foreign parts; continental goods must
go to the colonies through England; goods going from one colony
to another must pay customs duties at the English rates; Irish ships
and Irish trade were progressively penalised for the alleged benefit
of their English rivals. On the other hand unenumerated colonial
goods could go freely to many parts of the world in English or
colonial ships; desirable colonial goods, and notably tobacco, were
assured of a highly protected or exclusive market in England,
where some of them also received bounties; no customs tribute
was taken on continental goods destined for the colonies, and
liberal refunds were made of the duties paid on colonial goods in
transit through England.

As the system hardened there was grumbling in some colonies,
but compared with the mercantilist and still more the bullionist
practices of other European Powers the system was fairly liberal.
By the close of the seventeenth century it was working well enough.
England was after all the obvious landfall for incoming colonial
ships on the North Atlantic route, a convenient starting point for
the return voyage; the colonial mercantile marine flourished and
colonial-built ships were soon being sold more cheaply than English
ships in the very Thames; imperial shipping was as a rule sufficient

for imperial trade. Besides, by a kind of tacit bargain, England gave the colonies defence by her warships at all times and by troops in time of war in return for the restraints on their trade, and the said restraints could usually be evaded if they proved too irksome. Governors could not enforce them for lack of adequate police and customs officers, and hesitated to call in the troops or the Navy too often. By 1700 many colonial towns, notably New York and Boston, were the scenes of systematic smuggling even by the 'best families'.

The contempt for part of the law thus bred in the colonists was an evil by-product of the Old Colonial System which would seem to have persisted in American society as late as the days of Prohibition. Another evil, a growing evil as the eighteenth century wore on, was the tilting of the balance of trade in favour of the Mother Country which drained the colonies of hard money and forced them back on depreciating paper currencies. A third evil was the growing temptation to British politicians, merchants and industrialists to manipulate the old colonial system in their own favour. As Parliament gained the upper hand of the King, and the moneyed Whigs the upper hand in Parliament, that temptation was yielded to more and more frequently.

The Parliament which now controlled the old colonial system, and the public interested in its manipulation, were both much larger than in the seventeenth century. The Scottish Parliament had got rid of the Lords of the Articles and displaced the Kirk Assembly as the first authority in the land after the Revolution of 1688, and had begun to make serious commercial and political trouble for England. The English, as their manner has so often been, prudently came to terms while they were yet in the way. In 1707, in the midst of the War of the Spanish Succession, they induced the Scots to forswear the Stuarts and promise to accept a Hanoverian monarch when Queen Anne should be dead, in return for retaining their law and gaining an entry to the ground-floor of the English colonial system. The Scots themselves specially safeguarded their established presbyterian Kirk. Both parties agreed to merge their Parliaments in a Parliament of Great Britain which should control the largest free trade area in the tessellated Europe of those days. Henceforward the British Empire was to be run by Englishmen, Welshmen and Scots. It was a formidable combination.

The members of the Empire outside Great Britain fitted into the

colonial system with varying degrees of comfort to themselves
and safety to the enlarged Mother Country. The West Indies and
the southern mainland colonies with their gentleman proprietors,
droves of slaves and dependants, tropical products, and steady
demand for British goods and money, were prized as perfect colonies.
The Middle Colonies were also regarded as imperial assets; but New
England, with its products so like Britain's own, its growing
tendency to embark upon manufacture, its lack of slaves and
reputed lack of gentlemen, was regarded as a danger second only
to Ireland, whose proximity and comparatively low standard of
living aroused in the British the fears that are awakened in South
Africans to-day by non-European neighbours and competitors.

The tendency displayed by the earlier Navigation Acts to limit
Ireland's trade and industry and shut her out from the Colonial
System became more marked after the battle of the Boyne. The
Irish woollen industry was dead by the end of the seventeenth
century. Thirty years later Ulster's linen industry was dying, and
Ireland could send nothing direct to the overseas Empire except
provisions nor receive most articles of colonial origin save through
Great Britain. Nor could she look for relief to the corrupt Dublin
Parliament, which since 1704 had been recruited exclusively from
the Anglican 'garrison' and could never stand up to pressure from
Westminster for fear of jeopardising its own privileges and even its
safety. That pressure could be overwhelming. Not only had the
British Parliament taken to itself, since 1719, the right to legislate
for Ireland over the head of the Irish Parliament in the spirit of
Poyning's Laws, but Ireland had to pay for that 'standing army
within this kingdom in time of peace' which had been the nightmare of Englishmen, Scots, Irishmen and Americans since the days
of Cromwell's Major-Generals; an army 12,000 strong and
Protestant, ready to enforce the penal laws against Catholics and
the land and trade laws against Catholics and Protestants alike, with
two-thirds of it ready to serve overseas also if need be.

The same House of Commons that had claimed power to legislate
for Ireland frowned upon colonial manufactures since these would
lessen the dependence of the colonies on Great Britain. During the
generation that followed this resolution of 1719 Parliament tended
to apply to the transatlantic colonies, especially to unpopular New
England, something of the jealous policy that was being applied
to Ireland. It of course encouraged the production of naval stores

and raw materials, but it limited direct trade with Europe to West Indian sugar and the rice of Georgia and the Carolinas, and then only to countries south of Cape Finisterre. It did not admit the bar and pig iron of the Middle Colonies freely to the home market until 1750, and throughout showed itself anxious, though unable, to check the illicit trade in timber and provisions which the colonists, and above all the New Englanders, carried on with the foreign sugar islands. Nor did the colonists' excuse that they must do so to balance their trading budgets avail to turn away imperial wrath when some of them supplied the enemy during the Seven Years War.

Hard things have been said of British imperial policy during the thirteen years which elapsed between the end of that war and the Declaration of American Independence. Not all have been deserved. 'Ireland I risked and lost America' . . . but King George's men saved French liberties and British rule in Canada, gave the newly-annexed foreign colonies the best form of government they knew, extended Crown colony rule to West Africa, began to make Company rule a beneficent thing in chaotic India, outlined a Red Indian policy that foreshadowed much that is now the pride of British Native administration, and saw Lord Mansfield strike the first effective blow against the grim front of British slavery and lay down constitutional principles of the first importance for the governance of the non-British and even non-European dependencies that were soon to constitute so great a part of the British Empire. What wonder that some of the dust raised by this imperial spring-cleaning proved to be explosive?

Notable changes were made in the eastern or trading half of the Empire. After a long struggle the trade of the Levant Company had already been virtually thrown open to British subjects in 1753; now, in West Africa, the well-nigh useless Company of Merchants was thrust into the background. Their stations on the Gold Coast and the Gambia were combined with Senegal in the Province of Senegambia under the Crown and furnished with as near an approach as possible to the customary colonial institutions. No such assertion of sovereignty could be made in India, where sovereignty still lay nominally with the Mogul and power with the Nizam, Nawabs, Rajahs and John Company. It was well that the British Government rejected Clive's naïve suggestion after Plassey that Bengal should be milked, Dutch or Spanish fashion, to help the British to pay for the late war; events proved that it was not so well that it should have rejected his advice to extend its own rule over Bengal. That vast province proved to be more than a mere trading company could manage. For eight years a puppet Nawab was allowed to misgovern the unhappy country, while the Company's servants, Indian and European, disclaiming responsibility but relying on the troops, lined their own pockets and sent dwindling remittances home to the shareholders.

Clive came back to India in 1765 with authority from the Mogul to administer Bengal, Bihar and Orissa, and for the next year or two did something to put matters on a better footing; but, on his retirement with health impaired, evils reminiscent of the Dutch East India Company at its worst recurred. Anglo-Indian nabobs returned home with their spoils to affront the county by setting up as country gentlemen, outrage honourable members by buying coveted seats in the Commons, challenge the zealous righteousness of Wesleyans and Evangelicals, and alarm merchants and shareholders for the future of the trade with an India that was being looted by men like these. Warren Hastings was therefore appointed Governor of Bengal, and had already instituted reforms when the financial troubles of the Company enabled Lord North to pass the Regulating Act of 1773. That famous measure did not provide for regular parliamentary control over the Company, for the tradition of the times was strong against touching vested interests and chartered rights; but it did cut short the growth of a practically independent state in India ruled by Europeans on lines of more than oriental luxury and corruption. It reorganised the Company's governmental machinery in London, made Warren Hastings Governor-General of the three Presidencies of Bengal, Bombay and Madras, and set up at Calcutta a Council with wide powers and a Court to administer for all alike the law which was the pride of eighteenth-century Englishmen and Americans.

While better days were thus dawning on the Company's Indian provinces, Lord Mansfield delivered three resounding judgments. He declared first that 'whatever inconveniences' might follow from his decision, slavery could not exist on English soil, a salutary dictum that was promptly extended to Scotland by the Court of Session; next, that the inhabitants of an annexed dependency had the same right of access to the Courts of the Empire as the true-born Englishmen, and, conversely, that an Englishman in such a dependency had 'no privileges distinct from the natives' but must submit himself to the law of that dependency whether it be French, Spanish, Roman-Dutch or what not; finally, that although the Crown had power over a conquered dependency limited only by the articles of capitulation, once it had granted constitutional privileges it could not withdraw them.[1]

The British Government's immediate and chief concern was, however, with the enlarged colonial empire in the Western Hemisphere. Chatham had won the Seven Years War regardless of expense. George Grenville, the young King's chief adviser, therefore proposed that imperial trade should be made to converge, as it had always been intended to do, upon the Mother Country and thus help the British taxpayer to carry a burden which was immeasurably heavier than that borne by his American fellow citizens. Grenville proceeded on the familiar give and take lines. He offered additional bounties to many colonial products, allowed colonial timber and pig-iron to go freely to all parts of the world other than Europe north of Cape Finisterre, and, in spite of the grumbling of the provision-producing northern colonies, permitted Georgian and Carolinian rice to be sent to the West Indies and Central and South America. But he also revived in a milder form an old and moribund Sugar Act which had been intended to check the colonists' illicit trade with the foreign Antilles, and called in the all-conquering Navy to help the civil authorities to enforce the Navigation Acts against the swarming smugglers of Great Britain, the Isle of Man, Ireland and the Colonies.

This attempt to enforce that side of the tacit imperial bargain which primarily benefited the Mother Country and restricted the colonies came at an ill time. The colonists, seeing the Bourbon fleets dispersed and their garrisons driven beyond the Mississippi, felt so much the less need of defence by British arms. Nor did the Sugar Act confine itself to the accustomed regulation of trade, but talked of 'giving' His Majesty a revenue. At once the constitutional and economic sides of the Old Colonial System began to run together towards deadlock. The Americans' very human dislike of taxation as such was reinforced by their traditional resolve never to submit to 'taxation without representation'. Their resentment was redoubled when Grenville announced that, since they were unwilling to tax themselves, he must impose a Stamp Act to defray part of the cost of the imperial troops on North American soil.

[1] *Vide infra*, pp. 34, 102, 121.

Proposal and prospect were alike distasteful to the Americans, whose dread of a standing army was deep-seated. Regulars had never been stationed on the mainland in any numbers until the eve of the Seven Years War, and the fact that they had thereafter borne the main burden of the fighting had not endeared them to those many colonists who had failed to support them adequately, nor erased, from the memories of those who had, recollections of the friction that had arisen between the regulars and their own part-time soldiers. Besides, colonial frontiersmen, traders and land speculators disapproved strongly of the Indian policy the regulars were there to uphold. The troops had indeed put down a post-war Indian rising single-handed and were now policing the long indefinite western border; but the British Government was claiming custody of all lands between the settled area and the Mississippi, forbidding the purchase of Indian lands or trade with the Redskins except under licence, and generally proposing to extend over the hinterland of all the colonies the humane and liberal policy which the New Yorker, Sir William Johnson, had tried since 1755 to carry out among the Iroquois in one corner of the triangle that lay between the Ohio, the Mississippi and the Great Lakes. In the main the imperial authorities failed to carry out their frontier plans; but Americans argued, as Cape Colonists were to argue later on, that if they wished to pursue such policies let the British taxpayer finance them.

Meanwhile the Sugar Act and Stamp Act were doing what all else had hitherto failed to do; they had begun to drive the jealous, dispersed and heterogeneous colonies together. Delegates from nine of the thirteen mainland colonies met at New York to concert common action. During the fiery debates even the validity of the laws of trade were called in question and when, in 1765, the Stamp Act was passed, it was met by a boycott of British goods and mob violence against those who sold the stamps and those who bought. The stop-gap Rockingham ministry repealed both Acts, whereupon the quarrel over the laws of trade died down. Not so the more radical constitutional quarrel; for repeal had been accompanied by a Quartering Act which bade the colonists find billets for the redcoats, and a Declaratory Act which claimed for the British Parliament the right to legislate for the colonies over the heads of their own legislatures. Doubtless the Declaratory Act was good law, though Lord Camden was to tell the House of Lords, in the true spirit of English politics, that there were certain things that even a sovereign Parliament must not do; certainly it was in keeping with the then current 'Austinian' theories of ungraded sovereignty of which the Empire to-day is the most notable refutation. But it was bad policy. The claim was word for word that which had been made against Ireland nearly half a century earlier, and there were plenty of Irishmen in America to point the moral. There were plenty of other colonists ready to listen presently when Charles Townshend, during 'one slight day on American taxation', levied port dues payable in America on tea and a few other commodities going thence from Great Britain, and induced the amenable Dublin Parliament to increase the size of the Irish contingent for service anywhere.

The additional troops, too few to overawe and too many to be welcome, arrived in Boston to find patriots eschewing tea and drinking repellent substitutes. From that moment the two parties drifted towards war amid increasing violence and a general misunderstanding of each other's case. Even the good the British Government sought to do to other members of its widespread empire had unhappy repercussions in the American colonies, especially in New England. As compensation for the restrictions of the Regulating Act, Lord North allowed the financially embarrassed East India Company to ship tea direct to America at rates of duty which would give Americans their tea more cheaply than Englishmen. The tea ships were met with successful obstruction at the principal ports and with violence at Boston. There patriots who resented imperial taxation combined with chartered monopoly, and this at prices which would undercut those for their own illicit foreign teas, sent a mob on board to throw the chests into the harbour. The British Government thereupon closed the port of Boston and otherwise penalised recalcitrant Massachusetts. All the mainland colonies, save Georgia, retorted by sending delegates to a Continental Congress at Philadelphia to concert measures of defence.

The year of the Massachusetts penal laws, 1774, was also the year of the Quebec Act which New Englanders regarded simply as one of the series. During the Seven Years War, Nova Scotia had been given a constitution of the universal British American kind, a step that had been made easier by the recent deportation of the scanty French population after long years of friction induced by zealots

C

from French Canada. At the close of the war the British Government had promised similar institutions to the annexed foreign colonies. Between 1763 and 1775 these promises were fulfilled in St. Vincent, Tobago, Grenada and Dominica, while even the little Virgin Islands in the Caribbean and the new Province of Senegambia on the West Coast were given some semblance of colonial institutions. But the only inhabitants of widespread and thinly-peopled French Canada who wanted or even understood an elective assembly were the handful of newly arrived traders, speculators and lawyers from Old and New England or New York. Successive Governors, recalling past troubles in Nova Scotia, played for time. In the event the Quebec Act gave them what they had wanted.

The Quebec Act marked a great departure from earlier colonial policy. It gave the Governor a permanent revenue sufficient, presumably, to maintain the executive and the bench, and bade him nominate a large council of officials and non-officials, French and British. It retained the French civil law and, at a time when British and Irish Roman Catholics were still subject to grave disabilities, recognised Catholicism as the lawful religion of French Canadians. Puritan New Englanders and legalistic New Yorkers naturally looked with suspicion on all these things, while they and the Virginians farther south were incensed that their hinterland between the Lakes, the Ohio and the Mississippi should now have been included in Canada. Their indignation deepened when they learned that the Quebec authorities were talking of raising French Canadian regiments to uphold the royal authority on North American soil.

The first shots of the War of American Independence were fired at Lexington on 19 April 1775, but the struggle had dragged on half-heartedly for more than a year before Congress hesitatingly published its Declaration of Independence on 4 July 1776. A year later, however, Burgoyne surrendered at Saratoga to a combination of American troops, the autumn backwoods and War Office incompetence. Forthwith an Irish revolution began to march in step with the American rebellion. In response to pressure by Grattan, Flood and other members of the 'Garrison', the British Government sanctioned the relaxation of the Catholic penal code and itself abolished some of the restrictive laws of trade. At the same time it tried to conciliate the Americans by carrying the Renunciation Act which promised that never again would a British Parliament tax the

West Indian or American mainland colonies save for the regulation of trade, and even then it would spend the revenue in the colonies that provided the trade. It was too late. France, which had hitherto given the Americans indispensable aid surreptitiously, was now allied with them openly, and what had been a civil war within the Empire became France's return match for the Seven Years War. As Spain first, and then Holland, joined the hostile alliance, and Russia rallied the Baltic Powers against Great Britain in the Armed Neutrality of the North, the American war became merely a costly and distracting side-show. The British held New York to the end; but Cornwallis's surrender at Yorktown to American and French troops and a French squadron that had gained local command of the sea practically finished the fighting in North America. Early in 1782 Minorca and some of the West Indies were lost. North's ministry fell and, with it, George's Patriot King system. It was symbolic that the bottom should now have fallen out of the *Royal George*, the pride of the fleet, as she lay at anchor at Portsmouth.

And then the tide turned. Ireland, which had passed under the control of Grattan's Volunteers when the regulars went overseas, had recently seen her Nonconformists enfranchised and many commercial restrictions swept away. She was now pacified by the grant to the Dublin Parliament and Courts of untrammelled jurisdiction 'in all cases whatever'. In India, Hastings more than held his own against a combination of the French, the Mahrattas, Hyder Ali of Mysore and, at one time, ordinarily friendly Hyderabad. Above all, the Navy, much larger now than in the early stages of the war, was used intelligently at last. Lord Howe, equipped with brave Kempenfelt's new signalling code, relieved Gibraltar at the end of its three-year siege, and Rodney, scornful of such new-fangled devices, smashed the French battle fleet off The Saints in the West Indies. At the close of this year of recovery Great Britain came to terms separately with the Americans and therefore fared much better at the general peace settlement in 1783 than had at one time seemed possible. She recognised the independence of the United States and ceded to them their hinterland as far westward as the Mississippi, including the coveted Ohio Triangle; she restored the Two Floridas to Spain, who also retained Minorca; she gave back to France Tobago, Senegal, Goree, and her Indian stations unfortified.

It might have been, it very nearly had been, much worse; even so this Treaty of Versailles marked the end of the First British Empire.

II

LAW, ORDER AND SECURITY, 1783-1833

MOST foreign observers in 1783, and not a few British and American subjects also, prophesied a gloomy future for the two halves of the broken British Empire. Their belief was reasonable, for the thirteen thinly-peopled, financially embarrassed and loosely confederated North American republics were the first European colonies to have severed themselves from their Mother Country and had thus far given little proof of their ability to stand on their own feet in peace or in war, while Great Britain's prestige was tarnished, her resources depleted, her hold on the Mediterranean weakened by the loss of Minorca and her colonial empire reduced to a thing of shreds and patches. In that continent towards which her colonising efforts had been directed for 175 years past, she still held isolated Bermuda, some West Indian islands to the southward of the United States, and to the northward of them a broken fringe of dependencies consisting of neglected Newfoundland, struggling Nova Scotia, overwhelmingly French Canada and the well-nigh empty Hudson's Bay Territories. Nearer home she held the Rock but was not quite sure whether she still held Ireland, a doubt that was shared by many Irishmen; in West Africa the Province of Senegambia had collapsed with the loss of Senegal, and the old British stations had passed once more into the nerveless hands of the Company of Merchants; in India John Company ruled somewhat enlarged but sorely battered provinces. Few men saw hope of a great imperial future in remnants such as these; rather did they expect that Great Britain would sink to the level of a second-rate Power.

These depressing prognostications were soon belied by the event. The people of the Old Thirteen, realising from bitter experience that mere independence was not enough, agreed presently to surrender part of their state sovereignties to a national government. Drawing avowedly on their long memory of freedom as British colonists they framed a notable constitution, and in April 1789, one month before the States General met to inaugurate the French Revolution, installed George Washington as President of the first large-scale democratic and federal republic in the history of the world. Within two short generations 'these United States', thirty-one strong, had stretched out from the Atlantic seaboard to the shores of the Caribbean and Pacific, and had already exercised a powerful influence on the Second British Empire. American pressure and commercial competition during the long French Revolutionary and Napoleonic wars helped to produce those radical changes in British imperial fiscal policy that made colonial self-government possible; the mere proximity of a great and growing republic to the British North American colonies was a constant reminder that independence was the alternative to self-government in the British colonies of settlement everywhere. Presently the success of the American federation was to serve as an example, and in some respects as a warning, to the future British Dominions in North America, Australia and South Africa, while throughout the nineteenth century, as in colonial days, the great majority of the emigrants from the British Isles found their way to Philadelphia, Baltimore, or New York. It is hardly too much to say that, next to Great Britain herself, the most actively formative force in the making of the Second British Empire was the part that broke away from the First in 1783.

For there was to be a Second British Empire. The picture of British decline was soon shown to be misleading; not for the last time Great Britain surprised her friends and confounded her enemies. During the fifty years that elapsed between the signature of the Treaty of Versailles and the passing of the Slave Emancipation Act in 1833, she laid the foundation of another empire more widespread and varied than that which had just gone to pieces. The work of that pregnant half-century passed through three stages. First, a time of recovery and cautious liberal reform from 1783 till 1794; then a dogged period of law, order and security while the British, as their custom was, were once more 'fighting the French'; lastly, as the battle smoke cleared, the stage of expansion combined with social, economic and political reforms that heralded the great Victorian Age.

The economic recovery and revival of British naval power which marked the decade of peace between the American and French Revolutionary Wars were due mainly to the careful finance of the younger Pitt and the nascent mechanical and agricultural revolutions. As a disciple of Adam Smith, whose *Wealth of Nations* had been published in the year of the American Declaration of Independence, the Prime Minister saw more clearly than most contemporary politicians the bearing of the Industrial Revolution on the future of the Empire, and cared more for trade than for the plantations which had proved to be so unfilial. He wanted free trade wherever he could find it, especially with France and the United States, the principal enemies late in arms, and with Ireland which had enjoyed since 1782 the powers of a modern Dominion save that the Dublin executive was still controlled in practice from London.

Pitt succeeded in concluding an advantageous commercial treaty with France which ended only with the outbreak of war in 1793, but his plans for a general Anglo-Irish settlement were defeated by jealousies and suspicions on either side of St. George's Channel. He had proposed the reform of the rotten boroughs in both kingdoms and the admission of Ireland to complete free trade within the Empire in return for an Irish contribution to the Royal Navy; but all that came of it was the tardy grant by the Dublin Parliament of the franchise to the Catholic majority without the right of sitting in either House, a limited privilege similar to that which is still retained by some non-Europeans within the Cape Province of the Union of South Africa. Incidentally many difficult Dominion-like questions arose. Could the Kingdom of Ireland have her own ambassadors, make her own treaties, control her own navy, maintain neutrality in the event of a 'British' war? Was, perchance, the Crown divisible? How was an autonomous Ireland to be kept within the ever-changing British laws of trade? No answers were found to these questionings, and in 1791 Wolfe Tone, the advocate of neutrality, began to enrol Catholics and Protestants in his society of United Irishmen to press for a repeal of the penal laws and the full enfranchisement of the Roman Catholic majority.

Pitt's American policy was hardly more successful than his Irish. Anxious to conciliate the Americans, wean them from their French alliance and do good business, he followed Shelburne in proposing that they should be allowed to resume on pre-war terms the trade with the West Indies which had long been so vital to both parties. He and the hitherto all-powerful West Indian interest were, however, defeated by Lord Sheffield, who summoned British shipowners and the Tory rank and file to an Empire crusade. The 'Yankees' were shut out from the British West Indies, at all events on paper, and for a full decade this display of classic mercantilism towards ex-colonists exacerbated Anglo-American relations. These were already strained by Great Britain's retention of military posts in the rich fur-bearing Ohio Triangle until such time as the helpless Confederate authorities should induce the State governments to honour those clauses of the Treaty of Versailles which promised redress to aggrieved British subjects. Towards the end the British had visions of an Indian buffer state in this region, but the creation of a stable American government and the renewal of war with France paved the way for a settlement. Political and economic disputes were more or less disposed of simultaneously by the Jay Treaty of 1794. The American Senate indeed threw away the proffered right of limited entry into the West Indian trade and had to wait until 1830 before it was accorded under very different circumstances; but the redcoats did withdraw from the North-West Posts, and for ten years to come the United States was given most-favoured-nation treatment in the markets of the British Isles and the right, denied even to British colonies, of entry into the East India Company's immense sphere eastward of the Cape of Good Hope and westward of the Straits of Magellan. And, sure enough, the French Directory was so angered at this Anglo-American rapprochement that it denounced its American alliance, the only formal alliance the United States was ever to have with an Old World Power for more than a century.

The exclusion of the Americans from the West Indian trade meant that distant Canada, which had never been able to meet the needs of the French islands while she was still under the *fleur-de-lys*, was now called upon to provision the much more numerous British islands with such help as struggling Newfoundland and Nova Scotia could afford. One reason why this costly effort was made to foster the trade of British North America at the expense of the West Indies was that numerous American Tories, who could not endure the political and social revolution in the Old Thirteen, had gone thither. Some indeed found refuge in the West Indies or Great Britain herself; but the great majority, resolved to die as they had been born on British soil, migrated to the western half of Nova Scotia or to Ontario on the Great Lakes beyond the settled parts of French Quebec. The British Government and people found large sums for the assistance of these United Empire Loyalists who had deserved so well of them, and perhaps did too much for too long to find official posts in the colonies for them and their sons. Be that as it may, the immediate result of this loyal American invasion was the extension of freer institutions to British North America. In 1784 the western half of Nova Scotia became the colony of New Brunswick with privileges similar to those of the parent colony; in 1791 the naval control which had persisted in Newfoundland for the past fifty years was modified by the creation of a civil court; finally, in the same year, the Constitution Act relieved Canadian Loyalists of the unfamiliar French civil law, and sought to give them as little as possible to gain from cutting the painter by separating Anglo-American Ontario from French Quebec. Each of the Two Canadas was given a colonial constitution of the time-honoured type, with aristocratic modifications which, it was vainly hoped, would neutralise the democratic ideas that were so prevalent in the United States and France. It was the last such parliamentary constitution to be granted for thirty years.

So much for the West. Meanwhile British interests had been turning eastward since Clive's conquest of Bengal in 1757 and Captain James Cook's discovery of New South Wales and much else in the South Pacific a dozen years later. Now that the principal American colonies were gone the centre of gravity of the overseas empire shifted to the East and remained there for a full century.

The loss of the Old Thirteen led indeed directly to the formation of the most easterly of British colonies. Great Britain had sent convicts to the American plantations almost from the beginning and was still sending thither some five hundred annually at the outbreak of the War of Independence. She was now obliged to look around for some other 'receptacle' and found it in the reasonably fertile and happily far-away eastern shores of Australia. Hence, in January 1788, Captain Arthur Phillip founded Sydney with a company of marines and several hundred convicts, male and female, and annexed Norfolk Island and half the continent of 'New Holland', firmly believing that this 'New South Wales' would one day compensate his countrymen for the loss of the American colonies. For the time being, however, New South Wales was to be a self-supporting colony of peasants. Convict 'emancipists' who had served their time were offered small holdings in their new home, and presently it was resolved to 'clear the parishes' by sending after them folk who had been thrust off the land but were not yet marked by the broad arrow. So the shiploads of unfortunates, bond and free, went halfway round the world at irregular intervals, and the new colony struggled into being under the more or less benevolent autocracy of a naval Governor, a military court and a system of state socialism based on a currency of corn or rum and directed by officers of the New South Wales Corps. By 1796 Captain John Macarthur, the most energetic and avaricious of these officers, was experimenting with woolled sheep, whalers were putting into Sydney, and already, two years since, traders had opened up intercourse with Maori New Zealand twelve hundred miles to the eastwards. Meanwhile, in 1790, the mutineers of H.M.S. *Bounty* had planted themselves with their Tahitian brides on far-away Pitcairn Island, lost, they hoped, in the wastes of the Pacific Ocean.

In spite of North's Regulating Act and Hastings's reforms it was still an open question at the close of the American War whether the Company's administration in India was, in Burke's words, to bring the British 'great disgrace or great glory'. Pitt sought at least to make it 'a blessing to the native Indians'. His India Act of 1784 neither claimed for the Crown nor conferred on the Company the sovereignty which still lay in the feeble hands of the Great Mogul, nor did it deprive the Company of its cherished patronage or the monopoly of the India and China trades; but it did increase the power of the Governor-General at Calcutta over the three Presidencies of Bengal, Madras and Bombay by permitting him to override his Council, and subjected the Company to continuous parliamentary supervision exercised from London by a Board of Control responsible through its President to Parliament and competent to legislate over the Company's head. Such was the Dual Control under which British India was destined to be ruled for three-quarters of a century till the Crown superseded both Mogul and Company after the Indian Mutiny.[1]

Lord Cornwallis, first Governor-General under the new Act from 1786 till 1793, carried through far-reaching fiscal and administrative reforms, particularly in Bengal, and pushed on vigorously with the cleansing of the Company's service. Therein he was helped by the impeachment of Warren Hastings for high-handed and dubious acts committed during his dangerous term of office. That famous trial, begun in 1788, degenerated into a political persecution and ended in 1795 in an acquittal; nevertheless it was a salutary lesson to a corrupt generation that extortion, though for

[1] *Vide infra*, p. 77.

worthy public ends, simply could not be done even in an India inured from time immemorial to extortion for quite other purposes. Cornwallis also acquired coastal Indian territories wherever possible and gained an increasing control over the Indian Princes by means of the subsidiary treaties outlined by Clive. In terms of these treaties the Company guaranteed the signatory Princes against attack from without and revolt from within. In return it took charge of their external policies, stationed in their territories British and Indian troops subsidised by them, and sent them British Residents whose degree of authority would depend mainly on their own wisdom and character. Treaties such as these governed the long relations of the Crown with the greater Princes of India and, by analogy, still govern those with potentates in Malaya and other parts of the tropical Empire. It was prophetic of things still far distant that, in 1786, the Company should have leased Penang, its first foothold in the Malay Peninsula.

The British conscience stirred thus by the impeachment of Hastings was roused by reports of the horrors of the Slave Trade, the great scandal of the First British Empire. Poets and other thoughtful men in Great Britain, and Quakers on both sides of the Atlantic, had been crying out against it for some time past when Thomas Clarkson formed the Anti-Slave Trade Committee in 1787. The Evangelical philanthropists who rallied to his side found their parliamentary leader in William Wilberforce and an unexpected ally in Wilberforce's friend, the Prime Minister himself. At first Pitt hesitated to do more than limit the number of slaves that might be carried on a ship of a given tonnage, for opposition was strong, the prosperity of the West Indies, the West African stations and a great shipping depended on the Trade, and it was certain that France and other foreign rivals would snap up any of the traffic that Great Britain let drop. In 1792, however, as popular and parliamentary support stiffened, he persuaded the Commons in the finest speech of his life to resolve on gradual abolition; but the premature freeing of the French slaves by the Revolutionists led to what a British Governor called, in a triumph of meiosis, the 'inconveniences' of a ferocious rising of the blacks against their white masters in St. Domingo. Then Great Britain joined her allies of the First Coalition and for some years thereafter sent the bulk of her small army to fight French Jacobins, rebellious Negroes and the Yellow Jack in the rich, panic-stricken and strategically vulnerable West Indies. In face of that there could be no serious talk of the abolition of the Trade for a season. The Anti-Slave Traders must be content to preach with discretion, and meanwhile seek to save the settlement which some of them had founded in 1788 at Sierra Leone for ex-slaves who had been set free in England under Mansfield's famous judgement of 1772 or been taken by Loyalist masters from the United States to bleak Nova Scotia.

There is good Biblical authority for the doctrine that the law must precede liberty. That certainly was the belief of the British ruling classes after the excesses of Revolutionary France had driven Burke and the other Portland Whigs into the arms of Pitt's Tories. For fully twenty-five years after 1794 the watchwords of successive administrations were law, order and security.

Those principles had underlain the now superseded Quebec Act and had recently been asserted in their crudest form in the convict colony of New South Wales; they were now applied to Ireland side by side with a large measure of economic reform. Matters there drifted from bad to worse during the long French war. Tone's United Irishmen, disappointed of Catholic relief, began to work for a republic with French aid; pressed Irish sailors played a leading part in the wanton mutiny at the Nore during the Black Year of 1797; two unsuccessful French attempts to invade Ireland were followed by a desperate rebellion and fierce repression. Pitt, who had long ago contemplated the step, carried the legislative union of the two kingdoms. A federation might have brought more happiness to both partners; but federation was still an unproved 'Yankee notion', foreign to the traditions of a society which agreed with Blackstone, Chancellor Thurlow and Dr. Johnson that 'in sovereignty there are no gradations'. So, in 1800, the Irish were given liberal representation at Westminster and complete free trade within the Empire; but the bad old land laws remained, and the King forced Pitt to resign by his refusal to hear of Catholic emancipation. That came later, a generation too late to save the Union; for the rest, Ireland ceased to be part of the overseas Empire and was submerged rather than incorporated in the new United Kingdom of Great Britain and Ireland.

Law and order were necessarily the principles which guided the East India Company; the search for security was the motive which led its Governors-General, as a rule in defiance of the Directors' wishes, to extend the Company's authority either directly by annexation or indirectly by subsidiary treaties with the Princes. Between 1798 and 1805 Lord Wellesley conquered Mysore, pensioned the Mogul and defeated the Mahrattas; by 1818, after the final overthrow of the Mahrattas, Lord Hastings found himself Mayor of the Palace to the *roi fainéant* at Delhi and real ruler of all India up to the frontiers of Sind and the Punjab of Ranjit Singh. Thereafter the Company's power spread eastward. In 1819 Stamford Raffles acquired for it the splendid harbour of Singapore; five years later neighbouring Malacca was secured from the Dutch in exchange for Bencoolen, the Company's last station in the Spice Islands, and in 1826 both these acquisitions were placed under the jurisdiction of Penang which had been raised in 1805 to the rank of a Presidency equal to Bombay and Madras. In 1826 again, in revenge for an invasion of Bengal, the Company obliged Burma to yield to it some of her provinces fronting on the Bay of Bengal.

Meanwhile the Company was becoming more and more exclusively a ruling agency on behalf of the British Government. In terms of the Charter Act of 1813 it indeed retained its patronage and the monopoly of the China Trade, but it lost the monopoly of trade in India itself. At the same time and with many heart-searchings it admitted Christian missionaries to its Indian provinces, and set an example to the Imperial Government by making a small grant to public education. All was in keeping with Wellesley's warning that the Company's cadets must be trained, not as mere employees of a trading concern, but as representatives of a government charged with 'sacred trusts' for the welfare of the governed.

During the Revolutionary and Napoleonic Wars, and for some years thereafter, High Tory ministries with bitter American memories and present French fears, inevitably favoured strong official rule even in the colonies of settlement that still remained to them in North America. Governors of the Two Canadas, whose predecessors had looked upon the French Canadians as their defenders against *les Bastonnais* of New England, now relied upon the Family Compact of United Empire Loyalists to uphold the King's authority on the one hand against the French of Quebec, who were supposed to have Napoleonic sympathies, and on the other against the subversive doctrines of British and American immigrants of the 'lower orders' in Ontario. The loyalty of British and French alike during the American war of 1812–15 quieted these fears; the Napoleonic scare, never substantial, died away with the fall of the Emperor, and all immediate risk of American intervention ceased when Great Britain and the United States, in 1817–18, fixed their common frontier for most of the way from the Atlantic to the Rocky Mountains, and, thanks mainly to Castlereagh's wisdom, agreed to leave it undefended. But, for all that, neither Ministers nor Governors would hear of the colonial 'ministry' of which some French Canadians and their Anglo-American friends were talking.

British ministries of those days were much more interested in naval bases and commercial entrepôts than in colonies of settlement. In their eyes colonies were mainly factors in the problem of war, and it was no accident that in 1801 'Colonies' were transferred from the Home Secretary to the newly-created Secretary of State for War and remained in his hands for more than fifty years. Britain's hopes of victory in the long French wars had lain, as ever, in her ability to hold the seas, to deny to her enemies the use of their overseas bases and the produce of their colonies, and to finance herself and her continental allies by finding markets for the swelling output of her Industrial Revolution in the United States, her own overseas possessions and the colonial empires of other Powers to make up for the European markets which Jacobins and Napoleon alike tried to close against her. During both wars she had swept up the colonies of her enemies and, though she handed most of them back from a prudent liberality and a desire to achieve a satisfactory European settlement, some she kept. At the close of the Revolutionary war in 1802 she retained Spanish Trinidad, mainly as a centre for her growing trade with the eager Spanish and Portuguese colonists, and Dutch Ceylon, less for its cinnamon than for the harbour of Trincomalee which commanded the near approaches to both shores of India. At the end of the Napoleonic Wars in 1815 she kept Danish Heligoland as a stepping-stone to the Baltic and mouth of the Elbe, and Malta and a protectorate over the Ionian Islands to strengthen her hold on the Mediterranean and the overland route to India by way of Suez. It is true that in the Caribbean area she retained part of Dutch Guiana for the sake of its tropical produce and the heavy investments made there by British subjects; but she kept St. Lucia for the sake of its fine naval base, and Tobago for its anchorage and proximity to Trinidad. In African waters she annexed Ascension as a naval station and inaccessible Tristan da Cunha as a temporary military post on either side of Napoleon's prison of St. Helena. Finally she held on to the Dutch Cape Colony and French Mauritius, Rodriguez and the Seychelles to guard the long ocean route to her growing empire in the Indian and Pacific Oceans.

There could be no question of granting anything like the old type of colonial constitution to conquered colonies such as these, for they were inhabited by foreigners attached to their own languages and systems of law, unaccustomed to elective assemblies and as a rule outnumbered greatly by non-Europeans, bond and free. The British allowed such semi-representative institutions as there were to stand in Guiana and the Cape Colony, but there and elsewhere they imposed rigid Crown colony rule with as much power as possible concentrated in the hands of the Governor.

This policy of strengthening authority had the support of the Evangelicals, in whose ranks many officials were to be found, and of the Protestant missionaries. That missionary tide was at full flood in the early years of the nineteenth century with the London and Church Missionary Societies in the van, a cosmopolitan movement but so largely British in personnel and inspiration that jealous France regarded it as a political plot engineered by perfidious Albion. As a rule the missionaries, in India, southern Africa and the Pacific islands especially, looked to the executive authorities to make it possible for them to do their work, much as the Catholic Church had once looked to the Holy Roman Empire; hence they opposed the grant of local legislative powers to mixed colonies where the white inhabitants might be tempted to oppress their coloured fellow subjects, and often advocated the annexation of tribal areas in which they themselves had failed to buttress an effective native government lest uncontrolled European immigration, that most deadly solvent of tribal polities, should induce chaos.

The philanthropists sought especially to strengthen official control over the seventeen slave-owning colonies of the Empire, all of which, with the exception of Cape Colony and Mauritius, were in the Caribbean area. The British Government had been strengthening its hold there for some time past. In 1786, side by side with its reorganisation of the governments of British North America, it had appointed a Superintendent to control the logwood cutters on the Honduras coast who had been free to elect their own magistrates since 1638. A few years later it broke up the century-old

General Government and elective legislatures of the Leeward Islands, and shouldered the cost of the landward defence of Jamaica rather than let control of policy slip into the hands of the colonial Assembly. Presently it restored to oft-captured Tobago the free colonial institutions which had been first given to it after the Seven Years War; but it placed newly annexed Trinidad and St. Lucia under purely official rule, and when it regrouped the Leeward Islands under two governments in 1816 made no attempt to revive the federal legislature. On the contrary, officials and philanthropists were already talking of drastically amending the West Indian representative constitutions, some of the oldest in the Empire, as the only means of protecting the slaves against their owners.

By this time the British Slave Trade was a thing of the past. It had been forbidden in 1807, the year in which the United States Congress forbade it in vain to American citizens, and at the Vienna peace conference of 1814–15 Castlereagh had persuaded the Powers to pass a resolution against the 'traffic in human flesh'. Thereafter he and other British statesmen strove by all means to induce those Powers to honour their engagements, and extended a firmer control over the British stations on the slaving grounds of the African West Coast. The Crown had already relieved the philanthropists of Sierra Leone in 1808, and now, in 1816, it founded the tiny colony of Bathurst at the mouth of the Gambia. Five years later it took over the stations on that river and the Gold Coast from the Company of Merchants and grouped them under the Governor of Sierra Leone. This experiment was spoiled by a disastrous war with the fierce Ashanti which led the British Government to consider seriously the abandonment of all the posts on the threatened Gold Coast; but in the event it transferred these in 1828 to a London Committee of Merchants which ruled them tolerably well during the next fifteen years with the help of a meagre subsidy.

Meanwhile Sierra Leone continued to rule the Gambia and became the headquarters of the British 'sentimental squadron' which waged a costly, single-minded and thankless crusade against slavers of all nations. Chiefest of these were Americans in defiance of their own federal authorities, for the insatiable demands of the Lancashire and New England mills had given slavery a new lease of life by making cotton king of the Southern States. On the other hand slavery was fighting a losing battle within the British Empire. Neither the West Indian interest at home, faced with the competition of the French

Antilles and Spanish Cuba, nor the island legislatures, haunted by fear of their own blacks, could stand up to insistent pressure. Urged on by Wilberforce, the British Government first obliged the West Indian Assemblies to adopt the laws against illicit slave traffic, which it was imposing elsewhere, by threatening to legislate over their heads. Then in 1823 Fowell Buxton, supported by the ageing Wilberforce, opened his campaign for gradual emancipation. At first he worked along the line desired by Canning and his Young Tories of seeking to 'ameliorate' the lot of the slaves, and during the next few years saw this prudent policy imposed upon those colonies which had no Assemblies and pressed with scant success upon those who had. When, however, the victorious Whigs had carried the great Reform Bill, Buxton, sure of immense popular support, decided to force the pace. Hence the Emancipation Act of 1833 set free 800,000 slaves at the cost of £20,000,000 to the British taxpayer. To the slaves and the British public it was an act of the purest liberalism, but to the slave-owners it was a threat of ruination and a decisive step in the process of constitutional 'reform backwards'.

It was fitting that in this same year the Houses at Westminster, which were thus undeniably making good their claim to be an imperial legislature, should have constituted the Judicial Committee of the Privy Council the final court of appeal for the whole Empire outside the limits of the United Kingdom. Meanwhile the Secretary of State for War and the Colonies, whose effective power was increasing steadily, had built up a much better organisation at headquarters than ever before. During his long tenure of office from 1812 till 1827 Lord Bathurst revived a short-lived experiment of the unappreciated Shelburne by appointing two Under-Secretaries in his department: one for the Colonies, the other for War, and each with his own staff. Thus came into being the 'Downing Street' anathematised by the Colonial Reformers of the next generation, but, for all that, an unrivalled school of administration and a storehouse of experience wider and more enduring than that of any one of its critics.

Long before the period of law and order ended there were signs that the Empire was returning to the tradition of freedom that had been its glory and perplexity from the beginning. The High Tories, who had won the war and then carried the Corn Laws and muzzled popular liberties during the dangerous post-war years, fell in 1822. They were succeeded by Canning's Young Tories who reformed the fierce old criminal laws, repealed the war-time combination laws which had banned trade unions, removed old seventeenth-century restrictions on emigration and, within limits, on the export of machinery, enfranchised Catholics and Nonconformists in the United Kingdom, and then handed over to Grey's Whig ministry which was pledged to a sweeping reform of the electoral system.

The Reform Act of 1832 aimed primarily at giving full weight to the new middle class which had risen to affluence on the crest of the Industrial Revolution. That revolution had gathered strength fast during the French wars and was now spreading overseas. Home supplies of wool had failed to meet the home demand for the first time in the year in which Great Britain went to war with Revolutionary France; by the time Napoleon fell cotton had displaced woollens as Britain's chief export and the power loom was beginning to drive out the handweavers; when the Young Tories took office Yorkshire was drawing its wool from distant New South Wales, and cotton was promising to recompense Lancashire for the loss of the slave trade by finding its way into the immense Indian market. Moreover, communications were fast reducing the size of the world measured in time. The famous stage coaches of Pickwick's days and the less spectacular canal barges had reached their zenith only to be challenged by the steamboats and loco-motives which had first been proved practicable while Napoleon's Army of England was massing at Boulogne. In 1819 a paddle-steamer helped out by sails crossed the Atlantic; during the next decade similar ships made their way to Bombay and Sydney round the Cape of Good Hope, and England and the eastern United States were busily building railways.

The old mercantilist framework of the Empire could not stand the strain. It had already been warped almost out of recognition by internal lesions and external pressures since the days when Pitt had fought for free trade in vain. Long-continued privileges had been granted to useful neutrals during the French wars; both then and in the years immediately following the peace free ports were multiplied at which foreign ships might exchange goods of their own countries for British products; in the year of Waterloo Great Britain and the United States mutually abolished the differential harbour dues and

D

duties levied on their respective shippings. Not only so, but the outer world had changed. Very little remained of the old French colonial empire; Holland indeed still held large possessions in the East and West Indies, but was no longer financier and common carrier to half Europe; Ireland was now a problem within the United Kingdom instead of outside it. Beyond the Atlantic the United States had set up a tariff to protect the industries which had sprung to life behind the British blockade during the war of 1812–15; on the other hand Brazil had separated herself from Portugal at British instigation during the Peninsular War, and most of the Spanish-American mainland colonies had revolted with the aid of Englishmen and Americans zealous for liberty and commerce. These colonies secured their independence behind the shelter of the Royal Navy and the Monroe Doctrine. In 1823 Canning warned half-hearted France that Great Britain would resist all attempts by the Holy Alliance to restore Bourbon authority beyond the Atlantic. He failed, however, to secure United States co-operation, for President Monroe contented himself with disclaiming any intention of interfering in Europe and informing the European Powers, including Russia, that they must confine their transatlantic activities to their existing possessions. Canning, without assenting to this new 'Doctrine', presently followed Monroe's example by recognising the Latin American republics, and then set himself the easy task of preventing the formation of a Pan-American *bloc* under United States hegemony.

It is no wonder that in this changing world the Nova Scotian legislature should have called upon all British North America to demand the freedom of trade enjoyed by the United States, and the London Chamber of Commerce, in 1820, asked bluntly for free trade. No Tory could grant that, but William Huskisson took the lead in substituting reciprocity and imperial preferences for a decayed mercantilism as the fiscal basis of an empire which he hoped might prove to be the greatest political force for good in the world. The chaos of customs duties was reduced to order; the excise was overhauled so effectively that Scotch whisky became an Englishman's drink; obsolete Navigation Acts were jettisoned, and the Anglo-American abolition of differential harbour dues was extended by treaty to all the Powers of Europe except Holland, who, in Canning's opinion, proposed to give too little and asked for too much. Britain carefully reserved the long haul between her own ports and those of Africa, Asia and the Americas, and, on the analogy of the jealously guarded United States coasting traffic, confined to imperial shipping the trade between herself and her colonies, and one colony and another; but she gave her colonies much greater freedom than before to send their goods in their own ships to foreign ports, and permitted the republics of North, Central and South America to trade in their own ships direct with British ports. She also extended widely the principles of free ports and reciprocity by allowing foreign ships, whose governments gave British ships similar privileges, to carry to specified British colonial harbours everything except such goods as could compete with basic British manufactures. Finally she gave large preferences in the home market to colonial goods to make up for the bounties which were being steadily dropped, and in return gave herself similar favours in colonial markets. The United States was moved to retaliate against these imperial preferences; but 'the Tariff of Abominations' nearly split the Union, South against North, and in 1830, the year of Huskisson's untimely death, the United States agreed that the system was reasonable enough. In return she was admitted at long last to the West Indian trade on the same footing as the privileged British North American colonies.

While the United States, now twenty-four strong, was thus regaining bit by bit the benefits of the British connection which the Old Thirteen had forfeited in 1776, the English chartered companies, the oldest of which had seen the foundation of Virginia, passed away one by one. The eighteenth-century West African Company of Merchants, never a monopoly, expired in 1821; four years later the Elizabethan Levant Company handed over to the Crown its powers and responsibilities in the widespread Ottoman Empire; in 1833, the year of slave emancipation, the Elizabethan East India Company lost its one remaining monopoly of the China trade. In this age of freer trade only the Restoration Hudson's Bay Company retained its full and exclusive commercial vigour, for the Committee of London Merchants which administered the unwanted Gold Coast between 1828 and 1843 was obviously a stop-gap.

Meanwhile emigrants had begun to pour out of the United Kingdom alongside the swelling flood of goods, their sufferings mitigated by native good humour and hope. The modest stream of emigration which had flowed to British North America and New

South Wales before 1793 had dwindled thereafter to a mere trickle, mostly of dispossessed Highlanders, Irishmen and convicts, for the seas were dangerous in spite of the Nile and Trafalgar and the authorities were anxious to conserve man-power. The outbreak of war with the United States in 1812, however, impelled them to encourage migration to British North America to strengthen the frontier guard, and then the post-war slump suggested to them, as to their early seventeenth-century predecessors, that emigration might also be a cure for unemployment. With both ends in view they tried at first to direct the flow towards the Cape Colony of which great things were expected now that Capetown and neighbouring Mauritius, whose commercial connection with the Colony had always been close, were being declared free ports. In 1820 the British Government planted a considerable number of British settlers at the public charges in Albany on the dangerous eastern or Kaffir frontier from which a large proportion of the garrison had recently been withdrawn. These 1820 Settlers gave to the Eastern Province a British quality which still persists in a predominantly Afrikander colony; but very few unassisted British emigrants followed them. On the other hand some of them, from 1824 onwards, helped to found an unauthorised trading and ivory hunting centre far to the eastward at Port Natal (Durban) by leave of the Zulu Kings.

Distant New South Wales, which was to have been a self-supporting colony, had cost the British taxpayer a cool £10,000,000 by 1821; but it had grown steadily and could count some 30,000 inhabitants, half of them free men or 'emancipists'. Free settlers had also followed the convicts to Van Diemen's Land (Tasmania) which had been occupied in 1804 to forestall the French, and squatters, whose sheep-runs sometimes surpassed in size even the Afrikander farms of the period, were beginning to send wool to the London market from the island and the mainland. In 1821, therefore, New South Wales was opened to settlement by folk of means and their dependants, who came at the rate of 1,000 annually and changed markedly the character of the little-esteemed dependency in a decade. In 1829 free settlements, the luckless beginnings of Western Australia, were planted near the Swan river at the other end of the continent, while, far away to the eastward, British whalers, traders, beachcombers, escaped convicts and devoted missionaries were settling in such numbers among the Maoris of

the North Island of New Zealand that already, in 1817, the New
South Wales courts had been given criminal jurisdiction over
British subjects in those parts provided the accused and the witnesses
could be brought back for trial on colonial soil.

Nevertheless, in spite of official wishes and the call of Australian
wool, the main stream of British emigration flowed as ever across
the North Atlantic. Most of these west-going emigrants still set
out for 'Philadelphia in the morning', but from 1824 onwards a
notable proportion proceeded to Ontario where John Galt's
Canada Company was opening up good lands along the Great
Lakes. British folk were soon going to the North American
colonies at the rate of 20,000 annually, rising in 1831, the year of
the Great Immigration, to no fewer than 34,000.[1]

Emigration, combined with political and economic reform at
home, led necessarily to constitutional changes in the colonies.
Reforms in the slave and convict colonies, which made up so much
of the overseas Empire of those days, were in large measure inspired
by the Royal Commissions of Inquiry which reported between 1819
and 1831. The Commissions which visited the harassed West
Indies and the well-nigh derelict West African stations could effect
little; but those which inspected the Cape Colony, Mauritius,
Ceylon and New South Wales achieved much greater success.
The same men served on more than one of them, and all treated
these colonies bordering on the Indian Ocean as members of a single
class with mixed populations, bond and free, the convicts and
emancipists of New South Wales answering to the slaves and more
or less tribal majorities in the other dependencies.

In many respects the reforms in this group of colonies were
based on those which had been carried out long ago in Ceylon.
On its conquest in 1796 that island had been entrusted to the East
India Company, but the Madras officials with their swarms of alien
Indian underlings had soon bred rebellion. In 1801, therefore,
Ceylon was placed under the Crown and in the course of the next
few years its administration was framed on Company lines. Power
was concentrated in the hands of the Governor, who was assisted but
in no way controlled by an official Advisory Council; a civil
service, the first and for a long time the only one of its kind in a
colony, was formed of young Englishmen trained on the spot; an
elaborate judicial system was set up. A Supreme Court of two

[1] Some 226,000 emigrants left the United Kingdom between 1821–31.

English judges dealt with cases in which Europeans were involved; both judges were bidden to go on circuit; they and the Governor formed the court of appeal from the native local courts over which European officials presided; appeals from the Supreme Court and this local court of appeal lay to the Privy Council. Full weight was given to native custom, and the introduction of the jury system inevitably entailed the adoption of a good deal of British procedure, but in the main, on the analogy of the French law in Quebec, the Roman-Dutch law was retained.

One notable reform had been effected in New South Wales as early as 1812 by the appointment of a fully qualified judge who took civil cases out of the hands of the highly unsuitable military court and served as a court of local appeal. The Royal Commissioners now came to Sydney heralded by Brougham's reminder that even in convict settlements 'the common law is the birthright of Englishmen'. On their recommendation the transportation system was rendered less inhumane and, in 1823, Parliament enacted the first colonial constitution which it had essayed since Pitt's Canada Act thirty years back. An official Advisory Council was set up similar to that in Ceylon, and the military criminal court was superseded by a Supreme Court and Court of Appeal with circuits and jury complete. Two years later Van Diemen's Land became a separate colony endowed with similar institutions, and unofficial nominees were added to the New South Wales Council. Presently the legislature of each colony was divided into an Executive Council and a Legislative Council of officials and unofficial nominees whose majority could at least restrain His Excellency. Finally, an official Advisory Council was set up in struggling Western Australia, and in 1832 a helpless magistrate was sent to New Zealand to control as best he might British subjects in the North Island.

Tentative reforms had been set on foot in the Cape Colony also before the coming of the Commission of Inquiry; such were the institution of circuit courts in 1811, and the gradual substitution from 1822 onwards of English for High Dutch as the official language of a dependency in which it was expected that British immigrants would soon outnumber the scanty Afrikander population. Some of the reforms now carried through on the Ceylon model were of the law and order variety. The debased and mixed currency was linked to British silver; magistrates and civil commissioners were substituted for the semi-representative local boards of the Dutch East India Company's days, and a professional Supreme Court and Court of Appeal superseded the clumsy and amateur Dutch courts; but though the recently reformed English criminal procedure and mercantile law came into use, the Roman-Dutch civil law was retained. Other reforms were of a more liberal character. An official Advisory Council was created in 1825 and reinforced presently by unofficial nominees, as in New South Wales, while at about the same time the powerful Dutch Reformed Church was allowed to meet in Synod, a free press was guaranteed, and 'free persons of colour' were put on a footing of virtual equality before the law with white 'Christian men'.

An official Advisory Council was also set up in Mauritius in 1825, but there the French courts administering Bourbon law and the civil Code Napoleon were continued with very few changes. Finally, between 1832 and 1834, Legislative Councils of officials and unofficial nominees on the New South Wales model were established in the Cape Colony, Mauritius and Ceylon. In spite of Cape Colonists' demands for representative institutions, backed by the appeal of one Scottish enthusiast to 'American example', H.M. Government could not and would not do more for such mixed communities at a time when 'elected persons' in many of the West Indian islands were sabotaging its efforts to ameliorate the lot of their slaves.

The demand for constitutional reform was naturally strongest in the Two Canadas, and here it had the best hope of being met; for the European population was already considerable, there were neither slaves, convicts, nor tribesmen worth mentioning to complicate the issue, and always, south of the Undefended Frontier, lay the United States offering the democratic republican alternative to free institutions within the Empire. Fast-growing Ontario might resent the retention by stagnant Quebec of the customs dues levied at the ports of Quebec and Montreal which served both provinces; but democratic British and American newcomers were at one with nationalist *Canadiens* in their hostility to the United Empire Loyalists who shared with British officials a monopoly of seats in the Executive and Legislative Councils. The dissenting majority in Ontario complained that only the Anglican and Scottish Established clergy benefited from the large clergy reserves of land in each township, while French Catholics followed Louis Papineau, Speaker of the Quebec Assembly, in condemning the seigneuries as a useless burden

and demanding an elective upper house and control of all revenues.
The Assemblies of both provinces refused, as obstinately as those of
the Old Thirteen had done in days gone by, to vote a permanent
civil list to the local officials whose resources, secured though they
were by the laws of 1774, had long been inadequate.

At last, in 1822, Parliament gave Ontario its fair share of the
customs revenue, but failed to induce either province to agree to the
reunion of the Two Canadas, the installation of four non-voting
officials in the combined Assembly to explain policy and, as in the
Cape Colony, the gradual adoption of English as the sole official
language. Then the new Whig ministry of 1830, anxious to be
conciliatory, endowed Quebec and Montreal with municipal
institutions, but threw away its trump card by giving the provincial
legislatures control of nearly all the revenues. Appeasement failed.
Ontario indeed fulfilled its side of the tacit bargain by voting an
adequate civil list; but the response of the anti-British and isolationist Assembly of Quebec was nugatory, and forthwith men like
Robert Baldwin of Ontario, Lemuel Wilmot of New Brunswick,
and Joseph Howe of Nova Scotia echoed in more moderate tones
Papineau's demand for ministers who had the confidence of the
elected Assembly. It was small consolation to these reformers, in
the year of Britain's great Reform Act, that Newfoundland, which
had been given a civilian Governor and Supreme Court on the
Ceylon-New South Wales model in 1825, should now be given
old-fashioned representative institutions, or that New Brunswick
be brought into line with its neighbours by the separation of its
Upper House from the Executive Council. What they wanted was a
full parliamentary constitution similar to that which the Mother
Country had only achieved for herself as recently as 1784. And
already Ontario men had found a name for it: responsible government.

III

RESPONSIBLE GOVERNMENT, 1833-1874

THE achievement of colonial self-government and much else of lasting importance to the British Empire belongs to the great Victorian Age. Heralded by the Reform and Emancipation Acts, this formative period of middle class ascendancy fairly began with the happy accession of a young Queen who restored the waning prestige of monarchy by ending the monstrous regiment of uncles; it reached its climax forty years later in a further burst of reform which covered the House of Commons once more, Irish land, popular education and the safety of merchant seamen.

In the middle eighteen-thirties new imperial problems were coming to the front; during the next four decades those problems were to receive at least tentative solutions. By the middle 'seventies the United Kingdom and the still dependent portions of the Empire had almost forgotten Huskisson's reciprocity and learned to take free trade for granted; the Queen ruled an Indian Empire greater and more closely-knit than any Mogul or Company had known; convict transportation was an evil memory, and slaves in the tropical colonies had long since made way for free men and indentured Indian coolies; questions of Native policy had supplanted Emancipation as the first interest of philanthropists; slaving by white men had ended at last, and Europeans were preparing to deal justly in Central and East Africa with the Arab slave trade whose horrors had been revealed by explorers of all nations. Finally the British at home, themselves accustomed to reforms, had been ready to grant the reforms demanded by their fellows overseas. It is true that many of the tropical colonies had made no constitutional advance, and others, among them the oldest, had been 'reformed backwards'; but an unprecedented system of governance had been worked out in the colonies of settlement, and the chief group of those colonies had formed a federation within the Empire extending from the Atlantic to the Pacific Ocean.

Conditions were uniquely favourable for the free movement of men, goods and ideas that marked the rapid and, in most parts of the world, peaceful expansion of the Empire during these forty years. Great Britain exercised the naval monarchy, which Nelson and his captains had given her, with wise moderation and in the international spirit that suited her world-wide political and commercial interests; she seemed to find sufficient occupation for her unrivalled Navy in routing out pirates, chasing slavers and mapping the coasts and waters of the globe in charts that do not lie for the good of all who 'pass on the seas upon their lawful occasions'. For the rest the Navy kept war at a distance. The small British Army saw fighting in plenty in North-West India and Afghanistan, and waged minor campaigns against South African tribesmen, Boers, Maoris and Chinamen; but even when Great Britain took part in the Crimean War, which broke the forty years of peace between the European Powers that had followed Waterloo, the conflict was localised in the Baltic and Black Seas. The cycle of nationalist wars which scourged Europe and North America between 1859 and 1871 touched neither Britain nor her Empire directly.

It was now that Great Britain reaped the full benefits of her island position at the main cross-roads of the world's trade routes. The Great Exhibition of 1851 showed her for what she was: a land with a growing population fit and able to people the waste spaces of the earth, fed by a sufficient and highly-skilled agriculture, enriched by finance, industry and commerce far in advance of those of its rivals, well equipped and eager to trade with a world which had not yet heard the blessed word 'autarky'; the home of a *laissez-faire* utilitarian philosophy that regarded intercourse as a good in itself; the guardian of philanthropic traditions towards slaves and tribesmen; the only begetter of those parliamentary institutions and practices which her people regarded as the highest political achievement of man and a boon to be shared as widely as might be with others; a land fitted as no other land had yet been to be the centre and inspiration of a liberal Empire.

Critics from Carlyle and Dickens downwards have jeered at these Victorians as humbugs, smug and self-satisfied, caring more for distant dark-skinned folk than for the pale-faced poor of their own towns, too often saying 'Christ' when they meant 'Cotton'. There is truth in the jeer; but a generation, like a man, may claim that its work be judged as a whole and pray that in mercy its good deeds be remembered rather than its ill. Let it be recorded therefore that these same Victorians showed the world how to control the violence of the Industrial Revolution by means of factory and mines Acts, trade unions and co-operative societies; that they began to solve by their public health laws the age-old problem of how men were to live and not die in great cities; that they believed with Fowell Buxton and David Livingstone that cotton could be made the obedient servant of Christ by furthering the legitimate commerce which should kill the slave trade, raise the savage from his degradation and give the official, missionary and planter a possible field to work in. Let it be remembered also that they staked their fortunes on the belief that the free trade which suited British merchants, manufacturers and urban workers would suit all the world in the long run, and meanwhile do away with the struggle for closed mercantilist empires which was, as Adam Smith had noted in less happy days, one of the most certain causes of war. And who considering the latter-day scramble for *Lebensraum* dare say that they and Smith were wholly wrong? As for self-satisfaction, were not these Victorians doing things in all directions that had never been tried before? They may be forgiven if they believed that the special favour of Milton's God shone upon 'His Englishman'—and Scotsman—of whom He was demanding so much. Certain it is that they made the Second British Empire, setting their mark indelibly upon it and, in spite of manifold shortcomings and backslidings, holding to standards of liberty, the potential equality of all men and the supreme importance of the human soul that can only be rejected by the Empire and the world at their peril.

The Empire that the Victorians made was a threefold empire: the self-governing colonies, India, and the dependent colonies. Long before the end of the period in 1874 the political relations of the United Kingdom with the self-governing colonies were guided by the idea that subordination should give way to association on equal terms, and with India and the dependencies by the necessary conceptions of law, order and security tempered by trusteeship.

Trusteeship, one of the finest legacies of the Victorian Age to the modern Empire, had been foreshadowed in a measure by Pitt and Burke in their speeches on the India Bill of 1784, and, twenty years later, by Wellesley in his directions for the training of the Company's servants; but what those men had had in mind was good governance in keeping with the principles of justice and mercy that dictated the abolition of the slave trade. The full conception was first set out in the eighteen-twenties by Thomas Munro, the great administrator of Madras, who looked forward to the time when the British should have trained Indians to manage their own affairs and would then probably find it best for both countries that they should gradually withdraw their control over India.[1] A decade later, while the British were freeing their slaves, abolishing the legal colour bar in the Cape Colony and forbidding it to find a place in the East India Company's service, Macaulay could merely look forward to the proud day when an enlightened India should demand British institutions; but in the 'forties, at a time when the colonies of settlement were moving fast towards the self-government which should designedly enable them to stand upon their own feet, Henry Lawrence of the Punjab and Rajputana was to re-affirm Munro's full doctrine. Meanwhile thoughtful men sought to apply the idea to Africa. The Commons' Aborigines Committee of 1837 and, even more explicitly, Fowell Buxton in 1840, could doubt whether the British could 'rescue Africa' if the burden were to fall wholly and permanently on them, but could hope that they were 'competent to achieve the much less onerous task of calling forth her powers, and enabling her to stand alone'. A few years later Earl Grey was to declare that it was Britain's interest gradually to train the peoples of West Africa 'until they shall grow into a nation capable of protecting themselves and of managing their own affairs'. In 1865 a West African Royal Commission was to envisage the same high end.

There was to be less hopeful talk of trusteeship in the full sense for India after the shock of the Mutiny in 1857, and slower progress in tropical Africa than enthusiasts had hoped. Nevertheless, by 1874 the British had imperial achievements of the first order to their credit: the advancement in power, wealth, cohesion and political status of their colonies of settlement and the organisation of India as an empire within the British Empire.

When Englishmen of those days talked of 'the colonies' they usually meant the colonies of settlement. The growth and advancement of these were made possible by a great outpouring of folk from Western Europe: from Great Britain always, then from Catholic Ireland also and from the German and Scandinavian lands.

[1] *Vide*, pp. 156–171; 228–9; 236–8; 261–7; 306–321.

The main stream flowed as before to the United States, but a considerable volume was directed towards British territories.[1] Much of it was literally directed. As in the early seventeenth century, men hoped to ease the dislocations of British society, and now also to defeat the prophecy of Malthus that population must always tend to press upon the means of subsistence, by sending surplus capital and labour to build up New Britains in the vast open spaces overseas, new fields of exchange which would benefit the colonies, the Mother Country and foreign nations alike. The Colonial Reformers developed their ideas from 1830 onwards. Men like Gibbon Wakefield, Charles Buller and Lord Durham taught that land, the chief asset of new colonies, must no longer be squandered in lavish grants but auctioned periodically at a 'sufficient price'. This would give the colonies a general revenue and a land fund with which to finance further immigration, and meanwhile oblige newcomers to develop the already settled parts by hiring themselves out as labourers till they had saved enough to buy land for themselves a little farther out. Thus would self-supporting colonies expand automatically.

Wakefield was destined to complain that the scientific colonising system which bears his name was never fully tried anywhere, though the British Government did appoint first an Agent-General for Emigration and then, in 1840, a Colonial Land and Emigration Board which more or less directed the peopling of the overseas Empire during the next three vital decades. To be sure, neither Lord Ripon's decree of 1831 that colonial Crown lands were to be auctioned nor Wakefield's scheme was ever applied to British North America. Immigration there was guided by the local authorities who adapted to their own needs the effective United States system of selling moderate-sized blocks of surveyed land on easy terms. By 1840 the Huron Company was planting settlers by the thousand in western Ontario; a few years later famine-stricken Irish folk were trooping into eastern Canada, while men of all sorts were racing United States citizens overland or round by Cape Horn to Oregon on the Pacific Slope.

Nor did the Ripon principle or emigration schemes of any kind have much influence in South Africa with its poor soil, chancy

---

[1] Some 5,932,000 emigrants left the United Kingdom between 1831 and 1871, about 750,000 of them for the United States.

rainfall and numerous Cape Coloured and tribal Bantu inhabitants. One small and fruitful 'Wakefield' settlement was made in newly-annexed Natal in 1849;[1] one officially assisted emigration scheme brought a considerable number of British to the western Cape Colony between 1844 and 1847, and another a decade later planted British and Germans in the eastern districts and the adjacent little colony of British Kaffraria; but European expansion in South Africa was due mainly to the Great Trek of the Afrikander pastoralists northward out of the parent Cape Colony from 1835 onwards. This was a dispersal rather than a colonisation. Only in the early 'seventies did gold and diamonds attract overseas immigrants in any number to the interior and the ports which grew in sympathy with the mining centres up-country.

Australia and New Zealand were the fields in which the Emigration Board and scientific colonisers found most scope. Even so, much of the planting of the continent of 'New Holland' was done on the old haphazard lines. Just when the Great Trek was beginning in earnest in South Africa, the New South Wales authorities set their squatters and their sheep free to go where they would. Soon pioneers from the older settlements round Sydney had gone north into what is now Queensland, or southward to Port Philip (Victoria) where they met pastoralists coming north from Van Diemean's Land, while, during the 'mania' of land speculation which accompanied this migration, eager newcomers poured in from overseas so fast that, when the boom broke in 1840, New South Wales had been transformed from a convict settlement into a free colony. In witness of that fact the British Government ceased to transport convicts thither. On the other hand South Australia centring upon Adelaide had been founded in 1836 as a completely free colony on Wakefield lines, and in 1842 Parliament adopted Wakefield's main principle by directing that, though the New South Wales authorities might issue temporary occupation certificates to pastoralists, land in all the Australian colonies must be auctioned at an upset price and half the proceeds be devoted to the financing of immigration.

These same years saw a notable eastward extension of British authority. Since 1830 H.M. Government had been coming to the conclusion reluctantly that it must assume responsibility for at least the North Island of New Zealand to preserve order there, support the missionaries, encourage lawful traders many of whom had New

[1] Annexed in 1843.

South Wales connections, and safeguard Maori society from dis-integration at the hands of uncontrolled white settlers. Hence in 1840 the Crown signed the Treaty of Waitangi with some of the Maori chiefs and annexed the whole of New Zealand. Forthwith Wakefield's New Zealand Company began to plant coastal settle-ments which were presently reinforced by others organised on similar lines by the Anglican Church and the Established Church of Scotland. When the New Zealand Company resigned its charter in 1850 the new colony was on its feet. Twenty years later white settlement had penetrated far inland.

Side by side with this free expansion of British settlement over-seas went the freeing of British imperial trade. In the middle eighteen-thirties the imperial fiscal system rested upon those Navigation Acts which had survived Huskisson's most-favoured-nation treaties, the Corn Laws of 1815 modified now by a jerky sliding scale which kept foreign corn out of the United Kingdom for the benefit of the landed interest until the price of home-grown corn had reached a certain level, the sugar duties which gave the failing West Indian interest a highly privileged position in the insatiable British market, and the timber tax, that 'premium on dry-rot', which favoured the United Empire Loyalist colonies of North America. These preferential quasi-monopolies of staple products were buttressed by many others; but the life had gone out of Huskisson's system of reciprocity and imperial preference since a railway engine, most typical product of the Industrial Revolution, had killed its creator in 1830. The time was now coming when the advancing Industrial Revolution was to sweep away the whole elaborate structure.

The Corn Laws were the key of the position, for if Great Britain, the one big importer of continental European wheat, abandoned these no one would be sufficiently interested or strong enough to maintain the rest: hence industrialists and urban workers, set upon cheap bread or at least stable wages and prices, rallied to Richard Cobden's Anti-Corn Law League. Sir Robert Peel, the middle-class Tory Premier, played for time by instituting a flexible sliding scale to regulate imports, but the rains of 1845 in Ireland 'rained away the Corn Laws'. The overburdened Irish potato crop failed; the Corn Laws had to be suspended in the fight against famine and disease, and in 1846 Peel broke his party by arranging for their abolition in 1849. In that year the remaining Navigation Acts were also repealed, and by 1863 all preferences were gone, even the tobacco preference, the oldest in the Empire. Customs duties followed them wholesale, and by 1874 nothing remained of the old fiscal order but a few duties on luxuries. The gulf in the revenue was filled unto this day by the income-tax.

Contrary to expectation the repeal of the Corn Laws neither ruined the British farmer nor reduced markedly the price of bread; but, helped by the discovery of gold in California, south-eastern Australia and British Columbia between 1845 and 1856, it stabilised that price and therefore wages. Nor did British shipping suffer from the repeal of the Navigation Acts, for not only was there a growing demand for its services, but steam-driven iron ships, slow in coming, had come at last and in such matters industrialised Britain had the advantage over her competitors. For a time also it seemed that one of the wider hopes of the Free Traders was to be realised when the United States and the Prussian *Zollverein* both adopted low tariffs, and Cobden's commercial treaty of 1860 with Napoleon III ranged France on the same side for twenty years to come. It is true that the victorious American Federalists, who bore England little love and had many war-time industries to cherish, showed signs of reverting to protectionism after the War of Secession; but on the whole the world of western civilisation remained a freely trading world, with its currencies linked to the British pound sterling, till the end of the 'seventies. The other great hope of the Free Traders was, however, disappointed almost at once. The Crimean campaign of 1854 and the subsequent nationalist wars on both sides of the North Atlantic were a sorry commentary on their dreams of a pacific new order.

Before the Crimean war broke out, however, the British Empire had evolved its system of colonial self-government. If immigration to the colonies of settlement made this unique experiment desirable, Free Trade made it possible. Pitt's failure in Ireland in the old mercantilist days had proved how hard it must be to confine an autonomous member of the Empire within the British laws of trade. Even Huskisson's much more flexible and generous preferential system could not resolve that difficulty since it was after all imposed by the Westminster Parliament upon the United Kingdom and her dependencies overseas. The situation was radically different in a free trade Empire. If colonies were no longer to be rated above foreign states as contributors to the wealth and power of the Empire, why burden the Mother Country with the cost and anxiety of governing, sustaining, placating and defending them? The most admired writers on colonial topics, recalling Adam Smith's prophecy that ex-colonists would become 'instead of turbulent and factious subjects . . . faithful, affectionate and generous allies', could urge that colonisation should aim at commerce rather than dominion.

There were other considerations. Most of the Utilitarians regarded colonies as undertakings calculated to bring the greatest misery to the greatest number. Radicals, like Cobden and Bright, not only hoped to see the British come out of Asia before India had corrupted them as the provinces had corrupted republican Rome, but condemned colonies as a positive danger. The Tory and imperially-minded Huskisson, with the example of the United States and the Latin American republics before him, had agreed with eighteenth-century Turgot that colonies would one day be 'free nations'; now Whigs could reflect that little harm would come of separation except possibly to Britain's honour and more certainly to the stability of the ministry, while, as late as 1867, the Conservative Disraeli, no longer young, could wonder what was 'the use of these colonial dead-weights which we do not govern'. If the colonies were sure to go their own ways sooner or later, still more if they were to be sent about their business at the first reasonable opportunity, they must be taught to govern themselves so that the parting might be cordial and unspoilt by subsequent recriminations. Even the Colonial Reformers, who almost alone insisted that colonies of settlement could and ought to continue within the Empire, were at one with their opponents in desiring self-government for them.

Colonial self-government was evolved from representative institutions in typically British fashion: a minimum of theory and legislation, considerable discussion and the tackling of each workaday problem as it arose. It was worked out first in the British North American colonies. The propinquity of these colonies to the great American Republic made it hard for British ministers to refuse the demands of Baldwin and Papineau, Wilmot and Howe, for local executive councillors who had the confidence of the legislatures; but the prevalent Austinian theory which could not admit 'gradations in sovereignty', the fact that the Empire was still treated as an economic unit, and the fear that the bosses and spoils system of the

E

new Jacksonian democracy would come north across the Undefended Frontier forbade them to yield. Matters came to a head
in Quebec and Ontario in 1837. While West Indians were mutter-
ing sullenly and Afrikander trekkers leaving the Cape Colony in
dudgeon, sputtering rebellions broke out in each province, headed
respectively by Papineau and William Lyon Mackenzie. Both
risings were easily put down, the two ringleaders fled to the United
States, and the British Government suspended the Quebec constitution. It then sent out the Whig colonial reformer, Lord Durham, as
Governor-General.

In his famous Report of 1839, the Magna Carta of colonial self-
government, 'Radical Jack' aimed at encouraging something of a
Canadian nationality to counteract the southward pull of the United
States. He therefore recommended the union of the Two Canadas
so that the combined British vote might outweigh that of the
'stationary French', and the grant of self-government in local
matters to this predominantly British and presumably trustworthy
legislature. But for all that he made four imperial reservations. He
insisted that the British Government must retain the sole power to
alter the colonial constitution, control of foreign policy, the regulation of trade, and the administration of the Crown lands, 'the rightful
patrimony of the English people' which had been won largely by
British arms and defended at British cost.

Durham's programme was by no means carried out at once.
Lord John Russell's Canada Act of 1840 did indeed unite the Two
Canadas, giving each the same representation in the Assembly and
ensuring to that house full control of local revenues; but it made no
mention of self-government. Indeed Russell told Durham's
successor that he must remain responsible only to H.M. Government,
observing with truth that 'every political constitution in which
different bodies share the supreme power, is only enabled to exist
by the forbearance of those among whom this power is distributed.
. . . Each must exercise a wise moderation'. But then, having thus
begged the question, Russell conceded the essence of self-government in his next despatch. Impressed by Joseph Howe's arguments
he directed the Governor-General to allow his heads of departments,
other than the judicial, to retire whenever 'public policy' rendered
it advisable, and to see to it that the present permanent holders of
such offices were pensioned on retirement for political reasons.
As a rule successive Canadian Governors-General tried to solve

Lord John's riddle by emulating young George III and acting as their own prime ministers. Some trusted the French of Quebec, some did not, and more than one died under the strain. To make matters worse relations with the United States caused anxiety. The New Brunswick-Maine frontier dispute, which had persisted since the time of the separation, was happily settled in 1842 by the Ashburton-Webster treaty; but Anglo-American rivalry for the control of the projected Panama canal was serious at times, and bickering over Oregon gave rise to a risk of war that was only dispelled in 1846, when, the presidential election being safely past, the territory was partitioned, the northern half becoming British Columbia and the southern half United States territory. In that year also Earl Grey began his notable tenure of the War and Colonial Office and declared himself in favour of raising the colonies of settlement 'from the position of inferiority to that of association'. He had in mind nothing more than representative institutions, but he gradually came round to the idea that 'it was neither possible nor desirable' to govern British North America in opposition to the opinion of the 'inhabitants'. Hence, there must be responsible government, that is, control of internal colonial affairs, not, as hitherto, by permanent officials but by local politicians who would hold office only so long as they had the confidence of their legislatures or electorates. Little by little this new system was worked out till it quietly became a reality first in Joseph Howe's Nova Scotia (1848-49). At about the same time, the Governor-General, Lord Elgin, Durham's Scottish son-in-law, established responsible government in Canada at the cost of destructive rioting in Montreal, the then capital. For Elgin trusted the French and was 'possessed' with the idea that colonies could find an abiding place within the Empire, even on 'this soil of North America, and in the face of Republican America,' if British institutions were given 'freely and trustingly'.[1]

Elgin's stand in support of French ministers on a highly controversial issue drove some English-speaking Canadians to talk that winter of secession to the United States, for it had come at a time when Canada was angry at the loss of the wheat preference in the British market, the influx of unwelcome Irish famine refugees and the British Government's refusal to guarantee an intercolonial railway loan. Such talk died away when the Navigation Acts were repealed and the St. Lawrence ice-pack broke. Russell, Earl Grey,

---

[1] Nearly all the governments in the Americas were republican.

and Elgin's fellow Colonial Reformers silenced critics at Westminster, and the Bulwer-Clayton treaty of 1850 cleared the Anglo-American horizon. That treaty, which was destined to stand for a full half-century, provided that the Panama canal, desired more than ever by the United States now that she had taken gold-bearing California and much else from Mexico, should be neutralised and managed internationally. Sailing thus on smooth waters, the last of the five eastern North American colonies became self-governing in 1855, and next year the Hudson's Bay Company's Governor summoned an elective assembly in far-away Vancouver Island off the coast of British Columbia.

The achievement of responsible government by Nova Scotia and Canada at a time when no dependencies other than some of the West Indies possessed fully elective assemblies witnessed to the fact that the British North American colonies were in a class by themselves. But emigration was steadily bringing colonies of settlement elsewhere nearer to the North American level, and thus enabling the British authorities to grant them more liberal institutions. Four unofficial nominees were added to the Western Australian Council in 1838; four years later the nominee Council in Van Diemen's Land was enlarged and a similar body set up in South Australia. Meanwhile the Cape Colony and New South Wales were drawing ahead of Mauritius and Ceylon with which they had been grouped hitherto. The creation of a nominated Legislative Council at the Cape in 1834 had been followed by the widespread grant of municipal institutions elected on a 'civilisation franchise', by further egalitarian reforms as between white and coloured, and by a decade of comparative prosperity based upon wool; in 1842 elected members were given two-thirds of the seats in the legislature of a New South Wales that was waxing rich on its fleeces and was now closed to convicts. Then, in 1846, Earl Grey, side by side with the inauguration of his progressive policy in North America, invited the Cape Colony to submit a draft representative constitution and himself drew up elaborate plans for the governance of the Australian colonies and New Zealand.

Constitutional advance in Australasia was a more difficult problem than in North America. Convicts were still being transported to Van Diemen's Land and Norfolk Island, and the remaining convicts and emancipists of New South Wales dreaded rule by free and intolerant newcomers who were already taking up the cry against transportation, which had hitherto only been heard in Great Britain, and attacking the lordly squatters, who liked cheap convict labour on their immense sheep-runs. In Australia again and New Zealand the powers of the imperial Land and Immigration Board over Crown lands, and therefore immigration, had to be taken into account, while in New Zealand once more the claims of the Maori majority had to be balanced against those of Wakefield's Company if the Treaty of Waitangi meant anything.

The situation in South Africa was even more complicated. Not only must the British Government safeguard the Cape Coloured folk and such tribal Bantu (Kaffirs) as were within the borders of the Cape Colony from exploitation by the European minority, but it must face the extra-colonial problems posed by the Great Trek. At the outset, in 1836, it had merely passed the Cape of Good Hope Punishment Act rendering British subjects liable to trial for crimes committed southward of the 25th degree of south latitude, provided that, as in New Zealand and elsewhere, they and the witnesses could be brought back to colonial soil. Presently, however, it essayed to deal with the problem comprehensively. It first annexed Boer Natal as a detached district of the Cape Colony in 1843, partly to further colonial trade and ward off the acquisitive French but mainly to secure the peace of the Colony's eastern 'Kaffir frontier'. It then annexed the native territory of British Kaffraria beyond that frontier and, in 1848, proclaimed the Orange River Sovereignty which covered all lands and peoples, white, coloured and black, between the Orange and Vaal rivers to the northward of the Cape Colony.

In spite of every obstacle, reforms were carried out simultaneously in these widely scattered communities. There were delays, inevitably. Sir George Grey, the strong-willed Governor of New Zealand, managed to postpone the promulgation of a most intricate constitution largely because it virtually denied the franchise to the Maoris and left them at the mercy of the settlers; two Kaffir wars and trouble in the Orange River Sovereignty delayed the completion of the Cape Colony's draft constitution; in 1849 Earl Grey caused further delay and much ill-feeling in the Cape Colony and New South Wales by his well-intentioned efforts to relieve British gaols and the local labour shortages by sending ticket-of-leave men thither. Neither colony would have convicts at any price, though the squatters in semi-tropical northern New South Wales succeeded in securing some, and isolated Western Australia, having been denied leave to import Chinese or Indian coolies, accepted them with outward reluctance and inward satisfaction. The anti-convict agitation soon subsided at either end of the Indian Ocean and thereafter progress in Australasia was rapid. The Australian Colonies Act of 1850 created partially elective councils on the New South Wales model in Van Diemen's Land, South Australia and the Port Phillip district which now became the colony of Victoria centring upon Melbourne, and empowered all the colonial legislatures to submit to the Privy Council constitutions providing preferably for bicameral parliaments.

While the Australian constitutions were still under discussion the situation was revolutionised. The rapid extension of responsible government in British North America and the grant, in 1852, of representative institutions with a non-racial franchise to New Zealand were accompanied by the discovery of gold in New South Wales and Victoria. The rush of newcomers thither ended convict transportation to eastern Australia and carried the colonies swiftly forward to self-government.[1] The last convict ship sailed for Van Diemen's Land at the close of 1852, and four years later the ex-convict station of Norfolk Island was handed over to New South Wales. By that time Van Diemen's Land had become Tasmania and responsible ministries were at work in all the eastern Australian colonies and New Zealand. When northern New South Wales became the colony of Queensland in 1859 it was endowed with similar privileges. Crown colony rule, however, survived in Western Australia, and convict labour also until British and eastern Australian pressure ended it in 1867. Even so, three years later, the isolated colony was only given a single-chamber legislature with the strong elective majority that had once been the rule in other parts of the continent.

The solution of the South African puzzle was much less clear-cut. The British Government wearied of its spasmodic attempts to control the inaccessible tribes and Trekkers beyond the Orange river. It recognised the independence of the South African Republic (Transvaal) in 1852, allowed most of the Sovereignty to become the Orange Free State in 1854, and watched the two republics adopt constitutions which showed clear signs of United States influence and excluded non-Europeans from all hope of equality with white

---

[1] In 1852, some 65,000 British emigrants left for Australasia.

men in church or state. Meanwhile the first Cape Colony parliament met in 1854; a legislature of two houses, both elective as in most of the Australasian colonies, and both elected on a non-racial franchise which entitled men of whatever race or colour to a seat in either chamber. Natal, cut off geographically from the parent Cape Colony by the Orange Free State, became in 1856 a separate colony with a Legislative Council, more or less on the New South Wales model of 1842, in which elected members had a majority so overwhelming that they soon found means to exclude their swarming Bantu tribesmen from the nominally non-racial franchise. The one connecting link in this politically disrupted land was the High Commissionership which, since its creation in 1846, had given the Governor of the Cape Colony powers that ranged from direct rule in British Kaffraria to the exercise of a vague traditional paramountcy over the Afrikander republics.

Self-government came to the Cape Colony some twenty years after the grant of representative institutions. Elective divisional councils had been set up in 1855 to school the rural folk in the art of self-government, and copper had supplemented wool in the middle 'fifties; but responsible government was withheld so long as the Colony was poor and dependent mainly on the Mother Country for its landward defence. When it came, self-government was the result of an economic revolution, as in New South Wales and Victoria. The development of the ostrich industry in the Cape Colony, the discovery of diamonds in Griqualand West where Kimberley now stands and the finding of a little gold farther north gave the Colony sufficient revenues for the first time, while the opening of the Suez Canal in 1869 reduced the strategic importance of the Cape Peninsula. The Gladstone ministry therefore proposed to withdraw the garrison, as from the other colonies of settlement, and reorganise South Africa politically. It hoped that the Colony, which had been induced to take over British Kaffraria in 1865, would now relieve Great Britain of Basutoland and Griqualand West, which had been recently and reluctantly annexed under local official and popular pressure, and then, having achieved self-government, take the lead in federating South Africa from within. These hopes were by no means fulfilled. The Cape did indeed take over Basutoland and accepted self-government without enthusiasm in 1872, the last British colony to become autonomous for nearly twenty years to come; but it declined to touch Griqualand West or move in the matter of federation. Growing friction with the tribes and the Republics soon led to an increase rather than a diminution of the British garrison.

Thus by 1860 colonial self-government, effective first in 1848, had become a well-established system, and two of the powers which Durham had reserved for the imperial authorities had gone by the board. Control of Crown lands and therefore of immigration had passed to New Zealand in 1852 even before she became self-governing; 'the rightful patrimony of the English people' in other colonies passed to the 'man on the spot' either on or soon after the achievement of autonomy. Next, control of trade had begun to pass to the colonies in 1846 when all those that enjoyed representative institutions were permitted to abolish the British preferences in their own markets. They had done so with such readiness that British statesmen hoped that they would henceforward follow the Mother Country along the peaceful paths of free trade; but lest there should be backsliding the Australian Colonies Act of 1850 forbade the colonies concerned to grant trading preferences even to each other.

The first warning of what was to come was sounded in North America. In 1854 Lord Elgin helped to arrange a reciprocity treaty with the United States on behalf of all the North American colonies, a proof that self-governing colonies could come to terms with a foreign Power without involving the rest of the Empire. Then, in 1859, Canada levied substantial duties on certain goods from the United Kingdom, and, in response to protests, declared that, if her fiscal policy was to be dictated to her, she must be reduced to the rank of a Crown colony. H.M. Government gave way to this assertion that responsible government could not be limited, and, since it was already well understood that powers gained by one self-governing colony would be shared by the rest sooner or later, left such colonies free to accept British defence and at the same time tax the Mother Country for the regulation of their own industry and commerce. It mattered little to an imperial Power whose old colonial system had thus been turned upside down that the Australian colonies should ask leave to offer each other reciprocity. The British Parliament gave the required permission in 1873 and perhaps regarded it as a tribute to the validity of its own free trade principles that none of the jealous and dispersed colonies acted upon it.

Durham's third 'reservation' was also being whittled away. The sole power of the imperial authorities to alter colonial constitutions was not challenged by the invitation to the Cape Colony and the Australian colonies to frame their own constitutions, since these must be submitted for approval to the Queen in Council: but in 1857 New Zealand was given wide powers to alter her constitution, and in 1865 the Colonial Laws Validity Act empowered any representative colonial legislature to amend its constitution, powers and prodecure so long as it did not defy such British Acts, Orders in Council, Letters Patent or Colonial Acts as were still in force. True, the Canadians, especially the privileged French of Quebec, saw to it that the British North America Act of 1867 which established their Dominion, should be alterable only by the Westminster Parliament. But this was a federal measure, a virtual treaty calling for special safeguards. In ordinary self-governing colonies the practice came to be that the legislature could do what it chose at the risk of seeing its work vetoed by the Governor or by the Queen, that is, the British ministry, or set aside after reservation for the Queen's pleasure. Both vetoes, sparingly used from the first, were falling into desuetude by 1874, while the withholding of assent after reservation was used less and less as time went on. Even so the day was still distant when a colonial parliament, relieved of the trammels of the Colonial Laws Validity Act, should be free to act in all respects as seemed best to it.[1]

Control of native policy in the colonies of settlement also passed out of imperial keeping. Experience in eighteenth-century North America had suggested that it was better for the Red Indians, and often for the Palefaces also, that frontier policy should be conducted by disinterested British officials rather than go-ahead colonial legislators. Two generations later the problem had become pressing in many parts of the expanding Empire. At first the imperial authorities took a high line. In keeping with the declaration of 1833 that, in all legislation for India, it was 'an indisputable principle that the interests of the Native subjects are to be consulted in preference to those of Europeans', the Commons Aborigines Committee of 1837, the first to deal comprehensively with Native policy, recommended that the Crown should stand between the tribes and the colonists. Ten years later Gladstone, who had served on that famous committee, reaffirmed its ruling as 'an undoubted maxim'.

---

[1] The Colonial Laws Validity Act held good for the Dominions until the passing of the Statute of Westminster in 1931; *vide infra*, p. 146.

But the representative institutions for which Gladstone pleaded in the next breath weakened that principle; the grant of responsible government soon left colonists as free in practice as the Boer republicans to handle their own native policy. Control in New Zealand passed from the Governor to the local parliament by default in 1858, and the first of a decade of land wars against the Maoris ensued in 1860. In that year the expiry of certain British treaties with Red Indian chiefs freed the hands of the Canadian authorities; meanwhile control of such native policy as there had ever been passed to the colonial legislatures in eastern Australia, a land where the Black Fellows were few and elusive and the last Tasman obligingly died in 1876. In South Africa the British Government gladly entrusted the Cape Colony with British Kaffraria and Basutoland in 1865 and 1871 respectively, and thereafter encouraged it to extend its well-tried liberal Native policy over the tribes that dwelt between its own borders and those of Crown colony Natal.

Further, far fewer redcoats were to be seen in the colonies of settlement in 1874 than in the middle 'thirties, when the Duke of Wellington was still seeking to maintain an adequate army by hiding large portions of it overseas. In the 'sixties, after long deliberation and on sound strategic and administrative grounds, the British Government decided to withdraw its colonial garrisons as far as possible, and revert to the practice of the Old Empire by requiring colonies with representative institutions to see to their own landward defence and pay for such regular troops as they might desire in time of peace. It was confirmed in its resolve by the New Zealand ministry's use of British soldiers paid by the British taxpayer to implement its own warlike policies against the tribes, and the undisguised reliance of many Cape Colonists and Natalians on the regulars for like purposes. By 1870 the imperial garrisons were gone from New Zealand, Australia and nearly all federal Canada outside the naval bases of Halifax and Esquimault, while their strength was being reduced in South Africa.

But some things stood in 1874 as Durham had known them. No one questioned the right of the British Government to control the Royal Navy or the duty of the British taxpayer to pay for it, and few as yet agreed with Gavan Duffy of Victoria, the spiritual successor of his brother Irishman Wolfe Tone, that an autonomous colony should make its own treaties and have the right to be neutral in the event of a 'British' war. Newfoundland had indeed been promised in 1855 that she would be consulted whenever changes were to be made in the French and American treaties affecting her fisheries; but that was all. Until the self-governing colonies should ask for a share in the direction of external policy the Second British Empire would present an unbroken naval and diplomatic front.

The constitutional and economic development of the self-governing colonies was thus all in the direction of separateness and distinctness. That process was hastened by the federation, between 1867 and 1873, of the leading group of these colonies as the Dominion of Canada.

Federation had often been talked of in this protean British Empire, and even practised in a fashion. Seventeenth-century Massachusetts had been head of a loose New England federation; throughout the eighteenth century the Leeward Islands had had a Governor-General and a common legislature as well as island legislatures; and, when all is said, men who had grown up as British subjects made the federal United States. An unappreciated Loyalist had suggested the federation of British North America in 1822, and Durham had only set the idea aside nearly twenty years later till the railways should make it possible. Earl Grey's endeavours to federate the Australian colonies in 1847 to avert the trade wars and other inconveniences which he foresaw were indeed defeated by Australian apathy, fear of 'Sydney domination' and the opposition of Colonial Reformers at Westminster, who feared justly that a strong federal government would trench upon imperial prerogatives; but this defeat did not deter Grey from contemplating a federation of the Cape Colony, British Kaffraria, the Orange River Sovereignty and Natal, or assisting his successor to start New Zealand on her parliamentary career in 1852 as a federation that was to endure for a quarter of a century. The talk of closer union for defence that arose in Australia after the arrival of the French in New Caledonia in 1853 soon died away, for the French were more than 800 miles distant and Britannia ruled the waves; but in South Africa, soon after the two Boer republics had been recognised, the Colonial Office itself proposed to federate the three coastal British colonies. This scheme was ended in 1859 by the recall of the Cape Governor, Sir George Grey of New Zealand fame, for trying to include the unwanted Orange Free State at its own request, and all that federation meant to South Africans during the next decade was the possible separation of the Eastern Province of the Cape Colony from the Western and the superimposing of a federal government on both. Meanwhile, from 1863 onwards, delegates from various Australian colonies met from time to time to discuss tariffs and other matters of common concern; but little came of that, since free trade New South Wales could never agree with protectionist Victoria, and each of the colonies, centring upon the port which was also its capital, thought more of connections with far-away Great Britain than with its neighbours. Each emphasised the fact by building its railways on the gauge that took its fancy.

During the early 'sixties, while the American War of Secession was raging, 'confederation' became a live issue in British North America. Just as the Old Thirteen had found that independence was not enough, so these British colonies began to realise that closer union alone could give full meaning to autonomy within the Empire. In Canada proper men began to discuss general federation or, failing that, a local federation of Quebec and Ontario as the only means of ending constitutional deadlock. Dual premiers and cabinets, British and French, relying on dual majorities were becoming an unworkable farce; equal expenditure on both halves or the colony regardless of need was a costly nuisance: equal representation in the Assembly had long been an injustice to fast-growing Ontario.

Closer union, especially a general confederation, was certain to be no easy matter in British North America, for many of the factors which were making for it in other parts of the world at that time were lacking. Propinquity was to seek. Newfoundland was a distant island. The Maritime Provinces of Nova Scotia. New Brunswick and Prince Edward Island were separated from Canada by many hundreds of miles of dreary waste. Canada itself was widespread and sparsely peopled. Westward of Ontario lay the little Highland and French-Indian Red River Settlement just within the territories of the Hudson's Bay Company which swept thence, almost untenanted, up to and over the Rocky Mountains; beyond, on the Pacific Slope, lay isolated British Columbia and Vancouver Island. Provincial feeling was strong everywhere; the gulf between *les Canadiens* and *les Anglais* in Canada was wide;

popular interest in 'confederation' was markedly absent throughout. The chief operative motives were three: first, Kipling's 'ties of common funk', in this case funk of the United States; secondly, the insistent pressure of bad times; lastly, the decisive influence of a few politicians, notably of the Conservative John Macdonald and the Radical George Brown of Ontario, of George Cartier, leader of Catholic Quebec, and always of Edward Watkin, director of the reorganised Hudson's Bay Company, which had bought out the old shareholders in 1863, and of the Grand Trunk Company which he was resolved should build a railway by hook or by crook between Toronto and Quebec.

As Durham had foreseen, railways played a dominant part in the federating of British North America. In 1864 delegates from the Maritime colonies met to discuss a local federation which should finance the long-desired intercolonial railway that was to link them with each other and with Canada. They were joined by Canadians who persuaded them to discuss the larger scheme. Potent arguments were advanced at the subsequent Quebec Conference: the prospect of enhanced credit; joint defence in face of the heavily armed North that was clearly winning the Civil War and was resentful of British and Canadian sympathy with the South; the formation of an economic *bloc* strong enough to resist the southward pull of the United States; the creation of a state able to stand on its own feet in the event of separation from the rest of the Empire. The conference had little difficulty in laying down the main lines of confederation, and though the Maritimes, led by Howe, soon repented of their haste, British encouragement and American hostility helped the federalists to wear down opposition. H.M. Government offered its guarantee to an intercolonial railway loan and other financial aid, while, at the close of the Civil War, the American Government denounced the reciprocity treaty of 1854 and American-Irish Fenians raided Canada. The British Parliament duly passed the British North America Act, and in July 1867 Quebec, Ontario, Nova Scotia and New Brunswick became provinces of a federal state that was named the Dominion of Canada since the title of Kingdom, which Macdonald desired, might have outraged American susceptibilities.

The outstanding features of the new constitution were two: the closeness of the federation as contrasted with that of the United States and the entrenchment of the privileges of Quebec. The central government at Ottawa consisted of a Governor-General appointed by the Queen, a ministry, a Senate whose members were not elected two for each state as in the United States but nominated for life in numbers more or less proportionate to the populations of the various provinces, and a House of Commons elected on the usual population basis. The colonies became provinces, each with a Lieutenant-Governor appointed by the Governor-General and a legislature which was a continuation of its colonial parliament. In sharing out governmental powers, the hallmark of a federation, the Canadians took a course diametrically opposed to that followed by the United States which had just had to assert by force on the grand scale the powers of the federal authority against the 'state rights' of the seceding South. Not only did the Governor-General exercise considerable powers of disallowance over provincial legislation, but the federal authorities were, by intention, to enjoy all powers present and future that were not specifically allocated to the provinces. This division of powers was, however, made in such an involved and legalistic manner that, in the event, provincial patriots and the lawyers, who abounded in Canada as in the United States, were able greatly to increase provincial rights to the grave embarrassment later on of the social and economic policies of Ottawa. Provision was made for a system of federal courts as in the United States, but none of these was ever set up except the Court of Appeal in 1875 from which a further appeal lay to the Judicial Committee of the Privy Council in London. For the rest Quebec was given a permanent equality with Ontario in the Senate, and a fixed number of seats in the Commons that was to be taken as the basis on which the representation of the other provinces would be reckoned. Largely to safeguard the political and social privileges of the French province, and at Canada's own desire, amendments to the British North American Act were to be made only by the British Parliament.

The new Dominion grew rapidly. In 1867 the United States bought up Russia's rights in Alaska. Thereupon Canada, with imperial aid, purchased the vast intervening territories of the Hudson's Bay Company lest Americans flow in from the south and cut her off from the Pacific Slope. The Company survived, and still survives, as a powerful trading concern, but in 1870 Manitoba, the first of the Prairie Provinces, was carved out of the old Hudson's Bay sphere at the cost of some fighting with the Red River people.

The turn of the Pacific Slope came next. British Columbia and Vancouver Island had been removed from the Hudson's Bay Company's jurisdiction in 1858 soon after the discovery of gold on the Fraser river, and had been united in 1866 under the style of British Columbia. As the alluvial gold petered out there was talk of secession to the United States, but such talk was ended by the grant of an elective majority in the legislature and the promise of a railway linking the colony with the Canadian East within ten years. In 1871 British Columbia duly became the sixth province of the Dominion and only the fate of the eastern islands remained to be decided. Financial stress obliged little Prince Edward Island to join in 1873. Newfoundland stood out for three-quarters of a century.

IV

THE DEPENDENT EMPIRES, 1833-1874

IN view of the remarkable growth of the colonies of settlement it was well that the Colonial Office had been separated from the War Office amid the stresses of the Crimean campaign. The duties of the Colonial Secretary were now twofold: he must learn to behave toward the self-governing colonies, and *a fortiori* the Dominion of Canada, like a Foreign Secretary and yet rule the rest in the old style. Even in this familiar field he must exercise varying degrees of tact, for the numerous dependencies of the Empire were advancing unevenly upon the constitutional front and in some sectors were actually retreating.

In the middle eighteen-thirties, at a time when such colonies as the Cape, Mauritius, Ceylon and New South Wales must be content with nominee legislatures, it was natural that little St. Helena should continue under purely official rule after the Crown had taken it over from the East India Company to bring it within the scope of the Emancipation Act; natural also that the Falkland Islands, over which the Crown effectively asserted old claims in face of French and possibly American ambitions, should have been subjected first to naval control and then, in 1842, to official civil administration. The reorganisation of governmental machinery in the Caribbean area also proceeded along official lines. The Emancipation Act, passed over their heads, had been a heavy blow to those of the West Indian islands which had so long enjoyed representative institutions. That drastic measure was followed by the institution of an official General Government, and presently of a local Appeal Court also, for the Windward Isles of Barbados, Grenada, St. Lucia, St. Vincent and Tobago, by the appointment of a Governor-in-Chief for both groups of the Leeward Islands together with Dominica, and by serious thoughts of suspending the free constitution of recalcitrant Jamaica side by side with that of rebellious Quebec.

The slave compensation paid to the sugar colonies did little more than wipe out the debts of planters whose estates were becoming exhausted by primitive cultivation. The breakdown of the apprenticeship system, which was to have introduced the ex-slaves to freedom gradually over a term of years, and the competition of East Indian and Mauritian sugar sent the West Indies downhill rapidly. The importation of Indian coolies by Mauritius and British Guiana in 1837 awakened hopes; but these were dashed when the Calcutta authorities stopped recruitment and forced planters to seek in vain for suitable labour in the United Kingdom, Continental Europe, Madeira, Sierra Leone, St. Helena, China and the most over-crowded of the Antilles themselves. The India Government presently permitted recruiting under stricter control. Though the methods of Indian touts aroused resentment in India and the failure of some colonies to carry out the terms of the indentures led to temporary and local suspensions, the system spread and tided the sugar colonies over a difficult period. Between 1842 and 1870 fully half a million Indian labourers went to British colonies, including Natal after 1860, besides a further 50,000 to Dutch and French possessions. Many of them returned home with unaccustomed money in their pockets, but many more settled in their new homes as free men thus linking India with other parts of the Empire.

The partial recovery of the sugar islands coincided with the evolution of self-government in British North America and the recommendation of the Privy Council in 1849 that representative institutions should be given wherever they would do more good than harm. Thus encouraged, the British Government not only set up a partially elective Council in the island fortress of Malta and instituted democratic reforms in the Ionian Islands, but created legislative councils with large elective majorities in Natal in 1856, and in British Honduras four years later after the settlement of long-standing boundary disputes with the republics of Nicaragua and Honduras. In 1856 again it made a near approach to responsible government in St. Vincent and Grenada by giving elected Assembly members seats on the executive councils.

It was false dawn in the Caribbean. The hopes of the old planter class were swept away with the British preference on their sugar in 1854, and presently reform backwards set in. Elected members disappeared from the St. Vincent and Grenada Executive Councils in 1859; two years later Montserrat had to come down to the Natal-British Honduras level, and in 1866 the ancient constitution of Jamaica was abrogated after a Negro rising. Island after island had to submit to strict Crown colony rule; even Honduras succumbed, and though the eighteenth-century General Legislature of the Leeward

F

Islands was at last revived, with power to override island legislation, it contained a strong official element and three of the five island councils which sent up the elected members were of the nominee variety. In short, by 1878 the representative institutions of the Old Empire survived only in Antigua, the Bahamas, Barbados, Bermuda, Dominica and, in their antiquated Dutch form, in British Guiana. Meanwhile two other colonies with mixed populations had seen their liberties in jeopardy; the depressed Cape Colony during the later 'sixties just before the diamond discoveries came to the rescue, and Natal, whose legislative council was given a stronger official minority for a time in 1875 to clear the way for a reform of native policy and, it was hoped, South African federation.

The fortunes of the West African dependencies moved more or less in sympathy with those of the West Indies. The Crown colony of Sierra Leone and the stations of the London merchants on the Gold Coast drew their exiguous revenues from ivory, gold and palm oil, while from about 1830 onwards Sierra Leone's dependency on the Gambia began to rely on its ground nuts. Farther east Macgregor Laird and other Liverpool merchants of the African Steamship Company opened up trade in palm products on the Oil Rivers which had recently been shown to be the Niger Delta. At the same time Governor George Maclean of the Gold Coast instituted a pregnant innovation by making peace with the neighbouring Ashanti and exercising an unauthorised protectorate over the coastal Fanti tribes with the concurrence of their chiefs. Maclean thus went against repeated declarations by H.M. Government that it was resolved to limit its commitments in Africa, and the recommendation of the Aborigines Committee of 1837 that treaties with native chiefs were inadvisable; but the tide turned in his favour when Fowell Buxton convinced the authorities that treaties and the encouragement of 'legitimate trade' under official control were the best means of killing the slave trade. The official assistance given to Buxton's disastrous project of a model civilising colony on the lower Niger, coinciding with the Maori Treaty of Waitangi in 1840, marked a reversal of British policy which was emphasised by the treaties with local chiefs that virtually ended the slave trade in the regions between Sierra Leone and the Gambia.

Meanwhile attacks on Maclean by philanthropists and others called forth a Royal Commission. This upheld Maclean and paved the way for the Foreign Jurisdiction Act of 1843. That far-reaching measure was passed primarily to settle judicial difficulties that had arisen since the Crown took over the functions of the old Levant Company in the Ottoman Empire in 1825, or that might arise from the extension of Britain's consular powers in the newly-opened Chinese treaty ports. But the Act also regularised the position on the Gold Coast. It marked a great advance on the Punishment Acts on which the British had relied hitherto, for henceforward the Queen was empowered to exercise any jurisdiction she possessed or might acquire in a foreign country as fully as if this jurisdiction had arisen 'by the cession or conquest of territory'. In 1850 Earl Grey ruled that areas in which such jurisdiction might be exercised included those covered by treaties with local chiefs. Thus the Foreign Jurisdiction Act became the main root from which the vast protectorate system grew up during the last quarter of the nineteenth century.

The Gold Coast passed under the Crown once more in 1843 and was attached for a time to Sierra Leone, from whose control the Gambia on the other hand was freed. Better times seemed to have come for the 'White Man's Grave'. The Gold Coast's turn for a separate career as a colony came in 1850 when the neighbouring Danish stations were added to it by purchase, and presently the Gambia acquired French Albreda in exchange for British trading rights in the Senegal area from which Faidherbe's men were thrusting out in all directions. The annexation by the Crown in 1861 of Lagos, the principal surviving slave market on the Coast, laid the foundations of the Nigeria of the future; two years later Sierra Leone was deemed worthy of a nominee legislature; to crown all, the belated co-operation of Lincoln's United States with Great Britain, and the new British steam-pinnaces which could run down the slavers in shallow waters, made a swift end of the white man's share in the Slave Trade.

Then came the world slump of the middle 'sixties. Soon a Royal Commission could express regret that it might not recommend the abandonment of all the West Coast dependencies other than the freedman's settlement and naval base of Sierra Leone, and at least saw to it that Lagos, the Gold Coast and the Gambia were subordinated to that colony. Thereafter there was talk of rounding off the Gold Coast colony by acquiring adjacent French territory in exchange for the isolated Gambia; but though the garrison was withdrawn from Bathurst as from so many other more important parts of the Empire, the exchange was never made. And then the tide turned. The British made up their minds that the West Coast must be governed. They gave their consul at Spanish Fernando Po criminal jurisdiction over British subjects on the Oil Rivers, secured the Dutch stations on the Gold Coast in 1872 in exchange for ancient rights in Sumatra, and beat the Ashanti soundly when they tried to upset this transfer. Finally, in 1874, they separated Lagos and the Gold Coast from Sierra Leone, placing both under the Governor of the Gold Coast and giving each a nominated legislature.

If Great Britain, with half the world to choose from, troubled to acquire but few colonial dependencies between 1833 and 1874, she resolutely extended and consolidated her power in India and the parts adjacent. The East India Company's Charter Act of 1833 initiated revolutionary changes. It allowed the Company to retain Indian patronage for a further twenty years, but made it exclusively an administrative agent for the Crown by bidding it wind up its commercial activities in India and depriving it of its last monopoly, the China trade centring upon Canton. Further, the renewed charter gave the Governor-General and Council at Calcutta legislative powers over the other Presidencies of Bombay and Madras, and laid down the principle that no Indian should be debarred from holding any office in the public service 'by reason only of his religion, place of birth, descent, colour, or any of these'. Indians, of course, had held numberless minor posts from the beginning; but now the prospect of more responsible work was held out to them, and after much anxious debate the British authorities decided that Western education would be necessary to fit them for that.

This was a grave decision to be taken by a Government which had always been careful not to interfere more than it must with the social organisation and religious customs of its subjects. The Company had only admitted Christian missionaries reluctantly in 1813 and had been ill pleased to see them busy with their printing presses; it had not begun seriously to repress thuggee and suttee until the eighteen-thirties although these practices were as repugnant to millions of Indians as to itself; it wore down Indian slavery very gradually. It did so, first, by rigidly regulating the traffic after the abolition of the British slave trade in 1807, and thereafter by means of restrictive treaties with the Imam of Muscat-Zanzibar who controlled the East African supply; but it did not destroy the servile status in British India by withdrawing the protection of the courts until 1843, nor make slave-owning a punishable offence until 1860. Nevertheless, in 1835, the Company opened the floodgates of India to a torrent of Western ideas. Acting on the report of a commission presided over by Lord Macaulay it substituted English for Persian as the language of government and higher education. Next year it freed the press, which was destined to remain free throughout the nineteenth century except during 1857, the Mutiny year, and the short period from 1878 to 1882. It was symbolical of these changes that King William's head should replace that of the Mogul on the standard rupee.

This reforming era was followed by a period of annexation designed to buttress British power in India on both sides. To the westward Aden was taken in 1839, partly by treaty and partly by force, to strengthen Britain's hold on the Suez route along which the P. and O. steamships were beginning to ply on either side of the isthmus. Disaster in Afghanistan, where the Indian Government had tried to check Russian penetration, was offset between 1843 and 1849; first by the annexation of Sind with its fine harbour of Karachi at the mouth of the Indus, one of the very few acts of real though salutary aggression which can be charged against the British in India throughout the nineteenth century; and secondly by the annexation of the chaotic Punjab at the price of two hard-fought wars forced upon the Company by the over-confident Sikhs. During the 'fifties the British forestalled the French at Perim Island in the very jaws of the Red Sea near Aden, acquired by treaty the little Kuria Muria islands as a guano field and cable station on the road to Bombay, and began their long task of clearing the pirates out of the Persian Gulf and building up an informal suzerainty over the sultanates on its shores. In 1856, moreover, the Treaty of Paris forbade the Russians to launch warships on the Black Sea and thus removed one potential danger from Britain's Mediterranean route to the East.

British interests and control also increased steadily to the eastward. Singapore had grown so fast on its once scarcely inhabited island that in 1836 it became the capital of the Penang Presidency. Then the commercial quarrels over opium in the main, which arose from the recent opening of the China trade to all British subjects, and less widely known political difficulties with the Pekin government led to a war with China. This ended in 1842 with the cession to Great

Britain of the barren island of Hong Kong near Canton and the opening of Shanghai and other treaty ports to Western traders. The gap between Southern China and India was soon bridged by more or less British stepping-stones. In the year of the ending of the China war James Brooke became Rajah of Sarawak in North Borneo by treaty with the Sultan of Brunei, who in 1846 also ceded to the Crown the neighbouring desolate island of Labuan. At the close of the second Burmese war in 1852 John Company annexed the delta of the Irrawaddy with its splendid port of Rangoon, while five years later the Crown acquired the Cocos Islands midway between Ceylon and Western Australia.

Great economic changes were taking place in India meanwhile. There had been a time when Indian handicrafts had been exchanged for British silver and luxuries, but from the eighteen-thirties onwards Indian raw materials began to be exchanged for Lancashire cotton and other British staple manufactures. These developments were furthered by the unification of the coinage of British India, the centralization of finance, cheap postage as in Rowland Hill's England, and the steady disappearance of the preferences once accorded to British goods. Lord Dalhousie did much to draw India together between 1848 and 1856. Railways were laid to his planning; the Grand Trunk Road moved forward from Calcutta towards Peshawar by way of Delhi and Lahore; the Ganges canal soon outstripped in length any that Europe could show; telegraph lines raced ahead of the railway tracks; harbour improvements were undertaken at the great ports of Calcutta, Chittagong, Madras, Bombay, Karachi, and Rangoon; famine became less of a recurrent menace as administration and means of communication improved.

From 1850 onwards the British attempted to encourage local government in India, as in so many other parts of the Empire, by setting up nominee councils in the larger towns other than the three Presidency capitals which had long enjoyed municipal institutions, but they did not accede to the novel demand of some Indians in the Bengal Presidency that Indians should rule their own country. The renewal of the Company's charter for the last time in 1853 was, however, the occasion of notable changes in the administration. A legislative council of officials was set up in Calcutta, and the Governor-General was relieved of a crushing burden by the cutting up of the overgrown Bengal Presidency into Provinces each under a

Lieutenant-Governor or Chief Commissioner. The twenty-year-old proviso that there should be no colour bar in the public service was renewed; the Company's rights of patronage were modified by the partial introduction of competitive examinations for the higher posts, and, in spite of the laments of die-hards that education would weaken Great Britain's hold on India, Sir Charles Wood, President of the Board of Control, drew up plans in the spirit of Macaulay's report for the encouragement of university, vocational and vernacular primary education for boys and girls alike. In 1857 universities were created at Calcutta, Madras and Bombay on the examining model that had already been developed on a large scale in London and was taking shape in Capetown, the half-way house to India.

These liberal reforms were interrupted disastrously. The speed with which Dalhousie had pressed them in all directions, and his high-handed treatment of the Moslem ruler of Oudh and some other Princes, unsettled a conservative people; well-founded rumours that his successor, Lord Canning, intended to abolish the shadowy office of the Great Mogul incensed them. Part of the sepoy army, which far outnumbered the British troops, revolted in 1857 and before the Mutiny was ended a year later both Mogul and Company had disappeared. A Secretary of State and Council took the place of the President and Board of Control in London, and 'Clemency Canning', who now earned his honourable nickname, became Viceroy as well as Governor-General. To make all safe the army in India was reorganised on the basis of one British soldier to two Indian and the field artillery was concentrated in British hands; to ensure the health and efficiency of the central administration the Viceregal Court was transferred from Calcutta to the hill station of Simla during the summer months from 1864 onwards.

Other reforms marked the first dilution of purely bureaucratic rule and the beginning of the indianisation of the governance of India. In 1861 official and unofficial nominees, all at first British, were given seats on the Central Legislative Council. Similar councils were created for Madras and Bombay and, in 1862, for Bengal also, but in these the majority of the unofficial nominees were Indians. None of these councils, central or presidential, might question governmental policy nor discuss anything beyond the draft measures submitted to them by the executives, but within these rigid limits they could at least tell the authorities what Indians were thinking.

At the same time Indians were admitted to the civil service examinations, though the requisite preliminary attendance at an English university and the fact that the examinations were held in London shut out many who could not face the expense or feared to lose caste by crossing the ocean. Nevertheless the reform was a real one and in 1869 competitive examinations more or less on Indian lines were prescribed for the civil services of Ceylon, Hong Kong and the Straits Settlements in Malaya.

Great Britain's position in India and on its approaches was very strong on the morrow of the Mutiny. It was well for her that this was so, for Napoleon III, the ally of the Crimean campaign, had now become the danger in British eyes. It is true that he joined with Great Britain in a war against China which compelled the Son of Heaven to receive the ambassadors of the Western Powers, open yet more treaty ports, admit Western traders and missionaries to the interior of his dominions and cede the Kowloon peninsula opposite Hong Kong to the British; but, on the other hand, he built steam and iron-sheathed wooden battleships, urged on the cutting of the Suez Canal on lines which the British feared would make it a thinly-veiled French possession, intervened successfully in troubled Syria, acquired a wedge of Somaliland opposite Aden, showed an unwelcome interest in Madagascar and the East Coast of Africa, annexed Cochin-China and Cambodia and outraged the eastern Australians by sending convicts to New Caledonia.

The British met the Napoleonic challenge where necessary point by point. They outbuilt the new French navy with all-iron steamships, saw to it that the Canal should be under Egyptian control and open to shipping of all nations in peace and in war, modernised their dockyards at Gibraltar and Malta and, this done, yielded gracefully to the wishes of the Greeks and the local inhabitants by handing over the Ionian Islands to Greece in 1864 on condition that the base at Corfu was dismantled. Farther afield they revived old claims against Portugal and in 1861 hoisted the Union Jack over the southern shores of Delagoa Bay, partly to promote their campaign against the slavers and partly to ward off possible French activities. In Indo-Chinese waters they organised Singapore, Malacca and Penang as the colony of the Straits Settlements free from all connection with India, recognised Rajah Brooke's Sarawak as an independent state and presently saw their own traders busy elsewhere in North Borneo. Finally in 1868 an Anglo-Indian force enhanced the prestige of the British and Indian Governments in all the Red Sea lands by carrying out a punitive expedition into the mountainous heart of Abyssinia. Next year 'the Ditch' was opened formally by the Empress of the French, and forthwith the prophecy of the greatest of Egyptian Pashas was fulfilled that the French might cut the canal but the British would use it. Ships flying the white, blue or red ensign began to pour along the now unbroken waterway that had brought Great Britain so much nearer to her growing empire in the Indian and Pacific Oceans.

Thus stood the liberal and threefold British Empire in 1874. Far more of the map was now coloured red than in the days of Melbourne and Peel, but most of this represented peaceful settlement in well-nigh empty continents or the reconstruction by Company and Crown of the unity of India which had once been maintained by the Moguls. In other parts of the world the new red patches recorded reluctant annexations to forestall Orleanist or Napoleonic France, or to placate restive British colonists, merchants, missionaries and proconsuls. The map made no record of the many territories which Great Britain had relinquished outright or had refrained from taking.

As yet few British politicians or electors had any wish to assume new powers and responsibilities by enlarging the Empire. Having regard to the scattered nature of that Empire and their own free trade principles, most of them desired merely to maintain the political *status quo* behind the bulwarks of a supreme navy and a small but highly trained professional army. Another conception of empire was, however, being entertained by men who were moved by the expansion of the colonies of settlement, a conception which was destined to give a sinister flavour to the honourable word 'imperialism'. Durham had taken it for granted in 1839 that there was no hope for Canada till the 'Anglo-Saxons' had dominated the French of Quebec, and Carlyle, proclaiming the virtues of the strong silent man in the organ tones of an Isaiah a few years later, had counselled England, so narrow for her own people, to bring new markets within her Empire, by force if necessary, against the day when the hostile tariffs advocated by the German List should be raised against her. Now, in 1869, Charles Dilke had a vision of a *Greater Britain*, which indeed embraced the United States but ignored mainly

Afrikander and non-European South Africa and would fain have shut out the Irish and other cheap-living races; while in 1870 John Ruskin told his Oxford audiences, in tones more dulcet than those of Carlyle but equally assured, that the British, 'still undegenerate in race, a race mingled of the best northern blood, . . . not yet dissolute in temper but knowing how to govern and obey', must plant colonies of picked men on 'every piece of fruitful waste ground' they could secure, and teach the colonists that their first duty was to advance Britain's power by land and sea.

These dangerous thoughts of superiority and domination were balanced in the minds of their best exponents, however, by those moral considerations which, to the annoyance of rivals, have rarely been lacking when the British think aloud. Just as Huskisson had hoped to see a strong British Empire the greatest political force for good in the world of the eighteen-twenties, so Carlyle and Dilke believed that their Anglo-Saxons had a civilising mission. Ruskin indeed made haste to disclaim all ambition for mere size, wealth or power. His imperial Britain was to be 'a source of light, a centre of peace; mistress of learning and of the Arts, faithful guardian of time-tried principles under temptation from fond experiments and licentious desires, and amidst the cruel and clamorous jealousies of the nations, worshipped in her strange valour of goodwill towards men'.

Such thoughts led naturally to schemes for the federation of the Empire. That idea, first mooted in 1853 while the last remnants of the old economic unity of the Empire were being swept away, was brought forward again at the close of a decade that saw the unification of Italy, the federation of Germany and of Canada, and a long war to maintain the unity of the United States. By this time colonial self-government had been a fact for twenty years and yet none of the colonies of settlement had seceded; interest in those colonies was very real among thousands of voters, newly enfranchised under the Reform Act of 1867, who had friends there or even contemplated going thither themselves. One sign of the times was the foundation in 1868 of the Colonial Society, parent of the present Royal Empire Society, to study colonial problems; another yet more striking was Disraeli's Crystal Palace speech four years later. Disraeli foreshadowed the new imperialism. 'England', he cried, 'has outgrown the continent of Europe. England is the metropolis of a great maritime Empire extending to the boundaries of the farthest Ocean'. All that was lacking to make such an empire strong to extend its civilisation and authority was the cohesion that could be found in a common scheme of defence, an imperial tariff and a central federal council.

V

RIVAL OVERSEAS EMPIRES, 1874–1914

THE ideal conditions under which the liberal British Empire had been built up during the two preceding generations were passing away when Disraeli became Prime Minister in 1874. Henceforward the British were to find it more and more difficult to push their trade and, where needs must, enlarge their borders leisurely and unhindered. They learnt almost at once that their imperial policy was to be influenced directly by the course of events on that continent which Disraeli had so recently boasted their country had outgrown. Bismarck's German Empire, even more militaristic and far more efficient than the Second Napoleonic Empire, swayed the balance of power in the new Europe of the Armed Peace. A defeated and resentful French Republic, a consolidated Italy bound closely to Germany, and a Russia who had rearmed on the Black Sea with Prussian connivance during the confusion of the Franco-German war threatened to make it less easy than it had been for Great Britain to control the Mediterranean route to the East.

The facts of the situation were revealed during a crisis precipitated by Russia's designs upon the Straits, for it was Bismarck who presided at the Congress of Berlin that effected a Near Eastern settlement. Thereafter Germany, Austria-Hungary and Italy formed a Triple Alliance to dominate the Continent; Russia, furious at her check in the west, turned towards India and became Britain's bugbear in Asia for thirty years to come; France, egged on by Bismarck, sought colonies as a consolation for the loss of Alsace-Lorraine and preferably at Great Britain's expense; presently Germany entered the colonial lists. By 1893 at the latest France and Russia had allied to counterbalance the Central Powers, but Great Britain maintained her traditional isolation for another decade. She then allied herself with Japan, primarily to check Russian activities in Asia, and thereafter began to swing over to the side of the Dual Alliance. She entered the Kaiser's War of 1914–18 as the uneasy partner of France and Russia, taking the whole of the Empire with her.

The British were somewhat slower to learn that the halcyon days of free trade were also drawing to a close in the middle 'seventies.

Unprotected British agriculture, far outstripped at home by industrial interests, first endured a run of bad harvests and then suffered an irremediable blow at the end of the decade, when British steamships and railways, financed largely by British capital, began to flood the home market with the produce of the vast and mechanically worked wheatfields of the New World and southern Russia. At the same time nationalism, inflamed by the recent wars, joined forces with the Industrial Revolution. Foreign governments began to protect their industrialists as well as their farmers. Germany and, more significant from the British imperial point of view, Canada also frankly adopted protectionism in 1879; France reverted to her instinctive policy on the expiry of the Cobden treaty in 1881; the United States customs barrier rose steadily till it reached the forbidding heights of the McKinley tariff of 1890. By that time the north-eastern United States, Germany, France and Belgium were well equipped to compete with Great Britain's basic industries in a world that was tending to think of trade as a 'white war' filling in the intervals between 'red wars' of the Prussian type rather than as an exchange of goods and services.

Britain's naval supremacy was not to be threatened till Germany began to build a High Seas Fleet in the early years of the twentieth century, but her mercantile supremacy was challenged much earlier. The United States mercantile marine, more numerous than hers in the eighteen-fifties and the best of it much faster, had dropped out of the race when iron and steam ousted wood and sails and the development of the Middle and Far West absorbed even American energies; but steel began to supplant iron in the 'seventies and presently the subsidised shipping of the newly industrialised nations of Europe, led by that of Germany, began to press Great Britain hard. This pressure became still harder when the Americans remembered their great maritime tradition in the years immediately preceding the war of 1914–18.

Abundance of steel marked a revolution in human affairs to which the British Empire must adapt itself as best it could. Cheap, long-wearing rails and rolling stock, steel ships in which the new compound engines and water condensers developed unexampled power and saved valuable cargo space, all spelt speed and ability to carry men in numbers, and inexpensive goods in bulk, across a world whose ends were being drawn together by the spreading network of telegraphs and submarine cables. The improving means of communication also made it possible to hold together greater states and empires than ever before at a time when some of the continental Powers began to desire empires overseas.

Great Britain, the United States and Russia alone had territories more or less under their control which could absorb a high proportion of the capital that was piling up at home, and varied enough to give them the supplies they needed for their growing populations and factories, but only Great Britain had the resources, shipping, experience and *laissez-faire* faith that enable a people to buy, sell and lend in all parts of the earth. Other nations, burdened with protectionist armour, found it hard to compete with British free traders. They therefore desired reserved sources of raw materials, privileged markets for their products, and areas for investment under their own flags. There were other considerations. Governments and army chiefs wished to keep their hold on migrating taxpayers and recruits; scores of well-to-do folk looked for official or business careers in the Fatherland overseas; men of all ranks were taught to covet the prestige which overseas empire conferred, and to envy the British their wide dominions, which, like so many Englishmen in those days, they regarded as the heritage of an imperial people. Hence, these Powers began to press upon the British Empire and shut out British traders from spheres in which they had hitherto been free to make their way, and of all rivals France was the most persistent and exclusive since some of her republican leaders were persuaded that she could not remain a first-class Power unless she drew from her dependencies all that she required to that end.

Great Britain joined in the ensuing scramble for territory overseas with reluctance and outstanding success. She did so primarily to safeguard her own colonists and to keep the door open for the benefit of herself, her Empire and, she firmly believed, mankind. Between 1874 and 1902, when the last important annexations were made, she added to her Empire 4,750,000 square miles of territory inhabited by close on 90,000,000 souls.[1]

Her colonies of settlement had staked out their claims long ago, and she made few additions to them other than the two South African republics and the highlands of tropical Southern Rhodesia and Kenya. Similarly the political map of India underwent few changes. Baluchistan was taken over in 1876 with the consent of

[1] Including Egypt, 1882–1922.

its rulers; Upper Burma was annexed ten years later, partly at least to forestall a French advance from Indo-China, and the restive North-West Frontier was readjusted periodically after 'little wars' with the hill tribes; but at the close of a costly campaign in Afghanistan in 1878 the Government of India was content merely to retain control of the Amir's external policy, and in 1902 it duly withdrew the exploratory expedition it had sent into mysterious Tibet.

On the other hand the internal development of India and the colonies of settlement was imposing. 'The Colonies' busily peopled their open spaces with their own vigorous progeny and the swarms of immigrants that came from all parts of Europe as well as the United Kingdom whence some 300,000 souls were going overseas each year during the decade before the war of 1914, an increasing proportion of them bound for Canada or other lands within the Empire.[1] Settlement was often closer than in days gone by, for improving means of communication, advancing agricultural knowledge, and the perfection of cold storage enabled the waste spaces of the earth to supply distant Europe with the perishable beef and mutton of the ranches and the fruit and dairy produce of small holdings as well as durable wheat and timber. India, for her part, witnessed a phenomenal increase of population thanks to prolonged internal peace, more exact administration, extended health and famine services, and the numerous opportunities of earning a living which commerce and the embryo industrial revolution were bringing to her ports and the towns round which the fighting during the Mutiny had been heaviest.

The huge increase in the square mileage of the British Empire and its rivals took place in tropical or subtropical regions in Africa, South-Eastern Asia and the Pacific islands. Inevitably so, for these were the only parts of the world that offered annexationists scope for their energies so long as the Royal Navy guarded Australia, New Zealand and South Africa, and that Navy and the Monroe Doctrine together cordoned off the Americas. Further, it was here that the governments of the West could extend their rule most easily, for modern firearms had given them an inestimable advantage over savages or men of other civilisations less adequately equipped. Again, they could remain to rule now that railways were defeating

---

[1] Assisted United Kingdom emigration fell away after 1870, and all kinds of emigration diminished. Between 1891 and 1900 what are now Dominions took 28% of this emigration; they took 50% between 1901 and 1910, and an even higher proportion between 1911 and 1914.

the tsetse fly that had hitherto barred vast tracts to draught animals, and cold storage, tinned foods and the advances in sanitation and medical science effected by Pasteur, Koch, Ross, Bruce, Manson, the Cuban doctor Carlos Finlay and a host of others were making life in the tropics more tolerable for white men. Lastly, these regions could furnish products desired by the Western world, especially the vegetable oils, tin, rubber and copper needed by the new electrified industries.

Critics who condemn this extension of Western rule as sheer acquisitiveness would do well to contemplate the brutal alternative. These regions were going to be exploited in any event, and, since it was plainly impossible to set up ring fences around continents and the myriad islands of the sea, the choice lay between allowing irresponsible Westerners, armed with all the resources of their civilisation, to work their will in tribal areas or lands whose native rulers were too weak to check them, and taking charge of this penetration either by buttressing up such native governments with the element of control that this implied or by imposing direct rule upon all concerned. Inevitably the powers took this latter course and the proof of their essential humanity in so doing lies in one fact. Much of the preliminary work, in Africa particularly, was done by joint stock companies and chartered companies, Belgian, British, French, German and Portuguese, and the more fully these associations were controlled by their home governments and public opinions the better their record. There can be no question that control by the strongly organised national governments which presently superseded most of these companies made for the greatest good of the greatest number, or that the more enlightened governments hoped that the exploitation of the tropics would benefit the local inhabitants as well as their own people.

The scramble for Africa began in the Moslem North, which, with its prolongation up the Nile Valley, belongs to the Mediterranean world, and almost immediately thereafter in the region to the south of the Sahara. The African islands had long been in European occupation, except Madagascar, the largest of them, where, however, the French and British had long-established interests; but in 1874 European possessions on the mainland were dotted far apart along the coasts. The Spaniards were at Ceuta and Melilla, the

British on the Gambia, at Sierra Leone bordering upon the down-at-heel American Negro republic of Liberia, on the Gold Coast and at Lagos; the French were in Algeria, Senegal, the Ivory Coast and the Gaboon; the Portuguese still held Angola and Mozambique. The only two solid blocks of European settlement were in the temperate regions: in Algeria at one end of the continent and South Africa at the other. Morocco was independent; Tunis, Tripoli (Libya) and Egypt with her dependencies in the Sudan and the Equatorial Provinces bordering on independent Abyssinia owed a more or less nominal allegiance to the Ottoman Sultan. Farther south Moslem emirs or sultans ruled in the middle Niger valley and the parts around Zanzibar, and one or two well organised Bantu tribal monarchies held sway in Uganda and Barotseland; but the rest of Africa was sparsely dotted with loosely-knit tribes utterly unable to stand upon their own feet 'under the strenuous conditions of the modern world'.

The prelude to the scramble in North Africa was Disraeli's purchase from the needy Khedive of forty per cent of the Suez Canal shares on behalf of the British Government in 1875, and his acquisition, at the Berlin Congress of 1878, of the right to administer Cyprus under the suzerainty of the Sultan for so long a time as Russia should hold certain Turkish territory in eastern Asia Minor. Next year Italy founded her first colony of Eritrea by occupying Assab next door to French Obok and opposite British Aden; but it was France who set the ball rolling in good earnest by proclaiming a protectorate over Tunis in 1881 and thus driving disappointed Italy into the waiting arms of Germany and Austria-Hungary.

Meanwhile France and Great Britain, representing the Khedive's principal creditors, had set up a dual control over Egypt's finances in 1876. This foreign intervention, followed as it was by the dethronement of the spendthrift Khedive by his Turkish suzerain, called forth a nationalist military movement against all outsiders, Moslem and Christian. Several hundred Europeans were killed in a riot at Alexandria in 1882, and, since France refused to go with her, Great Britain occupied Egypt single-handed with the Sultan's leave. She then encouraged Italy, who alone of the Continental Powers was friendly, to forestall French activities on the Red Sea coast by occupying the Sudanese port of Massowah, and in 1885, after the defeat of two Egyptian armies and the destruction of Gordon and his garrison at Khartum by the Dervishes, herself

G

abandoned the whole of the Egyptian Sudan with the exception of Suakim and other Red Sea ports. She thus left the Equatorial Provinces farther south in the air and even offered to evacuate Egypt provided her troops might march in again if anarchy threatened; but the Sultan would not hear of her departure, nor France and Russia of possible reoccupation. So British officials, backed by British troops, remained in the valley of the Nile to rule Egypt through the Khedive and raise it to a prosperity unexampled since the days of the greatest of the Pharaohs, in spite of French obstruction and the complications arising from the international courts and other extra-territorial privileges guaranteed to foreigners by the old Turkish capitulations. Presently the British annexed Socotra and proclaimed a protectorate over part of Somaliland to strengthen their hold on the Red Sea, leaving the Italians free to take the remainder of Somaliland and proclaim a protectorate over Abyssinia.

Embarrassed by the jealousies which the unwanted burden of Egypt inflicted on her, Great Britain was further embarrassed by failure and loss of prestige in South Africa. In 1875 the Disraeli ministry had launched a campaign to federate the British colonies and the two Boer republics, and to secure among other advantages the adoption of a liberal native policy in those parts. The federation and native policies conflicted disastrously with one another. The self-governing Cape Colony refused to move, and a French arbitration court weakened Great Britain's hold over the republics by awarding to the Portuguese the whole of Delagoa Bay, the Transvaal's natural outlet to the Indian Ocean. Then, in 1877, Lord Carnarvon, the Colonial Secretary, sanctioned the hasty annexation of the Transvaal for a variety of reasons, including the fear that the imminent collapse of that republic would precipitate a general native uprising. On the other hand, at the close of a Cape Colony-Kaffir War, which delayed promised reform in the Transvaal, his successor refused to extend British control over neighbouring and confused tribal territories beyond annexing Walvis Bay on the west coast and Port St. John's between Cape Colony and Natal. The British then became involved in a harassing Zulu campaign; the Basuto rose against their Cape rulers, and the Transvaalers took up arms. In 1881 the British withdrew from the Transvaal, retaining certain rights of intervention but resolved to have as little as possible to do with the interior of South Africa.

The scramble for tropical Africa made mock of the British self-denying ordinance. Eighty years of exploration by men of various nationalities from the days of Mungo Park onwards had revealed the great African system of waterways, and lately the reports of David Livingstone and Henry Stanley had told the world something of the horrors of the Arab slave trade which went on behind the East Coast in spite of British treaties with the Sultan of Zanzibar and the efforts of the 'sentimental squadron' off his coasts. Something also was known and much more believed of the wealth of the interior. In 1876, therefore, Leopold II of Belgium summoned an international conference to Brussels to consider the opening up and civilisation of the vast Congo Basin, and, when the other branch sections forbore to take action, sent Stanley to sign treaties with Congolese chiefs on behalf of the mainly Belgian committee that he himself dominated. The French, who had recently been extending their hold on the Guinea Coast and the upper valley of the Niger, promptly sent de Brazza to secure a footing for them on the lower Congo. Portugal thereupon reasserted ancient and extensive claims to that area, and the British, fearful lest the French should oust their traders there as from the Gaboon and Guinea Coast, recognised some of these claims and arranged with Portugal that the Congo should be open to the shipping of all nations on equal terms and under joint Anglo-Portuguese control.

At this stage Germany descended upon Africa. In 1884 she snapped up Togoland next door to the Gold Coast, the Cameroons where British trade had hitherto predominated, and South-West Africa to the northward of Cape Colony around Walvis Bay. She also sent her agents into the hinterland of Zanzibar and the native areas on either side of Natal, and showed signs of desiring to reach out from South-West Africa to join hands with the expansive Transvaalers who had recently been freed from all British control other than the Queen's veto on their treaty-making powers. The British Government, which had just wearily relieved the Cape Colony of Basutoland, forestalled the Germans in the Natal region and, in 1885, prevented them and the Transvaalers from blocking the road from Cape Colony to Central Africa by annexing the southern portion of Bechuanaland and extending a protectorate over the remainder with the consent of the chiefs concerned.

Meanwhile Bismarck had decided to work with the French. In face of this the British and Portuguese set aside their Congo

treaty and attended a conference of the Powers on Africa, the first
of its kind, at Berlin. There Bismarck found to his surprise that the
comparatively internationally-minded British were his friends and
not the nationalistic French. Germans and British therefore worked
surprisingly well together behind the doors of the conference room,
and in the event the Congo Free State, fruit of Stanley's treaties,
was entrusted to Leopold II, neutralised and under international
guarantee. France was given the right of pre-emption over the new
State and gained also the large area which de Brazza had staked out
for her on the north bank of the Congo, while Portugal was allowed
to reach the south bank near the estuary. Slavery was forbidden
and freedom of trade and navigation proclaimed in the Conventional
Basin of the Congo, an area very much larger than the natural
basin, as well as in a wide extension along the East Coast which
included the Shire river and the Zambesi delta. But, whereas
control in the Conventional Basin was to be international, control of
the Upper Niger was entrusted to France and of the Lower Niger
to Great Britain on whose behalf George Goldie Taubman had for
several years past been consolidating local British mercantile
interests with consular backing.

The British had already had experience of agreements in South
Africa and elsewhere whereby chiefs had signed away rights without
fully understanding what they were doing in view of the radical
differences between tribal and western law, especially in the vital
matter of landholding; but the sheaf of Congolese treaties with
which Leopold and the French confronted the Berlin Conference
was something new. These documents were cessions of vast
territories and sovereign rights in return for trifling payments which
the chiefs must have regarded merely as recognition money for
leave to settle on the lands in question. High-minded administrators
like Lord Lugard have commented since that annexation would
have been the more straightforward course, and subsequent treaties
arranged by men like himself and Sir Harry Johnston were fair
and reasonably well understood by both parties; but the fact
remains that, in spite of British and American heart-searchings,
international recognition was given to the Congo treaties, and
most of the necessary extension of civilised rule in tropical Africa
was carried out henceforward by means of similar treaties, horribly
liable to abuse.

At Berlin the British tried to regularise the scramble by insisting that 'effective occupation' must mean the occupation of a given territory in sufficient strength to secure respect for acquired rights and freedom of trade and travel. The continental Powers, led by France and Germany, refused. They limited this rule to the coasts and maintained that the possession of such coasts constituted a right to the interior for an indefinite distance inland. The Conference did indeed accept the British invention of the 'sphere of influence', a delaying device by which a Power should give notice to the rest that it claimed a prior right in a particular area and proposed to set up a civilised authority there within a reasonable time. But British hopes that the scramble might thus be slowed down were speedily disappointed. Hardly had the Conference dispersed than Germany produced a bundle of treaties which had been secured during its sittings by her new East Africa Company. Thereupon the French turned right round and, claiming that effective occupation everywhere was after all the only sure test, led the Powers in a rush to secure more chiefly signatures.

Roughly speaking each Power tried to mark out a belt across Africa which would ensure to its possessor, among other advantages, a route for the trunk African railway and telegraph with which those of other Powers must link up on terms. The Portuguese and Germans worked from east to west to the southward of the Congo Free State, the French from west to east to the northward of it, and the British, in so far as they had a plan at all, mainly from north to south to the eastward of this central internationalised obstacle.

The British soon found that their West African possessions were wedged in coastwise by French acquisitions and the new German colonies; nevertheless they began to build up not inconsiderable protectorates behind Sierra Leone and the Gold Coast, and, in recognition of the Gold Coast's growing importance, separated it from Lagos in 1886. Two years later they freed the isolated Gambia colony from Sierra Leone control; meanwhile, in 1885, they had proclaimed a protectorate over the Oil Rivers and, in the following year, had given a charter to Sir George Goldie's expansive Royal Niger Company.

Chartered companies also carried through the main British drives in southern and eastern Africa. The British South Africa Company was organised by Cecil Rhodes and chartered in 1889 to operate in a sphere that covered Bechuanaland, Matabeleland-Mashonaland (soon to be known as Southern Rhodesia) and an indefinite area to the northward of the Zambesi river. Rhodes's base in the south had been strengthened recently by the Cape Colony's annexation of most of the Native territories that lay between itself and Natal, by the Imperial Government's annexation of all that the Transvaalers had left of Zululand, and by the inclusion in the British sphere of influence of tribal lands that linked Zululand to Portuguese Delagoa Bay. Now, in 1890, while the British Government was settling with the Germans the line that was to separate South-West Africa from Bechuanaland, the B.S.A. Company occupied Mashonaland. It also laid the foundations of North-Western Rhodesia by acquiring in Barotseland extensive mineral and commercial rights which promised to compensate it in some measure for its failure to forestall the Congo authorities in the rich Katanga copper belt farther north.

This thrust from the south overlapped a British advance from the east. In 1887 the Portuguese reasserted old claims over Lake Nyasa and the Shire river valley, where British missionaries and traders had long been at work, and over Mashonaland also on the southern bank of the Zambesi. Sir Harry Johnston, consul at Mozambique, promptly proclaimed a protectorate over the Shire area, and Lord Salisbury cleared the way for him and the B.S.A. Company alike by sending an ultimatum to Lisbon. After much discussion and some little scuffling the frontiers were fixed by the Anglo-Portuguese Convention of 1891. Johnston ruled Nyasaland as Commissioner of the British Central African Protectorate, administered the Chartered sphere to the north of the Zambesi and south-west of Lake Tanganyika, and dealt so vigorously with the Arab slavers who had recently come to the Zambesi valley that, by 1898, that evil business was a thing of the past.

Meanwhile the Imperial British East Africa Company, chartered in 1888, had made its way successfully in the regions to the north of German East Africa and gained a footing far inland by a treaty with the Kabaka, the King of Uganda. In 1890 the Anglo-German frontiers in this part of Africa were fixed. H.M. Government extended a protectorate over the Company's sphere, and also over Zanzibar and Pemba to which Germany gave up her claims in exchange for Heligoland, and France her's for the recognition of the exclusive right to coveted Madagascar.

Thus by 1890 the first breathless scramble for Africa was ended. The event was celebrated by a second general conference, this time at Brussels, which had to face the fact that the Congo Free State was fast becoming, to its sorrow, the preserve of King Leopold and his financial friends. Undismayed, it reaffirmed the rulings of the Berlin Conference, forbade the importation of firearms and spirits into the whole of tropical Africa between the Sahara and the northern border of the Transvaal, and, now that the British 'sentimental squadron' had been withdrawn at last, prohibited the slave trade in the eastern waters covered by Great Britain's treaties with the Moslem rulers of Eastern Africa, the Red Sea and the Persian Gulf.

It was only a breathing space: the French and Rhodes were soon off again on their respective sides of the equator. In West Africa the French pushed out boldly towards Lake Chad across the 'rather light soil' of the Sahara, and pressed close to the British coastal colonies and sphere of influence on the Lower Niger. The British replied by putting the protectorates behind the Gambia colony and Sierra Leone on a regular footing, organising the Northern Territories behind the Gold Coast, forcibly annexing the neighbouring blood-stained Ashanti Kingdom, and renaming their enlarged protectorate on the Oil Rivers the Niger Coast Protectorate. Relations with the French were very strained for a time in the Niger valley where the Royal Niger Company was steadily extending its authority, not without fighting against the traders of Brass, the bloody monarchy of Benin and the southern Moslem emirs. A general West African settlement was, however, effected in 1898–99. Boundaries were fixed and, by an arrangement which was soon to become general under the numerous most-favoured nation treaties of the day, French and British subjects were assured of equal rights of trade and navigation in the Gold Coast, the Niger Coast Protectorate and part of the Anglo-Egyptian Sudan on the one hand, and the Ivory Coast, Dahomey and part of French Equatorial Africa on the other. This done the Niger Company surrendered its charter to the Crown, which organised its now greatly extended sphere as the two Protectorates of Northern and Southern Nigeria (1899).

In East Africa the reluctant British Government first proclaimed a protectorate over Uganda and then, in 1895, took over all British East Africa from the chartered East Africa Company, which, having enjoyed neither the commercial opportunities of the Royal Niger Company nor the mineral, land and railway assets of Rhodes's Company, had come to the end of its financial tether after six years of admirable administration. Five years later Johnston, as special commissioner, concluded treaties which defined the powers of the Native monarchies of Uganda. Thereupon British taxpayers advanced the money for, and Indian labourers built, a railway from the coast to Kisumu on the Victoria Nyanza. On the completion of this Uganda railway in 1902 the healthy Kenya Highlands, which it traversed, were transferred from Uganda to the East African Protectorate and opened to settlement. The Zionists declined to found a New Jerusalem there, but settlers were drawn readily enough from Great Britain, South Africa and Australia.

Decisive events had meanwhile taken place in the valley of the Nile. While the French were moving eastward from Lake Chad and an Anglo-Egyptian army marching southward towards the Sudan building railways on the South African gauge as it came, the Italians tried to assert their authority over Abyssinia. The disaster of Adowah drove them back to their coastal possessions, and their going hastened the advance of Kitchener's army from Egypt. Kitchener beat the Dervishes at Atbara in 1896 and, two years later, overthrew them at Omdurman and took Khartum. At the grave risk of war between Great Britain and disappointed France he induced a small French force to withdraw from Fashoda higher up the Nile, and had the satisfaction of seeing an Anglo-Egyptian condominium established in the reconquered Sudan.

The political future of southern Africa also was not settled without heavy fighting. Rhodes's British South Africa Company became the almost independent ruler of Southern Rhodesia after the conquest of Matabeleland in 1893–94, and next year took over North-Eastern Rhodesia from the Nyasaland Commissioner. Meanwhile the development of great goldfields around Johannesburg in the southern Transvaal, and the construction of a railway from the mines to Portuguese Delagoa Bay by a monopolistic Dutch-German syndicate, led Germany to display an unwelcome interest in this part of Africa. President Kruger of the Transvaal was inclined to reciprocate that interest; hence, in 1895, the British Government agreed indeed that he should extend a protectorate over Swaziland but cut his republic off from the Indian Ocean by annexing tribal lands that lay beyond. At this stage Rhodes, who had just added southern Bechuanaland to the Cape Colony of which he was Prime Minister, tried to force on the federation of the colonies and republics south of the Zambesi. The consequent Jameson Raid into the Transvaal ruined Rhodes's plans, led to a crisis with Germany and weakened Great Britain's position in all Africa. The French took advantage of the confusion to annex Madagascar outright, but by 1898 H.M. Government had recovered its balance. Having handed Zululand over to newly self-governing Natal, it imposed strict imperial control over the Chartered Company in Southern Rhodesia, allowed it to exercise effective rule in North-Western Rhodesia, and itself came to terms with the Germans. By a partially secret agreement Great Britain and Germany arranged to support loans to the needy Portuguese Government and, in the event of default, to divide Portugal's mainland African colonies between themselves, Great Britain earmarking *inter alia* Delagoa Bay, the key to her South African puzzle, and Germany the lion's share together with the Portuguese half of Timor as the price of her 'abandonment of the Boers'. This elimination of Germany as an active factor in South African politics left Great Britain free to bring pressure on the Transvaal with which she had many points of difference. War ensued in 1899. At the end of it, in 1902, both Republics were annexed and the Transvaal's Swaziland protectorate was taken over by H.M. Government.

For nearly a decade after 1902 there was a lull in the partition of Africa by the Powers; certainly Great Britain made no significant annexation but rather carried out a work of political integration. That work was made possible by the railways. These advanced rapidly. For instance the Egyptian line, starting from Wadi-Halfa in 1897, had linked Khartum with the Red Sea by 1905 and, a few years later, had thrust far into the heart of the Sudan. Before war came in 1914 rail and river had connected Lagos with Kano in the extreme north of Nigeria, while Rhodes's so-called Cape-to-Cairo railway, which moved out northward from Kimberley in 1889, had traversed Bechuanaland and Rhodesia and reached the Congo copper belt.

Thus supported, local governments gained strength and cohesion. In 1906 Zanzibar was subjected to more effective control and all East Africa was placed under a Governor, who, in 1913, became also High Commissioner for Zanzibar. In West Africa, in 1906, the Southern Nigerian Protectorate was combined with the colony of Lagos, as soon as Sir Frederick Lugard had brought Northern Nigeria under British control partly by negotiation and partly by force, and early in 1914 Lugard at last succeeded in uniting the Two Nigerias under himself as Governor. Similarly North-Eastern and

North-Western Rhodesia were unified under Chartered rule as Northern Rhodesia in 1911. Finally all the British territories south of the Zambesi joined in a customs union in 1903, and in 1910, a year or two after H.M. Government had given the Transvaal and the Orange Free State self-government, these two colonies combined with the Cape Colony and Natal to form the Union of South Africa. The Governor-General of the new Union was also to be High Commissioner administering Basutoland, Swaziland and the Bechuanaland Protectorate and exercising Imperial control over Chartered Southern Rhodesia.

The link between the stage of the partition of Africa which ended in 1902 and that which almost completed the work before the war of 1914 was supplied by the Anglo-French *entente cordiale* and the web of secret agreements that was woven round it. In 1904 Great Britain and France settled many outstanding differences including the French fishing rights in Newfoundland. They agreed above all that France was to have a free hand in Morocco in return for recognising Great Britain's special position in Egypt. Presently, while the relations of Germany with Great Britain and France grew worse and worse, an anxious conference of the Powers, including the United States, discussed Morocco at Algeciras, Germany began to reform her heavy-handed colonial administration, and in 1908 Belgium took over the Congo Free State from her king and effected many salutary changes. Then, in 1911, Italy gave the signal for the cycle of wars that was to come by seizing Turkish Tripoli and the Dodecanese. Thereupon France occupied Morocco, leaving Spain a share behind the internationalised city of Tangier opposite Gibraltar.

Thus, in the course of thirty years, Great Britain, France, Germany, Italy, Spain, Portugal and Belgium had shared out the control of all Africa save only Abyssinia, and Liberia whose finances were now under United States surveillance. One final repartition was, however, never carried out. In 1913 British and German representatives agreed upon the division between their respective countries of Portuguese Africa in the expected event of Portugal's collapse. The German Government refused to make known the terms, and thus it was that the German people entered the Kaiser's War persuaded that the British would do nothing to meet their colonial aspirations.

A scramble for control of lands that border on the South China Sea and Western Pacific Ocean had run side by side with the scramble for Africa, interlocking with it and sometimes facing the British with a choice between success in one area and failure in the other.

Great Britain had begun to extend her control over the Malay Peninsula behind the Straits Settlements in the still spacious days before either scramble had set in. She had evolved a novel method of governance in the process, for in 1874 she signed treaties with anarchic Perak, Selangor and one of the nine states of the Negri Sembilan Confederacy whereby the Sultans and the State Councils were to retain sovereignty but admit Residents whose advice must be 'asked and acted upon on all questions other than those touching Malay religion and customs'. The scramble in these parts began some ten years later. Simultaneously with their arrival in Africa the Germans appeared in New Guinea, whose western half had long been held by the Dutch. Their coming alarmed the Australians, and when Great Britain showed herself slow to move, Queensland declared a protectorate over the eastern half of the great island. In the event Queensland was obliged to relinquish her prize, and in 1885 the north-eastern area went to Germany; but meanwhile, once some of the Australian colonies had undertaken to contribute to the maintenance of a territory whose acquisition would primarily benefit themselves, Great Britain had proclaimed a protectorate over the south-eastern portion. She annexed it outright a few years later.

The establishment of the Germans in New Guinea, followed as it was by the extension from Indo-China of French authority over Annam and Tong-king, impelled the British Government to strengthen its hold in and around Borneo. The British North Borneo Company, which had united all the British trading interests in those parts, had been given a Royal charter in 1881, the first of the new British companies of this kind and the one that survived longest as a ruling power. In 1888 its sphere of operations and the independent state of Sarawak, still under the Brooke dynasty, were given British protection, and the neighbouring Sultan of Brunei was persuaded to place his external policy under British control. Nor was the meaning of these developments lost upon the rulers of the Malay Peninsula. Between 1883 and 1895 Pahang and the remaining eight states of Negri Sembilan accepted British Residents, while the Sultan of Johore admitted a Consul. This done the four 'advised' Malay principalities became the Malay Federated States, each retaining its own government and Resident, but all subject now to a Resident-General whose advice must be taken. The Federated States were further pledged to help each other with loans, and to join in each others' defence and that of the Straits Settlements, whose Governor became High Commissioner and president at the periodical meetings of the four Sultans at one or other of the State capitals. Next year Great Britain and France ended a long dispute by defining their respective spheres of influence in Siam which lay between Indo-China and the Malay States.

The storm centre then shifted to China. There Russia, Germany, France and Italy were seeking privileged spheres of interest, while Japan, victorious over China in 1895, was watching nervously for a chance to do likewise, but the United States and Great Britain were insistent that the door for trade and finance in the Celestial Empire must be kept open. In 1898 the British leased a potential naval base at Wei-hai-wei as a counterpoise to the Russians at Port Arthur and the Germans at Kiau-chau on the approaches to Pekin, and leased additional land in the Kowloon area of Hong Kong to meet the needs of that expanding port and counterbalance the French at Kwang-chow. Then, having taken part in the international expedition which crushed the desperate Boxer rising around Pekin, they made a treaty with Japan for the mutual safeguarding of interests in Far Eastern waters. After her new ally had driven the Russians out of Port Arthur and Manchuria in 1905, Great Britain withdrew the bulk of her China Squadron, but reinforced her position in Malaya and the parts adjacent. In 1906 she handed over 'Papua', her share of New Guinea, to the new Australian Commonwealth, induced the Sultan of Brunei to admit a Resident of the Malayan type, and in 1909 persuaded the four federated Malay Sultans to join in forming a federal Council, under the chairmanship of the High Commissioner, which should consider drafts of laws affecting more than one of the States and exercise supreme financial control over the federation. At the same time she extended a protectorate over the Unfederated Malay States of Kedah, Perlis, Kelantan and Trengganu, from all of which Siam withdrew her suzerainty. On the eve of the Kaiser's War she sent a Resident to the court of Johore.

The islands of Polynesia and Melanesia were as dust in the balance beside the masses of Africa and Asia; but some were valuable for their copra, some were worth having as naval bases, and far too many were a reproach to the civilisation which allowed their peoples to be decimated by disease, drink, sheer boredom and the black-birders who supplied the Queensland sugar planters with Kanaka labour. After repeated requests from local chiefs Great Britain delighted the Australians by annexing the Fiji Islands in 1874, and in due time afforded less pleasure to blackbirders and others by giving the Governor of Fiji jurisdiction over British subjects on neighbouring islands as High Commissioner of the Western Pacific.

Great Britain and Germany then began to compete for the control of Samoa, where their respective traders had been long established. The United States complicated the situation in 1878 by securing the naval base of Pago-pago, the best harbour in the group of islands, and in that same year, to the alarm of the Australians, France challenged Great Britain's lien upon the New Hebrides. These difficulties were shelved by the extension of joint Anglo-French naval control over the New Hebrides in 1887, and joint Anglo-German-American control over the Samoan islands two years later at the close of a Native civil war. During the next few years the British extended protectorates over the Gilbert and Ellice Islands, Tonga and many of the Solomon Islands, and in 1898 at last recognised distant Pitcairn Island of *Bounty* fame[1] as a 'British colony by settlement', which it undoubtedly was.

The death of the king then brought matters to a head in much-disputed Samoa. The Germans, who had already annexed some of the Solomon Islands and were now negotiating with the British for the reversion of Portuguese Timor, were angered that British warships should have demonstrated alongside those of the United States and against their own in the Philippines during the recent Spanish-American war. They were angered still more when British and American cruisers bombarded the Samoan capital and damaged the German consulate in the course of the civil war which their own Consul had stirred up. After a long period of strain, during which Great Britain was hampered by growing difficulties in South Africa, an agreement was reached at the close of 1899. One of the Samoan islands went to the United States and the other two to Germany, while Tonga and most of the German Solomons went

[1] *Vide supra*, p. 32.

to Great Britain as compensation for her withdrawal. It only remained for the British and French to set up an uneasy condominium in the New Hebrides under British and French Residents, each with his own staff, and a common executive and joint court for certain specified purposes. So it was that on the eve of the war of 1914 Great Britain found herself responsible for numberless islands south of the equator scattered from the neighbourhood of New Zealand far out along the road to South America.

VI

THE TROPICAL DEPENDENCIES AND INDIA, 1874–1914

THE acquisition of these extensive and varied possessions between 1874 and 1914 faced the British Government with continually changing problems of governance. Apart from India and one or two shadowy protectorates, there had been only two classes of dependency at the beginning of this period; the self-governing colonies covering many millions of square miles, and the Crown colonies, comparatively few in number and for the most part small. Forty years later the number of Crown colonies had increased and two new classes of dependency had been added to the Empire: the vast protectorates of the modern type and the protected states.

The powers of a colonial Governor and the status of a colony and colonists had always been clear. His Excellency was responsible to the Westminster Parliament through the Secretary of State for the Colonies; a colony was as much an integral part of the Crown's dominions as the United Kingdom itself, and its inhabitants British subjects; but the powers of the High Commissioner, Chief Commissioner, Resident or Agent who, each in his degree, ruled a protectorate or protected state, and the international status of those territories and their peoples, had to be determined step by step.

During their long imperial career the British had had experience of many systems of control that fell far short of sovereignty. From time to time since 1634 they had applied Punishment Acts or their equivalents to territories so far apart as Newfoundland-Labrador, Honduras, Sierra Leone, the lands adjacent to the Cape Colony, New Zealand and various Pacific islands; but these were merely an extension of criminal jurisdiction over English or British subjects which could only be enforced if the delinquent and the witnesses were brought back to English or British soil. The Foreign Jurisdiction Act of 1843, invaluable by reason of its flexibility, gave the Crown full jurisdiction on the spot over British subjects in foreign lands whose rulers would permit its exercise. Occasionally the Crown had promised native rulers protection on condition that they had no dealings with third parties without its consent, while the Indian subsidiary treaties not only gave the Princes a guarantee of security but made the Government of India responsible in a measure for the safety of British and foreign interests within their states. Here, however, the Resident was accredited to the Nizam or Rajah and must rely as a rule on influence rather than authority. Force of circumstances was now to oblige the British to go much further in many parts of the world.

The new departure in policy became plain between 1874 and 1884. Some of the Malayan Sultans were given Residents whose advice had to be asked and taken on most matters; the new High Commissioner for the Western Pacific was given legislative as well as full judicial powers over British subjects in all islands not subject to civilised rule; in 1878 the British Government, armed with the Foreign Jurisdiction Act, undertook to govern in the fullest sense all the inhabitants of Cyprus even though these were still to remain Turkish subjects. It then amended the Act to give the Crown wider powers than before over British subjects in uncivilised or otherwise unstable regions. From 1881 till 1884 the Queen exercised a novel suzerainty over the Transvaal with considerable powers of internal control, and in 1882 set up in Egypt a curious but effective system owing much to Malayan and Cypriote example, whereby the Khedive, himself a vassal of the Ottoman Sultan, was bound to take the advice of British advisers, who were nominally his servants, and especially of H.M. Consul-General who had a veto on all financial measures.

It was, however, the scramble for tropical Africa that gave a new and much fuller significance to the idea of a protectorate. The British, who were even then signing treaties of the familiar kind with chieftains in the Niger valley and along the Gold Coast, went to the Berlin Conference in 1884 holding that a protectorate gave security to the local rulers, warned off foreign Powers, and at most gave their own government jurisdiction over British subjects or such subjects of foreign states as accepted that jurisdiction. They found that the continental Powers, especially France and Germany, regarded it as something almost indistinguishable from annexation, and 'sovereign rights of influence' as including complete jurisdiction. The pace of the Scramble, the example of other Powers and the patent inability of most African and Pacific Island governments to stand against advancing Western civilisation without a considerable measure of support, hence of control, forced them round to the Continental view and practice.

The British, therefore, amended the Foreign Jurisdiction Act once more in 1890, the year of the first general settlement of frontiers in the new Africa. The Act now conferred on the Crown full powers in a protected territory, gave statutory force to an Order in Council issued under the Act and submitted to Parliament, and made the Colonial Secretary the final judge of the existence of the jurisdiction thus claimed. These principles were upheld by the Brussels Conference; they were embodied in the Order in Council of 1891, which gave legal backing to the advance of Rhodes's Company northward into Africa, and were applied presently to the hinterland of the Gold Coast and the Pacific Islands. In the later eighteen-nineties, significant of the fading distinction between a protectorate and a colony, the Foreign Office began to hand over to the Colonial Office those protectorates that were under its control, till, with the transfer of Zanzibar in 1913, it retained only the British share of the condominia of the Sudan and the New Hebrides. A protectorate still might not be strictly speaking part of the Crown's dominions nor its inhabitants anything more than 'British protected persons'; it might not be able to borrow in the London money market on favoured colonial terms; but, for practical purposes and in the eyes of foreign governments, it was a possession in which British officials exercised powers over everyone, powers which varied indeed according to the vigour of the native institutions, but usually equalled and sometimes surpassed the effective authority of officials in a Crown colony.

The protectorate administrations looked to the Crown Colonies and India for guidance; necessarily so, for their territories were nearly all tropical and inhabited by folk who had no knowledge of parliamentary institutions or British local government. Government, therefore, had to be at the very least predominantly official: by a Resident Commissioner or other representative of higher authority at the centre assisted as a rule by an Executive Council and, in some cases later on, a Legislative Council also. But, as in India and the Colonies, other than those Caribbean dependencies in which local administration had been done by the committees dear to the English heart since the seventeenth century, the officials who made daily contact with the inhabitants were the men-of-all-work of the dependent Empire: the District Officers or District

H

Commissioners who found their Indian counterparts in the Collectors.

The methods of protectorate administration became more and more flexible as time went by. In India, Company and Crown had interfered as little as possible with the ancient religious and social customs of their subjects, and this sound rule was followed now in the protected states of Malaya, Zanzibar and elsewhere. The dealings of British officials with primitive peoples in times past, however, had ranged from the policy, which lack of officials and police had forced upon Theophilus Shepstone in mid-Victorian Natal, of upholding or even recreating the chieftainship on which so much of tribal life depended, to the contemporary policy of Sir George Grey in New Zealand and the parts adjacent to the Cape Colony of planting European settlers among the tribesmen as a restraining and civilising force, and the supersession of the authority of the chief by that of the magistrate. Generally speaking Grey's policy had prevailed in tribal areas. Most nineteenth-century officials found that the Evangelical missionaries regarded tribal customs as 'the beastlie devices of the heathen' which must make way for the Christian civilisation represented by their several churches, a process which all but the most far-sighted of them believed would be swift. They noted, moreover, that tribal institutions crumbled away on contact with Western civilisation even when attempts were made to preserve them; they generally shared the growing opinion of the Indian Civil Service of their day that, if a thing was to be done well, they must do it themselves; they were prone to regard chiefs as dangerous rivals.

Hence rule in Crown colonies had usually been, and still was, direct rule when the problem of the protectorates arose. Inevitably the colonial practice was followed there in the early days, and chiefs, where they survived, became more and more mere channels for conveying the instructions of imperial or company officials to the tribesmen. Such a system was, however, expensive, for the protectorates were large and kept on growing. Adequate supplies of good men and money to pay them were hard to find, and the folly of using cheap men was soon made as clear in the sphere of more than one administration as in British municipal life. It was these brute facts far more than any theory of governance that led to the development of the system of indirect rule.

Indirect rule by an imperial power through dependent rulers was, of course, an ancient device of which the British were making full use in the protected States; but indirect rule as it is understood to-day was different. Its fundamental principle is that British Resident and native ruler, District Officer and district or village headman, shall all be parts of a single administration, one and indivisible. There had been premonitions of the system. Shepstone had anticipated something of it in the fifties; Sir Arthur Gordon, the first Governor of Fiji, had worked through native institutions even more systematically in the 'seventies, and Sir William Mac-Gregor, the first administrator of British New Guinea, had followed his example. In Africa, where the full development of the idea was to take place, Lugard had recommended as early as 1893 that rule in populous Uganda, with its coherent Bantu monarchies, should he 'through and by the chief'. This principle was adopted in the treaties which Johnston signed a few years later with the rulers of Buganda, Toro and Ankole in those parts, and also in that concluded by the British South Africa Company during the same decade with the chief of Barotseland in North-Western Rhodesia.

The most fruitful experiment in indirect rule was made by Lugard himself in Northern Nigeria from 1900 onwards. Equipped with a mere handful of officials and very little money, and faced with a huge territory ill-furnished with roads, Lugard was fortunate in that the local Moslem emirs were heads of governments on which it was possible to lean without fear of their collapsing utterly. He thus learned to regard the hereditary chief as the desirable foundation of his system, though, failing such a potentate, he was as ready as Shepstone had been to revive decayed chieftainships or in the last resort look for some other form of native authority. He therefore recognized the Emirs of Northern Nigeria as native authorities deriving their power from the British suzerain. As a 'first beginning' he set them to collect the tax imposed by the suzerain, whose payment marked at once the recognition of the chief by his people and of the suzerainty by the chief, and bade them pay at least fifty per cent of their takings into the central exchequer. The remainder was to be retained by the Emirs and their councillors in native treasuries, which Lugard, with a sure appreciation of the vital connection between finance and self-government, always regarded as the keystone of his system. Further, as the second essential of indirect rule, he empowered the Emirs and their judicial councils to administer justice according to their own law and

exercise a general control over native courts, all under the supervision of British officials.

The system grew and it worked. The British and the Nigerian
Moslems came to terms and saw their example followed by the
Germans, who introduced something very like indirect rule into
Samoa and New Guinea from 1907 onwards to check the chaos
that was the fruit of unduly rapid detribalisation. In typically
British fashion Lugard only explained to the world, and perhaps
to himself, what he had been doing long after he had done it,
making a theory of necessity. What he had done, at a time when
most anthropologists were more interested in the dimensions of a
skull than with what had once gone on inside it, was to prove that
African ideas were often sound, and that native institutions could be
revived, strengthened and adapted, as the Normans had realised
long ago in Anglo-Saxon England, to ease the shock of the sudden
impact of a strange civilisation upon a continent, the vast majority
of whose inland inhabitants had never had the chance of seeing a
white man before the middle 'eighties.

Whether rule was direct or indirect the spirit of the administration was the same in Crown colonies, protected states and protectorates. The typical government of a British dependency was, as it
had long been on the whole, fair-minded and incorruptible; not
as a rule inspired, since the supply of Lugards was bound to be
limited, but concerned for the welfare of its subjects and true to
Lord Mansfield's tradition of administering even-handed justice
to all men according to its power and knowledge. The system had
its weaknesses quite apart from inevitable human frailty. The short
tenure of office by most Colonial Secretaries bred humdrum
routine at headquarters and left reform in the colonies to depend
too much on the opinions and characters of the Governors; the
distance of the colonies from Downing Street encouraged the time-
consuming correspondence dear to the bureaucratic mind; service
for long years in one area tended to give local officials an outlook
so narrow that they often did not know what was happening in
neighbouring territories and sometimes, in an access of departmental
loyalty, regarded their colleagues there as objectionable rivals. Most
of the District Officers, recruited from the public schools, had the
virtues of their kind: the power of leading men that came of their
experience of the prefect system, and the strong sense of loyalty to
those above them and, equally important, those below that led

many of them to spend themselves utterly in the service of the people committed to their charge. But very many of them also had the failings: a certain difficulty in dealing with westernised natives, a reluctance to honour the traditional British condemnation of the colour bar by welcoming such men to responsible positions in the official hierarchy, an inability to distinguish clearly at all times between fair criticism of the existing political and economic orders and 'seditious agitation'.

Further, the Colonial Office, and therefore the administration in the dependencies, suffered from lack of continuous and informed criticism at home. The British Parliament and public could still be stirred to righteous and sometimes effective wrath by tidings of grave scandal as in Warren Hastings's days, for the Puritan tradition reinforced by Wesleyanism and Evangelicalism still ran strongly and memories of slave emancipation and the campaign of the 'sentimental squadron' off the African coast awakened legitimate pride; but there were few men to take a sustained interest in purely colonial affairs except members of the Anti-Slavery and Aborigines' Protection Societies whose zeal sometimes outran their knowledge and discretion. Again the dependencies were usually short of the money required for proper health, education, transport and agricultural services, for the tradition was that each colony must finance itself. Run thus in watertight compartments none could easily help or look for help to its neighbour. If the worst came to the worst, each must brave the Treasury watch-dog and appeal to the British taxpayer at the price of seeing its expenditure cut to the bone.

On the other hand the spirit of the Renunciation Act of 1778 had been extended far beyond the letter. Parliament must not tax dependencies except for the regulation of trade, and there was little enough of that in a free trade empire; the proceeds of taxation whether by the central or local authority must be expended on the dependency concerned. The Imperial Government took no direct tribute from its empire as the manner of some has been and still is. An indirect 'tribute' there was and in the nature of things must be. Inevitably British colonial agents and trade commissioners bought British goods when they could, especially as London was the centre of the Empire's and indeed of the world's finance; British investors, traders and the 'terrible younger sons', whose predecessors had so impressed the gallant Brigadier Gérard, naturally felt themselves more at home, more secure and more certain of welcome under the

Union Jack than elsewhere. But that was all. Great Britain did not seek even the indirect tribute that comes to a metropolitan people from a fiscally-closed empire. Her colonists and 'protected persons' might sell where they could and buy from whom they would; foreign nationals could trade, dwell and invest in British dependencies as freely as in their own. And they did. Imperial Germany could never have built up her commerce without the British Open Door.

Great Britain had her reward. The ubiquity of the Royal Navy goes far to explain why much more powerful military rivals suffered her to build up her immense tropical empire; but the international spirit of her open door policy goes almost as far, since each disappointed competitor could reflect that a coveted territory was better in Britain's hands than in those of another more prehensile. Be that as it may, the Americans found much to admire in the British colonial system and applied a good deal of it to their new acquisitions in Hawaii and the Philippines, and when the Allied and Associated Powers, the United States among them, came to frame the mandate system at the close of the war of 1914–18 they had in mind, *inter alia*, the British spirit and practice.

The Colonial Office which presided over this bewildering growth of empire itself underwent marked changes. In the days before the Indian Mutiny, when patronage was patronage throughout the public services, the Colonial Secretary had chosen the handful of officers who staffed his little-considered department; but thereafter, in line with reforms in the Indian Civil Service, his nominees were called upon to face a judiciously conducted examination. All this was changed during the reforming 'seventies, the decade that saw the institution of competitive examinations for the Ceylon, Hong Kong and Straits Settlements Services, the abolition of purchase in the Army, the drastic reform of the two old English Universities, the foundation of women's colleges there and in London, and the multiplication of provincial colleges teaching for the London degree. An Order in Council of 1870 divided the Home Civil Service into a small and highly paid upper division for the real work of administration and a lower division for routine clerical tasks, and decreed that, except for the Foreign Office and posts that required professional qualifications, all permanent appointments were to be made on the results of competitive examinations. These principles were applied to the Colonial Office in 1877 as part of the Home Service.

The only notable change that took place for nearly twenty years thereafter was the creation of a Colonial Audit Branch to relieve the Treasury. Then Joseph Chamberlain became Colonial Secretary, the first statesman of leading cabinet rank to take that office since Earl Grey half a century earlier and a much less rigid man than he, the first since Grey to hold it for more than a year or two. During his tenure from 1895 till 1903 he brought vigour and imagination to bear on everything connected with the Empire. Not only did he startle 'Downing Street' by importing up-to-date maps and the electric light, but he broke with the practice of allotting work of all kinds on a geographical basis to sub-departments. He formed instead a secretariat to deal with policy and administration as a whole and left only workaday matters to sub-departments. He concentrated all the financial and commercial business of the dependencies in the hands of the Crown Agents, bade these officers arrange for the engineering works that were so vital to the development of the dependencies, and appointed one of them, a kindly thought, to look after young colonials who came to chilly England with scholarships from their own governments. Then, encouraged by the combining of the examinations for the Ceylon, Hong Kong and Malayan Services with those for the Home and Indian Civil Services, he faced the formidable task of unifying the Colonial Services.

The territorial system of recruiting which prevailed in the overseas Empire was repugnant to a man who saw the Empire as a whole and was anxious to get the best officers wherever he could find them. Chamberlain could not touch the self-governing colonies which had long filled all posts locally except those of Governor or Governor-General, nor handle the Crown colonies as he could have wished since they too had always been staffed in large part by local men; but many of the higher posts in the older dependencies were at his disposal, and he hoped for a free hand in the new protectorates which could hardly be staffed locally yet, especially those in Africa. He used his powers of promotion to ensure that able men should not be stranded in Crown colony backwaters, but the chief obstacle to his wider schemes arose ironically enough from Africa. It would be manifestly unfair to transfer officers, and still more their families, from more favoured parts of the Empire to West Africa before medical science and communications had wrought great changes in the 'White Man's Grave'. Hence Chamberlain had to be content with forming an interchangeable medical staff for the West African dependencies and laying the modest foundations of a Promotions Branch at the Colonial Office. It fell to his immediate successors to systematise recruitment for the Colonial Services more fully and to provide short courses of training for officers who were going to tropical Africa, the promise of much bigger things to come.

African hardships also dictated a partial return to patronage with all its risks. The Colonial and Foreign Offices agreed that it was unreasonable to ask volunteers for a trying service in Northern Nigeria and the Sudan to face the rigours of an examination; hence they appointed men on their personalities and records in work and play, the very tests that Rhodes was then prescribing for his scholars from all parts of the British Empire, the United States and Germany. It was a policy which reflected the Englishman's deep-seated conviction that mere learning, and still less an examination, is not enough. Experience had shown them that, mercifully, brains and character usually went together, but their instincts and also the practice of their public schools from the days of Arnold of Rugby onwards taught them that, if the choice had to be made, character must come first. Most of the men selected for the new services abundantly justified the decision.

Meanwhile Chamberlain did all he could for the health of the tropical Empire on which so much beside the unification of the services depended. He threw all his weight into the founding of the now famous London and Liverpool Schools of Tropical Medicine, which were soon to be linked with the Colonial Office by bureaux and advisory committees on tropical diseases, medicine and sanitation. He gave official recognition to the Royal Botanic Gardens at Kew which had maintained an unobtrusive connection with his office for fifty years past, and formed the Department of Tropical Agriculture, forerunner of the Imperial College at Trinidad, in the course of his campaign to save the sugar islands. He was also responsible for the Acts which enabled Crown colonies to raise loans on easy terms for the improvement of their means of communication, and gave all colonies, self-governing or dependent, a similar advantage by allowing them to register their loans as gilt-edged trustee stock. Finally he set an admirable example by going to see parts of the Empire for himself, travelling to South Africa by way of Egypt and Zanzibar shortly after the close of the South African War. He was, however, gone from Downing Street before committees were set up to map the tropical Empire and wage war on its abounding insect life, and near his end when the next important change was made within the Colonial Office by the creation of a Dominions Division, the nucleus of the future Dominions Office and the outward and visible sign of the constitutional advance made by the great colonies of settlement during the past generation.

During the forty years of the Armed Peace the British Government and people remained true to the tradition of the 'fifties, itself a revival of a tradition much older, that local liberties ought to be given wherever they would do less harm than good. Nevertheless there were parts of the Colonial Empire which caused them to hesitate, and others to give an adverse verdict.

The constitutional fortunes of the sugar colonies varied according to the pressure of bounty-fed Continental beet sugar on their main industry. The Bahamas, Bermuda and Barbados kept their seventeenth-century representative institutions, and keep them still, and in 1884 Barbados was separated from the Windwards and given a more liberal franchise. But the scattered Leewards fared badly. Antigua and Dominica passed under strict Crown colony rule in 1898 and, four years later, the number of unofficial nominees in the Montserrat legislature was cut down and the Virgin Islands were placed completely under the control of the Governor at Antigua. The Windward Islands, which had long had their own appeal court, marked time. After losing Barbados the group was placed under a Governor-General stationed at Grenada and presently furnished with a common audit system; but the federation, lacking a common legislature, law and tariff, remained much looser than that of the Leeward Islands. In 1898, moreover, it lost Tobago which became a mere ward of neighbouring Trinidad.

Other sugar colonies were more fortunate. Liberal reforms were effected in the Mauritius constitution and British Honduras was freed from Jamaican control in 1884, while in 1892, the Honduras legislature was enlarged and direct election was substituted for indirect in the old-fashioned 'courts' of British Guiana. Jamaica also struggled upwards and by 1895 had been given what was then a unique constitution. The elective members, fourteen in all, together with the unofficial nominees gained a strong majority in the Legislative Council; nine of the fourteen could henceforward veto financial measures, while the opposition of all of them on other matters could only be borne down by the Governor's certificate that the rejected measure was of paramount public importance. Then, in 1902, better days began to dawn for the West Indies. After years of fruitless negotiation, the British Government, inspired by Chamberlain, shut bounty-fed beet sugar out of the home market. The rapid expansion of the banana traffic to the United States and Britain helped Jamaica and some other islands still further. One straw which showed the set of the wind was the restoration in 1909 of the number of unofficial nominees to their old strength in Montserrat.

All things considered, constitutional advance was rapid in the African dependencies. Minorities of unofficial nominees were given seats in the newly-created legislative councils of Lagos-Southern Nigeria and the British East African Protectorate (Kenya) in 1906, and of the British Central African Protectorate, now renamed Nyasaland, in the following year; on the eve of the Kaiser's War liberal reforms were projected in Sierra Leone also. On the other hand, when the Two Nigerias were amalgamated in 1914, Lugard saw to it that the Lagos legislature should henceforward confine its activities to the little colony, and set up a mere Advisory Council to assist him in the administration of the vast protectorate. Echoing the sentiments of the East India Company's Charter Act and the Aborigines Committee's Report of the 'thirties, he declared that it might be 'accepted as a principle of British colonial policy that the interests of a large native population shall not be subjected to the will of a minority, whether of Europeans or of educated natives'.

Events south of the Zambesi, however, suggested that Lugard spoke with pardonable exaggeration or at the most with hopeful anticipation. As far back as 1898, when hopes of gold were running high, a legislative council had been set up in Southern Rhodesia with a minority elected on the Cape non-racial franchise but representing in fact the tiny European population. Ten years later the elective members had gained a majority over the Chartered Company's representatives, a majority which was increased in 1914 out of all proportion to the increase in the European electorate. Meanwhile, far out in the Indian Ocean, the Seychelles, which had long been drifting away from Mauritian control, were constituted a colony with a nominee legislature of their own in 1903; farther east, in 1911, representatives of Europeans, mixed-breed Burghers and 'educated' Cingalese were elected to the Ceylon legislature in a safe minority and on the communal rolls that were now customary in neighbouring India; farther east still, unofficial nominees were given seats in 1909 on the newly-constituted Malay Federal Council.

The act of faith which gave such liberal institutions to so small a European community as that of Southern Rhodesia had already been surpassed in two other parts of the Empire. Western Australia and Natal had possessed legislatures with a strong elective majority since 1870 and 1856 respectively. Although their resources were still slight both began to agitate for self-government in the later 'eighties. Apart from a few primitive Black Fellows in the out-back, the small population of Western Australia was entirely of British stock and there was then every prospect of a federation of all the Australian colonies. Since there seemed to be no particular reason why the boon should not be granted, Western Australia was given self-government in 1890, and was presently cheered by the discovery of gold at Calgoorlie and Coolgardie. The British Government hesitated much longer in the case of Natal, for its handful of Europeans were ringed round by Bantu tribesmen, Boer republicans and blue water, equalled in number by Indians within their colony, and outnumbered many times over by natives. However, in 1893, Natal's tea and sugar were prospering, the Durban railway was advancing towards the Transvaal gold mines, and here again there was good hope that the colony would soon be incorporated in a South African federation. So Natal, too, was given self-government.

While so many members of the Colonial Empire were thus rising in the constitutional scale, some of them even passing into the ranks of the self-governing colonies, the Indian Empire was moving slowly but massively in the same direction and, in its progress, influencing the rest of the British Empire more directly than hitherto. There had been few signs that this was to be so in 1877 when Disraeli gratified Indians, angered Liberals and old-fashioned Tories, and delighted his Sovereign Lady by conferring on her the title of Empress of India. The mutual relations of British and Indians had changed subtly for the worse during the twenty years that had elapsed since the Mutiny. Most British parliamentarians had lost interest in Indian affairs now that there was no longer the Company to be watched and a Secretary of State, advised by a council of retired and sometimes crusted Anglo-Indians, had taken the place of the semi-independent President of the Board of Control.

Debates on India became as ill-attended as colonial debates fifty years earlier; initiative passed more and more to the Government of India. The Governor-General and his Council, for their part, felt that their freedom of action was hampered by the new submarine cable that bound them to London and, sitting as they did for half the year in isolated and purely official Simla, found themselves less closely in touch with public opinion than their predecessors who had spent the whole year in crowded and overwhelmingly Indian Calcutta.

The segregation of the British in India proceeded apace. The mere increase in the numbers of official and unofficial British tended to make their community more self-sufficient, and the *memsahibs*, always more exclusive than the males, saw to it that it should be so. Better sanitation and medical care were making life in a hot climate more tolerable for white folk; improving means of communication put the Cape Colony or, after the opening of the Suez Canal in 1869, England itself within easy reach of those on leave. European children might still be sent home to school, but wives remained in India more frequently and made it difficult for their husbands to find out what Indians were really thinking. To make matters worse, the shock of the Mutiny had opened a gulf between British and Indian society, and the unforgettable memories of things done then on both sides had infected the scattered British with anxiety if not for themselves at all events for their women folk. As for the Civil Service, since the age of entry had been lowered in 1878 from twenty-two to nineteen, recruits were coming more directly than before from public schools that laid stress on duty rather than upon imagination, while the sheer burden of administration forbade even those officials who would from asking what their toil was all about and whither it was leading India. The titles of some of Rudyard Kipling's best known works, *Departmental Ditties*, *For Simla Reasons* and *The Day's Work*, embalm the atmosphere in which 'Service India' then worked. No praise can be too high for the industry, probity and self-abnegation of that Service; it was the perfect bureaucracy. But it was a bureaucracy and an increasingly aloof one at that, shouldering the 'white man's burden' and jealously guarding its fine administrative machine from profane hands, which, it was convinced, would soon ruin it 'all along of abby-nay, Kul, an' hazar-ho'.[1]

---

[1] Not now, to-morrow, wait a bit. (R. Kipling, *The Seven Seas*, p. 210.)

The hope expressed by British administrators in earlier days that Indians might one day be ruling India thus made little appeal to most of their successors. But it did appeal to the growing number of Indians who were no longer content with access merely to nominee seats in the somewhat ineffective legislative councils or the municipal councils in the larger towns. A politically-minded class was growing up, Hindu and Moslem. Thanks to Macaulay's reform, English had become the *lingua franca* of the educated folk in all parts of the country, and good roads and railways brought them closer together than ever before; streams of graduates were pouring out of the examining universities founded after the Mutiny, and those many graduates who could find no official posts took naturally to the law, school-teaching or journalism. In the hands of men divorced from responsibility some organs of the vernacular press became more remarkable for invective than constructive criticism.

The elective principle was introduced between 1873 and 1883, and, rightly, at the bottom, by the creation of municipal and rural councils from half to two-thirds elective. The rural councils were a failure, since the country folk, as in many British colonies, regarded them as mere engines for extorting additional taxes, but the municipal councils became a valuable school of self-government. Presently a grave racial crisis stimulated Indian political activities mightily. In keeping with the colour-blind imperial policy, Indian magistrates were empowered to try Europeans on criminal charges. Many Europeans, especially those of the widely dispersed unofficial classes in Bengal and Bihar, demanded the maintenance for themselves, and still more for their wives and daughters, of the old right of trial by men of their own race that was secured to their fellows by the capitulations in the Ottoman, Chinese and Japanese Empires. Indians resisted this claim stoutly and, though a compromise was presently effected, some of them formed an Indian National Congress to uphold Indian rights.

Congress was founded in 1885 at the suggestion of A. O. Hume, a retired British official, with the approval of the Viceroy, Lord Dufferin. It soon became the main focus of Indian political life. It consisted chiefly of university-bred Hindus with a few Moslems and Parsees, and demanded, as a beginning, elective Indian representation on the legislative councils and simultaneous Civil Service examinations in India and London. A measure of service reform was granted at once. The Superior Civil Service was divided into two branches: a provincial service recruited by each Province just as in so many British colonies, and an imperial service recruited as before by examination in London. Further important changes which partially met both demands of Congress were made in 1892. Indians were given a better chance of competing for the I.C.S. when the age of entry was raised from nineteen to its old level of twenty-two, but they were still called upon to attend an English University, in practice either Oxford or Cambridge, which could give them so much that was essential to public servants beyond the mere book-learning that their own universities fostered. At the same time the legislative councils at the centre and in the provinces were enlarged, and the latter were at last permitted to discuss the budget though still not to vote upon it. Official majorities were retained in all of them, but most of the unofficial members were to be nominated, subject to governmental approval, by religious bodies, the universities, municipal and rural boards, and chambers of commerce, while the rest were to be nominated by the governments concerned to speak for unorganised classes. Nomination which was virtually election strengthened the elective principle, and the communal representation thus introduced was to have a profound influence on all subsequent reforms in a land of numberless castes and creeds.

No further constitutional advance was made for many years to come, though legislatures of the new kind were set up in the Punjab and Burma in 1898. Meanwhile the spirit of nationalism which was at work in so many other parts of the Empire manifested itself in India in a movement for *swaraj*. This Home Rule movement began quietly enough, and received legitimate encouragement from the resolution of the Colonial Conference of 1897 that there should be nothing in the projected Australian and South African immigration laws that might offend Indians, whose interests the British Government was defending against the single-handed action of the republican Transvaal and whose warriors had played such a stirring part in the recent Diamond Jubilee celebrations. A revolutionary party soon took shape, however, and threatened to split Congress, much as the quarrels of the Mensheviks and the Bolshevik majority were splitting the International. This party drew its strength from that middle class which has furnished the world with most of its revolutionists. Many of these ardent young nationalists were university men filled with English ideas *On Liberty*, the *Liberty of Unlicensed Printing* and (who knows) *Killing no Murder*, heady doctrines when taken neat in the glare of the Indian sun, and disappointed like the latter-day Fascist or Nazi rank and file of the recognition they held was their due. All of them, moreover, being nationalists, had constructed a legend of an Indian golden age that had passed with the coming of the alien forces they wished to be rid of. They took to violence as early as 1897; but matters did not become serious until about 1905 when the Viceroy, Lord Curzon, partitioned the unwieldy province of Bengal and proposed to reform the universities.

There were sound administrative reasons for incorporating the two halves of Bengal in the racially and socially similar provinces which bordered them; but the abrupt change ignored Bengal's ancient and distinctive traditions, and came at an ill time when Indian national feeling had been stimulated by Japan's abolition in 1899 of foreign extra-territorial privileges and her resounding victory over Russia in 1904–5. Similarly Curzon's campaign against the syllabus and the crammer was in line with salutary reforms in other parts of the Empire: first, the formation of federal universities, with the emphasis on teaching and research, in Lancashire, Yorkshire, Wales, and presently in London itself; then, from 1899 onwards, the creation of self-contained universities in English provincial cities headed by Chamberlain's Birmingham, and now the determined but unsuccessful effort of Capetown to break away from the examining University of the Cape of Good Hope. All this was a recognition of the fact that however successfully examining universities might have met the sudden demand of the mid-nineteenth-century public services of the Empire for graduates, their usefulness was passing and their weakness made manifest. But that was no comfort to Hindu students who saw themselves, in a period of depression, in danger of losing the advantage which their agile minds and highly-trained memories gave them in the examination room over the more matter-of-fact Moslems. To the horror of Parsees, Moslems and Hindu moderates who protested their loyalty to the King-Emperor, some of them perpetrated political murders, and the older men who egged them on were not placated when Congress adopted *swaraj* as its objective. Restrictions on the inflammatory press falling short of formal censorship gradually checked, though by no means ended, the campaign of violence;

meanwhile Gokhale's Moderates, who interpreted *swaraj* to mean the fullest colonial self-government, had gained the upper hand in Congress, and in 1908 leading Moslems, whose people cherished proud and recent memories of rule in India, formed a Moslem League.

This formation of rival parties was hastened by the knowledge that the Liberal Secretary of State, Lord Morley, and the Viceroy, Lord Minto, were inclined towards constitutional reform. These two statesmen went some way towards meeting the demands of the Moderates in 1909. In terms of the Morley-Minto Reforms one seat on the Governor-General's Executive Council was reserved for an Indian for the first time, and two on the Secretary of State's Council in London. The central and provincial legislative councils were enlarged and, though the official majority was maintained at the centre, nominated and elective unofficial members together were given a majority, as in Jamaica, in all the provincial legislatures except that of Bengal. There, the elective members were given a majority outright. All these legislatures were empowered to vote upon any matter of public importance including the budget, and in all of them 'weightage' was given to the Moslem minority.

The Morley-Minto Reforms were rounded off in 1911 by the visit to India of the King-Emperor George V, the foundation of New Delhi and the reunion of the severed halves of Bengal; but those who expected that these things would satisfy India's political aspirations were soon disillusioned. Protest they never so loudly that they had no intention of transplanting British parliamentary institutions to Indian soil, that is precisely what Lords Morley and Minto had done, not so much by strengthening the elective principle or granting liberty of debate as by giving the legislature of restive Bengal that elective majority which had been the prelude to self-governing institutions in more than one colony of settlement. British imperial experience had taught again and again that there could be no standing still for long under such conditions. India must either go forward as the Australian colonies and Natal had gone forward, or, like so many of the West Indian dependencies, go back.

Indian nationalists, moderates and revolutionaries, Hindus and Moslems alike, were resolved to go forward till they had achieved the recognition as equals which the people of the West had accorded to the Japanese. From 1907 onwards, therefore, they lent what aid they could to Gandhi in his campaign against the anti-Indian legislation of Natal and the self-governing Transvaal, and presently of the new Union of South Africa, and rejoiced in his partial success. Encouraged by the sympathetic Minto they also demanded an end to the recruiting of Indians for indentured labour, for, apart from other considerations, it galled nationalist pride that so many of the representatives of India's ancient cultures overseas should be untouchable labourers or humble storekeepers and small-holders. The Indian Government had always declined to encourage recruiting; but the system had attained large dimensions in British, French and Dutch tropical dependencies in the middle 'seventies, and had since been extended to Fiji and the outlying Indian Provinces of Assam and Burma. Some 2,000,000 Indians were now living overseas, the great majority within the Empire and a high proportion of them colonial born; they formed from one to two-thirds of the respective populations of Trinidad, British Guiana and Fiji, fully equalled in number the Europeans of Natal and, thanks to free but controlled emigration, were numerous in East Africa, Ceylon and Malaya. Their ranks were destined to be reinforced by further immigration, for though Gokhale's Moderates succeeded in limiting the scope of the coolie system, recruiting continued on a dwindling scale till just after the close of the Kaiser's War.

Meanwhile the Secretary of State and Government of India, reviewing with anxiety the position of Indians in certain self-governing portions of the Empire, had begged the Dominion representatives at the Imperial Conference of 1911 to remember that 'each Dominion owes responsibility to the rest of the Empire for ensuring that its domestic policy shall not unnecessarily create embarrassment in the administration of India'. That appeal was a sign of the times, a warning that the changeless East was changing fast: Japan a first-class Power in renewed alliance with Great Britain, China newly a republic, India politically awakened, and the Ottoman Empire in the hands of the reforming Young Turks. Asia was on the move, presenting new and grave problems to an empire more than three-quarters of whose inhabitants were Asiatics.

I

VII

INTEGRATION AND DOMINION STATUS
1874–1914

GOKHALE's demand for constitutional liberties equal to those of the autonomous colonies was a high one, for such colonies were advancing rapidly in power and international status. 'Daughter am I in my mother's house, but mistress in my own' . . ., and, as witness to that fact, the exercise of the Royal veto by the Governor-General had long been one of those many things in British public life which can be done but are simply not done; disallowance of a completed bill by the British authorities was falling into desuetude, while the reservation of bills for the Royal pleasure contained few terrors now for even the most radical of overseas legislators except in such obviously all-embracing spheres as those of copyright, cable communications and merchant shipping.

The federal Dominion of Canada had set the pace. In 1880 Canada took over from the British Government all British possessions in North America, other than Newfoundland, for the most part within the barren Arctic Circle. Sir John Macdonald's protective National policy of 1879, the outcome of the 'Canada first' campaign of the preceding decade, and Canada's reply to the challenge of the high McKinley tariff set up by the United States in 1890 promised to raise at least Ontario and Quebec out of the ranks of mere primary producers. The completion of the transcontinental Canadian-Pacific railway in 1885 had given the Dominion the spinal cord that it had hitherto lacked, and henceforward Canada's domestic history became the story of the filling in of her gigantic framework. District after district was organised as new and hardy varieties of wheat broadened the belt of cultivation northwards and gold gave a value to the distant Alaskan borderlands. Gold-bearing Yukon became a Territory on United States lines in 1898 under a Commissioner and a small elected legislature, while in 1905, the year in which the last imperial troops left Canadian soil, the Prairie Provinces of Saskatchewan and Alberta became full members of the federation. So fast did immigrants pour in from the United Kingdom and, latterly, all Europe west of the Urals that the 7,750,000 Canadians of 1914 fully expected to see themselves 30,000,000 within the next quarter of a century. In this access of confidence and amid a maze of political wire-pulling they committed themselves to two more transcontinental railways: the Grand Trunk Pacific, greedy of public subventions, and the costly National Transcontinental built at the public charges.

Meanwhile the Australasian and South African colonies of settlement followed Canada along the road to closer union, cautiously and with many halts by the way. Talk of closer union at periodical Conferences of the Australian governments long turned on the apparently insoluble problem of the tariff with an occasional glance at defence. In 1868, however, the year after the British North America Act had come into force, Henry Parkes stepped forward as the champion of federation. Parkes, an immigrant of 1839 who had become Prime Minister of New South Wales, the senior colony, added the argument of better ocean communications to those of defence and the tariff; but he made little headway during the 'seventies while self-government was finding its feet, Australian nationalism coming into being, and the welcome annexation of Fiji suggesting that the Mother Country intended after all to keep foreigners at a safe distance. In 1880 Parkes tried again, advocating a Federal Court of Appeal and a Federal Council with limited legislative and executive powers. In spite of the German annexation of part of neighbouring New Guinea, all that came of these proposals was the creation by the Imperial Government in 1885 of a Federal Council, a mere legislature lacking executive powers and revenues to which all the Australasian colonies, including Fiji, might send representatives to deal with a few matters of common concern. And for this ineffective machinery Australians had to thank Samuel Griffith, Premier of Queensland and Parkes's dearest enemy.

Henceforward this Federal Council, lineal descendant of the old Conference, met every other year; but it was weakened by the abstention of Parkes's New South Wales and New Zealand and the spasmodic attendance of South Australia throughout. Indeed, during the 'eighties Australians were interested far more in an imperial federation, whose advantages were obvious to separate colonies each facing outwards to the ocean, than in an Australian federation for which they felt no impelling need. Several of the colonies offered aid to the British Government during the Balkan crisis of 1877–78 and the Transvaal war of 1880–81, and all took part in the first Colonial Conference in 1887. It was the failure of that conference to face the federal issue which revived Australian interest in the problem of defence, while the United States embargo of 1882 on Chinese immigration inspired the growing Labour party to demand the exclusion of the Chinese and semi-servile Kanaka labourers. Parkes therefore took the field once more in 1889. This time he reinforced his tariff, defence, and communications arguments with the cry of 'Australia for the Australians', an Australia which, sharing the dreams of Rhodes in Africa and nationalist enthusiasts in Canada, he envisaged as one of 'colossal proportions'. His hopes ran high, for Western Australia achieved self-government and all the Australian colonies and New Zealand agreed to attend a federal convention in 1891. Inspired by study of the Swiss confederation and James Bryce's newly-published *American Constitution*, the Convention adopted a federal scheme; but the small colonies were afraid of the large, the tariff controversy and a general election delayed the decisive action by New South Wales for which all the rest waited, and the return after that election of the Labour Party, with its suspicions of imperialist and militarist designs, drove Parkes from public life.

Federation seemed to be dead; but, as in British North America and presently in South Africa also, hard times shepherded the Australians towards closer union. Labour demands for social benefits at the public expense, coinciding with the breaking of a land boom and the collapse of Australian credit on the London market, forced the politicians to take stock of the general situation, and public opinion, stirred by the enthusiastic Edmund Barton of New South Wales, soon ran ahead of them. Fired by the discovery of gold in Western Australia in 1892, a conference of Federation Leagues and similar associations resolved that the colonial parliaments be invited to pass enabling Acts authorising their elected delegates in convention to frame a constitution which should then be submitted to a referendum in each colony. A Premier's conference at last accepted this procedure with two important modifications; first, that the representatives be chosen directly by the electors; and, secondly, that the Federal Convention must refer the draft bill to the several parliaments and meet again to consider their comments before submitting the final draft to the electorates.

Delay followed delay and it was only in March 1897 that delegates from five of the seven colonies began to draft the constitution. Distant New Zealand held aloof, and Queensland, whose planters desired Kanaka labour, was strongly separatist; but before three years were out the constitution had been adopted by referendum in all the mainland colonies except isolated Western Australia. Early in 1900 an Australian delegation went to London. There they received an enthusiastic welcome, since imperialist feeling was running high and Australians were serving with the international force against the Chinese Boxers and against the Boers in South Africa. New Zealand declined finally to join; but Western Australia was brought in at the last moment by the persuasiveness of Chamberlain and the votes of the floating population on its gold mines, much of it from the federalist eastern colonies. So, in 1900, the British Parliament was enabled to pass the Australian Commonwealth Act.

The Australian federation was looser than the Canadian, for not only were the State Governors to be appointed by the Crown and not by the Governor-General, but the division of governmental powers followed the United States precedent by reserving to the States all powers that were not specifically handed over or listed for subsequent transfer to the federal authorities. United States influence showed itself again in the naming of the House of Representatives, the wide powers conferred upon the Senate which represented the States, and the elaborate procedure for the alteration of the constitution which called for the participation of the federal and state legislatures and the electors. Other notable provisions reflected local difficulties or advances in constitutional practice made during the thirty years that had elapsed since the federation of British North America. A compromise capital was founded at Canberra to resolve the ineluctable rivalry of Sydney and Melbourne. Ministers were bound by law, and not by the custom which sufficed at Westminster and Ottawa, to find seats in one or other of the federal Houses. Special provision was made for the automatic redistribution of seats in the Lower House, a salutary innovation within the Empire, and for solving deadlocks between the Houses. Very wide discretion was entrusted to the Commonwealth Parliament and High Court to check the flow of appeals to the Judicial Committee of the Privy Council, and yet another of Durham's 'imperial reservations' went by the board now that a Governor-General in a Dominion legislature was given virtually untrammelled power to amend the constitution, except for the first eight clauses of the Act which embodied the federal bargain.

The Commonwealth of Australia came into being on New Year's Day 1901. Forthwith its Prime Minister, Sir Edmund Barton, carried an immigration restriction law aimed primarily at Asiatics and Kanakas, for he agreed with the half-forgotten and much maligned 'Over-Secretary' James Stephen, who had taught long ago that 'there is not on the globe a social interest more momentous . . . than that of reserving the Continent of New Holland as a place where the English race shall spread from sea to sea unmixed'.[1]

The South African federal problem was much more difficult than the Canadian or Australian, for it had to be worked out by the imperial authorities, British colonies and Boer republics in a predominantly native area that was presently caught up in the European scramble for Africa. The first overt suggestion of federation, for it was little more, was made by Governor George Grey of the Cape Colony in 1859. Grey aimed primarily at safeguarding the scattered white communities in face of the tribes, and indeed fear of a general native war remained one of the main arguments for closer union until the growing numbers and superior weapons of the Europeans dispelled it in the middle 'eighties. Grey's scheme was rejected by the Colonial Office, but deepening confusion showed that he had been right. In 1871–72, therefore, Lord Kimberley tried in vain to induce the Cape Colony to give a lead so that the British garrison might be withdrawn, except from Crown colony Natal and the fortress of the Cape Peninsula, and territorial disputes between the British and republican governments be settled locally. Lord Carnarvon returned to the charge in 1875 for these reasons, and also in the hope of seeing a liberal Native policy extended throughout South Africa. As his campaign developed he realised that federation would ward off foreign intervention from a land in which Great Britain had long been the paramount power, and avert the railway war between the coastal colonies and the Transvaal that was already looming on the horizon. All these arguments were destined to hold good to the end; but once more the Cape Ministry declined to move and the hasty annexation of the Transvaal in 1877 did much harm. Even before the successful rising of the Transvaalers in 1880, the imperial federation policy had foundered amid a turmoil of

---

[1] James Stephen was Permanent Under-Secretary at the War and Colonial Office, 1826–47.

native wars, and Kimberley, in office once more, had laid it down that South African federation must come, if at all, from within. This attempt to federate from within was made by Rhodes ten years later. Meanwhile opposition to the Carnarvon policy had led many Cape Afrikanders to form the anti-British Afrikander Bond; the failure of that policy stimulated the self-reliant 'colonial' sentiments of many British South Africans, among them Rhodes himself. During the 'eighties however, while Rhodes was building up a virtual monopoly of South African diamonds centring upon Kimberley, Jan Hofmeyr weaned the Bond from its extreme opinions, but made it the dominating political party in the Cape Colony resolved to uphold colonial liberties and the Afrikander way of life. Hence, when Rhodes became Prime Minister in 1890 he was dependent upon Hofmeyr in Parliament for the furtherance of his policy. That policy aimed at the development of Southern Rhodesia as the reversion of the Cape Colony in the vast area to the northward of the Transvaal for which his British South Africa Company had just received a charter, the absorption by the Cape and Rhodesia of their respective shares of intervening Bechuanaland, and the formation of a customs and railway union south of the Zambesi. Economics and geography fought against Rhodes. The Cape and its republican extension, the Orange Free State, had indeed formed a customs union in 1889 which was presently joined by imperial Basutoland, British Bechuanaland and the Bechuanaland Protectorate; but President Kruger's Transvaal bluntly refused to join any such union, as did also Natal whose economic hinterland lay in the republics. Their aloofness had been accentuated by the discovery of the Witwatersrand gold mines on either side of Johannesburg in the southern Transvaal in 1886, discoveries which precipitated the dreaded railway war between the Cape line, the Natal line and the line that the Netherlands Railway Company was building between the mines and Portuguese Delagoa Bay. The railway which Rhodes was already laying northwards from Kimberley to Rhodesia could do little to solve his problem since it was shut out of the Transvaal.

Towards the close of 1895 Kruger attempted to force traffic away from the Cape ports to Delagoa Bay. This defiance of the London Convention of 1884, under which his republic enjoyed its independence, almost led to joint imperial and Cape intervention; but Kruger gave way in time. Meanwhile many of the cosmopolitan

Uitlanders who had flocked to the Rand, especially those of British or colonial origin, had become so restive under inefficient administration and the repeated withholding of the franchise that an armed rising was generally expected. Successive British ministers resolved to intervene in that event to ensure the peace of South Africa and the security of life and property in the mining area. Chamberlain now proposed to use the Chartered Company's police as the spearhead of intervention, while Rhodes on his own account arranged secretly with a few leading Johannesburg Reformers that there should be a rising. When these Reformers drew back, Dr. Jameson, administrator of Southern Rhodesia, invaded the Transvaal without leave to force on a rising and therefore the imperial intervention that should overturn the Kruger régime, the chief obstacle to federation.

The disastrous Jameson Raid embarrassed the British Government, ruined Rhodes's alliance with Hofmeyr, inflamed Afrikander sentiment and restored Kruger's waning prestige. Natal indeed joined the Cape-Free State customs union in 1898; but Rhodesia grew far too slowly to affect the political balance, and Rhodes's efforts to secure fairer representation in the Cape Parliament for the British towns as against the rural Bond met with only partial success. On the other hand, power steadily followed wealth northwards to the Transvaal as the republicans armed themselves and their foreign-owned railway drew away traffic and revenue from the coastal colonies and the Free State. Sir Alfred Milner, Governor of the Cape and High Commissioner, then tried to restore Great Britain's traditional paramountcy and thus avert the foreign intervention which the Transvaal seemed anxious to invite. In the end he joined battle with Kruger over the Uitlander franchise, and so moved on to a war that was to decide whether Great Britain or the Transvaal, with its reluctant Free State ally, was to be the dominant power in Southern Africa.

Towards the close of the long South African war Milner decided to press for federation. Now that the republics had been annexed all Southern Africa was under official control except the self-governing Cape Colony and Natal. Natal must do what the Transvaal did, and, if the Cape constitution could be suspended as Quebec's had been long ago, Milner believed he could secure the safe British majority south of the Zambesi, which, like Lord Durham before him, he held would alone make federation tolerable. He had long been considering the step, for the constitution had been broken by war and rebellion, and now Rhodes's followers were demanding suspension to ensure a thorough redistribution of seats. On Rhodes's death early in 1902 Milner took the lead openly; but though he gained much local support, Chamberlain and the premiers of Canada and Australia, as good parliamentarians, were as firmly opposed to the withdrawal of colonial liberties as Lord Mansfield had ever been. The suspension policy was rejected by the Colonial Conference of 1902, and, with it, Milner's proposal to federate South Africa from above.

Henceforward Lord Milner devoted himself to the development of the two ex-republics, financing the work with imperial loans and the vigorous exploitation of the gold mines even at the price of importing indentured Chinese labourers. Before his return home in 1905 he had built up much of the material framework on which the future Union of South Africa was to rest. He had also combined all the British territories south of the Zambesi in a customs union and more or less composed their railway quarrels. This artificial economic federation began to go to pieces as soon as the Transvaal became self-governing early in 1907. The Transvaal, under a mainly Afrikander ministry headed by Generals Botha and Smuts, and Natal began to strain against the customs and railway arrangements; the Transvaal became involved in trouble with its Indians, and Natal also had to face a Zulu rebellion which pointed to the need for a general South African native policy. Lord Selborne, the High Commissioner, and some of his advisers, who had been deeply impressed by Oliver's recently published *Life* of Alexander Hamilton, one of the chief makers of the United States constitution, issued a memorandum stressing the need for closer union.

This memorandum won Smuts's support. As soon, therefore, as the Orange River Colony (Free State) had passed under a strongly Afrikander ministry and the Cape Colony under another consisting of Afrikanders and colonial-minded British, Smuts pressed for instant action. The upshot was that a National Convention, representing the four colonial parliaments with assessors from Southern Rhodesia, met in October 1908. It drafted the South Africa Act, which, following the Australian precedent, was debated in the colonial legislatures before being put into final shape. Southern Rhodesia, like Newfoundland and New Zealand, decided to stand aside, but the draft Act was adopted by three of the parliaments and by a referendum, Australian fashion, in Natal. It was passed without amendment at Westminster in 1909, a notable year in the history of the governance of the Empire which saw also the Morley-Minto Reforms in India, the Federal Council in Malaya and the rejection of the budget by the House of Lords.

The South Africans, repelled by the bickering of rival authorities which afflicted federal Canada and Australia, formed a legislative union in which all power was concentrated in Parliament as fully as in the United Kingdom or New Zealand. The Senate representing the four Provinces was to be mainly elective by a process of indirect election, but eight of its forty members were to be nominees of the Governor-General, four of them for their special knowledge of the non-Europeans who were excluded from Parliament. The House of Assembly (the old Cape name) was elected on the existing colonial franchises; that is, the adult European male suffrage of the ex-republics, the virtually white suffrage of Natal with its property qualifications, and the non-racial franchise with its financial and educational qualifications of the Cape Colony. The Cape non-European franchise and the equal rights of English and Dutch as official languages were entrenched, and machinery for the automatic redistribution of seats in the Assembly was provided on an even more elaborate scale than in Australia. The various courts became branches of one Supreme Court, whose Appellate Division had powers surpassing even those of its Australian counterpart to deal with cases which had hitherto been remitted to the Judicial Committee. Each of the four colonies became a Province under a nominated Administrator and an elective Council exercising the powers delegated to them by Parliament. Outdoing the United States, Canada and Australia with their compromise capitals, the Union created three capitals: Capetown, the seat of Parliament; Pretoria, of the Executive; and Bloemfontein, chief town of what was again the Orange Free State, of the Appellate Division. A long chapter was closed by the unification of the railway and harbour administrations and their segregation as far as possible from the general finance and politics of the Union. Finally, provision was made for the future incorporation of Southern Rhodesia, and for the transfer to the Union of the governance of Basutoland, Bechuanaland and Swaziland on terms laid down in the schedule to the South Africa Act; but for the time being all these territories remained under the control of the Governor-General in his capacity as High Commissioner.

On 31st May, 1910, just after the last of the Chinese labourers had left the Transvaal mines, Botha became first Prime Minister of the Union of South Africa supported by an ill-compacted majority of Afrikanders and their British allies. The legislation of the next few years reflected at once the desires of the dominant parties and some of the troubles that awaited the new Union. Under Free State and Cape pressure bilingualism was pushed far further in the schools and the public services than the British, and many of the Afrikanders also, thought wise or tolerable; the customary colour bar against the skilled employment of non-Europeans in the ex-republics was stiffened; steps were taken to ensure a supply of native labour to the farms and prevent the Bantu majority, elsewhere than in the Cape Province, from acquiring land outside certain areas specified or to be specified; an immigration law on 'White Australia' lines was directed against Asiatics, and a much needed Defence Act hastened the withdrawal of the dwindling British garrison.

The generation that saw federal Canada going from strength to strength and the Australian and South African colonies moving towards closer union naturally envisaged also a federation of the British Empire. Milner, confessedly 'an Imperialist more than an Englishman' who desired British domination so little that he was prepared to see the capital transferred to Ottawa or anywhere else if thereby the Empire could be held together, had worked in South Africa always with this ultimate federation in view. To him, the complete administrator, an Imperial Council would have the additional advantage of taking 'things that matter out of the hands of that mob at Westminster'; but many others, who took a more kindly view than he of the Mother of Parliaments, shared his hopes that they might one day give 'the great British race throughout the world the one thing it still needs, political organisation'.

Imperial federation was an idea in keeping with the imperialist spirit of the times. Throughout the Western world men had interpreted Darwin's theory of evolution to mean that a struggle for existence was the rule of life for nations as for species, and, overawed as they were by the weight of German learning, had more than half convinced themselves that recent German victories proved that those Prussian historians were right who believed that the expansion of the 'socially efficient' nations was inevitable. This imperialist spirit manifested itself in widely differing forms, for though most men born of western civilisation were sure, as many now are not, that their civilisation was higher than any other, each naturally believed that his national variant of it was best of all. Frenchmen saw in their growing overseas empire an extension of France, in their eyes the only truly civilised land on earth. Italian imperialists were equally nationalist as a rule, though some of them were content merely to claim for their country something of the political primacy that had once been Rome's just as the ecclesiastical primacy was Rome's still. American expansionists were convinced that it was 'the manifest destiny of God's own country', already of imperial proportions, 'to run the earth' sooner or later; mystical Pan-Slav Russians saw Holy Russia cast for the leading rôle, and Germans, more laboriously schematic and romantic than the rest, saw in themselves the pick of the innately superior Teutonic race that was destined for first place under the leadership of the All Highest and *der alte gute Gott*. Britons and Americans of enthusiastic temper were ready to admit this Teutonic relationship, and at the close of the nineteenth century Chamberlain and Rhodes could look forward to a *pax Teutonica* imposed upon a naughty world by the United States, Germany and the British Empire, while Rhodes again could seek to draw these three political systems closer together by allocating his Oxford scholarships to their young men. But these Americans and British regarded themselves first and foremost as Anglo-Saxons. They agreed with Dilke that their race ought to be, and many of them with Chamberlain that it was, 'infallibly destined to be the predominant force', however much they might differ as to which branch was to have the final hegemony.

The British, with their small respect for theory and strong sense of humour, never systematised their imperialism nor carried it to such extremes on insecure premises as did some of their neighbours. The idea took hold mainly of London and the comfortable southern half of England; but even in those parts, and still more in the north and west, there were old-fashioned Tories who hated the Empire, Liberals who feared it, Radicals who affected to despise it, and Labour men who tried to ignore it. Nevertheless imperialism was a very real force among the dominant Conservatives, their Liberal Unionist allies and the imperialist wing of the shattered Liberal party.

Enthusiasm for this strange empire growing daily 'mightier yet' was not confined to any one social class. It was strongest perhaps among well-to-do folk whose sons and investments were finding openings in the Empire, and was reinforced by the numerous retired officials and business men who came back from the new tropical dependencies, as always from India, to play their part in local and national politics. But it provided a romantic outlet for the imagination of thousands of folk of all kinds, especially those who lived humdrum lives in the metropolis and larger cities. During the middle 'eighties, more than twenty years before Oxford had founded the first English Chair in colonial history, the Empire had been discovered to them by Seeley in his *Expansion of England* and Froude, literary executor and spiritual successor of Carlyle, in his *Oceana*. As imperial sentiment rose to its climax in the Diamond Jubilee of 1897 the new cheap London press stunted it and versifiers wrote incredible patriotic songs, often with rattling good tunes, for a people that had not known serious war since the Indian Mutiny forty years back. Nor were the poets behindhand. The laureate, Lord Tennyson, greeted royal and imperial occasions with odes on the theme of 'Fifty years of ever-widening Empire' and 'Britons, hold your own'; Stevenson and Henley sang from their sick-beds of the strenuous adventure that went with empire-building; Swinburne at the last outdid most of his contemporaries in praise of 'vigour everywhere, and rigour', while, from 1892 onwards, Kipling hymned the spacious glories of the outer world in contrast to the cramped squalor of 'awful old England'.

The motives behind British imperialism ranged from downright jingoism, a delight in mere size and painting the map red, to the purest humanitarianism. There was, of course, the economic incentive. The habit of investing overseas was more widespread than ever, and thousands of investors, great and small, desired to see the lands in which their money was sunk brought under the Union Jack, which Rhodes assured them was the 'best commercial asset in the world'. Manufacturers might hope for protection at home or favoured markets abroad, and workmen also, so that Randolph Churchill, prophet of Tory democracy, could boast that 'Little Englandism' and free trade were dead among the British working classes. Closely connected with the idea of gain was that of the duty of making the most of what Chamberlain called the 'un-developed imperial estate', an idea with which imperialists of the newly-founded socialist Fabian Society and even some avowed anti-imperialists could find no quarrel, provided this were done by a government intent on serving the civilisation of the world and elevating the backward peoples.

The extension of the *pax Britannica* appealed to many. They might not all agree with Chamberlain that the Empire had a right to impose its *pax* and civilisation on other folk, or altogether approve when Lord Cromer, teaching Milner the arts of autocratic imperialism at its best in Egypt, echoed the great von Moltke and prescribed for the people 'what is good for them, but not what they think is good for them'. Not everyone could honestly share Kipling's Old Testament view of themselves as a Chosen People divinely commissioned to teach their Law to lesser breeds; but all could rejoice with Kipling whenever, as at skull-strewn Kumassi,

> We broke a King and we built a road—
> A court-house stands where the reg'ment goed.
> And the river's clean where the raw blood flowed . . .

Here imperialism moved up to its higher levels. It has been a fashion latterly, especially among those who have never borne it, to sneer at the 'white man's burden' and allege that it was taken up for the sake of the loot it contained. That is not how it appeared to hundreds of young men and women who went out to spend the best years of their lives working for others in uncongenial and often deadly surroundings for the sake of a public ideal that was greater than themselves. They, and the churches, missionary societies, schools and universities behind them, answered to the call of the humanitarianism that had lived on since slave emancipation days, the realisation that there were less fortunate folk overseas who needed help, the hope that the world might be left a little better for all this imperial endeavour. Nor, since imperialism was a spirit that worked mightily in the British Empire, was the idea of liberty lacking. British and colonial publics alike regarded the South African war as a campaign to win, in Rhodes's famous phrase, 'equal rights for every civilised man south of the Zambesi', and heard once more with Kipling 'the trumpets round the scaffold at Whitehall'. The beliefs shared by Huskisson and Ruskin were not dead; the Empire must have a moral basis, for only so could its extension or maintenance be justified. Chamberlain taught that the Empire stood for peace and prosperity; Lord Rosebery prayed that it might be 'the greatest secular agency for good the world has ever seen', and Kipling in his *Recessional* bade the British recall, amid the exaltation of the Diamond Jubilee festivities, to Whom they owed their power and responsibilities.

If Chamberlain was right and 'the day of small kingdoms with their petty jealousies' was indeed past, it followed that the United Kingdom, which was small enough compared with the compact mass of Germany or the vast bulk of Russia or the United States, must federate the unrivalled Empire of which it was the centre. Thus would there come into being a state more extensive, more varied and potentially more self-contained than any the world had ever seen, a state so powerful that, as Rosebery prophesied, 'without its consent no shot will be fired in anger throughout the habitable globe'. The idea of imperial federation, which had stirred during the 'seventies, came to full life in the middle 'eighties under stress of bad times, fear of foreign pressure in Africa, Asia and the South Seas, and the realisation that the Navy through little fault of its own was not all that it should be. The idea found expression in the incorporation of the Colonial Society as the Royal Colonial Institute for the diffusion of knowledge of the Empire and the preservation of its 'permanent union', the foundation of the Imperial Institute to serve at once as a memorial to the Prince Consort and a centre for research into the Empire's commercial and industrial resources, and, in the sphere of politics, the formation in 1884 of the Imperial Federation League.

The Imperial Federation League received the support of members of all parties at home and in the colonies. It discussed many schemes that fell far short of federation, such as the inclusion of colonial representatives in the British Cabinet or in a revived Privy Council Committee for Trade and Plantations, or, an idea old as the days of Cromwell, in the Westminster Parliament. In the event only one of these suggestions bore fruit: the appointment from 1897 onwards of eminent colonial and Indian judges to the Judicial Committee of the Privy Council, the highest court of appeal for the overseas Empire. But the League also canvassed the formation of a true federal government for the United Kingdom and other autonomous parts of the Empire, which should control at least foreign policy, the armed forces, and perhaps also trade, currency, posts and telegraphs, and enjoy the powers of taxation necessary for the financing of its federal activities. Nothing precise came of it all, though the principle of devolution implicit in Gladstone's Irish Home Rule

Bills of 1886 and 1893 encouraged the advocates of formal federation. The League was divided on the desirability, let alone the possibility, of parcelling out to central and local authorities the legislative powers which the British majority of its members were accustomed to think of as the prerogative of one sovereign parliament. Hence, in 1893, the League broke up. But it had done its work. It had taught men to think of the British Empire, not as the last of a moribund class of political organisations, but as the first of a new class that was seeking definite constitutional form, an Empire that ought to be and could be somehow drawn into closer unity in diversity. It had, moreover, indicated how that end might be achieved by suggesting the summoning of a Colonial Conference on the occasion of Queen Victoria's Jubilee.

The first Conference of 1887, and the Colonial and Imperial Conferences which followed it at irregular intervals, showed more clearly than even the debates of the League the obstacles that stood in the way of imperial federation. The self-governing colonies were far away from the Mother Country and one another; all shared indeed common traditions, but each had many more peculiar to itself; they knew that, whatever 'colossal proportions' they might hope to attain to, their present wealth and numbers would only entitle them to small representation beside the British in an imperial legislature; they were too often competitors with each other to be easy partners in any fiscal or commercial combine, and those of them who were fostering secondary industries feared nothing so much as the competition of the highly developed industries of the United Kingdom. In short, they cherished their present liberties, desired more, and so long as Britannia ruled the waves saw no reason why they should part with any that they had.

The Jubilee Colonial Conference was an assemblage of notabilities from every part of the Empire who showed in their debates that the sense of common interest was far too weak to overcome particularist preoccupations. The British Government had ruled out the federal issue in advance. Hence the discussions turned mainly on defence, which concerned that heavily burdened Government most nearly, and to a less extent on the imperial preferences that were the hope of many colonials. No return to the preferential system was possible, however, in view of the faith in free trade which most of the rest shared with the British authorities, and the brute fact that the United Kingdom could favour colonial trade only at the price of penalising her own vastly greater trade with foreigners. Nothing more than polite interest greeted a proposal by the Cape Afrikander leader, Jan Hofmeyr, that the defence and preference problems should be solved together by imposing a small customs surcharge on foreign imports into the Empire, the proceeds of which should go to the upkeep of the fleet. The main tangible results of the Conference were that the Cape Colony agreed jointly with Great Britain to put the Cape Peninsula into a proper state of defence, and the Australian colonies promised to pay an annual naval subsidy on condition that a strong British squadron was stationed in their waters.

Hofmeyr's proposal was shelved again in 1894 at the next conference. This was a colonial conference in every sense, for the Canadian Government had summoned it to Ottawa and the British Government was represented merely by an observer. The main subjects of debate were intra-imperial cable and steamship communications; the main results the repeal of the clauses in Earl Grey's Act of 1850 which debarred the Australian colonies from offering preferences to other members of the Empire, and the blunt refusal of the British Government to join further in the crusade to divert foreign trade into imperial channels.

The Conference system began to take its now familiar shape at the Diamond Jubilee Conference of 1897, for this was limited to the Prime Ministers of the self-governing colonies under the chairmanship of Chamberlain, the Colonial Secretary. British imperialism was rising to its zenith, but Chamberlain's high hopes were disappointed. His suggestion that there should be 'a great council of the Empire', consisting of 'representative plenipotentiaries—not mere delegates', drew from nearly all the premiers a modest refusal to bear the cost and responsibility which this sharing of imperial control must entail; his plea for a common defence scheme to meet the pressure of European Powers and rising Japan was answered simply by small unconditional annual contributions to the Navy by the Cape Colony first and then by Natal. Again, his grateful reference to Canada's recent grant of a preference to United Kingdom goods as an example to the others was countered by the obvious retort that, if Great Britain desired such favours, she must first denounce her most-favoured-nation treaties of the 'sixties with Belgium and the German *Zollverein* since the colonies were not minded that foreigners should share in benefits extended to the

K

Mother Country. The Conference dispersed on the understanding that there should be no purely racial or colour restrictions in the immigration laws which 'White Australia' and the South African colonies were contemplating. It was a warning that self-governing colonies must consider their relations with India as well as with the United Kingdom and each other.

Imperial enthusiasm was still running high when the Coronation Conference met in 1902, for Canadians, Australians, New Zealanders and South Africans had served beside the British troops during the South African war, now happily ended, and federated Australia was represented at the Conference for the first time. Chamberlain returned to the charge with redoubled vigour and, since the Belgian and German commercial treaties had now been abrogated, proposed 'free trade within the Empire'. The horrified colonial Premiers would not hear of it, but asked once more for mutual preferences and at the least consultation before Great Britain made any more commercial treaties with foreign Powers, a first hint that the colonies might yet trench upon the last of Durham's imperial reservations: control of imperial external policy. Chamberlain's renewed suggestion of a representative imperial council or, as Arthur Balfour, the new Prime Minister, put it, 'something in the nature of a constitutional union', met with a unanimous refusal and a request merely that the Conference should meet every fourth year. Under the head of defence, a New Zealand proposal that each colony should maintain an imperial force for service anywhere was rejected in favour of a general overhaul of local defence forces; on the other hand, the Cape and Natal increased their unconditional naval subsidies, Australia increased her subsidy and New Zealand added her quota in return for a larger British squadron in the Antipodes, Newfoundland agreed to finance a training ship, and even Laurier's continentally-minded Canada evinced a platonic interest in naval affairs.

The lesson of this Conference was brought home to Chamberlain during his subsequent visit to South Africa. He announced there a new conception of empire, 'a group of free nations gathered round the Motherland' which should leave formal unity to look after itself. On his return home in 1903 he proclaimed that the hope of the future lay in co-operation rather than in centralisation, and then resigned office to lead a forlorn hope in favour of imperial preferences. Since these must involve the abandonment of Great Britain's free trade principles, Chamberlain's efforts merely helped to bring down the Conservative ministry with nothing done beyond the imposition, in 1904, of an export duty on Malayan tin to direct its flow towards the United Kingdom or Australia, an intimation that the open door into the dependent Empire might one day be closed. On the other hand, Milner's newly-formed South African customs union at once followed Canada's example by giving a British preference and, in due time, New Zealand and Australia followed suit; though, in Canada and Australia particularly, many of these preferences were given by raising basic tariff rates against foreigners and not by lowering them for the benefit of Great Britain. The system of inter-colonial preferences was also extended; by 1907 the South African customs union had exchanged preferences with Canada, Australia and New Zealand, and in 1913 Canada and the West Indies arranged mutual concessions in which the United Kingdom shared.

Meanwhile the imperial atmosphere had changed. Virulent outbursts in Continental newspapers against their country and Queen during the South African war had apprised the British of their isolation and unpopularity; the early disasters and continued muddle of that long and difficult campaign had been, in Kipling's phrase, 'no end of a lesson'. Whether or no that lesson was to do the Empire 'no end of good', it had certainly killed the flamboyant imperialism of the 'nineties and undeservedly degraded the word 'imperialism' to a term of reproach. Further, rising prices, due mainly to the inflow of Transvaal gold, and the check to rising wages which had set in just before the recent war led to unrest at home, aversion to overseas adventures and demands for social reform. Finally, the publication of two notable books hastened this change of outlook: Hobson's *Imperialism*, which analysed the mixed motives that underlay the imperial idea, and Jebb's *Colonial Nationalism*, which showed that the peoples of the self-governing colonies were already nations distinct from the British of the Old Country.

All these tendencies were reflected in the proceedings of the Conference of 1907, the last of the Colonial Conferences. The Liberal premier, Campbell-Bannerman, endorsed Chamberlain's plea for co-operation by declaring that 'the essence of the British imperial connection' was freedom and independence, and its method periodical conferences interspersed with subsidiary conferences on matters that called for detailed discussion. The Conference rejected out of hand the scheme, which had been put forward two years since by the outgoing Conservative Colonial Secretary, that it should transform itself into an Imperial Council with a joint permanent secretariat to collect information and prepare agenda. It talked little of defence beyond welcoming Haldane's projected army reforms, which included an Imperial General Staff, Dominion representation on Balfour's Committee of Imperial Defence, and the organisation of home defence forces everywhere more or less on the same lines. It also agreed to continue the naval subsidies, conditional and unconditional, without in any way admitting that these were a duty. A determined Australian demand for imperial preferences, *videlicet* preferences in the immense United Kingdom market, was turned aside by the Transvaal Premier, Louis Botha, who reversed Canada's famous reply to the protesting British Government of 1859 by suggesting that it was not seemly for colonies that were asking to be let alone to interfere with the Mother Country's fiscal arrangements. Finally, the Conference decided that it should become the Imperial Conference meeting every fourth year and consisting of the prime ministers of the United Kingdom and 'the self-governing Dominions beyond the seas', a category from which India was necessarily excluded. Since these Dominions claimed to be autonomous nations within the Empire on an equality with Great Britain herself, though to be sure this was at the moment 'a very disproportionate equality', a Dominions Division was set up to handle the relations of the Colonial Office with Canada, Newfoundland, Australia, New Zealand and the South Africa that was so soon to be united.

The new status of 'Dominion' thus recognised formally rested primarily on the notable advance towards individuality made by Canada, with all her comparative advantages of size and wealth, during the past forty years, and the custom of the Empire which ordained that all members of a given class of colony should share sooner or later in the powers and recognition gained by any one of them.

Thanks to Canadian example the self-governing colonies had already gone a long way towards winning freedom for their external fiscal policies; as Dominions they were destined to become almost distinct political entities in the eyes of the outer world before the outbreak of war in 1914. Elgin's reciprocity treaty of 1854 had shown that the British North American colonies could have special commercial relations with the United States without affecting the rest of the Empire; but that treaty had lapsed in 1866. Some years later the Canadian Premier had had much ado to induce the Washington authorities to admit him as an effective participant in their discussion of a commercial treaty with a British delegation, and to convince the conservative Spanish Government that the High Commissioner he was sending to London in 1879 was a good deal more than a mere colonial agent. Before that year was ended, however, the British Government had agreed that Canada might contract out of British commercial treaties. Twenty years passed before this privilege was enjoyed by any other self-governing colony; but by 1911 it had been extended to all, and Great Britain had persuaded most of the Powers concerned that it was right and proper for such colonies to offer preferences to whom they chose regardless of her own most-favoured nation treaties. Meanwhile Canada had cheerfully waged a commercial war against Germany without involving the rest of the Empire, and in 1907, armed with full powers from the King, had negotiated a commercial treaty single-handed with France, though the British Government insisted that this and similar documents subsequently completed must be countersigned by the nearest British ambassador. Anything less would, in its eyes, have been 'equivalent to breaking up the Empire'.

Further advances towards independence were registered during the years that immediately preceded the Kaiser's War. Anglo-American arbitration and conciliation treaties provided that the Dominions should not be bound thereby without their own consent, and should be represented on conciliation committees wherever their interests were in question; as the outcome of the first of the subsidiary conferences, Australia and New Zealand began in 1909 to build naval squadrons, the latter as part of the Royal Navy, the former semi-independent; from 1906 onwards the Dominions sent their own delegations to non-political international conferences on such matters as posts, protection of industrial property, radio-telegraphy and safety of life at sea, each signing the report or not as its government directed. Even so the British Government preserved diplomatic unity to the end by retaining its right to reject the international agreements subscribed to by Dominion representatives.

The grim problem of peace or war remained, the last argument of kings and the last of Durham's imperial reservations. That reservation had survived unimpaired because the Dominions with their sheltered pasts, inexperience of international affairs, and truly Washingtonian suspicion of the Chancelleries of Old Europe had been loath to touch it. The Australian Fisher might desire direct communication with the Foreign Office over the head of the Colonial Office, but the Conferences of 1897 and 1902 had refused to take a hand in determining policy for fear of the responsibility that this must entail. Later on the French-Canadian Laurier spoke for the rest when he bade them cherish their autonomy, avoid entangling alliances and, though he could not know of the fetters that military conversations with the French and Belgians were even then fastening upon British policy, beware of consultations with the Mother Country that might imply responsibility of 'the Day'. No one quarrelled with Laurier's claim that a Dominion need not become an active belligerent unless its parliament so decided, for that had been the privilege of the self-governing colonies in all Great Britain's wars unless the war had come to them; but when a Transvaal newspaper revived Wolfe Tone's and Gavan Duffy's claim to a right of neutrality, the veteran General Botha observed with prophetic insight that the enemy would be the judge of that. Hence the British Government did not trouble to consult the Dominions before making its alliance with Japan, the *entente cordiale* with France and the agreement of 1907 with Russia. Nor did it consult them before adhering to two Hague Conventions and signing the Declaration of London which arose out of the second of them and would, if it had been ratified, have gravely hampered the Navy in its task of cutting off the sea-borne commerce of an enemy.

It was this abortive Declaration of London that moved the Dominions to ask for some small share in determining the foreign policy of the Empire. The Imperial Conference of 1911, the most important conference yet held and the first at which the South African Union was represented, met under the shadow of the German naval menace. It said little of imperial preferences, though the Dominions wistfully recorded their unshaken faith in them and welcomed as a possible step in their direction the appointment of a Royal Commission to examine the resources of the Empire and suggest methods of stimulating intra-imperial trade. It rejected a New Zealand proposal that a representative Imperial Council should advise the King on matters affecting the Dominions, and all that came of a British suggestion that there should be a standing committee of High Commissioners or other representatives to keep London in constant touch with the Dominion capitals was the appointment of a Canadian Resident Minister on the eve of the Kaiser's War. Then, having discussed immigration and the bearing of Dominion policies on the governance of India, the Conference passed on to external affairs. It adjusted the relations of the Australian and tiny Canadian squadrons to the Admiralty with excellent results when the time came; the British Government promised to consult the Dominions on the policy to be pursued at future peace conferences and, where possible, in other international negotiations also, and the Foreign Secretary, behind closed doors, painted such an unvarnished picture of the world situation that he evoked 'an unexampled sense of solidarity'. Even so, all could agree with the British Prime Minister that the day to day conduct of foreign policy and, above all, decisions of peace and war must lie with H.M. Government in the United Kingdom.

Thus, when 'the Day' came suddenly in August 1914, the British Government declared war on Germany without consulting the Dominions. This done, all made haste to quit themselves like men in a struggle that was to change so much of the form and something also of the spirit of the British Empire.

VIII

THE BRITISH COMMONWEALTH, 1914-1939

NOTABLE changes were taking place in all parts of the British Empire on the eve of the Kaiser's War. The United Kingdom had begun to waver in its loyalty to the doctrine of free trade; the Dominions were emerging visibly as states in their own right; Ireland was within sight of Home Rule, and India on the road to parliamentary government; the recruitment of Indian coolies was doomed to extinction, the Protectorates were being assimilated to the liberal British colonial system, and indirect rule as yet unnamed was taking shape in Nigeria. The Empire was now called upon to face close upon half a century of world revolution. That revolution has still to reveal its full results; but even to-day it is plain to see that it marked the passing of the age of *laissez faire* and the twilight of the sovereign national State. The Empire did indeed escape the violent revolutions which marked a break with the past in so many other states and empires; its story is evolutionary throughout; nevertheless all the processes at work within it were speeded up. Changes which would normally have taken a leisurely generation for their accomplishment were hurried through in a few short years.

The Kaiser's War of 1914-18 which set this world revolution moving was itself the first climax of a Thirty Years War that began when Italy invaded Turkish Tripoli in 1911. By the time the principal peace treaties had been signed in 1919 the Austro-Hungarian Empire was gone, the Russian, German and Ottoman Empires had been curtailed drastically, and the balkanised continent of Europe was dominated by France and her satellites. Presently the United States withdrew into the isolation from which she had emerged in 1917 in an attempt to redress the balance of the Old World; but the marching of armed men did not end until the Kemalist Turks had secured peace more or less on their own terms and the French had evacuated the German Ruhr district in 1924. There followed seven years of uneasy peace and apparent world recovery; but the hopes of this lucid interval were shaken by the collapse of Wall Street in 1929 and shattered by the Japanese invasion of Manchuria (Manchukuo) two years later. That event marked the beginning of a fresh cycle of wars which swept ever nearer by way of Abyssinia, Spain and Central Europe and culminated in the world-wide Axis War of 1939–45.

Throughout these tumultuous and desperate decades the fortunes of the overseas Empire depended as ever on those of the United Kingdom, the centre of the Empire and in the last resort its defender. Britain's responsibilities in the strange new post-war world were heavier than before, partly because of the territorial additions that were then made to her dependent Empire and some of the Dominions; partly also because, as the most internationally experienced of the Powers, the Power that stood between Europe and the outer world and was regarded as the traditional world-policeman beyond the three-mile limit, she was marked out as chief supporter of the League of Nations to which the treaty-makers of 1919 entrusted the keeping of the general peace.

For all that the League lacked means of its own for enforcing its decisions and had been weakened fatally at the start by the abstention of the United States and the exclusion of Bolshevik Russia and Republican Germany, it was mankind's boldest attempt hitherto to set up a world control for world affairs. Generally speaking the peoples of the United Kingdom and the Dominions gave it their warm support, for the very idea of such a League had sprung from the minds of their own statesmen and publicists, and although much of the machinery was American and the inclusion of the League Covenant in the peace treaties was the work of the Democrat President Wilson, they hoped that the spirit and method would be those of the Imperial Conference and pre-war British colonial administration. The peoples of the Commonwealth saw in the League an invaluable means of co-operation and, even if all did not share the widely held belief that it would somehow make an end of war, they expected that it would at least slow down the appalling speed of modern warfare in its beginnings. In so far as it might be the keeper of the world's peace, they hailed it as the guarantor of the liberties and prosperity of the Empire's scattered communities.

Unhappily, Great Britain was less favourably situated than she once had been for discharging her imperial and international duties. Masses of her merchant shipping had been sunk; there was less demand for her coal in a world that was using more oil, electricity and water power; her basic industries of steel and cotton were out of

gear, burdened by ill-judged and often unscrupulous over-capitalisa-
tion, and subjected to the competition of rivals, in North America
and Asia especially, who had waxed gigantic in the forcing house
of war. Her numerous unemployed found emigration to the
Dominions less tempting and easy than in days gone by, and much
less so to the United States who had begun to exclude the Japanese
before the war and was now practically closing her doors to all
newcomers. Moreover, while tariff walls were rising along the
thousands of miles of new political frontiers and New York was
promising to compete with London as the world's money market,
Great Britain found herself financially embarrassed for the first time
these many years. Saddled with a huge internal debt, she owed
vast sums to the United States for nominal dollars advanced to
finance war purchases of American goods, largely on account of
allies who now were slow to repay her if only because they found it
hard to extract reparation payments from Germany. Nor would
Americans admit this connection between war debts and the
reparations in which they would not share, but only that between
war debts and expenditure on armaments by debtor governments.
As the United States President said, 'They hired the money, didn't
they?'

Nevertheless Great Britain instituted or furthered far-reaching
changes in the Empire during the dangerous years of the war and
the post-war slump. The Dominions, including now the Irish Free
State, achieved an international status equal to her own; the central
Indian legislature was given a strongly representative character,
and responsible Indian ministers were entrusted with many departments in the provinces; the recruiting of Indian coolies came to an
end; the doctrine of trusteeship was adopted as the guiding rule for
the governance of a dependent Empire that now contained mandated
territories, and the constitutions of many of the dependencies were
liberalised each in its degree. Meanwhile Great Britain herself
sponsored ambitious schemes of empire migration and subscribed to
the principle of imperial preference.

The tide seemed to have turned in the right direction at the close
of 1924. Eager, too eager, to restore the prestige of the pound ster-
ling, which had for so long been the world's standard coin, Great
Britain gave the lead to many other States by rejoining the United
States on the gold standard and funding her scaled-down debt to that
Republic. The United States persuaded Germany to accept a flexible

plan for meeting her heavy reparation payments; whereupon American money poured into Central Europe furnishing the means to pay reparations and therefore war-debts, and to re-equip Germany's industries and public undertakings on modern lines. Millions of United States citizens believed that they had entered a new 'economic era' based on 'wealth by production'—a delusion that was shared by not a few in the kindred British Commonwealth—and for a time it seemed that Geneva, the seat of the League, was really becoming the political centre of a regenerate world. In 1925 the Powers most nearly concerned reaffirmed the essential clauses of the League Covenant at Locarno, and Great Britain promised France and Germany that she would help whichever of them might be wrongfully attacked by the other. Next year Germany was admitted to the League and in 1928 the United States and Russia joined all the League members in signing the Kellogg Pact, which renounced war as an instrument of policy, save only a defensive war or a public war declared by the signatories against a law-breaker. But even less than the Covenant did this pact provide machinery for carrying out the ban.

All seemed well on the surface of a world made 'safe for democracy', though, to be sure, Mussolini's Fascists were in control of Italy and the executives were overshadowing the elective legislatures of Germany and many of the smaller European countries. Beneath the surface all was far from well. Rapidly improving techniques in industry, mining and agriculture had for some time past been giving ever greater output for the same expenditure of capital and labour, and now unprecedented production accompanied by a general and often premature return to the gold standard drove prices down and created unsalable surpluses. Governments therefore protected home industries energetically and thus imposed an impossible strain on gold as the solvent of commerce.

It was now (and it is best to say this plainly and without heat) that the policies of the United States pressed heavily upon Great Britain and finally proved disastrous to the world and herself. Possessed of enormous wealth and entrenched behind high tariff walls and gates barred to immigrants, the great republic built up a financial empire in Europe and declined to take a hand in its political and commercial ordering. Tides of useless gold were already surging back and forth across the Atlantic when, in the year of the Kellogg Pact, a wild boom broke out in the United States based this time on the gospel of 'wealth by speculation'. Money poured westward out of Europe, while the British banks tried to fill the gap with short-term loans; the continental banks pole-axed industry by shortening credit, and the United States, backed by France, insisted on substituting for the flexible reparations scheme a far more rigid scheme which benefited France, might help Germany and did no good to Great Britain. At this moment, while Washington was framing the ferocious Hawley-Smoot tariff, the bottom fell out of Wall Street.

The Wall Street crash of 1929 was the signal for a *sauve qui peut* in a world from which the volatile spirit of Locarno had long since evaporated. Banks and governments followed each other violently down a steep place till, in 1931, Great Britain was swept off gold, taking half the world with her, just as the United States was arranging to barter wheat for the coffee which Brazilians were burning for lack of buyers. Reparations perished in the stampede. And then the long-suffering British turned. They replied with tariffs to the tariffs of their neighbours and followed the example of their ex-allies by stopping payment of their well-nigh unpayable debt to the United States. Meanwhile the Japanese army chiefs had attacked Shanghai, to the grave peril of the international settlement in which the British had long enjoyed the predominant interest, and made good their hold on Manchuria in defiance of the League and the United States.

The changes already under way in the British Empire were carried still further during the seven-year interval between the end of the first Great War in 1924 and this virtual beginning of the second. The Balfour Declaration of 1926 explained the new Dominion status, and in 1931 legal precision was given to its generalisations by the Statute of Westminster; India rapidly advanced towards Dominion status; the indianisation of the Services proceeded apace and a beginning was made with the drafting of a constitution that should give a federation of British and Princely India almost complete self-government. The Colonial Services were consolidated, Nigerian indirect rule was extended to other parts of Africa, British money was provided for capital expenditure in the dependent Empire, and the governments of contiguous colonial territories were encouraged to co-operate with one another.

These hopeful developments were warped, though by no means

stopped, by the perils which now pressed upon the Empire. Early in 1933 the Nazi leader, Adolf Hitler, became master of the Reich, Japan gave notice of withdrawal from the League, and before that black year was out Germany had followed Japan's example. Great Britain, with her depleted armaments and embarrassed finances, was in no state to play a part commensurate with her responsibilities in an increasingly warlike world, and was handicapped further by an uninspiring sequence of predominantly Conservative National ministries. Those ministries, bent upon 'safety first', neither supported the League wholeheartedly while it stood nor rearmed with vigour while there was time, and at the last, hastily arming, were forced into a policy of appeasement reminiscent of the Danegeld.

The drift towards war was steady. By the spring of 1937 the system of collective security had broken down; the Berlin-Rome Axis had made contact with acquisitive Japan, and the United States had retired into ostentatious isolation behind neutrality laws which prohibited the sale of munitions to belligerents or even the extension of credit to those that were not fellow American republics, forbade its own citizens to travel in belligerent ships or aircraft, and warned them that they would venture into a war zone at their own risk. In other words, so that she might keep herself free from overseas embarrassments, the United States had jettisoned her cherished tradition of the freedom of the seas: the claim that her men, goods and ships were free to go anywhere in peace and in war, and let those who would hinder them see to themselves. Never had the principle of 'safety first' been given such a resounding affirmation.

But then each government in that dislocated world was seeking to make of its territory a Robinson Crusoe's island. The British Government was no exception. In 1932 it yielded to Dominion pressure and the ardent desires of some of its own members by joining with its Commonwealth partners in a campaign to divert trade into Empire channels;[1] but a halt was soon called to this attempt to tighten the economic bonds of empire, partly at the request of disappointed members of the Commonwealth, and partly at the instance of the United States which was being drawn out of her bristling isolation by the new Democrat President, Franklin Roosevelt, and launched upon a more open-handed commercial policy by his Secretary of State, Cordell Hull. Meanwhile Great

[1] *Vide infra* Chap. X.

Britain watched the external policies of the Dominions drift away
from her own and each others', and faced growing difficulties in
India, where she indeed gave the Provinces almost complete self-
government but failed to persuade the Princes and the rival political
parties in British India to adopt the scheme of federation on which
depended the extension of similar powers to the Central legislature.
On the other hand, after a disappointing start during which she was
obliged to withdraw more than one liberal constitution, she did
much good work in the dependent Empire. The Colonial Service
was raised to the high level of the Indian Civil Service; local
administrations were overhauled and, where need be, financed more
generously; the well-tried policy of encouraging elective institutions was resumed and, at the last, after the shock of renewed war
had begun to drive most of the members of the Commonwealth
closer together again, considerable sums were provided for the
social and economic welfare of the colonies, protectorates and
mandated territories.

Developments in the overseas Empire during the last quarter of
a century fall naturally under three heads: those affecting primarily
the Dominions and the Indian Empire, which together with the
United Kingdom formed the Commonwealth proper, and the
Colonial Empire.

Dominion status, as it is understood to-day, took shape rapidly
during the crisis of the Kaiser's War. The united front which the
Empire presented to its enemies in 1914 was broken at the outset
by rebellion in parts of the South African ex-republics and later on
by Sinn Fein rebellion in Ireland and trouble over conscription in
Canadian Quebec; but the dogged readiness of the vast majority
of the King's subjects to serve the common cause was such that it
raised the hopes of the imperial federalists. Those hopes were
dashed by Dominion politicians whose most effective spokesmen
were Sir Robert Borden, Prime Minister of Canada, and General
Smuts, second-in-command in General Botha's South African
ministry. Both men rejected on the one hand Laurier's programme
of local autonomy and isolation, and on the other a federal solution
on United States lines. Neither disputed the primacy of Great
Britain, 'the senior partner in this concern' in such matters as foreign
policy, but both sought the partnership on equal terms which Earl
Grey had envisaged two generations back. To Smuts the very word

'Empire' was misleading. 'We are not an Empire,' he declared, '. . . we are a system of states, . . . the British Commonwealth of Nations, . . . the only league of nations that has ever existed', a commonwealth that would secure to all its members 'a fuller, a richer, a more varied life' by consulting its experience and holding fast to its 'tradition of freedom, self-government, and the fullest development'.

The federal issue was postponed until after the war by the Imperial War Conference which met in 1917 with Indian delegates present for the first time since 1887. Sitting alongside an Imperial War Cabinet, which consisted of the standing British War Cabinet and Dominion ministers, this Conference reaffirmed Dominion autonomy, called for effective means of continuous consultation, and demanded 'an adequate voice' for the Dominions and India in the determination of policies that might oblige them to wage another war on the grand scale and at their own charges. Next year Borden and Smuts demanded full equality with the United Kingdom in every right of self-government, including 'an equal voice' in foreign affairs. If this was given the Dominions would have achieved the essence of Dominion status, that is, full international standing in the eyes of the Empire and the world.

Dominion status was achieved in 1919, the decisive year in the constitutional development of the post-war Commonwealth. In spite of questionings and protests by foreign Powers, the Dominions, except little Newfoundland, were given a standing at the Peace Conference superior to that of other small Powers, for not only did they appoint their own delegations but could send one representative between them to speak with the great ones of the earth on the British Empire delegation. Each of them, and India also, signed the peace treaties separately; next year, they and India were given separate representation in the Assembly of the League of Nations, while the Dominions became eligible to the more powerful Council, a distinction enjoyed by 'Canada first' in 1927. Presently the Allied and Associated Powers mandated to Australia, New Zealand and South Africa the German colonies each had conquered, and by that time foreigners were reassured to see that representatives from different parts of this curious Empire could contradict one another flatly in public, though it still passed the comprehension of most of them that they could then go out cheerfully to lunch together.

All that has happened since 1919 is that first one Dominion and then another has claimed for itself, and therefore by the custom of the Empire for its fellows, the right to exercise powers that were implicit in the status gained then. The most significant claims were made early and under ideal conditions; for now that Germany had been disarmed it was the heyday of the small Powers, especially for Dominions who were doubly secure within the British Commonwealth and the interlocking system of collective security centring upon Geneva. As a rule the lead was given in these early days by Canada, the senior Dominion, triply secure behind those two defences and the Monroe Doctrine.

Dominion ministers, anxious to be off homewards, would not perpetuate the Imperial War Cabinet. Hence the co-operation of half-a-dozen governments, which Milner declared bluntly was the real problem for the Commonwealth and not the achievement of a Dominion independence that nobody questioned, had to be maintained by consultation between widely-scattered Prime Ministers, assisted by their High Commissioners in London who now handed over most of their commercial duties to subordinates and themselves advanced towards the status of ambassadors. Noting the set of the wind, the British Government, as in 1887, ruled out discussion of federation in advance and made foreign policy the main topic of debate at the Imperial Conference of 1921. This Conference deplored the United States' naval ambitions and undisguised desire to engross the markets of Latin America, recommended on the whole the abandonment of the expiring Japanese alliance for which the United States and Canada were pressing with some support from South Africa, and advocated close co-operation with France so long as her policy made for European recovery. By so doing an Imperial Conference advised the King for the first time in its collective capacity, though its overseas members left His Majesty's taxpayers in the United Kingdom to bear the cost of the joint policy. The Dominions then sent their representatives to join the imperial delegation which discussed naval and Pacific problems with the Americans at the ensuing Washington Conference of 1921–22, and soon showed that they were determined to be consulted on other high matters. When, three years later, the first British Labour ministry recognised the Red Russian government without consulting them, they condemned its action as unconstitutional, and when it ignored them in its reparations negotiations with Germany, Canada protested.

Smuts went too far when he claimed that if war was to affect the Dominions in future they would have to declare it, and if peace was to be made in respect of them they must sign it. His wish was father to the thought, for even in 1939 Australia and New Zealand held themselves constitutionally bound to follow the King to war. But Great Britain made no attempt to saddle the Dominions with undesired international obligations. She left them free to decide whether or no they should adhere to the 1919 Anglo-French treaty of guarantee which fell away when the United States refused to underwrite it; she specifically exempted them from her Locarno guarantee of the Rhine frontier in 1925 unless they chose to share it, and none of them did. For the rest, the old pre-war rule held good that no Dominion need help the Mother Country actively in time of trouble unless it so desired. When, in 1922, the victorious Kemalist Turks were driving the defeated Greeks out of Asia Minor and pressing down on the British troops guarding the Straits at Chanak, Australia and New Zealand, with recent proud memories of Gallipoli, prepared to respond to Britain's call for aid; but Canada and South Africa asked in effect, 'Where is Chanak?'

Finally, as early as 1920, Canada was given the right to send a full diplomatic representative of her own to Washington. In the event, it was reserved for the Irish Free State to accredit the first Dominion minister plenipotentiary to a foreign capital four years later; but Canada and South Africa availed themselves of the right in 1927, and in 1941 Australia and New Zealand tardily followed their example. Meanwhile Canada had long ago concluded an immigration agreement with Japan and signed a fisheries treaty with the United States even before she had arranged for separate diplomatic representation. There could, of course, be no question but that each Dominion should sign the Kellogg Pact of 1928 for itself alone. But, for all that, the world-wide British ambassadorial and consular services remained as freely at the disposal of Dominion citizens as of all other of the King's subjects.

Canada was apparently satisfied by the time the seven years of world recovery had begun in 1924. The Irish Free State and South Africa were not. After two bitter disappointments in 1886 and 1893 Home Rule had seemed to be within Ireland's grasp on the eve of the Kaiser's War, though only at the risk of civil war in the United

L

Kingdom. The Act of 1914, however, had been shelved 'for the duration'; Sinn Fein republicans had rebelled in 1916, and at the end of the war the British found themselves burdened with an exasperating struggle in Ireland. Doubtless they could have worn down their opponents, but sick as they were of bloodshed, anxious not to outrage League, Dominion and United States opinion, and fundamentally more tolerant than the Irish, there came a time when they would rely on force no longer. Ulster, which had always been ready to resist Home Rule from Dublin, was given Home Rule from Belfast and, in addition, liberal representation at Westminster as part of the United Kingdom of Great Britain and Northern Ireland. The Southern Irish rejected similar terms. In December 1921 they signed a treaty with the British by which the southern three-fourths of the island was recognised as the Irish Free State with powers and status equal to those of Canada, then the most advanced of the Dominions.

Once they had reduced the fierce resistance of the irreconcilables of the Irish Republican Army to mere sporadic violence, the Free Staters sought to extend the powers and status conveyed by the treaty. They found allies in South Africa. There, the mixed Afrikander and British ministry, which Smuts had led since Botha's untimely death in 1919, was overthrown in 1924 by a predominantly Afrikander Nationalist-Labour coalition led by the Orange Free Stater, General Hertzog. This Pact ministry was bent on enhancing the Union's status and emphasising its freedom from the bonds of empire. The South African and Irish Nationalists, with their Continental taste for absolutes and legal precision so unlike the pragmatic instincts of the English, naturally joined forces at the Imperial Conference of 1926. To their pleased surprise they found themselves reinforced by the Canadians who had recently had a sharp passage of arms with their Governor-General. Canadians, Irish and South Africans joined with the other delegates at this conference in resolving that henceforward the Governor-General of a Dominion must represent only the King's Grace and in no sense the British ministry. They then demanded a definition of Dominion status.

Luckily the British delegation contained a philosophic Scot whose theological skill was equal to the occasion. The famous Balfour Declaration proclaimed in almost Athanasian terms that the United Kingdom and the Dominions were 'autonomous communities

within the British Empire, equal in status, in no way subordinate one
to another in any aspect of their domestic or external affairs, though
united by a common allegiance to the Crown, and freely associated
as members of the British Commonwealth'; but it added, with a
frank recognition of the brute facts, that 'the principles of equality
and similarity, appropriate to status, do not universally extend to
function. . . . (In) the conduct of foreign affairs generally—as in
the sphere of defence, the *major share* of the responsibility rests now,
and must for some time continue to rest, with His Majesty's
Government in Great Britain'.

The Dominions were quite ready to let the major share of that
responsibility rest where it had always rested, especially in the year
which saw Germany's admission to the League; meanwhile the
recognition of their individuality pointed to the need for formal
changes in the law of the Empire. Canada and the Irish Free State
had defined their own nationals long since, and, though they had
forborne to do likewise, Australia, New Zealand and South Africa
were careful to confer political rights only on certain specified
groups of British subjects. Most of the Dominions also had their
own flags which indicated the gradations of their enthusiasm
for the imperial connection: those of Canada, Australia and New
Zealand proudly showing the Union Jack in the canton, and that
of the Free State being simply the orange, white and green under
which the republicans had fought the British and each other.
Now, in 1927, South Africa defined her nationals in such a way
that they remained British subjects, as in other Dominions, and
adopted two flags as was fitting in a land of prudent political
compromise: the one the orange, white and blue of the House of
Orange with the Union Jack and old republican flags shown in
miniature on the white, the other the Union Jack itself to be flown
beside the tricolour at suitable points.

The next step was the adoption by the Imperial Conference of
1930 of the report of experts who had examined the Balfour
Declaration in detail. The changes in the position and duties of the
Governor-General were made forthwith. Henceforward His Excellency was to be appointed by the King on the sole advice of
Dominion ministers and must act in his Dominion as the constitutional monarch would act in the United Kingdom. His old functions
as representative of the British Government were to be discharged

by a High Commissioner equal in rank to a Dominion High Commissioner. In the special case of the Union, the High Commissionership of South Africa, which carried with it imperial control of Southern Rhodesia and the governance of the so-called protectorates of Basutoland, Bechuanaland and Swaziland, was to be transferred from the Governor-General to another British official. So it was done, though some years passed before New Zealand, who disliked this whittling away of the formal links of empire even more than did Australia, consented to receive a United Kingdom High Commissioner.

The legal changes desired by the Conference were embodied in the Statute of Westminster which the British Parliament passed at the request of the Dominions towards the close of 1931. Disallowance of completed Dominion legislation, except as touching the advantageous Colonial Stocks Act of 1900, had been decently buried by common consent in 1929. Now, the Statute recognised Dominion Parliaments as sovereign legislatures in all cases domestic and external by providing for the abolition of the long ineffective, though by no means defunct, reservation of bills for His Majesty's pleasure, placing future Dominion legislation outside the sphere of the Colonial Laws Validity Act and leaving Dominions free to repeal such British laws as might still apply to them. Further, it relinquished the British Parliament's power to legislate for a Dominion save at its own request, recognised the validity of Dominion extra-territorial legislation, and relieved the Dominions from the operation of the British Merchant Shipping and Colonial Courts of Admiralty laws.

It is now admitted almost universally that a Dominion to which the Statute of Westminster applies is legally a sovereign independent State within the Commonwealth. But the Statute did not take effect in them all at once by any means. The sovereign status defined in the preamble was conferred upon all the Dominions forthwith, but the operation of the Act itself was withheld from Australia, New Zealand and Newfoundland at their own wish until their respective Parliaments should determine otherwise. Australia, mindful of her jealous States, and New Zealand, as ever more trustful of the Mother Country than the rest, noted that the Act did not extend the already wide powers of their Parliaments to alter their respective constitutions, while Canada, with the entrenched privileges of French Quebec and other provincial interests to consider, stipulated that her constitution should be amended, as hitherto, only by the British Parliament which had enacted it as long ago as 1867. With this single limitation Canada at once received the full benefit of the Statute of Westminster side by side with South Africa and the Irish Free State.

These two latter Dominions hastened to exploit the formal freedoms thus recorded. Doubtless the Union would have gone further than it did had Hertzog's Nationalist-Labour ministry remained in office, for some Nationalists desired a republic out and out, and many more wished to go as far as they could in that direction without seeing their country absolutely independent and unprotected in a dangerous world. As it was, the republican-minded Nationalists formed a party of their own under Dr. Malan when the old rivals, Hertzog and Smuts, joined hands in 1933. In the following year the new United Party Ministry was content to secure for South Africa her own Great Seal on Irish analogy and adapt the South Africa Act of 1909 to the new conditions. In so doing, however, the Union Parliament ventured to amend the covering Statute of Westminster in its own favour by decreeing that no mere request but a South African Act would be necessary before the Westminster Parliament could legislate for the Union.

The Irish Free State for its part almost severed its connection with the Crown and Commonwealth. The republican Sinn Feiners, organised in the Fianna Fail party, took office under de Valera early in 1932 and promptly abolished the oath of allegiance. Then, having gained the majority in both Houses, they cut off appeals to the Judicial Committee of the Privy Council as all Dominions were now empowered to do, abolished the Senate, and decreed that within the borders of the Free State an Irish citizen was no longer a British subject even though he might share that status elsewhere with the rest of the King's lieges. They then moved many Afrikanders to envy by dealing drastically with the Governor-Generalship. That office had always been held by an Irish citizen, though Canada, which had been indicated as the model for the Free State in 1921, continued cheerfully to receive a Governor-General from the Old Country, and Australia, after one experiment on Irish lines, had once more welcomed a Governor-General, as well as her State Governors, from overseas. The Irish, however, first reduced their Governor-General to a cipher and then abolished his office altogether during the crisis that accompanied the abdication of Edward VIII in 1936. They presently elected a State President to discharge his formal duties for a seven-year term, and instituted a reformed Senate in whose selection de Valera, as Prime Minister and President of the Executive Council, had a considerable share. Meanwhile they had denied to the King all authority within the borders of the Irish Free State, described the Crown as the mere external symbol of the free association of a scarcely-veiled republic with the other members of the Commonwealth, and repudiated the title and status of Dominion as being unworthy of an ancient community and a Mother Country in her own right. It is no wonder that these drastic measures impelled the South African ministry to secure the appointment of a Scots-born Union citizen as Governor-General if only to quiet the clamour of extreme Nationalists for more far-reaching changes.

Thus, by 1939, Dominion status had come to mean to members of the Empire all that had been implicit in it from the first, that is, sovereign independence within the Commonwealth and, for the restive Irish Free State, an even more detached position than that which Massachusetts had enjoyed in the mid-seventeenth century. To foreign Powers it meant in time of peace all that members of the Commonwealth said it meant and in time of war whatever it might suit their own convenience to allow. It was to this high and novel status that India aspired.

India, like the women of the United Kingdom, owed her sudden advance in status and her steady enfranchisement mainly to her war service. True, the campaigns of violence in Bengal and the Punjab which had never quite died away since Curzon's day were stimulated by German agents on the spot and Sikhs domiciled in North America, while the Moslems were perturbed that the British and Indian Governments should be at war with the Ottoman Caliph; nevertheless, the Government of India prosecuted the war vigorously with the support of the Princes and the majority of the people, while Indian soldiers, recruited voluntarily and mainly from the martial north-western quarter of the country, served by the hundred thousand in East Africa, the Near and Middle East, and Western Europe. Hence, Indian representatives took their seats at the Imperial War Conferences and attended the War Cabinet from time to time. Indian delegates signed the peace treaties on behalf of

India; in 1920 India became a full member of the League of Nations and, as an outward and visible sign of her advance in status, sent a High Commissioner to London, an Englishman on the first occasion and thereafter an Indian. But, for all that, India's imperial and international respresentatives were nominated by the Secretary of State and the Governor-General in Council, for she still lacked the autonomy that had elsewhere preceded Dominion status.

Long before the close of the war, however, steps were being taken to bring India's powers nearer to her acknowledged status. Lord Chelmsford, the Viceroy, had announced in 1915 that if all went well India's destiny was self-government. The Left, therefore, returned to Congress, which it had abandoned in 1907, and agreed with the Moslem League at Lucknow that there should be the separate communal representation to which Indians had grown accustomed since the Councils Act of 1892, and a specified number of Moslem seats in the future legislature. Then, soon after India's admission to the Imperial Conference, the Secretary of State, Edwin Montagu, promised that there should be a progressive indianisation of the Services and 'the gradual development of self-governing institutions with a view to the progressive realisation of responsible government in India as an integral part of the British Empire', a development whose pace would be determined by the British Government in the light of India's response to new powers and responsibilities. Forthwith India began to stride rapidly along the road to responsible government which it had taken Canada half-a-century to traverse and Great Britain herself close upon two hundred years to mark out.

The constitutional portions of the Montagu-Chelmsford reforms were embodied in the Government of India Act of 1919, the year that saw also the effective creation of Dominion status. The Governor-General's Executive Council, consisting now of four Europeans and three Indians, retained wide powers of supervision over the Provinces, but relinquished its hold over much of their finance and such other matters as were transferred to provincial ministers. The Central legislature was divided into two chambers: a Council of State and an Assembly. In spite of friendly warnings both Chambers stereotyped the communal system of representation stipulated by the Hindu-Moslem Lucknow pact. Members elected on a high franchise were given the majority in the Upper House, while, as in some mid-nineteenth-century colonies, more than two-thirds of the seats in the lower house were allotted to members elected on a wider franchise, either by local constituencies or constituencies representing communities and special interests, and the remainder to officials or nominees representing unorganised interests. To resolve deadlocks, a bill which the Governor-General had certified as essential for 'the safety, tranquillity, or interests of British India or any part thereof' would become law if it were passed by one chamber or, failing that and subject to disallowance by the King in Council, by the Governor-General alone. In the event these powers, similar to those that had long been wielded by the Governor of Jamaica, were exercised only ten times in sixteen years, and then to defeat wrecking by Congress.

The approach to self-government was much more direct in the Provinces. Unicameral legislatures were set up in the eight Governors' provinces, and presently in Burma also, consisting, as in mid-Victorian Natal and Honduras, of a few officials and a large majority of members elected on a liberal franchise by local, communal and special constituencies. The relations of these legislatures to their executives were based on the principle of dyarchy. Departments such as education, public health, local government and economic development were transferred to Indian ministers who must be members of their legislature and responsible to it as in the United Kingdom itself; but the rest and notably law and order, finance, land revenue, irrigation, famine relief, control of the press, and labour disputes were reserved to the Governor, who could certify as absolutely necessary reserved measures that had been rejected by the legislature and refer them either to the King in Council or, in emergency, to the Governor-General. Finally, a consultative Chamber of Princes was set up, the outcome of the informal conferences of Indian rulers that had taken place during the war.

The constitution of 1919 was a bold venture in face of the dangerous state of the post-war world and India's very limited experience of parliamentary methods. With its mixture of Crown colony rule, representative institutions and responsible government it promised to be a difficult system to work. All would depend on the exercise of that 'wise moderation' to which Lord John Russell had appealed in the days before even Canada was self-governing. The auguries were not good. Most Indian politicians, and especially the younger men, stirred by the war, envious of the Dominions and eager for equality with the hitherto dominant West, were dissatisfied with the reforms and, still more, with the prospect of *swaraj* by instalments. Distress was widespread and famine conditions prevailed in some parts of a crowded land whose population had risen during the past twenty years from 293,000,000 to nearly 320,000,000 in spite of the ravages of the 1918 influenza. The mass of this swarming population lived, as it had always lived, in villages and in dire poverty according to Western standards, while, for all that war industries and banking had developed fast during the war, rising prices and the detachment of the rupee from the paper English pound bore hardly on the urban middle class from which extremists were drawn. Sporadic violence called forth the stringent Rowlatt Acts against which all sections of Indian politicians protested, and when the Moderates left Congress power passed to the Left under Mahatma Gandhi.

Gandhi, a baffling combination of the saintly ascetic and the astute party leader, wielded great moral and therefore political authority. Since his return home from South Africa in 1914, he had preached a quietist non-violence inspired by the Sermon on the Mount, communal harmony, and the removal of the stigma of untouchability from the fifty millions of no-caste Hindus which he saw, as clearly as did Gokhale's devoted Servants of India, was a fatal bar to self-government. He further advocated the spinning and use of home-made cotton cloth to mark at once the revival of India's chief village industry and her revolt against the forces of the West. But Gandhi also taught non-violent civil disobedience to objectionable laws, and was soon to show that he was ready to risk starvation to enforce his will on the authorities or his own followers. The day was still far distant when he was to reject self-starvation as a form of violence; meanwhile, he proclaimed civil disobedience against the Rowlatt Acts and thus let violence loose in Delhi and several cities of the Punjab. The Government replied to force with force, as governments must; but at Amritsar one of its officers at the head of a party of Gurkhas broke the long British tradition of handling a dangerous situation with firm moderation. His drastic action shocked all Indians and most Englishmen, and killed Gandhi's sympathy for the British *Raj*.

Led by Gandhi, Congress set itself to clear the way for *swaraj* on Indian lines by wrecking the new constitution. At first it gained the support of many non-Congress swarajists, including Moslem

Leaguers who were alarmed by an Afghan invasion of that part of India in which their main strength lay, and pleased that the Mahatma was championing the Ottoman Caliph whose Empire was threatened with partition by some of the Western Powers. During the next few years, the Moslem League functioned as a detached wing of Congress. But then the scene changed. The Leaguers were reassured when the Afghan Amir was defeated and not unduly perturbed by his recognition as an independent King with the control of external policy that had been withheld from his predecessors since 1878. Gandhi was imprisoned for proclaiming civil disobedience against such laws as he might indicate; assaults by Moslem Moplahs on their Hindu neighbours in the Bombay area alienated Congress from militant Islam, and the abolition of the Caliphate by the Kemalist Turkish Government robbed the Moslems of their main justification for resistance to the authorities. League and Congress drifted apart. Henceforward the chief incentive to violence and obstacle to constitutional advance was to be the growing hostility between Hindus and Moslems.

Nevertheless the Montagu-Chelmsford reforms marched. The Congress Left boycotted the first elections in 1920 and thus gave the Moderates a clear field, and although they stood three years later with the avowed intention of sabotaging the constitution, they were able to do so only in two Provinces. Meanwhile India gained more and more control over her own destinies. Advance on the economic side was rapid. Customs duties had been low before the war and the duty on Lancashire cotton piece-goods had long been practically balanced by an unpopular excise. Some duties had risen to protective levels during the war, and when in 1921 India was given a high degree of fiscal autonomy, her Government swept away the last remnants of the cotton excise and embarked on a policy of protection. The consequent industrial expansion, in which up-to-date steel works and cotton mills found in nationalism a common ground with Gandhi's archaic spinning-wheel, was upheld by a great influx of gold. Much of this treasure went into women's ornaments or underground as was customary, but part poured into the coffers of the Imperial Bank of India and, later on, of the Reserve Bank which, as in some of the Dominions, was established on the United States model. Indians launched forth into insurance and accountancy; co-operative societies and trade unions sprang up; the habits of investment and, with the advent of the motor-car, of travel became widespread, and, just as Milner's agricultural reforms of 1901–05 were only now bearing fruit in South Africa, so Curzon's contemporary work now gave its full benefits to Indian cultivators. Another 20,000,000 souls were added to the population in a decade, and by 1931 India ranked among the eight leading industrial countries of the world. Inevitably socialism made headway among the peasants in some parts, and communism spread to Bombay mill-hands and Congress intellectuals.

The promised indianisation of the Services was made possible by the extension and reform of the Indian universities on the teaching and residential lines that were being followed in South Africa also, and by the zeal for education displayed by Provincial ministers and soldiers newly returned from Europe. From 1924 onwards some branches of the All-India Services were transferred to the Provinces which had long recruited none but Indians; others, and notably the Civil Service proper, were recruited in India and the United Kingdom on equal terms with the understanding that the Indian element should be steadily increased. Again, following the admission of Indian cadets to Sandhurst first and then Woolwich, Indian officers began to take their places on equal terms in regiments with proud records that had hitherto been officered only by Europeans. The proportion of British to Indian troops was reduced to the level of one to three and Indians were entrusted with field artillery for the first time since the Mutiny; in 1934 a military academy was opened at Dehra Dun near Delhi. Further, the nucleus of an Indian Navy was formed on Dominion lines, the most recent of the many naval forces to be maintained in Indian waters since the Company had launched its first little squadron in 1613, and soon Indians were manning a small but efficient Air Force.

In view of all this progress Indian nationalists made it a point of honour to enhance the prestige of their compatriots in other parts of the Empire. They had the satisfaction in 1920 of seeing the last of that system of recruiting coolies for work in British or other tropical colonies which had long been an affront to them, however differently it may have been regarded by the people most directly concerned. That done, they took up the cudgels on behalf of the Indians in South Africa and Kenya.

The Imperial Conference of 1918 had agreed that India was as much entitled as any Dominion to enact her own immigration laws, and that of 1921, South Africa alone dissenting, had resolved that

Indians domiciled overseas were entitled to full rights of citizenship. Australia, New Zealand and Canada could report to the Conference of 1923 that the comparatively few Indians within their borders had access to all rights, except the state franchise in Western Australia and the federal and provincial franchises in British Columbia. South Africa, on the contrary, pleaded that her limitations on Indians' right of entry, free movement, trading rights and, in most parts of the Union, the franchise also, were not due to colour prejudice but to fear of an economic danger which she was trying to mitigate by persuading her own Indians to go away to Mother India. So far from relaxing her precautions South Africa proposed presently to stiffen them.

At this stage the Indian Government succeeded in opening direct negotiations with the Union authorities. At a conference held appropriately in the old halfway house of Capetown, India and South Africa rediscovered one another after sixty years of severance by the Suez Canal. The Indian delegates were fain to admit that South Africans had a right to defend their Western standards of life against Indians, most of whom would have been Untouchables in the land of their birth or ancestry; the South Africans, realising that not all Indians were coolies or storekeepers, agreed that domiciled Indians who wished to rise to the Western standard must be helped to do so; both agreed to work together to make the repatriation scheme a success. The Government of India thereupon set up a precedent for direct communication between one overseas member of the Empire and another by sending Srinavasa Sastri to South Africa as its Agent, the first of an admirable succession of Hindu, Moslem and Christian representatives, who, if they could not solve the Union's Indian problem, did much to ease the strain for all concerned.

That strain had been accentuated during the nineteen-twenties by the course of events in East Africa. The mutual relations of the handfuls of Europeans and Indians in Uganda were friendly enough, and in Tanganyika also where the authorities were resolved that, so long as the mandate stood, government must be kept out of the hands of 'alien settlers of whatever nationality'. It was otherwise in neighbouring Kenya. There some 10,000 Europeans of British, South African and Australian origins, whose pioneers had come in 1902, were struggling with 25,000 Indian immigrants of slightly longer standing over the heads of 2,750,000 tribal Africans. The

Europeans, who had been reinforced by ex-officers after the War, had a thoroughly South African programme: the exclusion of Indians from the healthy Kenya Highlands which they held had been reserved to Europeans since 1906, a check on Indian immigration, and the residential and commercial segregation of Indians in the towns. The Government of India, on the other hand, called for the application of Tanganyikan principles to Kenya, while local Indians and their nationalist supporters in India itself clamoured for equal rights and, regardless of the communal representation that was the rule in India, demanded a common voters' roll.

The India and Colonial Offices proposed a compromise in 1922. The leaders of the settlers, vigorous, vocal and in some cases connected with high military, governmental and parliamentary circles in Great Britain, promptly sent a delegation to sympathetic South Africa, looked hopefully towards Southern Rhodesia which was on the point of receiving self-government, and, like 1914 Ulstermen or Jamaica loyalists of an earlier day, threatened to rebel to the strains of *Rule Britannia*. The uproar died down when a British cruiser dropped anchor in Kilindini harbour; but it was renewed in the following year by Indians and Europeans in chorus when the British Government proclaimed the self-evident truth that Kenya was an African territory and concluded therefore that 'the interests of the African natives must be paramount'.

The Kenya settlers could do little against this White Paper policy which won widespread approval among such British folk elsewhere as heard about it; but the central Indian legislature demanded strict reciprocity of rights between India and other parts of the Empire, while its delegates to the Imperial Conference of 1923 urged that surrender to the settlers would be a denial of all the liberal ideals avowed by British and Indian Governments for a hundred years past. In the end the British Government imposed a compromise. It confirmed the settlers' right to the Highlands, rejected immigration restrictions and urban segregation as negations of British policy, and empowered the Indians to elect five representatives to the Legislative Council, and the Arabs one, on separate rolls but with privileges equal to those of the eleven European members. Henceforward the Kenya Indians recognised that their best hope of escaping local European domination lay in supporting the White Paper policy, a policy that was ratified presently by a Royal

Commission, two more White Papers and a parliamentary Joint Committee.

As the tension slackened in Kenya and the Union, excitement rose once more in India. Now that the recent Service reforms had put responsible posts within easier reach of Indians, and experience had shown that the powers of Provincial ministries were real, party lines hardened. Hindus and Moslems fought the 1926 elections with bitterness and frequent violence, and Congressmen jammed the dyarchical machinery amid a turmoil of communal rioting. The British Government therefore decided to overhaul the constitution forthwith instead of waiting for the elapse of the prescribed ten years. The efforts of an Indian All-Parties Conference to draft a unitary Dominion constitution died away in face of demands by Congressmen for immediate independence and by Moslem Leaguers for a carefully guarded federal solution. This failure left the field clear for the Simon Commission, which, in spite of a Congress boycott, was able to present its massive report in 1930. The report was prefaced by an assurance from Lord Irwin, the Viceroy, that 'the natural issue' of India's constitutional progress implied by the promises of 1917 was the Dominion status that had since been defined by the Balfour Declaration.

Thereafter three successive British and Indian Round Table Conferences sat in London, against a background of intermittent civil disobedience in India, to debate the governance by themselves as far as possible of nearly one-fifth of the human race. It was a problem beside which those that had faced Anglo-Scottish unionists, American and French revolutionaries, and advocates of closer union in the Dominions had been clear and simple. Could India, with her manifold creeds, colours, languages and customs, operate the democratic parliamentary institutions which had been evolved gradually by more or less homogeneous societies and which could be wrecked in a week by litigiousness or a desire to 'save face'? As it was, no topic consumed more of the Conferences' time than the allocation to the minorities of seats in the projected legislatures. Could India discharge duties that had been taken as pre-requisites of self-government elsewhere: the defence of her long frontiers or the maintenance of order in a country in which communal passions were rising and troops at the disposal of Indian ministers would not be given credit for the Gallio-like impartiality that was the distinguishing mark of the easy-going

British soldier? Be that as it may the labours of the Conferences issued in a White Paper, which set out the British Government's proposals, and a declaration by Lord Willingdon, the new Viceroy, that all was intended to 'help forward India to the goal of absolute equality with the other Dominions in the Empire'.

There could be no doubt about India's advance in strength and status. Her representatives attended the Imperial Conference of 1930 and, at the Ottawa Conference of 1932, exchanged preferences with the United Kingdom, acquired a privileged position beside 'the other Dominions' in many parts of the dependent Empire, and were promised that the British Government would encourage its manufacturers to buy Indian raw cotton. India then came to terms with Japan over duties and quotas and, though she presently abandoned the disappointing Ottawa agreements, made some concession to the Lancashire cotton industry which had been hard hit by her high protective policy. But such enthusiasm as any of her politicians may have had for the new constitutional proposals was chilled by the Secretary of State's warning that Dominion status of the Statute of Westminster pattern was not 'the chief immediate end', and that these White Paper proposals contained merely 'the seeds of growth into Dominion status, assuming that the distinctive conditions that separate India from the rest of the Dominions are eventually removed'. Enthusiasm was killed by the transfer of the final discussions to a joint committee of those Houses which were indeed alone competent legally to pass the necessary Act but most of their very nature exclude Indian collaborators.

It was under these depressing conditions that the new Government of India Act received the Royal assent in 1935. The second and eighth parts of that Act provided for dyarchy at the centre as soon as a federation of the Provinces and Princely States had been achieved. As before the central legislature was to consist of two chambers. Most of the members of the Council of State were to be elected on a somewhat extended franchise, either directly by Hindu, Sikh and Moslem constituencies, or indirectly by colleges of representatives of the smaller communities in the Provincial legislatures. Six members, however, were to be appointed by the Governor-General; six seats were reserved for women, a convincing proof of the political awakening of India, and a number of seats were reserved for the depressed Hindu classes. Similar reservations were made for these Untouchables in the much larger Assembly, some of whose members were to be chosen by the elected members of the Provincial councils, others by colleges drawn from the representatives of the smaller communities in all those councils, others again by chambers of commerce and labour organisations. The Princes were to nominate representatives to both chambers.

The powers of this Central legislature were to be much the same as those of the Provincial councils under the Act of 1919. Defence, external affairs, the care of tribal areas and control of British chaplains were reserved to the Governor-General, but all the rest were to be entrusted to parliamentary ministers subject to the overriding powers of the Governor-General whenever his 'special responsibilities' were endangered. Such were to be the maintenance of public order and the credit of the federal Government, the protection of the rights of the Princes, minorities, public servants and British subjects domiciled in the United Kingdom, and, to the anger of the powerful industrialist wing of Congress, the prevention of discrimination against British or Burmese trade.

As in 1919, so now, the greatest constitutional advance in India was to be made in the Provinces. The rest of the new Act provided for almost complete responsible government on the British model in Bengal, Bihar, Assam, Madras, Bombay, the North-West Frontier Province, the Punjab, the Central Provinces, the United Provinces and the newly-created Provinces of Sind and Orissa, eleven in all. The franchise was to be so liberal that it would give the vote to one in every eleven of India's millions, and self-government was to be limited only by the rare exercise of the Governor's 'emergency powers' in defence of his 'special responsibilities' for public order, the welfare of minorities and so forth.

· The projected federation was to be confined to India proper; it was to include neither far-away Aden, which was to become a Crown colony, nor alien Burma. The ending of Burma's fortuitous connection with India was long overdue, for not only was the country cut off from India by mountains and dense jungle but fully two-thirds of its 15,000,000 inhabitants were Burmese, different from Indians in race, language, traditions and interests, and a still higher proportion of them Buddhists, innocent of caste and *purdah*. Burma was to be given a system of government similar in some respects to that which the Indian Provinces were to have under the new Act and in others to that which they had had under the Act of 1919, for though most of the departments were to be entrusted to ministers drawn from and responsible to a bicameral legislature, the Governor was to take charge of defence, some aspects of external affairs and the like, and to have power to defend his 'special responsibilities' in other directions. Half of the Senate was to be nominated and the other half elected by the Lower House on a system of proportional representation, while two-thirds of the House of Representatives was to be elected on a wide franchise, either by local constituencies or by constituencies representing minorities, chambers of commerce or industry, and the University of Rangoon. The Secretary of State for India was to be also Secretary of State for Burma.

The sections of the Government of India Act which dealt with Provincial reforms, and the separation of Aden and Burma from India, came into force in April 1937. The Constitution made a bad start, for, as at the elections of 1923, Congress instructed its representatives to wreck it from within. Congressmen carried the day in Bombay, Madras, the United Provinces, the Central Provinces, Bihar and Orissa, and promptly refused to form ministries unless the Governors promised that their special powers should remain in virtual abeyance. In the end, however, realising that the stop-gap ministries were working unexpectedly well and that its own supporters were impatient for the execution of the advanced social and economic programme they had been promised, Congress allowed its members to take office in those six Provinces, and in the North-West Frontier Province also, though without disavowing its hostility to the constitution.

Ministers everywhere had to face great difficulties, for times were not good. The population was surging up towards the 390,000,000 mark at the rate of five millions a year; trade returns were falling so fast that Congress demanded that the rupee should go back from 1s. 6d. to its traditional level of 1s. 4d.; the peasants in many parts were restive and serious strikes were taking place in Bengal, Madras, Cawnpore and elsewhere where conditions in some of the new Indian-owned factories were bad. On the other hand office brought to Congressmen, as it usually does, the sobering sense of responsibility. Ministers found that their powers were real and, to the surprise of some of them, that British officials rendered them their traditional loyal service. Gandhi's moderating influence resolved constitutional crises in Bihar and the United Provinces; Congress ministers soon made it clear that they would have none of the

M

violence that had proved so embarrassing to the British *Raj*; both they and their non-Congress fellows busied themselves with the peasant and his eternal debts, village education, medical relief and the needs of the workers in the crowded industrial towns. Bengal even instituted an inquiry, presided over by an Englishman, into Cornwallis's rigid land settlement of 1790 on which its taxing system and much of its social structure still rested.

While self-government was thus taking shape in the Provinces, the Central Government had to be content with the old allocation of powers. The machinery of 1919 worked well enough as a rule, though the Congress majority did oblige the Governor to 'certify' the Budget of 1938 whose largest item was, as usual, military expenditure. But the central legislature must continue in its half-fledged state until an All-India Federation had come into being, and the obstacles in the way of that were formidable.

Like de Valera's followers in Ireland, Congressmen now regarded Dominion status under the protecting shadow of British imperialism as unworthy of a great nation; they had no mind to see India 'a hanger-on of semi-colonial status'. Many of them from Gandhi downwards knew that India was not yet well enough compacted to take over from the British or provide for her own defence; nevertheless Congress claimed independence, *purna swaraj*, as an abstract right, demanded the withdrawal of the new constitution as a fatal bar to that objective, and insisted that, if only the British would take a risk and trust an All-India constituent assembly, communal differences would fade away and India *faro da se*.

The anxious British could not share this optimistic view, especially as Congress could find no room for them, whose responsibilities were admittedly so great, in a constituent assembly dominated by itself. The Princes entertained no doubt on this score. Their Chamber, from which, however, some rulers, including the powerful Nizam of Hyderabad, still held aloof, approved cautiously of Dominion status, but declined to accept federation on the terms proposed. A few of the Princes effected reforms which went some way towards meeting the reasonable objection of Congress that autocratic states would be uneasy partners of parliamentary Provinces; but more of them showed anger at the invasion of their States by Congress enthusiasts and the agitation by local organisations for which Congress disclaimed all responsibility. For the rest the Princes, whether Hindu or Moslem, showed themselves determined to maintain their status, and opposed Congress's demand for an All-India constituent assembly which would put their States at the mercy of the politicians of the Provinces.

The Congress Left insisted that the Princes were mere creations of the British and accused the British of using them to bar India's constitutional progress; but the facts which the British had to face were that the Princes ruled fully three-eighths of the territory of the projected federation, and that some of them were bound to the King-Emperor by treaties that were much older than Congress itself and still older than the reforms of 1909 that had set India on the road to parliamentary government. Moreover the struggle was not between the Princes and themselves on the one hand and the Provinces on the other, since the politicians and the electorates of the Provinces were not at one.

There had been a time before the foundation of the Moslem League and the withdrawal of the Moderates when Congress could claim justly to speak for all politically-minded Indians. It still counted a considerable number of Moslems in its ranks, and, remembering past days and the great advance in status which India had made under its inspiration, clung to that claim. No one denied that Congress still constituted the largest, most highly organised, and, thanks to its newspapers, the most influential party in India; but the British could not ignore the fact that other parties insisted on being heard and had a right to be heard. The old Congress right wing, organised now as the National Liberal Federation, repudiated Congress leadership and was not ill disposed towards Dominion status; the ultra-Hindu *Mahasabha* took much the same line and was even ready to consider federation; in the background stood the Bombay Independent Labour Party, whose leader, Dr. Ambedkar, was also the organiser of the millions of Hindu Untouchables and, as such, doggedly resolved not to be subjected to the caste Hindus of Congress. Moreover there were renewed signs of a split in Congress itself. There the section led by Gandhi and the cultured, amiable and implacable Jawarharlal Nehru was challenged by the extremist Subhas Bose, the vigorous leader of a *bloc* which contained many socialists and communists, the would-be ally of the Bombay I.L.P. and the Moslem League.

But, when all is said, no cleavage in Indian life goes deeper than that between Moslem and Hindu with their radically different philosophies. Already in 1933, while the Round Table Conferences were in session, Moslem enthusiasts had banded themselves together to fight the alleged 'Anglo-Hindu *entente*', convert the 90,000,000 Moslems of India to the belief that they formed a distinct nation, and achieve the recognition of their land of Pakistan as a separate southern Asiatic state; that is, the Provinces of the Punjab, Sind and the North-West Frontier and the Administered Province and States of Baluchistan and Kashmir, all of which contained Moslem majorities and all of which lay adjacent to independent Moslem Afghanistan and Persia.

The new Provincial system of rule deepened this Hindu-Moslem cleavage dangerously. Hindus and Sikhs criticised bitterly the Moslem ministries in the Punjab and Bengal; Moslems in the seven Congress Provinces made the most of such grievances as they had, though to be sure no Governor was obliged to use his special powers in defence of a minority, while the champions of Pakistan were encouraged by the separation of Burma from India to claim as theirs Bengal, with its considerable Moslem majority, and also Assam at the further end of the Ganges plain. Congress and the Moslem League failed to come to terms early in 1938, and the *Mahasabha's* pungent criticism of this abortive pacification convinced the League that orthodox Hinduism's hostility to Islam was indeed implacable. A year later, therefore, the League was demanding home rule for the predominantly Moslem Provinces. Presently it was talking of independence for a Pakistan that might be linked perhaps in some federal relation with the rest of India, and condemning democratic institutions which must subject all minorities to Hindu domination. And this the Leaguers would not stomach, they whose people had ruled most of India for five hundred years before the British supplanted them.

The British could not admit the claim of the League's President, Mohammed Jinnah, that it spoke for all Moslems, for, quite apart from the Moslem members of Congress, there were various Moslem organisations independent of it. But it was their chief spokesman and, in any event, the mere counting of party members led nowhere. What the British had to reckon with were masses of humbler folk who could be stirred to furious action by the cry of 'Hinduism defiled' or 'Islam in danger'. Meanwhile Congress accused them, whose chief dread was communal arson and bloodshed, of inflaming communal differences so that they might divide and rule, and even asserted that there had been nothing of the kind worth mentioning before they had stepped into the shoes of the Great Mogul.

The element of truth in this version of India's troubled history was that, as in Palestine, communal differences had been inflamed by the prospect of self-government. Submission to a neutral and irremovable executive is one thing for a minority, obedience to ministers responsible to a popularly elected legislature quite another. Self-government has always called forth party strife, and parties in India had been formed inevitably on religious lines. The tragedy for the British, who with all their faults have understood political give-and-take better than most men, was that both the Moslem League and the predominantly Hindu Congress had a case and yet neither seemed able to meet the other even half-way. Had the struggle been, as Congress always tried to show it was, a straight fight between Indians and themselves with their gift for compromise, the solution might not have been difficult. As it was, the real issue lay between Indian and Indian. All the British could do was to effect a few changes in the central Government preparatory to federation, and urge all parties as earnestly as did Mahatma Gandhi himself to compose their communal quarrels and thus clear the way for further constitutional advance.

IX

COLONIES, PROTECTORATES AND MANDATED TERRITORIES, 1914–1942

PROBLEMS which faced the British in India were repeated on a smaller scale in those many parts of the dependent Empire that contained men of two or more races with different social systems and traditions. The situation was complicated in some of these by the fact that they were neither Crown colonies nor protectorates but mandated territories held under the supervision of the League of Nations.

The 'mandate' sprang from the idea of trusteeship. Its essence was a promise given publicly to administer a territory in the interests of the native inhabitants and of the commercial interests of at least a greater or smaller portion of the rest of the world, a specific undertaking to adopt within limits Great Britain's traditional liberal and free trade policy. That policy had been accepted in principle by the Berlin and Brussels Conferences of 1884–85 and 1890–92 whose Acts bound the signatories to prevent war, maintain equal rights of trade and navigation, and advance civilisation in a great part of tropical Africa for the benefit of Africans and Europeans alike; it was sponsored by the Fabians in the eighteen-nineties, practised by Lugard in Nigeria during the following decade, and expounded by him in detail soon after the close of the war of 1914–18. Lugard's doctrine of the Dual Mandate taught that the world had a right of access to the products and markets of tropical lands, and that the inhabitants of those lands in their turn had a right to an explanation of the new forces that were rushing in upon them, help in standing up to them, and means to provide the schools, roads and health services without which mere peace and security could avail them little.

The beginnings of the mandate machinery of government were contained in the Act of the Berlin Conference which handed over the Congo Free State to Leopold II and his associates as a trust and not as a downright possession. It was sketched more fully in 1906, when the United States, which had recently extended its guardianship over the new Republic of Cuba, proposed in vain at the Algeciras Conference of the Powers that Morocco should be mandated jointly to France and Spain who would render periodical accounts of their stewardship to Italy. The full mandate machinery, in whose planning General Smuts played a leading part, was only set up at the close of the Kaiser's War for the governance of certain ex-enemy territories.

The mandate system was embodied in three groups of documents. First, two conventions which took over the main clauses and the substance of the Berlin and Brussels Acts. These conventions bound the signatories of the League Covenant to maintain in the territories covered by those Acts sufficient authority to ensure safety of person, property, trade and transit, to further 'the moral and material well-being' of the natives, and to refer disputes to arbitration. Secondly, article XXII of the Covenant. This article affirmed that 'the well-being and development' of peoples who were 'not yet able to stand by themselves under the strenuous conditions of the modern world . . . form a sacred trust of civilisation'; it extended the principles of the two new conventions to mandated territories in tropical Africa, though by no means so fully to those elsewhere, and bade the Mandatory Powers render an annual report to a commission of the League Council. Thirdly, the actual mandates which were drafted in detail and at leisure by a committee presided over by Lord Milner amid such inter-allied bickerings and pertinacious questions by the United States that the first of them could only be issued in August 1922.

These mandates were grouped in three classes. Class A covered the ex-Ottoman Arab provinces of Syria and Southern Iraq (Mesopotamia) whose independence was provisionally recognised subject to the compelling kind of 'administrative advice and assistance' that Great Britain had given to Malayan sultans since 1874 and Egyptian Khedives since 1882. Monopolistic concessions were forbidden except where necessary for revenue purposes, but no further provision was made for the commercial open door. Great Britain, however, presently agreed to leave the door into her Class A mandated territories open to League members and Associated Powers.

Class B covered the ex-German tropical colonies. These mandates were the most comprehensive of all and could only be altered by a revision of the Covenant. They reaffirmed the principle of trusteeship, guaranteed the open door to League members and Associated Powers, and, bearing in mind one of the chief reasons given for depriving militarist Germany of her colonies, forbade the mandatories to erect fortifications, military stations or naval bases, or to train natives as soldiers except for the policing and defence of the territories. To be sure the French mandates left loopholes through which black warriors could be thrust for service beyond the frontiers, but in the event France never made use of them.

Finally, Class C covered Germany's Pacific Islands, which had been captured by Australia, New Zealand and Japan, and South-West Africa conquered by the neighbouring Union. These three Dominions and Japan had hoped that they would be allowed to annex their respective acquisitions outright; but after much argument at Versailles they had accepted them under mandates which, as Smuts said frankly, came as near to annexation as made no difference. Subject to the safeguards prescribed by the Class B mandates in the interests of the indigenous populations and the duty of reporting annually, the mandatories were free to rule their dependencies as 'integral portions' of their own territories and, since there was no mention of the open door, apply to them their more or less exclusive fiscal policies.

The weaknesses of the mandate system were manifest. The conception was new in international law; the title was long regarded as precarious; the national status of the inhabitants was uncertain, for it was hard to say where if anywhere sovereignty resided; above all, as in the ominous precedent of Leopold's Congo Free State, the fulfilment of pledges depended on the goodwill and good faith of the Mandatory Powers. Hence every effort was made to focus world opinion on the working of the system. After acceptance at the hands of the Allied and Associated Powers each mandate was debated by the League Assembly and endorsed by the Council, thus ensuring that the fifty governments which signed the Covenant affirmed the principle of trusteeship. Thereafter, year by year, the permanent and expert Mandates Commission of the League Council discussed the mandatories' reports in public and built up an imposing store of information and precedent. Presently the Commissioners' hands were strengthened by British authorities, who proclaimed that the principles of trusteeship held good for their African colonies and Protectorates as well as for the mandated territories,[1] and, recalling the hopes of Munro and Fowell Buxton, Henry Lawrence, Earl Grey and the West African commissioners of 1865, proposed 'gradually to train the people so that, however long it might take, they would be able one day to stand by themselves'.[2]

Great Britain alone of the members of the Commonwealth received mandates in the first two classes. Her Class A mandates, combined with war-time extensions of authority, gave her a potentially much stronger position in the Near and Middle East than ever before. Prior to 1914 her foothold in the Mediterranean had been confined to the fortresses of Gibraltar and Malta, the island of Cyprus which she administered nominally on behalf of the Turkish Sultan, and Egypt which she controlled through the Khedive who was himself a Turkish vassal. When Turkey joined the Central Powers the Ottoman suzerainty lapsed and Britain ruled Cyprus as a Protectorate and Egypt as a protected State. On the conclusion of peace she received mandates for Palestine, Transjordan and Southern Iraq.

This accession of power brought with it, however, grave difficulties. The shock of war had hastened the awakening of the Moslem world and stimulated nationalism not only among the defeated Turks but among the Arabs, some of whom had fought beside the Allies. Egyptian nationalists greeted the peace with riot and bloodshed because it did not bring them the independence they had done little enough to earn. They welcomed indeed the recognition of their country in 1922 as an independent kingdom under a constitutional monarch and a ministry responsible to a bicameral legislature on approved British lines; but they refused to accept the reservations which the British insisted on for Egypt's safety and their own: that is, the retention of British troops at vital points in the Nile valley and on the Suez Canal, the continuation of the old Ottoman capitulations and the mixed courts which protected foreigners and minorities, and the maintenance of the Anglo-Egyptian condominium over the Sudan. Nationalist violence was not checked substantially until 1925 and, even so, prevented the Egyptian Government from signing the treaty of perpetual alliance which Great Britain proposed five years later.

The Italian conquest of Abyssinia, with its implied threat to the Sudan and the sources of the Nile, convinced the Cairo authorities

[1] Kenya White Paper, 1923.   [2] Sir Donald Cameron in Nigeria, 1931.

at last that it would be wise to make friends with the British betimes. Hence, in terms of the treaty of 1936, Great Britain withdrew her garrison from the Nile valley and, to the fury of the French, used her influence successfully to ensure that the capitulations and the mixed courts should disappear within the next few years. But she kept her troops on the Suez canal until Egypt could provide for its defence against all comers, made herself responsible for the equipment and training of the Egyptian army, retained her share of the condominium over the Sudan, and was promised the use of Egyptian ports, aerodromes and communications in time of emergency.

The situation farther east was more complicated. During the war those Arabs who rallied to the ruler of the Hedjaz, whose capital was Mecca, had been led to expect the creation of a great Arab state from which the British proposed to withhold the coastal belt of northern Syria desired by France, and also, though with a lamentable lack of precise definition, that of southern Syria in part of which they presently promised the Zionists a Jewish National Home. There was a moment in 1919 when a general settlement seemed possible, for the Hedjaz was recognised as an independent State, and its representative, the Emir Feisal, agreed with Dr. Weizmann, the able leader of the Zionists, that Palestine should be set aside for special treatment provided the other Arab States received their independence. French and British claims to northern Syria and southern Iraq barred that solution and, to make matters worse, little heed was paid to article twelve of the Covenant which demanded that the wishes of the inhabitants should be a 'principal consideration in the selection of the Mandatory'. When, in 1920, Feisal was hailed as King of Syria and Palestine, the French drove him out of Damascus and the British suppressed a sympathetic rising in Iraq. In the end Feisal became King of Iraq with the British in military occupation to keep out the Kemalist Turks, while his brother became Emir of Transjordan, the one Arab state in which there was no fighting.

In the event neither Iraq nor Transjordan were subjected to a formal British mandate. The demand for independence was so strong in Iraq, even among Christians and Jews, that in 1924 Great Britain persuaded the League to accept a treaty which gave her control of Iraq's foreign policy and bound the Iraqi Government to do on British advice all that she herself would have done as mandatory. A representative Iraqi Constituent Assembly then imitated Egypt's example by instituting parliamentary rule. In 1928 a similar treaty was concluded with Transjordan whose Emir created a legislature with a strong elective majority.

Meanwhile, in 1925, the French had crushed a Syrian rising by bombarding Damascus, and Ibn Saud, the Puritan Wahabi ruler, had seized the Hedjaz with its Holy Places and brought most of Arabia under his sway. The British dissuaded Iraq and Transjordan from going to war to recover the Hedjaz, and then, having secured the oil-bearing Mosul area for Iraq by treaty with the Turks, signed a new treaty with King Feisal in 1930, the year of the abortive Egyptian treaty. Iraq became the ally of Great Britain for twenty-five years and promised to give British troops every facility in war-time, while Great Britain withdrew her garrison, except from one air-base near Baghdad and another near the port of Basra, and in 1932 secured Iraq's admission to the League. Thereafter Iraq rose rapidly in international status; in 1934 her ruler made a pact of Moslem brotherhood with Saudi Arabia, in which Yemen was presently included, and three years later joined Turkey, Persia and Afghanistan in an alliance of the Northern Moslem Powers.

The rapid progress of Iraq and Transjordan embittered racial, political and religious strife in Palestine. That little country, about the size of Wales though with a much sparser population, was a Holy Land to Jews, Christians and Moslems. Whatever Great Britain did or did not do there as Christian mandatory was sure to be scrutinised jealously by the 46,000,000 of Arabs everywhere, perhaps also by the 200,000,000 Moslems who were spread out from the African West Coast by way of the Middle East and Northern India to Malaya, and certainly by millions of Jews powerful in finance and all the means of publicity the world over and nowhere more powerful than in the eastern United States, South Africa and Great Britain herself.

There had always been some Jews in Palestine and, between 1881 and 1918, thanks mainly to Tsarist and popular persecution their numbers had risen from 25,000 to some 55,000. The Zionists had now been promised a National Home on the understanding that this should not prejudice the civil and religious rights of non-Jewish communities in Palestine nor the status and rights of Jews in other lands. The success of the experiment depended, like parliamentary government, upon reasonably stable conditions and the 'wise moderation' of all concerned. Neither of those conditions was realised and, in the end, the three parties, British, Arab and Zionist, each with much right on its side, had drifted into deadlock.

The expressed fear of the Arabs was that they would be swamped in their own country; but though Jewish immigration was thus the focus of the quarrel, the issue was really political throughout. The Palestinian Arabs, backed by their fellows beyond the frontier, would not accept the National Home and greeted the first Jewish newcomers with rioting. Undismayed, the British in 1922 proposed to take the first step towards the self-government envisaged by the mandate by setting up a Legislative Council with a nominated un-official majority. The Arabs would have none of it, if only because the balance would have been held either by the Jewish or Christian representatives. The British therefore appointed a mere official Advisory Council, assimilated the administration to that of a Crown colony, and worked as best they might with various Jewish local authorities, including the Jewish Agency which organised the Zionist immigration, and with the Supreme Council which super-intended the Moslem courts under the presidency of a Mufti who had long been hostile to themselves but for whose peaceful replace-ment no machinery had been provided.

At the outset the British Government, and probably the Zionists also, had expected nothing more than a gradual influx of picked settlers whose economic activities would benefit the local Arabs and thus win their friendship. Zionist immigration, however, almost trebled the Jewish population during the first decade. And it was no ordinary immigration. Not only were the newcomers Europeans of all ranks of society who sorted ill with the conservative and for the most part backward Palestinian Arabs, but they had behind them the pious patriotism of a nation-church widely dispersed *in partibus* whose Zionist members were ready to sink money at very low rates of interest in agricultural, social and industrial undertakings in the Promised Land. No praise can be too high for the zeal with which the Zionists developed their National Home in all its parts from the new Hebrew University at Jerusalem downwards. Their capital and enterprise provided employment; the prices they paid for land, whether to peasants or to the wealthy and often absentee *effendi* who were the leaders of the anti-Jewish movement, were so good that few Arabs came forward when state relief was offered to those who had 'lost' their land to the newcomers; the Arab population, stationary or even decreasing elsewhere, increased in the neighbour-hood of Jewish settlements. But man, even in Palestine, does not live by bread alone. The Arab rank-and-file were convinced that they were being worsted economically; they and their leaders were offended by the flamboyance of some of the younger Zionists in their new-found freedom, alarmed at Zionist demands that Trans-jordan should be opened to Jewry as being part of the historic Palestine, and angered that the self-government which had been accorded to other Arab communities should be withheld from them because of the National Home. They did not fail to note that the Jews of Baghdad under the constitutional monarchy of Iraq had no desire to see a Zionist branch establishment in their city.

The Arabs rioted in 1928 and again in 1929; wherefore a Royal Commission recommended that immigration be controlled more strictly. Immigration did indeed slacken for a time, but the financial crash of 1931 and the accession to power in Germany of the bitterly anti-Semitic Nazis sent a stream of immigrants pouring into Pales-tine. At that the Arabs proclaimed non-co-operation with the British on Indian Congress lines and pressed their demand for in-dependence. To make the situation more difficult, the French in 1935 promised Syria and the Lebanon their independence at some future date. The harassed British Government then proposed to set up a Legislative Council with a non-official majority under a neutral president. This time the Arabs were inclined to agree, but the Jews, whose more ardent members were talking for the first time of a Jewish State, refused. This was the signal for a renewed Arab strike of such sustained violence that the British Government was obliged to interrupt its long overdue military and aerial re-organisation by sending strong reinforcements to its depleted garrison in Palestine.

Nothing but the persuasions of the neighbouring Arab rulers, a dangerous precedent, induced the Arabs to appear before the Royal Commission which followed hard on the heels of the troops. This Commission did not mince its words. It declared that many of the grievances on both sides had little substance, however sincerely they might be felt, and pronounced the mandate unworkable and self-government unattainable since neither the 400,000 Jews nor the 1,000,000 Arabs, Moslem and Christian, had 'any sense of service to a single state', nor were like to have while their rival youth move-ments and systems of education remained 'schools of nationalism'.

The commissioners therefore proposed partition as the only alternative to a régime of mere law and order that could lead nowhere and was as distasteful to the British public in Palestine as in Ireland. A British mandate was to cover small areas round the Holy Cities of Jerusalem and Bethlehem with the port of Jaffa, and also Nazareth and the shore of the Sea of Galilee; but a Jewish State was to include most of the plains and coastlands, and an Arab State, united with Transjordan, was to take in most of the steppe and hill country. Both States were to be bound to Great Britain by treaties on the Iraqi and Egyptian model and be admitted to the League of Nations.

Had partition been effected forthwith there might, at least, have been a chance of it becoming the basis of a federation with adjacent Arab states, including Syria and the Lebanon whenever the French should have given these their promised independence. In such a federation the Palestinian Arabs would have had no fear of being swamped and the Jews would have possessed a territory of their own, small indeed but with full international status, able to accommodate thousands more immigrants under the intensive development of which they had proved themselves capable, and admirably placed for business purposes on the bridge between East and West. Unhappily the British Government hesitated; Jewish and Arab antagonism flared up, and the civil war smouldered on in spite of repeated attempts at negotiation in which the Arab States and Egypt played their part. At last, in May 1939, the British Government announced its decision. Henceforward Jewish land purchase was to be confined to specified areas. A further 75,000 Jews were to be admitted during the next five years to bring their numbers up to 500,000 as against 1,000,000 Arabs, and within ten years a Palestinian State was to be set up with representative institutions, controlling its own immigration policy and bound to Great Britain by a treaty which should *inter alia* safeguard the Jewish National Home. It was a solution that satisfied no one.

Unlike the A mandates those of the B class created no difficulties for Great Britain. Rather did they clear away obstacles to good government by reuniting tribes and border districts which had been cut up by the partitioners of Africa. In West Africa Great Britain took over the strips of Togoland and the Cameroons that remained after French claims had been satisfied; in East Africa she took the main mass of Tanganyika (German East Africa), leaving the Ruanda and Urundi districts adjacent to the Congo under Belgian mandate and a tiny wedge in the south-east under Portuguese sovereignty. Presently, as they had promised, she and France compensated Italy in a measure for these additions to their African empires by rectifying her Libyan frontiers and transferring the Juba river valley from Kenya to Italian Somaliland. The British administered their strips of Togoland and the Cameroons as parts respectively of the adjacent Gold Coast and Nigeria except where the mandates forbade; Tanganyika they ruled on protectorate lines subject again to mandate pledges, and in 1926 gave it a legislature with a nominated minority which included two Indians but as yet no representative of the Bantu tribesmen.

Great Britain's share of the C mandates was trifling: a mere joint mandate with Australia and New Zealand for the tiny guano island of Nauru whose administration was repeatedly entrusted to the Canberra authorities. Australia, on the other hand, took over German New Guinea and the adjacent Bismarck and German Solomon Islands, while New Zealand received the two German Samoan islands. Both Dominions followed British methods of native administration, but whereas Australia achieved good results by employing specially trained officials, New Zealand relied too much on inexpert civil servants and was thus able to do far less for the listless Samoans. On the other hand, as early as 1920, New Zealand had already set up in her comparatively advanced dependency a legislature with an unofficial minority consisting of two elected Europeans and two nominated Samoans. It was only in 1932 that Australia ventured to create a somewhat similar legislature in New Guinea.

The Union received the mandate for South-West Africa, Germany's one more or less temperate zone colony. After one passage of arms with the Mandates Commission for its heavy-handed suppression of a Hottentot rising in 1922, it did something for the broken Herero clans in the south and applied, later on, an effective system of indirect rule to comparatively untouched Ovamboland in the semi-tropical north. But South Africa's main preoccupations were with the Europeans of the territory. Constitutional advance was fairly rapid, though political rights were given only to the white ten per cent of the mixed population of some 300,000 souls. Nearly half the exiguous German population had gone home voluntarily or otherwise at the close of the war, but the gap was more than filled by immigration from the Union and Portuguese West Africa, of Afrikanders for the most part. As soon as the formal mandate had been given municipal institutions and an Advisory Council were set up, and presently, by arrangement with the German Republic, nearly all the remaining German residents became British subjects.

The governmental machinery was elaborated. An Executive Committee was created consisting of the Administrator and four members chosen by the legislature as in each of the Union's Provinces; the Advisory Council became a second chamber manned by the Executive Committee members and three nominees, one of whom was to have the special knowledge of the wishes of the non-Europeans that had always been required of the four nominee 'native' Senators in the Union; a Legislative Council was formed with a two-thirds elective majority similar to those of the mid-Victorian Australian colonies and Natal. The powers of this government were however strictly limited. Its railway and customs policies were directed from Pretoria, and soon the mandated territory was so closely bound up with the Union, its sole money market, that General Hertzog could cause a stir at Geneva in the year of the Kellogg Pact by looking forward to the day when 'South-West' should become the fifth Province of the Union. For all that, during the nineteen-thirties, the South African authorities refused repeated requests by the majority of the South-West African electorate for admission to the Union, and contented themselves from 1936 onwards with checking more and more vigorously the disruptive manoeuvres with which the Nazis were soon to make Europe disastrously familiar.

Constitutional advances in most of the mandated territories were accompanied by similar developments in the Crown colonies and Protectorates, for the Imperial Government was bent more optimistically than ever on giving representative institutions wherever possible in this brave new world made safe for democracy. These changes were preceded in some cases by the formal annexation of protectorates: the Gilbert and Ellice Islands (1915), Kenya (1920), Southern Rhodesia (1923) and Cyprus (1925), annexations which gave these territories, among other advantages, the right to borrow on the favourable colonial terms that were denied to protectorates and mandated territories until the passing of the Colonial Development Act of 1929. The changes themselves were hastened by the knowledge recently gained, and chiefly in India, that possibly indifferent popular government gave more satisfaction than the finest administration by outsiders, and that risks must be run for the sake of political education.

One dependency was favoured above the rest. Post-war opinion in Southern Rhodesia turned decidedly against either a continuation of chartered rule, for which indeed the British South Africa Company was not anxious, or Crown colony rule as a possible alternative. A large majority of the voters also declared at a referendum against incorporation in the Union of South Africa which had hitherto been regarded as the Protectorate's manifest destiny. Hence, though it contained a mere 33,000 Europeans as against 770,000 Bantu, Southern Rhodesia was given self-government of the pre-Dominion kind in 1923, subject to imperial control exercised through the High Commissioner for South Africa over native policy and dealings with the Chartered Company and the privately-owned railways. The new government bought from the Crown the extensive unalienated lands and public works for rather less than half the amount that the Crown paid or remitted to the Company for past administrative and war expenditure, and presently bought out the Company's exclusive mineral rights and the railways. Power was given to create an Upper House, but Southern Rhodesia has been content hitherto with a single chamber Parliament, in which the first woman Member of Parliament in the overseas Empire took her seat in 1924, and with the non-racial franchise which it had inherited from the Cape Colony. For the rest Southern Rhodesia succeeded in eliminating the High Commissioner and some other formal controls in 1937. She thus secured freedom of action except for the reservation of laws differentiating against non-Europeans, a safeguard which may be little more than an imperial invitation to think twice before acting.

Other dependencies received a smaller measure of autonomy, for here the British Government was resolved to maintain real checks and balances and to reserve decisions in the last resort to executives responsible to the Secretary of State and the Westminster Parliament. The island fortress of Malta, for all that its population numbered less than a quarter of a million, was given a dyarchy on the new Indian model in 1921. Military matters were naturally reserved to the Governor, but all others were entrusted to ministers responsible to a bicameral legislature of the familiar British type.

N

Cyprus was given a legislature with an elective majority on its annexation as a colony in 1925, in line with the contemporary reforms in Egypt, Transjordan and Iraq; but here the three Moslem members could combine with the official *bloc* to outvote the twelve Greeks.

Meanwhile, in 1920, Ceylon had been given a legislature with a considerable majority elected, as in India, either by local constituencies or by various communities; but the fact that representatives of small non-Sinhalese groups held the balance caused dissatisfaction. Accordingly a much more liberal constitution was granted in 1931 with the avowed intention of breaking away from the separate voters' rolls which were sharpening communal enmities in India, Kenya and Cyprus. This Donoughmore Constitution was modelled on that of the London County Council whose 'subjects' were indeed more numerous than the inhabitants of Ceylon. Legislative and executive functions were combined in the hands of a Council of State consisting of the Governor, three Officers of State, eight nominees and fifty members elected on a common roll by adult suffrage. Each of the Officers of State presided over a department; seven ministers took charge of the committees into which the Council was divided for administrative purposes, while the Officers of State, without the power to vote, and the ministers together formed a Board of Ministers to advise the Governor. This novel constitution worked, though it must be confessed that some elections were stained with blood and the Sinhalese majority complained that its desires were thwarted by the extreme dispersion of powers and responsibilities.

Another group of dependencies was given an equal balance between officials and the rest, the Governor wielding a casting vote. Constitutions of this kind had been conferred upon Grenada, Trinidad-Tobago and the Straits Settlements by 1924, and in 1928 the colony of Lagos and the Southern Provinces of the Nigerian Protectorate, whose joint legislature had recently been given an elective minority, were given the equal balance together with power to control governmental expenditure in the Northern Provinces. An Advisory Council appeared in Northern Rhodesia in 1918, but made way for a Legislative Council with a minority of seven elective members on the termination of British South Africa Company rule in 1924. Then, in 1938, the elective members were given an equality with the official *bloc*, and two seats on the finance committee of the

Executive Council; a little later, when the Axis war had made the demand for copper insistent, three of them and an unofficial nominee were given seats on the Executive Council itself beside the Governor and four other officials. Thus this tropical protectorate, whose permanent European population was far smaller than that of Southern Rhodesia and its Bantu population markedly larger, had been put within measurable distance of responsible government.

In the sugar islands the general tendency was to raise all to the Jamaican level by reducing the size of the official *bloc*, increasing the strength of the elective members, giving the balance of voting power to the unofficial nominees, and empowering the Governor to override the majority only on questions of 'paramount importance' subject to confirmation by the Secretary of State. The old Dutch Courts of British Guiana, where the remnants of the Roman-Dutch civil law had made way for a local code in 1917, were superseded by a legislature of this kind in 1928. Thereafter political unrest bred of bad times and the recommendations of a Royal Commission hastened the process elsewhere. Between 1933 and 1937 constitutions of a similar kind were given to Mauritius and British Honduras, to each of the Windward Islands (Grenada, St. Lucia and St. Vincent), and to each of the Leeward Islands (Antigua, St. Kitts and Nevis, Dominica, and Montserrat) whose Governor and General Government already possessed overriding powers over island legislation. In 1940 Dominica was transferred to the Windward group and the powers of its Governor adjusted suitably.

Meanwhile, in 1938, the Imperial Government had decided that all literate colonial citizens throughout the Empire must be enfranchised in some way as soon as possible. Two years later yet another Royal Commission urged that, in view of the serious social disturbances that had broken out in many of the sugar islands during the past few years, 'more and not less participation by the people in the work of government is a real necessity for lasting social advancement'. The imperial authorities hesitated to yield to the growing demand in the West Indies for a nearer approach to self-government, nor had the Commission recommended this; but they did propose to give the elective members in Trinidad-Tobago an equality with the officials and unofficial nominees combined, and to double the number of the elective seats in Jamaica and replace that island's restricted franchise with the adult suffrage of Ceylon.

In some dependencies again the balance was tilted down, nicely but effectively, on the official side. This was the line taken in 1924–25 in Sierra Leone, the Gold Coast and Kenya. Considering the sparseness of the European population, the constitutional advance of Kenya was rapid. On the annexation of the territory in 1920 the coast strip, which had once been the domain of the Sultan of Zanzibar, became a Protectorate ruled by the Nairobi authorities. The settlers in the new colony, who had long been accustomed to send elective representatives to an informal council, were now empowered to elect eleven of their number to a Legislative Council. Five Indians and one Arab were elected in 1924 on communal rolls with privileges equal to those of the Europeans, but ten years were to pass before two Europeans were nominated to speak for the vast native majority. Meanwhile, in 1929, far-away Fiji had been given a similar legislature in which elective members represented the European and Indian communities and nominees the Fijian.

Yet other dependencies were promoted to the rank of those whose legislatures, like that of Nyasaland, contained a minority of unofficial nominees. Two Europeans and one Indian were nominated thus in Uganda in 1920; on the termination of the Zanzibar High Commissionership and Protectorate Council in 1926 similar provision was made for Zanzibar itself and adjacent Tanganyika, as well as for Turk's Island, Jamaica's little dependency. Next year a dozen nominees representing the Malayan, European, Chinese and Indian communities were added to the Federal Council of the Malay States, an example which was followed in due course by each of those States. In 1921 even the Solomon Islands and the tiny European community in Swaziland were given nominee Advisory Councils.

Finally, during the past thirty years, the tendency has been to give unofficial members, whether nominee or elective, seats upon the Executive Council. This policy has been carried furthest in Northern Rhodesia and Kenya where there is equality between the official and unofficial groups under the Governor, but it has been followed also in many West Indian colonies as well as in Tanganyika, Mauritius and Fiji.

On the other hand, just as the depressed West Indies had been 'reformed backwards' during later Victorian times, so during the black nineteen-thirties three members of the Empire were obliged to take lower places in the constitutional hierarchy. Disturbed Cyprus lost the elective majority which it had enjoyed for six years past and, in 1931, was placed under the control of its Governor. Next, the responsible government of Malta, never much of a reality owing to the power exercised by the military Governor, came to an end. It foundered in the storm that beat up when the small educated bourgeoisie, under Fascist inspiration, pressed the claims of the Italian language upon islanders who for the most part spoke Maltese or English. Suspended for a time in 1931 amid the distant rumblings of Papal thunder, the constitution was abrogated two years later when it was seen how ill the pro-Italian party took the introduction of Maltese into the courts alongside of English and Italian, and its substitution for Italian in the elementary schools. Finally, proudly insular Newfoundland was overwhelmed by the world depression at the end of a long period of maladministration which its small population and limited resources were unable to bear. It fell out of the ranks of the Dominions, and in 1934 submitted voluntarily to rule by a joint British and Newfoundland Commission.

Those parts of the Empire in which Lugard's system of indirect rule prevailed were gaining a firm foothold on the lower rungs of the constitutional ladder. The interlocking system of rule by British officials and native authorities within the framework of a single decentralised administration had been applied to the highly organised Yoruba chieftainships of south-western Nigeria during the war; thereafter it was extended gradually into the less promising parts of the Protectorate. The work called for endless tact and patience; but now that Lugard himself had expounded them, the principles were better understood and had the support of the new school of social anthropologists and educationalists who believed in building on familiar foundations, of the growing body of missionaries who held that a good African was worth more to the world than an imitation European, and of the League of Nations which stood for the self-determination of peoples and the mandatory programme of training 'backward' folk to stand upon their own feet.

Indirect rule began to spread beyond Nigeria. In 1925 Sir Donald Cameron went thence to Tanganyika after sixteen years' service under Lugard and worked most successfully through the surviving chiefs, revived chieftainships, or failing them, native courts. The system was adopted in whole or in part in the Southern Sudan,

Northern Rhodesia, Nyasaland, the Gold Coast, and Sierra Leone whence a Governor carried it to Kenya in 1931, the year in which Cameron returned to Nigeria to institute it in the difficult Ibo south-eastern districts of the Protectorate. Far to the south the Union of South Africa introduced it with success into still tribal Ovamboland, the northern half of its mandated territory, and grafted the revived chieftainship and some other features of indirect rule on to its own system of native administration. Southern Rhodesia, whose white population was much smaller relatively to the black than that of the Union and its tribes much less broken up, followed a similar course.

The South African and Southern Rhodesian Government, however, had to face the same fundamental difficulty. Both were parliamentary governments and, however zealously they might try to exercise trusteeship for their native majorities, both must conform in the long run to the wishes of their electorates. Voting power lay almost entirely in the hands of Europeans, male and female, whose feckless poorer members, in the Union especially, feared nothing so much as non-European competition. Indeed, experience proved everywhere that the more numerous and influential the European settlers the more difficult it was to maintain a system of indirect rule. Authorities from David Livingstone downwards have admitted that European example stimulated Africans, and employment by a good master civilised them rapidly; but the fact remained that tribal society tended to disintegrate in contact with western society even where every effort was made to preserve it, and went to pieces with disastrous speed wherever the European demand for native labour was compelling. Indirect rule checked his headlong dissolution and, in the many vast areas of Africa in which conditions were still favourable, gave Europeans and Africans time in which to work out a new order together. In short, its main justification was that it was transition rule.

Even so, indirect rule had grave weaknesses. There was little or no place in it for Africans who had broken away from tribalism; where the European population was numerous it tended to encourage the growth of two distinct societies within the same state, the white inevitably having the advantage over the black; there was a real danger lest chiefs, upheld by European authority and freed from normal tribal restraints, should become irresponsible despots; above all, there was no guarantee that what was essentially a form of local government as far as natives were concerned would issue in self-government. To all this the exponents of indirect rule could reply that it was for Europeans to absorb westernised Africans into their own political, economic and perhaps even social systems; that the cure for chiefly misdemeanours was time, experience, education and, in the last resort, deposition at the hands of the European suzerain; and finally that it was early days yet to say that so novel and elastic a system could go thus far and no further. All British history suggests that in such things there is no finality.

The policy of integration which characterised indirect rule in Africa was foreshadowed on a more ambitious scale in other parts of the Empire. The arguments for federating the numerous small West Indian islands were strong: administrative economy, the advantage of common legal and fiscal systems, the educative effect of membership of one large though dispersed community as against the cramping experience of insular segregation. But the obstacles were many: distance, lack of communications, varying island conditions, vested interests, local patriotisms, scarcity of white folk and a superabundance of poor, ignorant and prolific non-Europeans. A West Indian appeal court was indeed set up in 1920 for all the islands except Jamaica, far and away the largest of them; but it was only after the great slump of 1931 that closer political union was discussed seriously when the newly-founded West Indian National League talked hopefully of a federal Dominion and a Royal Commission also recommended federation, though on a much less exalted plane. Trinidad opposition killed this comprehensive scheme, and the Colonial Office shelved the Commission's alternative proposal that the Leeward and Windward groups at least should be federated in favour of granting more liberal institutions to each of these islands. The Royal Commission of 1939–40, however, suggested once more that the Leeward and Windward Islands be combined 'as a practical test of the advantages of federation'; meanwhile the islands were to be encouraged to co-operate as closely as possible and, in any event, organise a unified West Indian Civil Service.

Repeated attempts were also made to achieve closer union in Africa. The widely separated West African dependencies achieved nothing better than annual Conferences of their respective Governors from 1939 onwards, nor did the more ambitious contiguous territories of East, Central and Southern Africa achieve much more. The Tanganyika Mandate had looked forward to the day when that territory should form part of a customs, fiscal and administrative federation or even union with Kenya and Uganda. Economic problems presented no barrier because all three territories were covered by open door international treaties, and the fact that Great Britain lacked in Tanganyika the sovereignty she enjoyed elsewhere constituted no real difficulty. The chief obstacle to closer union was political: the refusal of the dominant section of the Kenya settlers to subscribe to the Tanganyikan and Imperial version of trusteeship for the native majority. Undaunted by their failure to secure an elective majority in the Nairobi legislature in 1924, their leaders began to talk of a white man's federation running southward from the frontiers of Abyssinia and the Sudan to those of the Union of South Africa.

It was an ambitious scheme. The little groups of Europeans scattered on the islands of high ground in those tropical regions constituted barely one per cent of the total population as compared with the five per cent of the West Indies, and a high proportion of them were officials, missionaries, employees on mines, plantations or mercantile ventures, and other birds of passage. Again, though the number of white children born in these territories was increasing, it was by no means certain (nor is it yet) that Europeans living so high up under the actinic rays of the tropical sun and far from the calming sea breezes could raise families healthy in mind, body and spirit, generation by generation. It was undoubtedly possible to keep physically fit with reasonable care; but the nervous strain was severe, and reliance on numerous and cheap African dependants did nothing to stimulate the mental activity or toughen the moral fibre of the young folk. Be that as it may, the settlers' dream of empire aroused little enthusiasm in the southern dependencies, while all that came of their alternative proposal for a federation of Kenya, Uganda and Tanganyika were periodic conferences of the three Governors and the creation of a permanent East African Secretariat at Nairobi.

The Hilton-Young Commission of 1929 suggested the appointment of a Governor-General or High Commissioner for the three East Africa territories, who should discharge on the spot many of the duties of the Secretary of State, and the co-ordination of various departments to pave the way for federation. The praise which that report bestowed on the Tanganyikan theory of trusteeship moved General Smuts, lecturing at Oxford, to call for a conference of the

governments of East, Central and Southern Africa, which, drawing
upon the Union's long experience, should show the Imperial
Government a more excellent way in lands that might take 'an
appreciable number' of Britain's people and provide work for many
who remained at home. The British Labour ministry replied by
reaffirming the Kenya White Paper policy of 1923. It declared
that it had long been 'an axiom of British policy and now embodied
in the Covenant of the League, that the well-being and development' of the native peoples in such territories formed 'a sacred trust
of civilisation', and intimated, in words reminiscent of those of the
Aborigines Committee of 1837, that however anxious it might be to
share that trust with local governments it was not prepared to devolve
it upon them.

This stout reply caused a stir in all 'White Africa' from Pretoria
to Nairobi. Northern Rhodesians and Nyasalanders talked of
federation with each other and even with Southern Rhodesia to
escape the White Paper policy; a Kenya deputation hurried to the
Union, where Transvaal Nationalists envisaged a Dixie line drawn
well to the north of the newly-discovered copper mines in Northern
Rhodesia, thus cutting off the colour-bar States of the south from
the White Paper dependencies of the north, and another sailed for
London where General Hertzog was attending the Imperial Conference. The South African Prime Minister, thus encouraged,
asserted publicly the Union's right as a Dominion to manage its
own affairs, and then asked that all the Governments concerned
should consult together before any of them adopted a native policy
that differed too much from South Africa's policy of segregation.
The British Government, however, anxious that none of these
governments should adopt policies that differed too markedly from
its own, decided after further inquiry that Uganda, Kenya and
Tanganyika should develop separately for some time to come.
Then, to secure departmental co-operation wherever possible, it
bade the three Governors to meet annually and, when desired, to
summon to their councils the Governors of Northern Rhodesia and
Nyasaland and the Resident at Zanzibar. In spite of occasional
protests it adhered doggedly to that policy throughout the darken-
ing nineteen-thirties.

Difference of opinion on Native policy, the fundamental problem
for Africa, had hitherto caused the British authorities to discoun-
tenance East African federation. It obliged them, also, to refuse

their sanction to proposals for the amalgamation of the Two Rhodesias either with or without neighbouring Nyasaland, and decline
to transfer to the Union the governance of the three High Commission territories of Basutoland, Swaziland and Bechuanaland for
which provision had been made in the South Africa Act of 1909.

The native policies of Union ministries had been spasmodically
restrictive from the first, like those of the Republics and Natal
in days gone by. Then, in 1925, Hertzog, as leader of a Nationalist-
Labour coalition, proposed a thorough-going scheme of native
segregation. He carried much of it through, but was unable to deal
with land tenure and political rights as he wished until he had made
sure of overwhelming British and Afrikander support by joining
hands with Smuts in 1933. The upshot was that by 1937 the native
two-thirds of the Union's population could acquire land only in
scattered areas, of varying value and density of prior occupation,
which might one day cover some $12\frac{1}{2}$ per cent of the country's
surface if all that was projected were made available to them. Elsewhere they must be either short-term labourers or rent-paying
tenants-at-will (squatters), or labour tenants paying for the land
they lived on by working for their landlords up to 180 days each
year. They could be shut out from the towns except as visitors or
employees; they were debarred from many skilled or semi-skilled
occupations, and obliged, in common with the mixed-breed
Coloured folk and Indians, to make way for subsidised Europeans
in many state and semi-public undertakings. The natives of the
Cape Province, who had enjoyed the full franchise since its inception in 1853, must be content to be represented in the House of
Assembly by three Europeans elected by them on a communal
roll, while the unenfranchised natives in all four Provinces could
elect indirectly four Europeans to sit in the Senate beside the four
others who had always been nominated to speak for them there.
These unenfranchised natives could also express their wishes through
an Advisory Council consisting of European officials and native
nominees and elective members.

When, therefore, the Union Government began in 1933 to press
seriously for the transfer of the three High Commission territories,
the British Government demurred, and all the more since the
Nationalists desired to apply a segregation policy systematically
to Coloured folk and Indians. The Union's request was supported
by most of the white settlers in the three Protectorates and men of

influence in Great Britain, but it was opposed by others of equal influence there and in South Africa and by the articulate portion of the local native populations. After one or two moments of strain the issue was shelved and, as in East Africa, the Protectorates and Union native administrations resolved to co-operate as far as might be.

Meanwhile self-governing Southern Rhodesia had adopted a native policy similar in many respects to that of South Africa. Her Government divided their ample lands between white and black, keeping the high and more developed parts within the white sphere. They proposed to reserve the towns, in principle at all events, skilled occupations, secondary industries, and certain lines of agriculture as far as possible, for Europeans; but apart from these limitations, they were ready to let the Bantu majority make its own way, or, as the Prime Minister, Dr. Godfrey Huggins put it, Whites and Blacks were to have full scope to rise, each in their own pyramid. It remained to be seen, however, whether the Blacks would ever share fully in the political control of their country, the power that really mattered.

Side by side with this policy of 'parallel development' the Rhodesian authorities launched a scheme of amalgamation with their neighbours other than the overwhelming Union. Incorporation with the South had long been taken as the obvious destiny of a colony which had been settled from that quarter mainly by men of British stock but by Afrikanders also, whose civil law was based on the Roman-Dutch law of the Cape Colony, whose appeals had lain first to the Cape Supreme Court and then to the Union's Appellate Division. Southern Rhodesia had also been a member of the South African customs union since 1903, and her railways were a continuation of the South African system; but, for all that, she had drifted away and in 1935 left the customs union. On the other hand, when amalgamation with Northern Rhodesia had been suggested in 1916 by the Chartered Company, it had been resisted by advocates of self-government who feared to see themselves swamped by 'the Black North'. Times had now changed; the rich copper belt was attracting Europeans to Northern Rhodesia and swelling that territory's revenues, and in 1935 Northern Rhodesian police had welcomed the help of Southern Rhodesian troopers in suppressing an African strike on some of the mines. Huggins therefore proposed the creation of 'a large economic unit' centring upon his colony, which should include on the one hand Nyasaland and Northern Rhodesia, and on the other the northern half of the British protectorate of Bechuanaland and perhaps a railway corridor through the Union's mandated territory of South-West Africa to Walvis Bay.

The core of the scheme was the amalgamation of all Northern Rhodesia with its southern neighbour or, at the very least, its high ground which carried the chief centres of settlement and the railway that served the copper mines before this should become a 'black railway' giving employment in responsible posts to Africans as in the Belgian Congo farther north. In response to Huggins's summons the elected member of Northern Rhodesia were returned on a federal platform and, early in 1936, while many Nyasalanders hoped for their own inclusion in a 'great white Dominion', representatives of the Two Rhodesias agreed upon a scheme of federation with the good wishes of some of the South African authorities. The British Government declined to have it so, though it agreed that the Two Rhodesias should have a joint Appeal Court as an alternative to the Union's Appellate Division. Then the party which had always favoured incorporation with the Union rallied in Southern Rhodesia, and the Northerners drew back now that their copper was booming in a rearming world and the British Government had promised their elected members more substantial powers. It was partly for these reasons, but mainly because the European settlers were so few and Southern Rhodesia's native policy too divergent from Great Britain's, that the Bledisloe Commission reported in 1939 in favour of the now usual departmental co-operation and against federation, at all events for the present.

This Commission's report was not the only reaffirmation of the traditional British policy, which, for all its failures and departures from principle, regarded Africans as potential citizens in no wise to be held back by artificial barriers. A Conservative spokesman of the Colonial Office, reviewing labour troubles in Trinidad, had declared recently that no British ministry could tolerate anything like the South African colour bar in a British colony. That assurance was repeated presently by a Labour successor. Commenting on renewed bloodstained strikes on some of the copper mines of Northern Rhodesia, whose settlement was complicated by the exclusive demands of white miners from the Union and elsewhere, he announced that the 'accepted policy' of the British Government was to give Africans in all the tropical dependencies 'opportunities to qualify for any employment for which they are capable and to supply the requisite educational training'.

The Imperial policy was thus opposed in principle to those of South Africa and Southern Rhodesia, which, tempered though they often were by human kindness on the one side and loyalty on the other, tended to regard natives primarily as a means for the support of European society. There is no space here to debate the rights and wrongs of either policy, but merely to note their difference in principle and to record that South Africa was extending her influence steadily into the British territories to the northward.

The Union resembled these territories in many ways, notably in her mixed population of Europeans, Coloured folk, Indians and natives. It was natural, therefore, for her to regard herself, and to be regarded, as the most fully developed member of a class whose example could be followed safely and profitably by the rest. In reality, her unlikeness to them was far greater than her likeness. South Africa had been founded in the days of Cromwell and now contained close upon 2,200,000 European inhabitants in the proportion of one white person to less than four others; her European society was permanent and highly articulated and, though life on the Transvaal High Veld without periodic visits to the coast was apt to leave its mark, nearly the whole of her territory lay in the south temperate zone. In contrast the British territories to the northward lay in the tropics. Their European societies, the oldest of them with barely half a century of history, were comparatively simple in form and much less deeply rooted than the Union's; above all there were in those territories in 1940 only some 120,000 white folk in the proportion of one to 150 others, surely an inadequate force of brains and experience to carry the weight of a sovereign Dominion.

The connection of the Union with the precariously poised white communities and changing African society of this vast tropical region had long been close and was becoming closer. Some of the original Kenya settlers, British and Afrikander, had come from South Africa, and there were men of South African origin in every territory in between. The Union was pushing her trade in those parts energetically; she had sent military aid by air to Northern Rhodesia during the copper belt strike of 1935 and, since the Abyssinian crisis of that year, had learnt to regard the equator as the line of her strategic frontier. In 1935 and again in 1936 international conferences on matters of common African concern met at Pretoria representing all the British Southern, Central and East African territories, Portuguese Angola and Mozambique, the Belgian Congo and French Madagascar. The day was not far distant when the Union, the strongest State in its own right in Africa, was to watch its soldiers, and Southern Rhodesians beside them, fight their way through Italian Abyssinia and look down upon the blue waters of the Mediterranean at the mouths of the Nile.

Southern Africans were destined to achieve those triumphs during the Axis War of 1939–45, a total war. Total war changes much, even men's opinions. Early in 1942 Smuts showed, not for the first time, that he was not too old to learn. Impressed by the mutual respect that had sprung up between white Union and black African troops in the north, and no less by the patent results of neglected native health, housing and nutrition nearer home; conscious doubtless also of the impossibility of manning the Union's expanding industries if the colour bar were maintained in all its rigidity, he declared that, since segregation had been tried and had failed, Europeans and Bantu must learn to 'live together in helpful harmony' and thus 'fashion a variegated but harmonious race pattern' in their common country. It was a pronouncement full of hope for Black Africa, and for an Imperial Government which might now look forward to help rather than hindrance in the handling of its native problem on the liberal lines to which it had been committed for more than a hundred years past.

X

OTTAWA AND COLONIAL WELFARE, 1915–1941

GREAT BRITAIN's liberal imperial policy, challenged from one side by the colour bar, was threatened from another by an economic doctrine that received its fullest expression in the Ottawa preferential agreements of 1932.

The origins of the Ottawa policy lay far back, but the agreements in which it was embodied arose immediately out of the campaign for the development of the Empire's resources that was set on foot in the middle of the war of 1914–18. One important aspect of this campaign was the attempted redistribution of the white man-power of the Empire. That man-power was most unevenly distributed; close on two-thirds of it was concentrated in the British Isles and nearly one-ninth in London alone. The British Government sought to redress the balance by reviving the schemes of assisted emigration that had worked such wonders during the middle decades of the nineteenth century, hoping thereby to relieve social stresses at home, give the Dominions populations adequate to their new international status, remove the reproach that the Commonwealth consisted largely of jealously guarded 'great open spaces', and, by reinforcing the British element overseas, strengthen the cultural and sentimental bonds of empire, 'ties, which, though light as air, are strong as links of iron'. At the close of the war, therefore, it gave ex-service men and women free passages to Kenya and the Dominions and then, in terms of the Empire Settlement Act of 1922, undertook to bear for fifteen years to come half the cost, not exceeding £3,000,000 in any one year, of public or private emigration schemes that had been arranged in concert with the Dominion authorities.

This policy of directed emigration could not achieve much in tropical and tribal Kenya; it was never applied to South Africa with its mixed non-European majority, which lived for the most part at a low economic level, and its many Afrikanders and Labour men who looked askance at all newcomers. Nor did it effect anything like what had been expected of it in Canada, Australia and New Zealand. Truth to tell, conditions were not favourable on either side of the ocean. In spite of the acute post-war depression, the dole made life in familiar home surroundings tolerable for countless potential emigrants, and admirable social services raised the standard of living nearer to the high Dominion level for many more; on the other hand, Dominions with social and economic troubles of their own were only ready to admit immigrants of a kind that the Mother Country could ill afford to lose and were apt to regard those who did come as unwelcome competitors. In the decade following the passing of the Settlement Act perhaps 1,000,000 souls left the United Kingdom for other parts of the Empire; but more than three-fifths of them went at their own charges, while another 300,000 paid their way to foreign parts. The British Government never had occasion to spend even half the sum allotted for assisted emigration in any one year. Moreover, some 610,000 souls came into the United Kingdom from Empire lands during this decade, and, with the onset of the great depression in the nineteen-thirties, the homeward flow far surpassed the movement outwards. The revised Settlement Act of 1937, whereunder the British Government undertook to pay up to three-quarters of the cost of voluntary emigration, thus remained little more than the expression of a hope.

The abandonment of free trade by the United Kingdom which accompanied these emigration projects was a product of the Kaiser's War. True, a beginning had been made in 1904 when an export duty was levied on Malayan tin that was to be smelted elsewhere than in the United Kingdom, Australia or Malaya itself; but the first serious departure was only made in 1915 by the imposition of protective duties on certain key industries. Since war breeds tariffs the British representatives at the Paris Economic Conference of 1916 virtually jettisoned free trade principles by agreeing to join with their allies in a post-war economic campaign against Germany as a retort for her schemes for an exclusive *Mitteleuropa* and its overseas adjuncts. By the end of the war a growing body of British politicians and their electors, confirmed in their opinions by the resolutions of the two Imperial War Conferences, envisaged an Empire self-sufficient in food supplies, raw materials and essential industries, which should serve its own members first, its allies and associates second, and the rest of the world last. In keeping with this conception export duties were levied on West African palm-kernels, Nigerian tin and Indian hides, and small preferences were given to the Dominions, the West Indies and some other colonies on articles that were already dutiable. Before long those colonies that were not forbidden to do so by open door treaties had responded to a compelling invitation to give preferences in return.

These small preferences affected less than six per cent of the trade of the dependencies concerned, while the hide export duty lapsed when India secured virtual fiscal autonomy and the Nigerian palm-kernel duty was suspended presently as bad business. At the Imperial Conference of 1923, however, the Conservative British ministry formed an Imperial Economic Committee, on which all the members of the Commonwealth except Canada co-operated, to gather information on Empire products and market prospects. It also offered substantial preferences to the Dominions. A short-lived Labour ministry declined to implement that offer, and though the Conservatives soon regained power they did not venture to levy the duties on staple food-stuffs which would alone give room for the preferences that Canada and Australia especially desired. They merely stabilised existing preferences and, in 1926, set up an Empire Marketing Board on which some of the Dominions accepted a half-hearted and non-contributory representation. Financed by the British taxpayer to a maximum of £1,000,000 annually, this board called upon the various publics of the Empire to 'buy British' in the widest sense of that comprehensive term. Nor did it call in vain.

Thus encouraged, British protectionists, led by the Empire Crusaders, dwelt on the advantages of the economic imperialism which most of Great Britain's rivals pursued as a matter of course. They urged that common allegiance to the Crown and such British sentiment as survived overseas must be reinforced by appeals to mutual economic advantage now that emigration was failing to strengthen markedly the cultural and social links of empire, and the Balfour Declaration of 1926 had shown that the political ties of the Commonwealth were of the most tenuous character. Point was given to these arguments by the pressure of foreign tariffs and the brusque treatment that many investors were receiving at the hands of their foreign debtors. British investors learned to place a higher value than ever on the Union Jack as the guarantor of their dividends and interest, a point of view that was embodied in the Colonial Development Act of 1929 which empowered the Treasury to make loans or even grants to dependencies, whether Crown

o

colonies, protectorates or mandated territories, for capital expenditure that might benefit British trade and manufacture.

Then came the Wall Street crash to be followed by a catastrophic fall in world prices of the primary products on which the Colonial Empire relied almost entirely and the Dominions only less so, the damming of the flow of commerce by governmental obstacles of every kind, and the dumping on the Empire and still more the British home markets of the surplus products of peoples whose currencies were depreciating rapidly. At once the Dominions felt the full weight of their heavy public debts and saw the maintenance of their high 'North American' standard of living for white men threatened. Led by Canada and Australia, whose tariffs already nearly reached the United States level, they called out for help. This time the resentful British hearkened. The new National ministry, whose Conservative majority was very ready to implement the policy that had been Joseph Chamberlain's, set up considerable tariffs, if only as a means of bargaining with single-minded neighbours, and extended imperial preferences on a large scale at the Ottawa Economic Conference of 1932.

The Ottawa policy was the child of compromise. The British hoped not only to sustain the economic framework of the Empire but to organise imperial trade in such a way that it would help to free the choked channels of world trade and thus conduce to political stability. In these aims they had the support of the Indians and South Africans. But the Canadians and Australians, whose demands were echoed more modestly by New Zealanders and Rhodesians, insisted that the main object must be the engrossing of the trade of the Empire by members of the Empire, and on the whole they had their way. Not that there was any question of Empire free trade, for that would have opened Dominion and Indian markets to the dreaded flood of British manufactures. Instead the United Kingdom, India, Southern Rhodesia and nearly all the Dominions signed bilateral agreements with one another, the common factor being the granting, over a period of years, of the same terms to all by the United Kingdom. Even the Irish came to terms with the Canadians. Nor were the dependencies forgotten. The British Government sought with considerable success to secure for them advantages in overseas Commonwealth markets similar to those which it was gaining for Great Britain. In return it invited those of them that were free to do so to give preferences to Great Britain,

and privileges to the other members of the Commonwealth similar
to those which it was itself according to them.

Two years later an addendum was made to the Ottawa agreements.
On imperial invitation once more, and frankly for the benefit of
British and Commonwealth manufacturers and workmen, those
dependencies that were not debarred by treaty applied quotas to all
foreign cottons and rayons in such a way as to penalise especially
the incredibly cheap Japanese textiles, while the West African
dependencies imposed quotas upon Japanese textiles alone, and even
Open Door East African territories substituted specific duties for
the old *ad valorem* rates as a measure of anti-Japanese protection.

Each of the parties to the Ottawa system benefited up to a point,
especially during the early years. British manufacturers gained
somewhat as against foreigners in Commonwealth markets, though
little enough against their highly protected local competitors.
Canada displaced the United States in a measure as purveyor of
agricultural produce to the United Kingdom, and welcomed to
her side of the Undefended Frontier branches of American firms
who were anxious to secure the imperial preferences. Australia,
who ranked next after South Africa and India as Britain's best
customer, and New Zealand, long accustomed to do most of her
business with the Mother Country, both found the British preference
a powerful aid in their effects to maintain solvency. That preference
was more than useful to South Africa in the disposal of her sugar
and, together with the Canadian preference, made possible her
modest maize export in face of Argentine competition; it was the
making of Southern Rhodesia's tobacco export, which soon became
second in value to her gold at a time when the Union was shutting
out Rhodesian tobacco in defence of her own growers. India also
was no loser in respect of favoured exports.

Further, all the members of the Commonwealth reaped benefits
from colonial preferences, though critics of the Ottawa policy were
soon noting drily that more than half of Great Britain's total
exports to dependencies went to those which gave her no advantage,
and that these same dependencies were those that took from her
more than they sent home. Many dependencies also benefited from
the preferences they received, especially those which, like the sugar
colonies, produced less than the Empire markets needed. It was no
matter for surprise that, once the Ottawa system had come into

play, the Empire Marketing Board, its warfare accomplished, ceased to function.

The root causes of the Empire's troubles, however, lay deep down beyond the reach of any such palliatives as the men of Ottawa could apply. It was no real help to have brought new trade into imperial channels if the total volume of world trade remained the same as before or even dwindled, for this meant merely that foreigners had less to spend on Empire products. The British soon remembered that the Empire was not enough, and one by one their Commonwealth partners made the same discovery. Dominions realised that the United Kingdom could not possibly consume their growing surplus of primary products, for not only were her people increasing in numbers more slowly than they once had done and eating withal less wheaten bread than their fathers, but they were even minded to protect their own farmers against external competition regardless of the flag under which it might originate.

Moreover the Dominions and India were no longer mere primary producers. India's industrial advance had been notable of late years. Canada also, after bitter experience of bumper harvests in an artificially impoverished world, was supplementing her wheat with gold, base metals, wood pulp, the tourist traffic, and manufactures based on the splendid hydro-electric power of Ontario. Australia had reinforced her wool latterly with wheat nourished on the Nauru phosphates, and South Africa was enjoying an envied prosperity on her swelling output of gold; but both were making significant moves towards industrialisation, while New Zealand, faithful still to her mutton and wool, was also paying attention to the claims of secondary industry. The Dominions and India desired therefore to traffic with all the world and found to their dismay that the rigid Ottawa agreements, together with the new British policy of protection, impeded world recovery and their own freedom of action.

The Commonwealth was soon edging away from Ottawa. Canada took the lead. Her new Liberal ministry under Mackenzie King signed an agreement in 1935 with the United States whose investments in the Dominion and purchases of Canadian products outstripped those of Great Britain herself. This agreement was presently given a wider scope, since Franklin Roosevelt's administration at Washington was set upon liberal courses, and was accompanied by others with various countries including Germany. India denounced her Ottawa agreements in 1936; an Anglo-Canadian agreement in the following year set Canada free to adjust her tariff as she wished; Australia presently secured a similar freedom and came to terms with Japan. At the Imperial Conference of 1937 it was the Dominions who demanded in chorus that everything possible be done to stimulate international trade 'as an essential step to political appeasement', while friendly citizens of the United States, fresh from their enthusiastic contemplation of the imperial pageantry that had attended the coronation of George VI, observed that possessions so vast as those of the British were justified only on condition that the commercial policy which governed them should be 'eminently liberal'. The British, thus encouraged but abstaining tactfully from the obvious *tu quoque*, did indeed join with the Dominions in extending modified Ottawa agreements for a further five years, but they also signed a commercial agreement with the United States for themselves and their Colonial Empire towards the close of 1938. That notable agreement could contain nothing revolutionary in view of the hold the high tariff parties still had at Washington, and in London also; but it was at least a sign that the two greatest industrial and commercial Powers in the world, Powers which had once upon a time formed parts of the same empire, were prepared to pursue a mutual 'good neighbour' trade policy.

The Ottawa policy had thus failed to draw closer the ties that held the states of the Commonwealth together; instead of goodwill it had bred questionings and consciousness of divergent interests. Meanwhile it had succeeded only too well in awakening discontent in parts of the Colonial Empire and jealousy in the other world. It could hardly have failed to do so, for it involved a denial of the two great principles that underlay the Dual Mandate.

By swinging to the open door that had led hitherto into large areas of the Colonial Empire the British had lost the right to claim that they were developing the whole of their 'imperial estate' in the interests of the world. Not that the Ottawa system applied to all the dependencies by any means. Aden, as an international entrepôt, gave no preferences; the Central and East African territories were debarred from doing so by the Congo treaties, the Conventions of 1919 and, in the case of Tanganyika, the mandate; apart from discrimination against certain Japanese products, the same held good of those West African and Sudanese territories that were covered either by mandate or the Anglo-French agreements of 1898–99, and were still held to be covered thus even after the French had denounced those agreements in 1938. On the other hand, all the other dependencies gave preferences in some shape or form, either on the low range of revenue duties which obtained in the military stations and entrepôts of Gibraltar, Hong Kong, Singapore and the isolated Falkland Islands, or on the extensive and fairly high tariffs which had long been the rule elsewhere in immature communities which found it hard to levy direct taxes. Nevertheless, though barely three per cent of Great Britain's total exports received these colonial tariff or quota favours, the principle of the thing outraged British Liberals, United States citizens and League economists and played straight into the hands of the so-called 'have-not' Powers.

It was useless for the British to point out to Germans, Italians, Japanese and, at one stage, Poles also that the value of colonies as sources of raw materials was overrated, since 97 per cent of the world's supply of commercially important products came from sovereign States. The reply was only too obvious, and, moreover, tropical dependencies such as Malaya, Cyprus, Nigeria and Northern Rhodesia did supply a high proportion of the raw materials for the vital electrical and armament industries. Nor did it avail to assure such peoples that the British dependencies were anxious to sell and free to do so on equal terms for all except for the export duties on tin. The 'have-not' Powers regarded a dependent empire as a prize, a *lebensraum*, and the Ottawa policy naturally suggested to them that the dominant parties in the British Commonwealth were beginning to take the same view. They were thus given an additional incentive to attempt the partition of the British Colonial Empire before it could be closed against them still further.

Again, the virtual taxation of colonial peoples for the benefit of self-governing communities, and without consent other than the acceptance of an imperial invitation which could hardly be refused, was not in keeping with the principle of trusteeship. Already in 1919 the unofficial members of the Gold Coast and the Nigerian legislatures had pointed this moral against the short-lived export duty on palm-kernels; now Ceylon obliged the imperial authorities to carry the Ottawa preferences over her head, and the free-trading Straits Settlements grudgingly made the smallest possible concessions. In 1934 again, the unofficial members of the Gold Coast and

Nigeria objected to the anti-Japanese measures, the Malayans protested vigorously, and the Sinhalese board of ministers not only left the British authorities to impose the measure as one of 'imperial significance' but were hardly dissuaded from cancelling the Ottawa preferences.

Nor, with all its dangers and drawbacks, did the Ottawa preferential policy bring prosperity to the Colonial Empire as a whole. British preferences could do little to help the West Indian or West African growers of cocoa and palm products whose surpluses far exceeded the British public's power of consumption, while dependencies such as Ceylon, Cyprus, the Caribbean colonies and Mauritius, Malaya, Nigeria and Northern Rhodesia derived less help from preferences than from international agreements which limited the output, and therefore raised the world prices, of their copper, rubber, sugar, tea and tin.

Such agreements were, however, hard to arrive at and maintain and could only be applied to a small range of products; of their very nature they revealed a trouble that was world-wide. The British dependencies were exposed to the same forces that were straining even the greatest of industrial communities and, with their comparatively simple societies and reliance on one or two staple export crops, were less fitted than they to withstand them. Abounding production had trebled the overseas trade of the British dependencies during the two decades that followed the Kaiser's War; but improving health services, and, in tropical Africa, the cessation of tribal wars and the slave trade had increased the number of hands ready to work and mouths to be fed, and the failure of the industrialised countries to consume the swelling surpluses sent prices down and down. Those industrialised countries that preferred butter to guns and had currencies acceptable beyond their own frontiers of course enjoyed colonial products at cheaper rates than ever before, whether they possessed colonies or not; but the effect on the colonies was disastrous. For all that the revenues of the British dependencies had increased sevenfold during the quarter of a century that preceded the great slump of 1931, official and private inquiries during the nineteen-thirties showed undeniably that the colonial peoples were not reaping the social and economic benefits that the imperial policy of trusteeship was intended to bring them.

The truth of these findings was confirmed from 1934 onwards by widespread unrest. There were native strikes accompanied by bloodshed on the rich Northern Rhodesian copper belt; a strike of Native small growers of cocoa on the Gold Coast against the stranglehold of European merchants who were at once the importers of necessities and sole organised buyers of the staple crop; frequent displays of resentment in Nyasaland and the East African territories against the practice borrowed from some of the Dominions of setting up semi-monopolistic boards, from which natives were excluded, for the marketing of cloves, cotton, coffee and tobacco; complaints of low and stationary wages on Malayan plantations, and continuous grumbling, punctuated by strikes and rioting, in Barbados, British Guiana, Jamaica, St. Kitts, St. Lucia, St. Vincent and Trinidad.

These untoward events were a shock to a Colonial Office which had not been unmindful of its duty as it had conceived it hitherto. On the other hand, that office was better fitted than before to deal with the problem, for not only was it learning to view the dependent Empire as a single whole now that Dominion affairs had been relegated to a separate office in 1925, but since the close of the war it had consolidated the various colonial services and linked up with them the little Dominions Office service in the South African High Commission territories. Its Colonial Service had now become virtually one organisation, from which only the Sudan Service stood apart under the Foreign Office, and was attracting and training the carefully selected type of man who would have entered the Indian Civil Service a generation earlier.

Again, the Colonial Secretary had put the pre-war boards, committees, and institutes on a more permanent footing and given them wider spheres of usefulness. Such were the Imperial Institute of Entomology, the Colonial Survey and Advisory Medical Committees, and the justly famous Imperial College of Tropical Agriculture in Trinidad which arose in 1921 on the foundations of Joseph Chamberlain's Imperial Department of Agriculture. A Mycological Institute financed by all the governments of the Empire was founded at Kew in 1920, and an Imperial Forestry Institute supported by those of the dependencies at Oxford in 1924, while in 1929 the Colonial Secretary appointed committees at headquarters on Colonial Education, Agriculture and Animal Health, and Colonial Development. He also called upon the British taxpayer during the nineteen-thirties to provide £12,000,000 to meet colonial deficits in addition to the large sums advanced to the bankrupt ex-Dominion of Newfoundland, while loans and grants amounting to £6,600,000 were authorised for capital expenditure on materially reproductive schemes under the Colonial Development Act. From 1937 onwards a growing body of labour legislation appeared in the statute books of the Mother Country and various dependencies.

The conclusions of the inquiries of the decade, which were summed up in Lord Hailey's *African Survey* and the report of the West India Royal Commission of 1939, were that much more must be done if the claim to trusteeship was to be substantiated. Two main facts emerged: first, the decay of the old Caribbean colonies and the backwardness of the much more recent African dependencies; secondly, the utter inadequacy of local revenues to finance social services and foster the agriculture by which nearly all these colonial peoples lived.

It followed that there must be a sustained effort to make fuller use of the land, encourage the production of food for local consumption in greater quantity and variety even if that meant a smaller exportable surplus of staple crops, vary the colonial economy and enhance colonial self-respect by developing secondary industries as in the Dominions and India, press on with the organisation of trade unions under reasonable control, and, above all, extend education, public health services, housing and the like. Then, since everybody's business is apt to be nobody's concern and colonial legislation may be influenced unduly by a few interested men who know enough of local conditions to beat down uninstructed opposition, suggestions were made that room be found in the House of Commons for colonial members. The West India Commission did not go as far as that, but it did propose the creation of a standing Parliamentary Committee on the Colonies, if possible including colonial representatives as associate members, and at the very least the devotion of more parliamentary time to colonial affairs. Lord Hailey, for his part, realising the need for full and accurate knowledge, pressed for systematic research into all that pertained to the tropical dependencies.

It remained to finance the projected reforms. Plainly, social services and the rest could not wait until improving agriculture and expanding secondary industries had provided the funds locally. Two sources of revenue, however, lay ready to hand: in Africa some of the colonies were rich in base or precious metals, and in London there was always the Chancellor of the Exchequer. Hailey showed that, though African mining companies were in many cases sending great sums overseas each year in dividends or British income tax payments through their London head offices, they were not contributing anything like their fair share to colonial revenue from what were, of their very nature, wasting colonial assets. With a passing commendation for the very substantial taxation which successive republican, Crown colony and Dominion administrations had levied upon the Transvaal gold mines, he declared roundly that 'the largest possible share of profits' from such mining ventures ought to be made available for African welfare. The West Indies Commission, having no minerals to fall back upon other than the asphalt and petroleum of Trinidad, recommended a modest imperial grant for twenty years under imperial control.

The British Government bettered its Commission's instruction by carrying the Colonial Development and Welfare Act of 1940. That Act wiped out £11,260,000 of colonial debt, including £5,500,000 owed by Kenya for the Uganda railway, and promised to the whole dependent Empire £5,500,000 annually for the next ten years to finance social and economic development and the research which should ensure progress along sound lines. Experience alone could show whether the time allowed was enough; it was certain that the sums allocated would have to be increased greatly as the work went on; but at all events the Act was a step in the right direction, a declaration that, even if dependencies were to be regarded as liabilities and not the assets they had once been esteemed, the burden must be shouldered, a recognition that an imperial people is responsible for more than the mere safety and orderly governance of those committed to its charge.

XI

DEFENCE AND FOREIGN POLICY, 1919–1939

THE Colonial Development and Welfare Act of 1940, based on the Report of the West India Royal Commission, was passed under the shadow of the most grievous threat to the safety of the British Isles since the days of the Spanish Armada. Something of the story of the drift to catastrophe, so sudden at the last, is told by the preoccupations of the Imperial Conferences of the nineteen-thirties. The first, in 1930, debated defence and foreign affairs at some length, but, in spite of the recent Wall Street crash, felt itself free to concentrate on the high constitutional problems arising from the Balfour Declaration. The second, at Ottawa in 1932, attended strictly to business and, disregarding the cloud small as a man's hand that hovered over Manchuria, disposed of foreign policy in a few minutes. The third, the Coronation Conference of 1937, surveying the ruins of the system of collective security, devoted its labours to problems of defence and foreign affairs. It was high time, for though the overhaul of armaments had begun before the Conference met, the forces and equipment of the Commonwealth were still at a dangerously low level.

The nations of the Commonwealth had made haste to lay their arms aside on the conclusion of peace in 1919. All of them disbanded masses of their land forces; the United Kingdom and Canada gave up conscription, and though New Zealand retained that system till 1930 and South Africa a modified form of it throughout, each member of the Commonwealth allowed its regular forces and militia to dwindle down even below their reduced paper strength. Nor, while business men were 'axing' Great Britain's once dominant Air Force, did the overseas peoples give much thought to aerial arrangements.

The most significant reduction, however, was that of the Empire's sea-power, which had reached its peak after the surrender of the German High Sea Fleet on the morrow of the armistice. The United Kingdom could hardly maintain indefinitely her huge wartime navy virtually single-handed, especially since the United

States and Japan were threatening to find an outlet for their un-expended warlike energies in a naval armaments race. She therefore tried to spread the burden; but though Canada, Australia and New Zealand accepted the gift of a few cruisers and light craft, Australia cut down her naval establishment on balance and joined with the other Dominions in rejecting Lord Jellicoe's scheme for an imperial Navy to which each Commonwealth government should contribute its quota.

The Imperial Conference of 1921 referred the full discussion of naval problems to an international conference which was to meet soon after at Washington. Meanwhile Great Britain loosened her hold on several parts of the Empire of high maritime importance. She had withdrawn her effective garrison from South Africa during the war, and now she abolished her South African command and handed over local War Office property to the Union. She also agreed that South Africa should divert to coastal defence the naval grant which the Cape Colony and Natal had made first in 1898 and, in line with the agreement she had made with Canada when she was withdrawing her troops from the naval bases of Halifax and Esqui-mault in 1905, stipulated only that the Royal Navy should have the use of the Simonstown dockyard in the Cape Peninsula under all circumstances. She then left a mere handful of marines at half-forgotten St. Helena, transferred the small naval station of Ascension to a cable company, and withdrew her troops from the Irish Free State except for maintenance parties at three harbours guarding the North Atlantic route whose use in time of war was reserved for the Navy by the Irish Treaty of 1921.

At the Washington Conference of 1922 Great Britain accepted parity in capital ships with the United States and a superiority of 5 to 3 over Japan and of 5 to 1.75 over France and Italy respectively. That agreement forced her to scrap on a large scale, obliged Australia to weaken her squadron still further and enabled Canada to reduce her squadron to a shadow. It also faced the Empire with the likeli-hood of trouble from jealous France and Italy in the Mediterranean, left Japan, for all her apparent inferiority, mistress of the Western Pacific, and shared Great Britain's control of the rest of the seven seas with the aloof and continentally-minded United States. At the same time the United States and Canada, supported more or less by South Africa, induced Great Britain to abandon her Japanese alliance against her own inclination and that of Australia and

New Zealand, and to substitute for it multilateral treaties regulating the affairs of China and the Western Pacific.

The Commonwealth displayed a greater awareness of naval possibilities during the middle 'twenties. Great Britain announced to the Imperial Conference of 1923 that she was resolved to build a naval base at Singapore now that her alliance with ambitious Japan was gone. New Zealand promised an annual contribution, an example which the Straits Settlements, the Malay Federated States and Hong Kong followed; but Australia and India merely approved the plan, South Africa objected, and Canada, withdrawn into North American seclusion, declined to express any opinion. In the course of the next year or two Australia and New Zealand at least modernised their depleted squadrons, and India began to make her Royal Indian Marine a fighting service once more; for the rest, the Conferences of 1923 and 1926 resolved that Commonwealth defence should be based on co-operation in the Joint Committee of Imperial Defence, similar systems of organisation, drill and, as far as possible, equipment, special attention to the air arm, the traditional provision of landward defence by each government for itself, and the maintenance of harbours which formed vital links in the chain of imperial maritime communications.

So it was planned and so it was done, leisurely and more or less, though to be sure South Africa went to Germany for some of her aeroplanes, and the Irish Free State preferred to have her officers trained in the congenial atmosphere of the United States and buy arms in non-British markets. The Conference of 1930 discussed defence and foreign affairs with some anxiety, as well it might; for the French, having reorganised their army and planned the fortified frontier Maginot Line, were at daggers drawn with Mussolini's Italy over naval parity in the Mediterranean, and their belated withdrawal from the Rhineland had been followed by sweeping Nazi victories at the German polls. Moreover, after some years of increasing friction, Great Britain had recently agreed with the United States and Japan on the tonnage of cruisers and other light craft which each might have for six years to come, an agreement which faced the United States with a considerable building programme if she was to reach the desired parity and left the Royal Navy deplorably short of means for the defence of Britain's long trade routes.

This diminution of British sea-power was accompanied by failure on the part of Commonwealth politicians and publics to provide betimes for the aerial and mechanised land warfare which had already been worked out in theory by their soldiers. Meanwhile, as the Balfour Declaration of 1926 had prophesied, the overseas members had drifted back to the pre-war practice of leaving the effective provision of defence to the British Government, which, financially embarrassed as it now was and committed to costly social services, could draw only on the resources of the United Kingdom. If the Foreign Secretary had been right when he told the Commons in Locarno days that it lay with the Empire, 'detached from Europe by its Dominions, linked to Europe by these islands', to say whether or no war should come again, this failure to live up to imperial responsibilities foreshadowed disaster to the world.

The advent of Hitler to power and the breakdown of the League's disarmament machinery, the withdrawal of Germany and Japan from Geneva, withdrawals for which Russia's entry could not compensate, and Japan's denunciation of the naval treaties at the first opportunity stirred the Commonwealth to tardy action. Australia and New Zealand began to strengthen their naval squadrons in 1934; they and South Africa drafted schemes for the reorganisation of their land forces; Australia laid the foundation of an Air Force and armament and aircraft industries, while South Africa took steps to improve Table Bay as the halfway house to India in default of Suez, financed a steel industry at Pretoria and gave up her mine-sweepers in favour of an Air Force that should support the Royal Navy offshore and help in the defence of the British and even foreign dependencies far to the northward. Then, early in 1935, Great Britain announced a tentative scheme of rearmament in reply to Hitler's re-establishment of military conscription. Canada alone, reassured perhaps by Hitler's promise to be content with a fleet about one-third the strength of Britain's, took no steps to restore her decayed defences in spite of a recent flight over her soil of Italian war-planes on their way to the Chicago World Fair.

The rearming of the Commonwealth failed to keep pace with the breakdown of the system of collective security. Early in 1936, in the confusion that accompanied the abandonment of the League's attempt to enforce sanctions against Italy for her assault upon Abyssinia, Hitler remilitarised the Rhineland and put the restoration of the colonies in the forefront of his programme. The war now moved from Africa into republican Spain and, before the close of the year, General Franco's German and

Italian abettors had formed the Berlin-Rome Axis and signed an anti-Comintern Pact with Japan. Presently Kemalist Turkey, noting the way the wind was blowing, obtained permission from the dying League to fortify the Straits, and in the background Japan set out to conquer China.

Nevertheless, in spite of everything, the Imperial Conference of 1937 failed to frame a common plan of defence. The Irish Free State did not even trouble to attend and the rest merely affirmed the independent co-operative principles of 1923 and 1926, laying special emphasis on the air arm which had shown its deadly power in Abyssinia, Spain and China. As a result, those Dominions who had already begun to overhaul their armaments went forward with greater energy; Canada at last began to look to her coast defences and Air Force; India began to mechanise her army with the assistance of the British taxpayer, and Great Britain, who was already modernising part of her old fleet, laid down fine battleships which she might hope to finish by the end of 1940. If the precedent of Bismarck's war of 1870 went for anything, the Germans might be expected to make their big effort somewhat before that date.

The failure of the Imperial Conference of 1937 to subscribe to a cut-and-dried scheme of defence was inevitable. Such a scheme, alien to the traditions of the Commonwealth, could only have followed upon an agreed foreign policy, and that was lacking. The outlook of the Dominion peoples, shaped as it had been by their long colonial pasts, was necessarily different from that of the British. There were men of various origins in all the Dominions who were determined never again to be drawn into an imperial or 'British' war, and though the great majority of Dominion citizens by no means went so far as this, they did seek, United States fashion, to avoid European commitments and draw Great Britain away from the unspeakable Continent towards the open sea and themselves. Ever since 1921, they and many British citizens also had agreed with Smuts that Continental Europe's day was passing and that henceforward greater heed must be paid to Asia, where so high a proportion of mankind was 'on the march', and to the United States, with whom the Dominions had so much in common and to whom Smuts bade them look as a possible defender. Thus it was that Australia, in 1925, welcomed a visiting United States squadron almost as warmly as she and some other members of the Empire had recently welcomed Edward, Prince of Wales.

The Dominions, led by Borden's Canada and Smuts's South Africa, had at first taken a lively and even embarrassing interest in the Empire's foreign policy, but by the time of the Locarno treaties of 1925 Smuts and Borden were both out of office and imperial policy had become once more virtually British policy. Nevertheless all went well so long as the system of collective security stood, the counterpart of the Commonwealth and, for a growing body of Commonwealth opinion, the heir presumptive of an Empire that was nearing the end of its internationalising labours. Great Britain never pressed the Dominions to assume unwanted responsibilities, while her support of the League suggested that she had taken to heart the warning which Smuts had given, away back in 1917, that an imperial policy, to be a common policy, would have to be 'for one thing, far simpler. We do not,' he had said, 'understand finesse in other parts of the Empire. We go by large principles.'

Smuts was a true prophet. Principles of foreign policy would have to be simple and large indeed if they were to secure the loyal co-operation of widely separated communities who were becoming more aware of local problems than of general interests and felt themselves safe. The Dominions were hardly perturbed by Great Britain's failure to check the Japanese in Manchuria; Canada contemplated with satisfaction the United States warships at Hawaii and the vast width of the Pacific Ocean that lay between herself and Japan; Australia and New Zealand reflected that Manchuria was far away and that British Singapore and American Manila were comfortably close; even Afrikander Nationalists, who condemned the Empire and all its works, made an exception in favour of the base at Singapore which should guard South Africa's eastern approaches. As late as 1932 a committee of the Ottawa Conference could dispose of the Empire's foreign policy in twenty minutes by recommending in effect that there should be no such thing.

The Abyssinian crisis of 1935–36 proved the truth of Smuts's warning. An Italian invasion would threaten British, Indian, Australian and New Zealand interests in the Suez canal route and disturb the tranquillity of the British and South African communities in all Black Africa; hence Sir Samuel Hoare's rousing summons to defend League principles and the League's decision to apply economic sanctions to Italy in spite of French manoeuvres won a general election in Great Britain and widespread approval overseas. India, preoccupied with her internal problems, paid little heed to the danger; but the New Zealand Labour Ministry advocated sanctions to the limit and the mass of Australian opinion proposed to follow the British Government's lead. Far more significant was the awakening of isolationist Canada and the enthusiasm displayed by the Union and the Irish Free State. The majority of the Canadians approved of the cautious support which Mackenzie King's new Liberal ministry was prepared to give to the sanctions policy. In South Africa, Hertzog and Smuts, now in alliance, drove Malan's Nationalist extremists to decry the once-admired League as the tool of British imperialism by proposing, first of Dominion governments, to go to all lengths. Then, in spite of his many differences with the British authorities, de Valera committed the Free State to the support of sanctions as the supreme test of the League.

The Hoare-Laval negotiations, carried through without the customary Dominion consultations and issuing in a proposal to partition Abyssinia, came as a profound shock. Plainly the Commonwealth could not carry on in its existing form if British policy was to be thus secretive, inconsistent, savouring of finesse and guided by purely European considerations. The prompt repudiation of the proposal by the British ministry, Parliament and public and the resignation of the Foreign Secretary averted a Commonwealth crisis; but the subsequent half-hearted enforcement of sanctions, their final abandonment after the Italian victory, and the return of Sir Samuel to another office drove the members of the Commonwealth further apart than ever. New Zealand dissociated herself hotly from this reversal of British policy; South Africa protested and hurried her Defence minister off to London to discuss armaments, and the Irish Free State relapsed into disappointed isolation.

It was useless for Commonwealth governments to repeat the old Genevan formulae, or for Smuts and Joseph Lyons, the Australian Premier, to talk of reviving the League on the basis of the regional pacts which they had deprecated in happier days; matters went from bad to worse. Dominion governments watched, with growing bewilderment, the failure of the League to check the aid which Italy and Germany gave to Franco's men, or discussed fruitlessly with other members of the League and the United States projects for the appeasement of totalitarian peoples who had now been taught to regard commerce as a branch of power politics and

P

colonial areas as ministers to the exclusive prestige, strategic advantage and prosperity of their possessors. When, early in 1938, the Germans seized the northern end of the Brenner Pass and marched into Vienna, the Canadian Premier announced coldly that his government no longer regarded the sanctions articles of the Covenant as 'effective by general practice'. Plainly the League, which could not stop Hitler, could serve no longer as a bond of union to the Commonwealth.

The peoples of the British Commonwealth, the sole surviving system of collective security, were thus forced to take stock of their mutual relations. They found that the breakdown of the League system had given point to questions that had been asked long ago in Wolfe Tone's Ireland and then in Gavan Duffy's Victoria, and had since been held by many to follow from the Balfour Declaration. Debates on the divisibility of the Crown and the rights of neutrality and secession had been academic so long as the Covenant and the Kellogg Pact had had force, for those instruments prescribed the international duty of each signatory quite apart from possible duty to the Commonwealth. If wars were to be public wars sanctioned by Covenant and Pact and in no sense imperial or 'British' wars, there could be no conflict of loyalties for members of the Commonwealth, unless one of its own members were proclaimed the aggressor, a hardly likely contingency. No Dominion, therefore, would have just cause to challenge the unity of the Crown by remaining neutral, still less by seceding to preserve its neutrality. De Valera's stand for sanctions in 1935 was convincing proof that loyalty to the League could override intra-Commonwealth estrangements.

Now all that was changed and these three questions became of moment to the fissiparous Commonwealth. The admission was made little by little in various parts of the Empire that the Crown was indeed divisible. Edward VIII was once toasted publicly as 'King of South Africa' as well as 'King' *sans phrase*; the Union Act which ratified his abdication deprived him of one day of his short reign, the Irish Act added one day to it, and the Irish Free State edged his successor out to the three-mile limit without seceding. The coronation oath taken by George VI made mention of all the states of the Commonwealth as distinct entities; the Judicial Committee implicitly recognised divisibility in its judgment on a Canadian appeal, and certainly many Canadians regarded King

George VI and Queen Elizabeth during the royal visit in 1939 primarily as King and Queen of Canada, living symbols of the unity of the loosely-hung Dominion rather than of the Empire. Had not Sir John Macdonald in Confederation days thought of Canada as a kingdom?

Opinions differed as to whether secession would be the exercise of a legal right or the consummation of a probably bloodless revolution, but for a long time past few had denied the power of a Dominion, or for the matter of that the Mother Country herself, to part company with the rest of the Commonwealth if its people so desired. The practical point, however, was put by Smuts, who observed that, the world of the 'thirties being what it was, an independent Union 'would have to seek the guarantee of a Great Power, and the only one possible is Britain'. Smuts could have said the same for all the Dominions except Canada, which could turn naturally and easily to the United States for support. Meanwhile, the most widespread and practical debates turned on the right of neutrality, since this was most directly bound up with the issues of peace or war. Long before the Abyssinian crisis, the Irish Free State and the Union had insisted that the decision of those issues must rest with their respective legislatures. Now Canada was contemplating a similar stand, and it would be strange if Australia and perhaps even New Zealand did not follow her example.

Opinion was terribly confused throughout the Commonwealth. An increasing number of men and women everywhere accepted the persistent German allegations that the Versailles peace treaties were the root of all the world's present troubles and agreed that Hitler, then in his purely German and revisionist phase, had a case. In the United Kingdom the strain between Left and Right became more and more severe. Independent Liberals, Labour men and Communists clamoured for co-operation with China, Russia and republican Spain, while the National Government, more fearful apparently of anything even slightly red than of the Nazis, scorned the idea that totalitarian victory in Spain might endanger Gibraltar; objected that other folks' forms of government and society were no concern of theirs, and stigmatised as jitterbugs those who warned them that ideologies of violence which had their centres at Berchtesgaden, Rome and Tokyo to-day might soon have their circumferences everywhere.

These same currents of opinion cut across the deep undertows of sentiment which would determine Dominion policies in the end. Both parts of Ireland were bound closely to Great Britain, their one large market and source of supply; but whereas the Six Counties could be relied upon to go with the United Kingdom of which they formed part, the Irish Free State could be relied upon with equal certainty and for quite intelligible reasons to take the opposite course. Anti-British feeling and a sneaking admiration for armed resistance to government were traditional among large sections of her people; both sentiments reached their highest point in the Irish Republican Army which drew most of its funds from the numerous Irish of the United States and, ignoring outlawry by the Dail and the Irish Catholic hierarchy, gravely embarrassed de Valera's administration. De Valera himself had won office in 1932 largely on his anti-British record, and could be sure of retaining it so long as the Belfast Government displayed its suspicion of the Catholic minority in Northern Ireland and the British Government refused to thrust an unwilling Ulster under Dublin rule. Great Britain did indeed settle long-standing Anglo-Irish financial and trade disputes in April 1938 and, as a gesture of appeasement, gave up her claim to the use of the Irish harbours that had been reserved to her in time of war by the treaty of 1921; but the Dublin authorities made it clear that there could be no cordial co-operation while partition stood, and least of all co-operation in the event of war.

While the Free State nursed her grievances under the lee of the British breakwater, Mackenzie King's Canadian ministry, pledged to maintain national unity at all costs, trod the mazes of external policy as delicately as Agag. The vocal but diminishing groups of imperialists, strongest in Toronto, Ottawa and Montreal, gave the outside world a misleading picture of Canadian unity and resolution to support the Mother Country at all costs. In reality the Dominion was deeply divided by geographical barriers and lively sectional jealousies. Some seventeen per cent of Canada's population, in the western Prairie Provinces mainly, were recent comers from all parts of Europe with no feeling for the British Empire and little enough for Canada except as a refuge. The French of Quebec Province and the parts adjacent, thirty per cent of the whole and multiplying faster than the rest, regarded themselves as *les Canadiens* in contra-distinction to their fellow-citizens, *les Anglais*. Bad times fanned their nationalist ardour so fiercely that some of their younger folk, supporters of the *Union Nationale* provincial ministry, dreamed of

'Laurentia', an exclusively French and Catholic republic run more or less on fascist lines. Many *Canadiens* wished Franco well as a good fellow Catholic in opposition to the main weight of Canadian opinion; practically all of them demanded abstention from overseas adventures; they were resolved to a man that there should be no more conscription as in the Kaiser's War. Therein they had the support of those *Anglais* who shared the suspicions of Labour everywhere for 'capitalist wars', and of those many others who, forgetting their country's advance in status, regarded the casualty lists, debts and war memorials as Canada's only reward for her past endeavours. Nevertheless, however much some of them might dread the United Kingdom as a peril which was apt to drag their Dominion into war, the mass were ready enough to stand by her in a good quarrel, partly for old times' sake and partly because she was the largest purchaser of their products next after the United States; great numbers of them would even face the dispatch of another expeditionary force in spite of their fears lest U-boats and bomber aircraft should prevent its safe arrival 'over there'; come to think of it, the little-considered Royal Navy might be of some use to Canada in a matter like that! But, as North Americans first and foremost, they held that their country must march in step with its great republican neighbour and agreed with their Government that the defence of their own territory and territorial waters was the best contribution they could make to the defence of democracy everywhere.

The same doubts and fears played their parts in forming Australasian opinion. Some Australian Labour men had favoured neutrality ever since the Abyssinian crisis, while many more joined with members of other parties in advocating concentration on local defence; in New Zealand, the readiest of all the Dominions to look at international politics through British spectacles, the British enthusiasms of the Labour ministry had been damped by the readiness of some recent immigrants from the Old Country to accept low wages and the chilly attitude to itself of the City; be that as it might, Australians and New Zealanders as a whole were much more ready to co-operate actively with the British than were the Canadians. They recalled that nearly all their forebears had come from the British Isles which they still called 'Home', as do some Virginians also; they took little interest in the Statute of Westminster but a great deal in the British market and the Royal Navy;

most Australians were ready to take their full share as before, especially in the Mediterranean which, their Premier reminded them, was now 'almost as much an Australian sea as the Tasman Sea', and New Zealanders were not likely to lag behind. So reassuring was their attitude that British imperial federalists, who had remained silent since the shelving of their schemes in 1921, looked forward to a federation of the United Kingdom and the two Pacific Dominions which should control at least the ends of the Empire's central sea and airways.

Politically-minded India, midway along this Grand Trunk Road, was too fully occupied with domestic problems to pay much attention to international affairs; but once the new provincial institutions were at work, some of her leaders raised their eyes and looked outwards. Hindus, and a few Moslems also, peered eastward, dreaming of the day when India, China and perhaps a repentant Japan should combine to win 'Asia for the Asiatics'. The Moslems as a rule looked more realistically westward across the Khyber Pass to the stirring world of Islam, and especially to Kemalist Turkey which was seeking to safeguard the peace of the Near and Middle East by concluding treaties with some of her Christian Balkan neighbours and fellow Moslem states as far eastward as Afghanistan. As yet few of them seemed to realise that such dreams, and indeed all hope of retaining present constitutional liberties, were imperilled by the totalitarian combine that centred upon Hitler's Germany. Meanwhile the National Congress resolved that India must not take part in any war without the consent of her people, and the Moslem League demanded that no Indian troops be sent overseas without that consent.

The line that would be taken in the event of war by the Southern Rhodesians, few in number and intensely proud of their British origins, was no more in doubt than that of the Ulstermen; but the course that would be followed by the South Africans in the key position on the alternative route to the East was much less certain. On the face of it, close co-operation with Great Britain would seem to be the obvious course for an isolated European community whose standard of living depended mainly on the gold that it sent to London and its security on the Royal Navy; but the obvious course was cut across by acute national and party differences which had been exploited skilfully by Nazi propagandists ever since Hitler's advent to power in 1933.

These quarrels between British and Afrikanders, and still more between the two halves of the Afrikander majority, turned to an increasing degree upon the problems of the divisibility of the Crown and the twin rights of secession and neutrality. The original Nationalist party of 1913 had always upheld these three principles in its desire to be free from overseas entanglements, but its Labour allies of 1924 had said as little as possible about them, and Smuts's British and Afrikander following had denied them with varying degrees of conviction. Hertzog and Smuts agreed to differ on this score when they and the majority of their respective followers joined hands in 1933, for all three issues were then academic. On the other hand, the small Dominion Party, which broke away from their United Party, found much support in coastal Natal and the larger towns for its continued repudiation of these propositions as well as for its demand that the Union should subscribe to a precise scheme of Commonwealth defence, while the much larger 'purified' Nationalist Party under Dr. Malan reaffirmed them vigorously.

Presently the Malanites were calling for a general declaration of South African neutrality and advocating the return to Germany of her colonies, except South-West Africa which was to be treated as a 'special case' and a Union reversion since so many of its citizens were Afrikanders of their own way of thinking. They even contemplated the cession to Great Britain of the naval base of Simonstown as a southern Gibraltar lest the agreement of 1921 to defend it with Union batteries should imperil South African neutrality. The United Party, however, declined with growing emphasis to part with South-West Africa or to see willingly the transfer of Tanganyika to the Reich, and reaffirmed the Simonstown agreement. As early as 1935, even before the Abyssinian crisis, Hertzog had hailed the British Navy as the guardian of his country's liberties; now, as the war clouds gathered, he reminded the unheeding Malanites that Great Britain had been 'the greatest benefactor to South Africa in the last three hundred years', and Smuts gave it as his own opinion that the Union, with her gold and fine strategic position, could never keep out of a general war and must therefore 'stand by Great Britain'.

'The Day' that so very nearly came in September 1938 revealed the bewilderment of an unready Commonwealth in no part of which were the rights and wrongs of the Sudeten German problem generally understood. The British public supported its appeasing government with many heart-searchings and prepared itself hurriedly to meet mass air attacks. The Dublin authorities approved of the British policy, though some of them proposed to bargain for an end to partition in the event of war, while de Valera, presiding over the League Assembly at Geneva, encouraged Neville Chamberlain to be instant in peacemaking. The Canadian ministry said nothing until the last possible moment and then endorsed the British Premier's policy. In the Union opinion was sharply divided, for many Afrikanders and not a few English-speaking South Africans sympathised with the Sudeten Germans' demands for constitutional and cultural liberties, and Nationalist extremists worked up anti-British feeling to a dangerous pitch by their shameless abuse of the centenary celebrations of the Great Trek. Hence, though Hertzog declared that the Union, as a good member of the League, must go to Britain's aid if she were wantonly attacked, his United Party ministry decided to maintain neutrality at all events for a time. In India the Princes and warlike Punjabis proffered their services as usual, but in pursuance of Gandhi's policy of non-violence Congress merely expressed its sympathy with the Czechs, while some of its members, by their obvious readiness to use the coming war as a means of extorting constitutional concessions from an embarrassed British Government, drove the Moslem League, the crisis past, to mutter that it might have to imitate the Sudetens by calling in outside aid against Hindu domination. The most downright support for Great Britain came from the Antipodes. New Zealanders made up their minds to go to war if the Mother Country must, and the mass of the Australians resolved to stand by Britain in spite of the demands of some of their Labour men for neutrality.

Relief that war had been averted, though at a high cost to Czechoslovakia, was widespread, and Smuts, ever hopeful, looked for the restoration of the League on the lines of his original suggestion that effective control should be entrusted to the Great Powers who were, after all, the Great Responsibilities; but the speedy realisation that Hitler had gained most of what he wanted and was still set on violent courses called down fierce criticism on the men of Munich and undeserved scorn upon the League. For the rest, the Dublin ministry, thinking in terms of independence, informed Geneva that, pending the creation of an adequate system of collective security, it must decide for itself who the aggressor might be at any moment, and meanwhile took no steps to check the spate of I.R.A. bomb out-rages in Great Britain; the Australian Attorney-General Menzies, thinking in terms of the Empire, urged his colleagues to take more interest in foreign affairs so that they might learn to 'say useful things at the right time'; Smuts, thinking in terms of the world, said the most immediately useful thing by declaring that the best hope of peace now lay in 'the sea-power wielded by the Navy'.

Smuts was right. Events moved swiftly. On the Ides of March 1939, Hitler seized the remains of Czechoslovakia in defiance of his promises, and at once brought pressure on distant South Africa where Nazi preparations were well advanced. The Pretoria authorities were told, in words that were soon to become a formula, that Germany 'would not be responsible for the consequences' if they refused to admit a large party of German 'immigrants' into South-West Africa. The Union Government, however, stood its ground; in spite of Nationalist opposition it took prompt steps to forestall trouble in the mandated territory and saw to it that the immigrants moved on to a more hopeful sphere of activity. Mean-while Hitler's rape of Czechoslovakia had disillusioned most of those the world over who had believed hitherto that his aims were merely to undo the work of the Versailles peacemakers and gather all German Aryans within the bounds of the Third Reich. Now his demands for Danzig and a road across the Polish Corridor, following as these did upon Mussolini's seizure of Albania and the collapse of republican resistance in Spain, rallied the Democracies. Great Britain introduced military conscription, guaranteed Greece and Roumania against aggression, came to terms with Turkey, opened belated negotiations with Russia and agreed with France to 'fight on the Polish line'.

Great Britain and France were disappointed of their hitherto sure expectation of Canadian assistance. Mackenzie King had already announced that Canada's co-operation would depend on the decision of her own Parliament and must in no wise be taken for granted. Now, while isolationist lawyers debated the niceties of Dominion sovereignty, he was boggling over the British Govern-ment's proposal that an Empire air-training scheme be developed on Canada's safe and wellnigh boundless plains. On the other hand the Democracies were confirmed in their resolution by a reasonable hope of material aid from the United States in spite of the neutrality laws. President Roosevelt and his Secretary of State, Cordell Hull, had striven for some years past to persuade their fellow-countrymen that even they, favoured above all great peoples of the earth, could not live to themselves alone, and had induced Congress latterly to vote large sums for naval construction. The Munich debacle had strengthened the Americans' natural desire for isolation, but it had convinced many of them that they must supply their fellow democracies with warlike stores so long as the peace should hold. The Czechoslovakian crisis had set some of them talking, with presidential approval, of modifying the neutrality laws so as to permit the sale of munitions for cash down to those belligerents, obviously France and Great Britain, who could fetch them away. Be that as it might, both Democracies were reassured when the President sent his main fleet to the Pacific and denounced the expiring American-Japanese commercial treaty of 1912, and the British were encouraged further by the warm welcome given to the King and Queen in the United States on their way home from Canada. They replied to the startling Russo-German Pact with an Anglo-Polish Alliance, a well-meant gesture which could only awaken false hopes in the breasts of the inaccessible Government at Warsaw. Be that as it might, on 1 September, 1939, in spite of appeals by the Pope, President Roosevelt and Mahatma Gandhi, Hitler hurled his mechanised armies upon Poland. Two days later Great Britain and France took up the challenge.

XII

THE EMPIRE AT WAR, 1939–1945

THE Empire's response to the challenge of war, though far from unanimous, was more whole-hearted than it had promised to be in September 1938. In the United Kingdom the nation was solid in its support of the war policy. Its unanimity was hardly marred by the dissidence of an insignificant minority which was strangely compounded, as in so many other parts of the Empire, of pacifists, Nazi-minded traitors, and Communists who had hitherto called for strong action against Hitler and now condemned the 'capitalist war' against the unexpected partner of Stalin. The Liberal and Labour parties, holding that parliamentary institutions answered best when there was a vigilant opposition, declined indeed to join the National ministry in which they had had no confidence since its inception in 1931, but they did agree to an electoral truce and were confirmed by the Trade Union Congress in their resolve to 'stop Hitler'. With this the Chamberlain ministry seemed well content, for it did little to adapt itself to the new conditions beyond forming a small War Cabinet and calling Winston Churchill, Anthony Eden and Lord Hankey to its inner councils. The British public, for its part, awaited the German air attacks in some doubt as to what precisely it was fighting for, but stubbornly determined to fight to the last against 'the evil things' incarnate in Nazi Germany.

Once the United Kingdom was at war the dependent Empire, automatically at war also, gave proof of its accustomed loyalty by offers of service and gifts to numerous war funds. Social unrest died down in the West Indies and elsewhere, and even in Palestine the clamour of Jew and Arab was stilled by the thought of a possible German conquest that would spell common ruin to their rival aspirations.

Each of the overseas members of the Commonwealth made the expected response. The Australian and New Zealand governments, holding that when the King in London went to war they went too, made no declaration of war beyond asking their Parliaments to confirm the event. Fadden's Australian Country Party pledged its support to Menzies' minority United Party ministry; but Labour, which almost equalled these two parties combined, refused to enter the projected National Government. In New Zealand, on the contrary, it was the Labour ministry which rejected appeals for such a government. Nevertheless, both Governments had behind them peoples united in their conviction that the Germans must be fought, though many Australian Labour men still advocated merely local defensive action.

The shock of war, coming so soon after the inspiring visit of the King and Queen, went far to unifying Canada. True to its promise the Liberal ministry delayed its declaration of war for a week until Parliament could assemble, and then made it in the most formal manner to signify that it was the sole act of the representatives of the Canadian people. The solid French phalanx supported war upon Nazi paganism as soon as is was satisfied that there would be no conscription, and was rewarded presently by the defeat of the isolationist *Union Nationale* ministry in Quebec at the hands of French Liberals and English-speaking Conservatives. The Dominion Conservative Party promised full critical support; the Social Credit Party of the Middle West did likewise provided wealth was conscripted as well as men, and most of the members of the small socialist Co-operative Commonwealth Federation agreed at least to give the Allies help in food and credit. But here there was no question of a National Government. Mackenzie King's Liberals decided to carry on alone, and, early in 1940, increased their already unwieldy majority at a general election held in response to the Ontario legislature's criticisms of their leisurely prosecution of the war.

In South Africa the Hertzog-Smuts ministry foundered on the war issue. Parliament happened to be in special session. The Prime Minister, who regarded the invasion of Poland as a matter of merely European concern, proposed to honour the Simonstown agreement and, for the rest, maintain neutrality. Smuts condemned this modified neutrality as being utterly impracticable, asserted justly that Hitler was showing himself bent on world domination, and narrowly carried the day in favour of a declaration of war on Germany. He thereupon formed a ministry which included representatives of the Labour and Dominion parties and had behind it all English-speaking South Africans and perhaps two-fifths of the Afrikanders. It was sure also of the good wishes on this issue of the Coloured folk and natives, loyal as ever to the Crown, but lacked the moral support of many Indians who took their cue from Congress and regarded the war as a struggle between rival imperialisms from neither of which they had much to hope. Smuts's majority in either House was not large, for Hertzog and his personal followers joined with Malan's extremists to form a Reunited Nationalist or People's Party which attacked the ministry with a bitterness that was only equalled by that of one wing of the new party for the other; but that majority was large enough to throw out Hertzog's defeatist peace proposals early in 1940 and maintain in office the veteran international statesman who now became the spokesman of an Empire against which he had fought so doggedly as a young man.

Northern Ireland, of course, stood four-square with Great Britain under its unchanging ministry of Orange stalwarts, but her peace was troubled by the Catholic minority whose restiveness was stimulated by events south of the border. The Sinn Fein Dail at Dublin made its long-anticipated declaration of neutrality, thereby reflecting faithfully the wishes of the mass of its constituents who were as anxious to keep out of the war as were the people of the United States with whom they had such close ties. The British Government recognised the implications of this anomalous situation by sending a British Representative to Dublin, where the continued presence of the German minister doubtless enhanced in official eyes the value of Hitler's promise to respect the neutrality of their country.

In Dublin, as in Ottawa, there was no question of a coalition cabinet. The Labour party indeed drew nearer to the ministerialists by dropping the idea of a 'workers' republic' which savoured too much of Communist Russia; but Cosgrave's Opposition ignored the war as far as possible, and the Prime Minister contented himself with a mere cabinet reshuffle on the plea that expertise was less important than an understanding of the mind of the people. De Valera's Christmas message to the United States revealed that mind truly enough with its appeal to the administration to summon a peace conference before the combatants had bled each other white, and to Irish Americans to withhold funds from the I.R.A. whose bombing experts were at last being sent home from Great Britain. Meanwhile, in spite of gratefully acknowledged help from the British Government and the Bank of England in the matter of supplies and exchange facilities, rising taxation and the closing of the world-wide Irish Sweepstake proved the truth of de Valera's warning that the war would not leave neutral Free State unscathed, while the sight of her citizens streaming across the border and St. George's Channel to find work in Britain's expanding war industries or to enlist in His Majesty's forces with nothing said was a constant reminder that Irishmen would as ever be 'in the war' regardless of the attitude of their Government.

In India the war issue was inevitably confused by constitutional disputes and communal quarrels. In spite of Congress's recent warning that India's consent must first be obtained, the Viceroy simply informed India that she was at war with Germany. His action was constitutionally correct and doubtless any other course would have involved the risk of an embarrassing refusal, but the lack of even consultation played into the hands of the Empire's enemies everywhere. The Princes, however, offered their services and resources as before; volunteers for the Indian Army, Royal Indian Navy and Indian Air Force came forward faster than they could be trained or equipped, and money all unasked for poured into the Viceroy's War Purposes Fund. For a moment it seemed that all might go well, even on the party front. The Viceroy suspended discussions of federation, Gandhi declared for the fullest moral support of the Allies on whose victory the hopes of Indian liberties depended, and the Congress Working Committee rejected Bose's suggestion that it should break with the British and condemned Nazism in terms which the American President and the Princes could hardly have bettered.

On the other hand, the Congress Working Committee classed British imperialism with other imperialisms and announced that its active support would only be forthcoming if all British dependencies were given the fullest political freedom as soon as possible and India herself forthwith. That assurance the Viceroy could not give and soon the politicians were at deadlock with the Government and each other. The Princes and the Hindu *Mahasabha* repudiated Congress leadership, and Jinnah's Moslem League virtually claimed a veto on further constitutional advance. At that Gandhi urged Congress to demand immediate independence. The Viceroy tried to close the growing breach; but his assurance that Dominion status of the Statute of Westminster kind was India's goal simply disquieted the Princes, while his offer to set up a consultative committee at once and discuss changes in the federation scheme freely with Indians after the war failed to satisfy the Working Committee.

That Committee, which now controlled Congress's every act, reverted to its old wrecking tactics, the refusal to make the most of existing liberties which had done so much to delay *swaraj* during the past twenty years. It ordered the seven Congress provincial ministries to resign. This the ministers did with greater or less reluctance; the subsequent debate in the Commons did not mend matters, and Jinnah helped not at all by calling on Moslems to observe a day of thanksgiving for deliverance from Hindu rule.

So the quarrel ground on, to the dismay of all Moderates, while Indian soldiers did good service in Europe, the Middle East and Singapore with the consent of those Indian leaders whom the Viceroy had very properly consulted. At last Congress, persuaded by its Working Committee, resolved that civil disobedience must be 'the next step' against a Government which in its view was fighting simply to preserve an Empire based on the exploitation of Asiatics and Africans. In response to this proposal to trade upon Britain's necessities by the non-violent methods which, Gandhi had long ago lamented, so often led to violence, the Moslem League gave notice that on this occasion civil disobedience must lead to civil war.

Meanwhile the war dragged on its early indeterminate course. The Germans overran Poland, while the Russians began a private war against the Finns. The British, with markedly inferior forces, drove the German pocket-battleship, *Graf Spee*, to self-destruction at Montevideo (December 1939), but must themselves submit to aerial bombing of their outlying islands and distressing losses on the high seas at the hands of the U-boats. In the background President Roosevelt carried a Cash-and-Carry Bill which ensured to France and Great Britain such arms and other supplies as they could pay for 'on the barrel-head', and Cordell Hull induced the Pan-American Congress to mark out a 300-mile zone to the eastward of the Americas within which belligerent warships might not fight. For the rest, United States citizens, remembering the sustained and ponderous slaughterings of the Great War, and unimpressed by the air-fighting around Great Britain and the dispersed struggle at sea, complained that this comparatively bloodless war was 'phoney'.

American suspicions were shared by others. As the months went by dissatisfaction with the conduct of the war became more and more outspoken in all parts of the Empire. The British Government had admittedly shown imagination in its efforts to ensure supplies and ease the economic strain on other members of the Empire by purchasing, at prices good for the moment, Dominion wheat and meat, maize and dairy produce, wool, hides and skins, and the tropical produce of the dependencies in all its variety. Fruit alone of the Empire's staple crops it did not buy if only for lack of cold-storage vessels, and thus left the Australian, New Zealand and South African Governments to go to the rescue of their own fruit-growers. But at home, in spite of periodical changes of portfolios, it seemed unable to handle war finance, labour, rationing and food production decisively or goad industry on to make up in short time for the years the locust had eaten. Moreover, its unconvincing propaganda bred the fear that its post-war plans did not go beyond the restoration of as much of the old order as possible, and that was the last thing that a growing body of British opinion desired. Before long Labour was talking of ending the party truce.

While London thus failed to give the peoples of the Empire the lead they were looking for, the other Governments of the Commonwealth assumed or called into operation far-reaching emergency powers and proceeded to wage war with varying degrees of intensity.

The Canadian ministry waited for a month before giving an outline of its war policy: the strengthening of its exiguous naval squadron with patrol craft, participation in the defence of Newfoundland and the dispatch overseas of a volunteer division as well as a few airmen, doctors and technical experts. It agreed indeed at long last to the training of the Empire's airmen on Canadian soil, though on a much smaller scale than that originally contemplated by the British Government, but indicated that Canada's main effort was to be the supply of foodstuffs and munitions, a long-term effort suited to a protracted war.

Australia and New Zealand put their naval squadrons on a war footing at once. Australia also raised a volunteer division for overseas service and then, on its dispatch to the Near East at the New Year of 1940, resolved to expand it into an army corps. New Zealand, heavily in debt though she was, raised a few thousand volunteers for service beyond her own frontiers. At the outset, however, both devoted their main energies to local defence and supply. Australia called up large numbers of militiamen for home service, arranged to give her airmen most of their training on the spot before sending them to Canada, and pushed on with her war industries even to the extent of subsidising a monopolistic motor factory. New Zealand found that she must rebuild her decayed Defence Force from the foundations and, facing the probability of conscription if the war proved to be a long one, followed the British Government's example by taking a national register of man-power.

Smuts's South Africa, with its consciousness of imminent danger from within and without, showed the clearest comprehension of what had to be done. The ministry decided at once not to send an expeditionary force to Europe, but to make ready for the heavy task that would face it in Africa whenever Italy should enter the war on the side of the senior Axis partner. Swift and decisive steps were taken to make up the deficiencies of a Defence Force that had been neglected for years past by a teutophile Hertzo-gite minister, and to develop home supply based on the mining and State railway workshops and the subsidised Pretoria iron and steel works. Knowing that Nationalists would make trouble if the ordinary Defence Force regiments were ordered beyond the Union's frontiers, Smuts called in every rifle in the country, thus disarming the Nationalist backveld, and raised a Mobile Defence Force of British and Afrikander volunteers ready to serve 'anywhere in Africa' or, as many of its members signified, 'anywhere'. For the rest he began to enrol a Native Military Corps as an integral part of the Union's army, and decided to train the South African Air Force locally for African conditions, while neighbouring Southern Rhodesia pushed on with her warlike preparations to the same end and arranged to train British airmen as well as her own. Thus it was that the British public was able to welcome contingents from Canada and Newfoundland, Australia, India and New Zealand and often heard the unmistakable speech of Ireland and the United States in its streets, but as a rule and for sound reasons looked in vain for South Africans and Rhodesians.

Early in April 1940, while the Empire was thus preparing more or less at half speed for a long-drawn-out war like the last, the *Blitz-krieg* burst upon Scandinavia. A disastrous month later, with the rumble of the German invasion of the Low Countries drumming in its ears, the world learned with relief that the British Liberals and Labour had joined a truly national ministry under Winston Churchill. The Westminster Parliament welcomed the change by giving the new Prime Minister and itself something like a Roman

Q

dictatorship of the classical pattern in the short space of three hours. It was just in time. Within the month Holland, Belgium and Luxembourg had been crushed, France rotten from the head down had begun to crack, and the bulk of the British expeditionary force, and many thousands of French soldiers, had struggled back from Dunkirk. Then Italy, eager for easy spoils, leaped upon France as she fell and the world held its breath to watch if Britain would fall too. Britain did not fall. Distrusting the new Vichy Government which had abandoned her in spite of Churchill's last-minute offer of a joint British Imperial and French citizenship, she shattered French warships at Oran and Dakar. At home, while her people were putting forth an unparalleled effort to meet the needs of their fighting forces and civil defence organisation, the Royal Air Force, heavily outnumbered though it was, had, by the end of October, beaten the *Luftwaffe* out of her daylight skies.

Time had thus been gained by Great Britain to save herself by her exertions, as in Pitt's day, and the rest of the world by her example. In the glare of her burning homesteads and cities, friends and enemies saw her more clearly than at any time these three hundred years as the guardian of the world's main cross-roads. During those long years Britain had fought again and again to prevent the most powerful and highly developed of the continents, and especially its western seaboard, from falling into the hands of an ambitious Power, which, relieved of military preoccupations, might build a fleet that could overwhelm hers and sally forth to hold the outer world in fee. She was facing her appointed task once more against an overweening Power that had overrun nearly all Europe west of Russia, and this time she was facing it without a great Continental ally, against the power of the air which had gone far to rob her of the island position that was so much of her strength, and with the handicap of a neutral Irish Free State in her rear ill-equipped for self-defence but resolute to deny to her the use of the harbours which could best guard their common life-line to North America and the rest of the overseas world.

Most of that world beyond the seas had become over-night a far more friendly world to Great Britain than hitherto. Everyone knew that there were many dingy pages and some black ones in the long story of the British Empire; the British themselves would not deny that, being human, they had consulted their own interests first and foremost throughout; but most men were now ready to recognise

that Great Britain's record was not so bad after all by contrast with
the aims and achievements of the Powers to whom she had denied
world domination in the past, and still more those of the mechanised
tyranny against which she was now contending. Free English,
Spanish, Portuguese, Dutch and French-speaking republics, Dominions and colonies, who had waxed great and prosperous behind the
unobtrusive screen of her Navy for generations past, were fain to
confess, some of them for the first time, that her essentially international policies had been to their advantage as well as her own.
There was much less talk than there had been of one imperialism
fighting another now that Continental refugees were flocking to
Great Britain as the one comparatively safe and sane country within
reach, and exiled Continental governments, at work in London,
were making of the British capital a truly international city and
strengthening the claim of the Empire to be a league of free nations
by pooling their armed forces, shipping, and sometimes vast dependencies with those of the British. All the world over millions of
decent folk, desiring some approach to freedom of thought, speech,
and movement and the old kindly things, saw in Britain, the central
fortress of the Empire, their best and for the time being their only
hope.

The peoples of the Empire got from Churchill what they had been
waiting for: a courageous lead conveyed in gruff oratory, and as a
body those peoples responded. For here was an issue simple and
straight as a sword, principles large enough to move men of all
conditions to mutually pledge to each other in their defence their
lives, . . . their fortunes and their sacred honour. . .

> It's war we're in, not politics,
> It's systems wrastlin' now, not parties;
> An' victory in the end will fix
> Where longest will an' truest heart is . . .

No matter that the Government had to curtail the operation of
the Colonial Development and Welfare Act for lack of men,
materials and shipping; the governments of dependencies offered
to go entirely without 'for the duration' and those that had them
poured their surplus revenues into the Empire's war-chest, while
their peoples vied with one another in offers of personal services
and gifts ranging from thousands of pounds down to a few head of
sheep, even all that they had. If prices were disappointing in the

dislocation of commerce that was threatening the life of the Mother Country, colonial governments and peoples agreed to make the best of them and store their unexportable primary products against the day when a freed Europe could be fed.

It was the same story in nearly all quarters of the Commonwealth. The New Zealander who cried 'God help us all if Britain goes under' spoke for the rest. Money poured into Dominion war funds and those of the United Kingdom. Dominion and Indian governments redoubled their war effort. Canadian war industry began to get into its stride; the Air Training scheme was expanded to undreamed of dimensions; armed men from Canada trooped overseas to Newfoundland, Iceland, the West Indies and Great Britain, and with them went Newfoundland bluejackets and lumber-men. Australians rushed to the colours at the other end of the world, stung by the Italian threat to the Mediterranean, Australians' *mare nostrum*; Labour men, hesitations forgotten, called for strenuous efforts to defeat the Nazi menace and presently joined the War Council; the manufacture of warlike stores was pressed on. So it was also in New Zealand whose Government imposed conscription as in the last war. Soon the sons of the men who had fought at Gallipoli were more than upholding the Anzac reputation in the Balkans and North Africa.

The response from South Africa could not be so unanimous. On Italy's entry into the war the Malanites sought to show that the only way to escape Hitler was to proclaim a republic, while on the collapse of France Hertzog pressed hard once more for peace now that the war was presumably lost. The defeat of the ex-Premier's motion was soon followed by a defeat more final at the hands of his allies. The extremists of Malan's section, egged on by the *Ossewabrandwag*, a so-called cultural society framed on the Nazi model, demanded a republic in which there would be no place for English-speaking South Africans and little enough for Afrikanders who were not of their way of feeling. Unwilling to descend to this, Hertzog, Havenga and a few other devoted followers retired from the Nationalist Party and formed an Afrikander Party of their own to fight Smuts's 'holistic imperialism' on the one hand and Malan's enlarged 'Kruger republic' on the other. Almost immediately thereafter police fell foul of soldiers in the streets of Johannesburg after a riot induced by an *Ossewabrandwag* meeting. Smuts, wiser than his own zealots, declined to deal drastically with the *Ossewa-brandwag* beyond ordering civil servants and police to resign their membership. His patience was rewarded when Malan broke with this fifth column rather than permit it to dictate the policy of his Nationalist party. Malan first told Pirow that there was nothing Afrikander about his more or less Nazi New Order, and then, having reorganised his own party very much on *Ossewabrandwag* lines, gave such a broad hint to his followers that shoals of them made haste to come out of that fissiparous organisation. At this stage, Hertzog, who had recently resigned his very seat in the Assembly, committed himself to the strange assertion that the Union must adopt some form of that National Socialism on which he said the old Free State republic had been based because a victorious Führer could never have dealings with a mere parliamentary democracy. Havenga promptly repudiated this dangerous nonsense and was elected leader of the Afrikaner Party in place of his afore-time chief. Meanwhile Smuts prophesied confidently that the United States would come into the war one day and continued to drive on all concerned in the war effort with the consuming energy of his seventy years. He repelled with fitting scorn the Nationalist accusation that the Union was being made to fight for England. 'The truth is,' he cried, 'that England is fighting for the world, and where our freedom and our self-government are in the scales we will never be satisfied to let Britain fight for us. We will fight side by side with her.' Before long South Africans, equipped in large part by their fast-expanding industries, were forcing their way across the ruins of Mussolini's East African Empire beside British and Indian troops. With them went Rhodesians, settlers from the British East African territories and, colour bars forgotten, Cape Coloured transport drivers, Indian soldiers, Sudanese levies, Abyssinian patriots, and the black West African Frontier Force and King's African Rifles. Wielding now a Field Marshal's baton, Smuts rejoiced to know that Union troops had been the first to enter Addis Ababa and that, before the close of 1941, fully 160,000 South African volunteers had gone north.

The shock of events in Western Europe had repercussions in neutral Ireland. The threat of invasion impelled the Dublin authorities to round up dangerous characters, hang two I.R.A. murderers and call for recruits with considerable success. Common interest in defence brought inveterate political enemies together in peace, and de Valera touched the hearts of the peoples of Great Britain and Northern Ireland by twice offering hospitality to women and children from their bombed areas. But he quickly disappointed their hopes of active co-operation in the war. Smuts might pronounce neutrality a Nazi trap and Churchill promise to defend the whole of the British Isles; de Valera retorted that 'Eire' would protect her own neutrality against all comers. The most he would offer, while Germans dropped occasional bombs on her soil and shipping and no one seemed to have arms to spare for a democracy that was not resisting the totalitarians actively, was federation with the North on the basis of an All-Ireland neutrality.

It was an offer that could not be accepted, if only because acceptance would have robbed Great Britain of the Northern Ireland land base which flanked her vital north-western approaches and made possible the defence of Ireland against air-borne attack. Meanwhile the war pressed upon the Free State in the shape of heavier taxation, rising prices, the abandonment of the famous Dublin Horse Show, a growing shortage of coal and overseas supplies, and a censorship which protected the administration at the price of denying to Irishmen all real understanding of the forces that had been let loose upon the world. De Valera courageously warned his people that a small neutral community must tighten its belt, work harder and face unemployment as an apparently 'incurable blot' on civilisation, since Great Britain had little shipping to spare and the United States was forbidden by her own neutrality laws to send ships into the combat zone in which they indubitably lay. The best he could do was to arrange with the Washington authorities that a few ships sailing under Irish charter and with Irish crews should bring across cargoes of foodstuffs.

In India official rule functioned smoothly enough in the seven ex-Congress Provinces, the mixed Hindu and Moslem ministries did well in the remaining four including Bengal and the Punjab, and the extension of the war to north-eastern Africa turned the thoughts of millions away from political controversy. The Indian Army had been greatly enlarged by the end of the first year of war, the personnel of the Indian Navy trebled, and that of the Air Force quadrupled, while a Supply Board under an Indian minister was furnishing these forces with many articles of equipment and sending the growing surplus to the Dominions and the United Kingdom.

Meanwhile, the Government of India had enhanced the international status of their country by summoning an Eastern Group Supply Conference to concert measures against the Axis. That Conference, so much more comprehensive and significant than the Colonial Conference which had once been summoned to Ottawa by the Canadian Government in 1894, met at Delhi in October 1940. It represented Palestine and all the important British territories in John Company's old sphere of influence eastward of the Cape of Good Hope: the Union of South Africa and Southern Rhodesia, the East African dependencies, India herself, Burma and Ceylon, Hong Kong and Malaya, the Australian Commonwealth and New Zealand. The fact that it had been summoned to the Indian capital witnessed to India's swift advance towards equality with the West. India was quietly taking her place as a Power by sheer weight, and no one in the British Empire would have it otherwise; certainly not Smuts's South African Government which arranged that the Indian Agent to the Union should become a High Commissioner, and assuredly not an Imperial Government which presently welcomed the dispatch of an Indian Agent to Washington, India's first diplomatic representative to a non-British capital, and was fully prepared to see the governance of India carried on 'by India, for India, in India', and not necessarily on British parliamentary lines if Indians desired otherwise.

The Churchill ministry tried to resolve the political deadlock in August 1940. In spite of Gandhi's warning that a Congress which claimed to speak for all India could not be expected to come to terms with those who did not echo its demand for immediate independence, it proposed to give Indians forthwith more seats on the Central Executive Council, to set up a War Council on a similar broad basis, and to summon a convention representing all the chief political parties to devise a new constitution as soon as the war was over. The *Mahasabha* and the Untouchables, the extremes of Hindu society, were inclined to co-operate; the Moslem League and the Hindu Moderates of Sir Tej Bahadur Sapru's Liberal Federation at least did not condemn, while the Chancellor of the Chamber of Princes, echoing the words of Lord John Russell a century ago, expressed the hope that participation in the workaday tasks of the proposed councils would build up those traditions of mutual confidence and fair play which were the only sound basis for parliamentary self-government. The Chancellor might have added that, if the experience of Great Britain and many other parts of the Empire went for anything, the real powers of the councillors would soon be far greater than their nominal authority and issue naturally in *purna swaraj*.

The Congress Working Committee thought otherwise. It accused the British of seeking to avoid the surrender of power by exploiting India's divisions, and demanded, as the price of its support of the country's war effort, the immediate creation of a provisional government responsible to all the elected elements in the Central Legislature among which Congress-minded members were in the majority. The authorities refused and presently Gandhi, dismayed at the repudiation of his policy of non-violence implicit in the Working Committee's open bid for power, launched a pacifist campaign which must obstruct the war effort. Hence, three thousand of his followers, including Nehru, speedily achieved arrest and the dreaded communal troubles flared up in the crowded Bombay area.

The war ground on, whatever Indian faction leaders might say or do. The United Kingdom, relieved in great measure of fear of destruction from the air or invasion by sea, did well enough for a time. Her warships sank the giant German battleship, *Bismarck*, in the Atlantic and beat the Italians at Taranto and Cape Matapan in the Mediterranean. Farther east, Imperial forces dealt drastically with Axis supporters in Iraq and chased the Italians out of Cyrenaica (December 1940 onwards). But then came a setback. Troops had to be rushed from North Africa in a gallant attempt to save Greece and Crete from German and Italian invaders. The North African army, thus weakened, was obliged to fall back to the very frontier of Egypt, and had thereafter to watch the enemy bomb Malta unmercifully and, by virtually blocking the direct route, force supplies and reinforcements to make the weary voyage round by the Cape of Good Hope.

Holding on doggedly thus, the Allies were heartened by signs of dawn in the West. There, President Roosevelt began to swing his people over from rigid neutrality to a policy of all possible help for that Britain which most of them had been taught at school to regard as Enemy No. 1. In working this long-drawn-out miracle, he was hampered by anti-British and pro-Nazi groups which played upon the isolationist instincts of a highly individualistic community that held firmly to the anti-militarist tradition that was part of its British tradition and disliked the restrictions inseparable from the New Deal whereby he was seeking to restore the strained fabric of United States society. The North American sense of blessed isolation was bred of geography and history. There was the broad Atlantic and there the century-old Monroe Doctrine together drawing a sanitary cordon between God's own Country and that City of Destruction from which Americans or their ancestors had fled that they might become Americans. United States citizens had been confirmed in their belief that European entanglements only led to trouble by their experiences during the Kaiser's War, and were now repelled by the growing confusion of the Old World even more strongly than the peoples of the Dominions. Few of them realised as yet that their own economic policies and diplomatic aloofness were largely responsible for this world-wide collapse of morals and stability. Isolationism and neutrality were, moreover, the lines of least resistance for a huge, racially mixed and highly sectionalised community which occupied a territory as large as the Australian continent. A positive external policy which should enlist the support of a convincing majority was as hard to come by in the Republic as in the British Commonwealth, whereas a negative policy put no strain on national cohesion.

Nevertheless, in this crisis of the British Empire, the isolationists found themselves fighting a losing battle against the American tradition of liberty which is also the British tradition. Half-forgotten memories began to stir in the hearts of countless citizens of the United States. After all, the oldest of the thirteen foundation members of the federation had been British colonies for more than half their history and, though less than half the blood of the inhabitants of the forty-eight States derived from the British Isles, the British stock had always been the formative force in the Republic, the framework on which the United States had been built up. To this extent the long centuries of British history meant more to all Americans than that of any other European land. English was the speech of Americans from Harvard to Hollywood; American literature, now making its own strong and distinctive contribution, was rooted in the *Canterbury Tales* and soaked through and through with the language and imagery of the *Authorised Version*, Shakespeare's *Plays*, *Paradise Lost* and *The Pilgrim's Progress*. Americans' ideas of right and wrong were those of the British;

the English Common Law was the basis of their own except in once-French Louisiana; their political institutions, local, state and federal, were fundamentally those of the British everywhere. These deep-running currents of sentiment came to the surface and drifted the United States ever closer towards the islands which had given her birth.

Sometimes the President gave the lead, sometimes he waited to be pushed on; but the direction was always the same, towards informal but effective co-operation with the British Empire. When Denmark surrendered Roosevelt sent a diplomatic representative to Danish Iceland on the heels of the Canadian garrison and extended the sphere of the Monroe Doctrine to include Danish Greenland; when Holland fell fighting he warned Japan that interference in the Dutch East Indies would be regarded as an unfriendly act. The American public, for its part, cheered at the news of Dunkirk and heaved a sigh of relief when the Royal Navy struck hard at the Vichy warships at Oran and Dakar. In mid-1940 the Democrats threw aside one of the most jealously preserved of Washingtonian traditions and nominated Roosevelt by acclamation for a third term, while the Republicans put forward a candidate whose foreign policy marched in step with that of the President.

Confirmed thus in his course of action the President carried a military conscription bill and redoubled his armament drive, while Cordell Hull, his Secretary of State, engaged all the American republics to help any of their number that might be attacked and to take over jointly for the duration of the war European possessions in the elastic Western hemisphere whose security had been imperilled by the conquest of their metropolitan countries. Roosevelt further agreed with the Canadian Prime Minister that there should be a permanent joint board to organise the defence of all America north of the Rio Grande. He then struck a notable bargain with Churchill. In return for fifty invaluable destroyers Great Britain leased to the United States naval and air bases in the Bahamas and the once jealously guarded West Indies; in Antigua, St. Lucia and Trinidad screening the approaches to the Caribbean Sea, and in Jamaica and British Guiana covering the western outlet of the Panama canal. But she freely gave the Republic similar facilities in Newfoundland and Bermuda, her two oldest island possessions in the New World.

This was a deal that must have made the Empire-crusading Lord

Sheffield of Pitt's day turn in his grave. But times had changed since 1783, and now American citizens and British subjects, who still prized their liberties, the rule of law, democratic representative institutions and plain dealing, watched each others' fortunes with growing sympathy and understanding. Americans were dismayed at the failure of the British and Free French to seize Vichy Dakar, a short seven hours by air from Brazil where Germans did much abound, and elated by the shattering of the last heavy German daylight raid on London; the whole British Empire rejoiced when the American electorate gave Roosevelt his third term backed by Democratic majorities in both Houses of Congress. There was good reason for this rejoicing. Roosevelt had already shown that the fifty destroyers were a mere instalment from an administration and people resolved now on giving 'all possible aid to Britain short of war'. While the Empire's troops were sweeping across Italy's African provinces, he carried a Lease-and-Lend Bill in March 1941 which gave Great Britain the means to place immense new orders in the United States and endowed himself, as President, with wide discretion to transfer finished goods of all kinds to her or any other country, such as China, whose continued resistance to the Dictators he might consider 'vital to the defence of the United States'. By signing this 'Bill No. 1776' he gave to those well-known figures a happier connotation than they had had hitherto in the story of Anglo-American relations.

The United States might thus be ready to send Britain 'the tools to finish the job', but week by week the German submarines and long-distance bombers took heavy toll of those tools in transit. The President extended patrols by American warships indefinitely beyond the 300-mile safety line in an attempt to relieve the strain on the shipping and naval escorts of the Empire whose widely dispersed armies had lost Libya and their foothold in Greece and were now fighting Germany's supporters in Iraq. It was not enough, and the cry went up, irrespective of party, from the leaders of a nation which still hoped to keep out of 'the shooting war' that somehow, and never mind how, the tools must be ferried across the Atlantic safely. The issue was put most plainly in May 1941 by the outspoken Secretary for War. Henry Stimson told his fellow-countrymen and the peoples of Canada and Latin America that they owed their freedom and way of life to the 'friendly control' which the Royal Navy had so long exercised over the North Atlantic.

He warned them that, if ever they wished to see the surrounding oceans safe again, the United States Navy must be used to supplement the British Navy to ensure the flow of supplies that would sustain Great Britain as a fortified naval and aerial base, and win for the United States the year she must have in which to build up an adequate Army and Air Force.

This American rendering of classical British grand strategy and plain hint at convoy were greeted by German and Japanese threats, but the next impetus to collaboration between the neutral Republic and belligerent Empire was given by the half-willing subservience of Vichy France to her conquerors. At last the President spoke to his people with 'hard-headed concern' for the safety and future of their country. He made no mention of convoy nor any threat of war; but, speaking in the presence of representatives of every government in the New World, he promised all possible aid, short of shooting, to the fighting democracies of the East and West and reasserted 'the ancient American doctrine of freedom of the seas. We will not,' he added quietly, 'hesitate to use our armed forces to repel attack.'

These were epoch-making pronouncements from the spokesmen of a great people, who, above all others in the outer world, had been content to cultivate their incomparable garden on the assumption that there would 'always be an England'. Stimson's candour had made it possible for fair-minded British and Americans everywhere to talk to one another with fewer inhibitions than at any time since the sundering volleys were fired at Lexington in 1775; his President's stand for American rights and proclamation of a state of 'unlimited national emergency' were a warning to the common enemy that it lay with him whether or no the United States should enter 'the shooting war'. Roosevelt made his meaning clear by sending United States troops to garrison Iceland alongside the British and Canadians, and using American warships to keep the sea lanes thereto open for the passage of American and Empire shipping to within a short thousand miles of Great Britain.

As they listened to these voices of sanity and hope rising above the clatter of workshops and shipyards pouring out the material means of victory around the seven seas, some Englishmen at least began to wonder whether this might not be the last time that their storm-beaten ships would be called upon to stand between a European conqueror and the dominion of the world. At the close of the last war Smuts had bidden them note how the balance was beginning to tilt against 'the Continent' and in favour of the more spacious world overseas; now they could see for themselves that this outer world, already more powerful in 1939 than it had been twenty years earlier, was going from strength to strength under the stimulus of war. Doubtless Europe would long remain the most densely populated and highly developed of the continents unless it were wasted irremediably during the current conflict; but once the United States and the Dominions, China, India and the Latin American republics should have armed and supplied themselves adequately from their own abundant resources, they need have little to fear from the hallooing and stamping of mere Continental warlords provided always that sufficient of them elected to stand together. But time must be granted for all this to come to pass. The British in their island fortress braced themselves to win that time.

For there was no discharge in this war, and less than ever after Hitler, towards the close of June 1941, had flung the main weight of his armies against his Russian associate. Within the day the British Government, old fears and prejudices laid side, promised all possible aid to the Soviet Republics in their struggle against the monstrous German recrudescence of tribalism, and on the morrow the Governments of the United States and the Dominions underwrote that promise.

Nevertheless, the tide still ran strongly in favour of the enemy as Hitler's *Grande Armée* swept onward to the very gates of Leningrad and Moscow. For all this, however, the Germans, by their own act, had saddled themselves with the dreaded war on two fronts. They were given speedy reminders of that ugly fact when the Empire's airmen scourged the enemy wherever they could find him, British and Free French forces made Vichy Syria as safe as neighbouring Iraq now was, and British, Indian and Russian troops cleared Germany's *avant-couriers* out of Persia. When Japan brought the American public markedly nearer the shooting stage by occupying Vichy Indo-China, Great Britain at once joined with the Republic and the Dominions in freezing Japanese credits and promised to march with the United States in defence of British Malaya, the Dutch East Indies and the American-protected Philippines.

There were signs that this co-operation between the two halves of the First British Empire was not to cease with the gun-fire.

American and British statesmen began to make plans suited to the
'broader lands and better days' that would be open to the world
once the Dictators had been sent to their own place. The recent
policies of the United States administration had paved the way
for a joint advance. In the course of his New Deal campaign, itself
a revival of the first Roosevelt's Square Deal, the President had
brought American social services, collective bargaining and control
of big business more nearly into line with British and Dominion
practice than ever before and to that extent had rendered post-war
co-operation in such matters possible; his Lease-and-Lend Act, a
modern version of the eighteenth-century British system of subsidies couched in terms of things rather than currencies, was a
promise that this time post-war Anglo-American relations were not
to be bedevilled by whirling legions of dollars and pounds sterling.
Cordell Hull also, an American Huskisson come to judgment in an
autarchic world, embodied his hopes in five points which drew the
ready response from the British Government that it too looked
forward to a time when commerce should once more be a 'trading
of goods and services', and social security 'the first object of policy
abroad not less than at home'. Finally Churchill, himself an
American on his mother's side, confessed that he had long been
regarding with satisfaction the process by which the British Empire
and the United States were becoming 'somewhat mixed up'.

It would be too much to say that no examination of the structure
of the Empire could now be complete which failed to take into
account the colossal flying-buttress of the Republic, but undoubtedly
the mixing-up process had been going on rapidly. It was carried a
long stage further by a meeting of the President and Prime Minister
on board a warship 'somewhere in the Atlantic' (August 1941).
The two men outlined their joint peace programme at the end of a
three days' conference in these appropriate and congenial surroundings. The eight points of this Atlantic Charter repeated, though in
terms less precise, President Wilson's Fourteen Points of 1918, his
accompanying message to Congress and the speech in which Lloyd
George, the then British Premier, had narrowly anticipated these
pronouncements. There was the same disavowal of all desire for
the aggrandisement of their own States or any territorial changes
undesired by the peoples concerned; there were the same promises
of a restoration of sovereign rights and self-government to those
who had been deprived of them forcibly, of liberty for all peoples

to choose their own forms of government, of freedom for all men to sail the high seas and oceans without let or hindrance, of every effort to lighten the crushing burden of armaments since the nations, 'for realistic as well as spiritual reasons, must come to the abandonment of the use of force'. But the Eight Points, reflecting the bitter experiences of the intervening quarter of a century, dwelt far more emphatically than the Fourteen on the necessary economic foundations of a stable political peace and the immediate steps that must be taken to establish that peace. First, a promise that, 'with due respect to their existing obligations', the two great democracies would see to it that all nations, 'great or small, victor or vanquished', should have equal access to the trade and raw materials of the world, and every encouragement to enhance their 'labour standards, economic advancement and social security' by collaboration in the economic field; secondly, a hope that the peace would be such that all men could 'live out their lives in freedom from fear and want'; finally, a warning that peoples who had shown themselves to be incurably aggressive would be disarmed, 'pending the establishment of a wider and permanent system of general security'.

Critics were not lacking who objected that this Atlantic Charter was too vague, too much like the mainly negative programme of 1918, to serve as an inspiration to a desperate generation that demanded positive and constructive action. It was, they said, a document that might mean much or little according to what was read into it at the peace conference and, even so, paid unmerited deference to the national sovereignty and restrictive economic policies that had wrought such havoc during the years between the two wars. Be that as it might, the Eight Points, by their very likeness to the Fourteen, were proof that American and British statesmen tended to think alike in times of crisis and might be expected so to think when the time came for greater precision; at the least it augured well for the treaty-making and the winning of the peace thereafter that the President should be so plainly resolved that this time the United States should play her part in both.

That hope of collaboration was made certain a short four months later. On 7 December, 1941, Japan struck without warning at the American Pacific fleet at Pearl Harbour in Hawaii. The British declaration of war upon the aggressor followed 'within the hour'. All branches of the English-speaking folk were now in the shooting war together, and American isolationism perished over-night except among the anti-British minority who now only dared to urge that their country should concentrate on local defence or, at the most, throw her weight into the new Pacific struggle. The President's reply came short and sharp. He sent United States troops to Northern Ireland, one of those 'islands in the North Atlantic' that had played such a great part in his long-term strategy, the nearest support to that other island which was at once the bulwark of the New World and the bridgehead leading from the New World to the Old.

The United States might now be fairly 'in the war', but it would be long before her troops were fit to take the field in any numbers, and, meanwhile, her Pacific Fleet was virtually out of action. Indeed, 1942 was destined to be the Black Year for the Allies. Three days after Pearl Harbour, the Japanese sunk two great unescorted British warships in the Gulf of Siam, and, ensured thus of command of the Pacific and Indian Oceans as far westward as Ceylon, speedily swept up the Philippines, the Dutch East Indies (Indonesia), Malaya with its splendid naval base of Singapore, and Burma also. Commonwealth and Free French forces, indeed, managed to occupy Vichy Madagascar about the same time as United States warships broke the back of Japan's carrier flotilla in the Coral Sea and off Midway Island, thereby relieving Australia and New Zealand of all immediate fear of invasion; on the other hand, U-boats sank Allied shipping wholesale in the Atlantic and along the vital Archangel supply-route to the U.S.S.R., while the Germans poured far down into the Caucasus in search of oil and even tried to take Stalingrad on the lower Volga during which time their Japanese allies were marking time on the eastern frontier of India; finally, in North Africa, where the Allies had gone forward again, Rommel's heavy tanks overran Tobruk and pressed the Commonwealth forces back to within a day's march of Alexandria. And then the tide turned. Montgomery saved the Suez Canal by routing Rommel at Alamein (2 November, 1942) and thereafter chased him out of Libya; large Commonwealth and American forces landed in Algeria, and the Russians not only cut off 300,000 Germans at Stalingrad but drove them out of the coveted Caucasus and most of their territorial gains in western Russia and the Ukraine. The Führer might send his men into hitherto unoccupied Vichy France, but he could not stop French officers from scuttling most of the Toulon fleet, and still less prevent Churchill and Roosevelt from sketching at Casablanca the main lines of the peace settlement that was surely drawing nearer now that Australians were winkling the Japanese out of New Guinea and Americans smashing yet more of the Mikado's Navy in the Bismarck Sea and then 'island-hopping' along the road to Tokyo. Presently, the Germans, now 250,000 strong, surrendered to Montgomery in Tunisia (May 1943) and the Allies, helped by their rapidly-growing airfleets and improved radio-location, at last began to get the upperhand of the U-boats.

When vigorous fighting was resumed after a lull of three months, it went more favourably than ever for the Allies. They sank the battle-cruiser, *Scharnhorst*, and put the giant battleship, *Tirpitz*, out of action for good, steadily mastered the U-boats thanks largely to the use of the Azores as a base permitted them by the Portuguese, and battered Berlin, Leipzig and the huge German steel centre of the Ruhr. The Russians regained the Crimea and nearly all their other lost territories, while Anglo-American forces landed in Sicily amid such popular enthusiasm that Mussolini fell and a now friendly Italian Government signed an armistice. Crossing over to the mainland, Montgomery's Eighth Army encouraged Italy to declare war on Germany, saw the Resistance flare up as it had already flared in France, and itself took Naples before the winter rains bogged down the campaign. Far away to the east, Americans and Australians drove the Japanese back and back, while, on the Indian front, British and Indian troops beat off a full-scale Japanese attack and, by reconquering most of Burma, joined hands with the Chinese. So well were world affairs shaping that Churchill and Roosevelt ventured to Cairo to talk with Chiang Kai Shek and the Turkish President, and thence to Teheran to make plans with Stalin for the coming year.

During most of 1944 all went as the Allies had hoped. The Russians surged forward beyond their old western frontiers and forced the Germans out of Finland; the Allies entered Rome and thereafter shattered Germany's last organised line of resistance in Italy by taking Florence, while, to crown all, huge Anglo-American armies made a surprise landing in Normandy on D Day (6 June, 1944) and, presently, also gained a footing on France's Mediterranean shores. In August, while Allied troops were liberating Marseilles, Free French soldiers marched into Paris under the Arc de Triomphe. Nevertheless, the Germans hit back by loosing flying-bombs and rockets over 'southern England' and making a

R

partial break-through in the Ardennes which ruined the Allies' hopes of ending the war that year. However, the Allies soon restored the situation and crossed the 'German Rhine'. The end in Europe and on the high seas followed quickly. Mussolini was murdered by infuriated Italians, Hitler committed suicide, and once the Allies had joined hands with the Russians in Vienna and Berlin, Churchill could broadcast on VE Day that the war in the West was over (8 May, 1945).

The news of this great deliverance came just in time to hearten the Allies who had already assembled in the San Francisco Conference to prepare for the post-war world by framing the United Nations Organisation (April 1945). This Organisation gave *ex officio* seats on its Security Council to the five Great Powers (the United Kingdom, the United States, France, Russia and China) side by side with a majority of others elected by the much less powerful General Assembly, that is, by all the Member States. In spite of the resistance of Canada, Australia and New Zealand as spokesmen of the so-called 'Middle Powers', a far-reaching veto was given to each of the Big Five on the Security Council, while the failure of Australia and New Zealand to elicit a corporate pledge to resist aggression at once made it plain that U.N.O. was to be no more of a real world government than the dying League of Nations had been. This last fact was emphasised by the Colonial Charter which the Conference accepted after much debate. This Charter decreed that, in line with the now traditional British policy, the interests of colonial people must be paramount, that those peoples must be assisted to become self-governing, and that, with the consent of the Powers directly concerned, all Dependencies were to become Trustee Territories enjoying the advantages conferred by the Charter and offering to all comers the Open Door prescribed by the A and B mandates. This system was to be supervised by an elaborately constructed Trusteeship Council, which, unlike the Permanent Mandates Commission of the League, was to be merely a political and not an expert body. Lacking executive power, its sole duties were to be to advise the Assembly in the light of reports sent in by the administering Powers and of information furnished by them at its request, and to inspect Trusteeship Territories by arrangement with those Powers. France, Belgium, Australia and New Zealand at once agreed that their Mandated Territories should pass under Trusteeship; South Africa merely promised not to change the status of her C mandate of South West Africa till the local Europeans and Africans had been consulted; while the United Kingdom accepted Trusteeship for all her Mandated Territories except Transjordan, which was to become independent, and Palestine which was already being surveyed by an international Commission. Then, saddened by the death of Roosevelt, the San Francisco Conference dispersed.

Almost at that very moment, Japan collapsed (August, 1945). She had already been far gone when the ruthless Americans dropped the new atom bombs on Hiroshima and Nagasaki with devastating effect. At that, the Mikado surrendered on VJ Day, just as the Russians, who had hitherto held only a watching brief in those parts, swooped down to claim a voice in the Pacific settlement and incidentally to secure indirect control of industrialised Northern Korea.

The swaying fortunes of the war inevitably affected the several parts of the British Empire differently. Undismayed at the naval disasters in the Pacific at the close of 1941, Churchill hurried off to Washington and Ottawa. Returning thence, he sought to steady panic-stricken Australia and to cope as best he might with the harm done to the Allied cause by Lord Beaverbrook, his Minister of Production, who was echoing the insistent demands of Stalin that the United Kingdom must 'violently and recklessly' rush masses of divisions which she did not possess to the rescue of the hard-pressed U.S.S.R., and, once he had been relieved of office, started a press campaign for a general election on the morrow of the fall of Tobruk and Singapore. Churchill dashed off to restore the situation at Washington and thereafter at Moscow with whose masters he had recently concluded a twenty-year treaty. Back from his Odyssey, he set the long-silent church bells ringing for Alamein, created a Ministry of Town and Country Planning, and accepted schemes for agricultural education and for the vastly improved social services recommended by the Beveridge Report; but when he appealed for a post-war Coalition to carry out reconstruction, he was told by Labour that, once the war in the West was over, the party truce must end. Despite this rebuff, the patient British carried on sick to death of rationing, controls, hostile aerial missiles, sporadic strikes and the chronic failure of the miners to furnish enough coal. Farmers, again, grumbled that controlled prices bore no fair relation to rising wages, and many Labour men, as they watched the Prime Minister hurrying hither and thither from Washington to Teheran by way of Cairo for talks with Allied leaders, complained that he seemed to care about nothing but the winning of the war. In face of these internal strains not even Butler's Education Act of 1944 could save the Coalition. This broke up soon after VE Day, and the British public, 'very tired,' was plunged into the turmoil of a general election from which Clement Attlee's Labour Party unexpectedly emerged victorious though only with a minority of the votes cast.

Little need be recorded of the Two Irelands, save that in the North the inevitable Unionist Ministry plodded on troubled by strikes, a recalcitrant Belfast Municipal Council, and periodic I.R.A. raids from the South directed to driving from the Six Counties the British and United States troops 'at present in occupation'. To check these desperadoes, the Northern authorities tightened controls along the Border that separated their country from the Irish Free State whose rulers paraded neutrality as a proof of independence, claimed repeatedly as 'national territory' the whole of the island which they had shown on their stamps almost from the first, and refused to take part in any Commonwealth or international affairs so long as Partition stood. In mid-1943, Sir Basil Brooke and a group of comparatively youthful colleagues supplanted their veteran and exhausted predecessors at Stormont, and relations between the Free State and the United Kingdom became somewhat better if only because the latter respected her neighbour's neutrality under all the provocation of seeing her ships sunk right and left off the undefended southern shores of Ireland. De Valera, having won a general election, piped down on Partition; on the other hand, though he strove to check spying by their superabundant staffs, he refused to send the German, Italian and Japanese ambassadors packing at Roosevelt's behest, and was rewarded by victory at yet another election. And if the drain of emigrants away to the United Kingdom went on unabated, it at least kept unemployment figures low on either side of the Border.

For some time, the record of Canada, the senior Dominion, was not impressive. Mackenzie King, her veteran and semi-isolationist Liberal Prime Minister, had indeed taxed and controlled prices vigorously, but he had thereby alienated swarms of his *laissez-faire* fellow-countrymen and had even driven farmers, who held that Canada's primary duty was to grow food for the Allies 'over there', to threaten to hold back their produce until they were given prices more in keeping with the rising cost of living. Under such circumstances, voluntary recruiting for service overseas had been so poor that on the eve of Pearl Harbour the country's 11,500,000 souls could show only some 500,000 in uniform and a trifling list of 3,000 casualties. Mindful of the storm that had burst when conscription had at last been enforced during the Kaiser's War, the Prime Minister had long ago promised the frankly self-regarding *Quebec-quois* on whom his Ministry depended that they need fear nothing of the sort this time. When he was freed from his 'no conscription' promise by an immense over-all majority at a plebiscite which he had at long last been forced to hold by Japan's entry into the war and English-speaking Canadian pressure, the only immediate result was an uproar from Quebec which alone of the Provinces had registered an adverse vote, a protest from sixty-five *Quebecquois* members of the Federal Parliament, and the resignation of the senior French-Canadian Minister.

The conscription struggle together with widespread Socialist successes impelled the old-established Conservative Party to set its house in order. Alarmed by the steady drift of the isolationist *Bloc Populaire* of Quebec towards the Co-operative Commonwealth Federation in its stronghold in the Prairie Provinces and the defeat by the latter party of the Conservative leader himself in a 'safe' constituency in central Canada, the younger Conservatives saw to it that their party should demand full conscription, soft-pedal its traditional protectionism, rename itself the Progressive-Conservative Party, and elect as leader the Liberal-Progressive John Bracken (December 1942). The Liberals, on the other hand, strong in their dominance at Ottawa and in six of the Provincial capitals, merely comforted themselves with the thought that no one could produce a satisfactory alternative administration and that their present leader had won for Canada a status equal to that of the United Kingdom herself. They were hardly moved when the stalwart liberal *Winnipeg Free Press* thundered that Mackenzie King must come off the fence unless he wished to see the British Commonwealth go forward leaving Canada behind in not-too-splendid isolation and impotence. They were, however, so shaken from their complacency by the rally of the Progressive-Conservatives and the eastward sweep of the C.C.F. into the French-speaking coal mines of Quebec that they only gave the Prime Minister his customary vote of confidence at their party's grand assize under the threat of having to face a general election. They were then spurred into positive action by external forces. Smuts at Westminster and Lord Halifax at Toronto both said that the Empire-Commonwealth must strengthen itself if it were to speak on even terms with the United States and the U.S.S.R. The French-dominated Legislative Assembly of Quebec promptly condemned Halifax's 'new imperialism and dangerous tendencies'; the *Winnipeg Free Press* fulminated against his tampering with Canada's independent status, and the Prime Minister, who desired an international system of peace-loving states rather than a balance dependent on a few great Powers, deprecated debate in Parliament.

This unexpected stimulus came just in time for the general election towards which a divided Canada was drifting with many of her business-men so frightened at a recent decisive C.C.F. victory in Saskatchewan that they were talking of a merger of their two great capitalist parties to check the onrush of collectivism. There was also the problem of bread and butter. Join the British-dominated sterling *bloc* dollar-using Canada could not and would not, while many of her farmers and Ontario exporters looked so unkindly on the United Kingdom's attempts to protect her own agriculturalists that they asked whether the British could not be bribed to drop a 'conspiracy' which might forbid Canada to resume her pre-war practice of selling to the United Kingdom far more than she bought from her and then balancing accounts by buying from the United States. Finally, the oft-discussed problem of the Centre *versus* the Provinces could not be postponed indefinitely; yet, if there was now to be a readjustment of financial powers and responsibilities, masses of Protestant and English-speaking Canadians might have to see a French and Catholic-dominated Federal Parliament go off with the chief Provincial sources of revenue, distribute the proceeds as it thought fit, and thereby increase the power of the Centre at the expense of the Provinces. On one point only were all parties now agreed: Canada must stand in with both the United Kingdom and the United States, and fit her external relations into an international framework that would restore the multilateral commerce on which her vital export trade depended. In the event, just as the war was ending, the Progressive-Conservatives carried Ontario, but over-all the Liberals somewhat unexpectedly struggled home to Ottawa though with a reduced majority.

Australia, by contrast with Canada, had pulled her weight from the first. Relying on the unobtrusive help of John Curtin, leader of the Labour Party, her Prime Minister, Robert Menzies, had pressed forward so vigorously that by the close of 1941 some 400,000 of her 7,500,000 inhabitants were on service either as volunteers overseas or conscripts in the Home Militia, and another 200,000 at work in the war industries which were sending much to other members of the Eastern Supply Group. In the background, farmers had done well in spite of the drought. On the other hand, since the *Blitzkrieg* of 1940 in Western Europe, Menzies first and then his successor, Arthur Fadden, conscious of their country's isolation, had clamoured for the return of the Australian division from North Africa. On assuming office, Curtin took up the cry (October 1941); hence, the division was sent home at the heavy cost in British and Allied men and ships foretold by Churchill, just as urban Australia was staggered by the news of Pearl Harbour, the British naval disaster in the Gulf of Siam, and the loss of the *Sydney*, Australia's one sizable warship. Sorely shaken at thus finding themselves in the front line for the first time in their corporate lives, far too many Australians greeted the fall of Singapore with laments that they were stranded now that the Royal Navy could no longer protect them, and Curtin, though himself no isolationist, demanded the return home of most of the four remaining divisions serving overseas. He got them as soon as the hard-pressed British could furnish transports, escorts and replacements. Thereafter, having successfully asserted the right of his Government to tender separate advice to His Majesty, he readily agreed that Australia's local forces should join those of New Zealand under the new American South Pacific Command and helped to form a Pacific War Council of the Powers directly concerned. Australians gradually recovered their balance as United States soldiers poured in, and made ready to follow their Prime Minister's advice to look to the Great Republic as the universal provider. The distant United Kingdom proved Curtin wrong, for she at once diverted to Australia sorely needed American supplies intended for herself and, during the next six months, sent from all sources supplies equal to half

Australia's own production and many times more than those that came under American Lend-Lease.

The Curtin Ministry was in a difficult position, for though it had a satisfactory majority in the Senate, it must rely on two Independents for its majority in the House of Representatives. Everywhere, producers and businessmen dreaded lest the Atlantic Charter should imperil their cherished protectionism and imperial preferences; wool-growers were worried because Australia alone could never consume the whole of their output; urban workers struck from time to time, and farmers as a body demanded the right to make 'a good living' out of anything they chose to grow. Then there were the problems of financing the war and providing for post-war reconstruction. Under the former head, Parliament relied mainly on the income-tax, but was hampered by the fact that each of the six States had its own income-tax, all varying so greatly in weight and incidence that swarms of citizens escaped altogether. Early in 1942, Curtin strove to draw these folk into the net by following the ill-fated example of his two immediate predecessors and asking the States to give up their income-taxes in return for Federal grants. The States declined to do any such thing. Under the second head, Curtin desired wider powers than the Constitution gave him to regulate commerce, production and employment in time of peace. Rather than attempt the cumbrous amendment of that rigid Constitution, he 'referred' the matter to the States by asking each of them to give the Centre the requisite powers for five years after the war. Some of the States bluntly refused to pass such an 'agreed' measure unless all the rest did. One step, however, the Canberra Parliament could take of its own mere motion. Holding that Australians might as well be masters in their own house as long as it was theirs, it implemented the Statute of Westminster.

News of mounting victories raised the spirits of the Australians as 1943 went by, though a temporary recrudescence of the Japanese peril frightened their Labour majority into sending conscripted militiamen overseas to specified areas close to their own shores. Then, despite rocketing prices, Labour gained a new lease of power at the elections, re-elected all the old Ministers, cut down excessive munitions production, directed women into canneries and food-processing plants, and, generally, began to concentrate more on the production of food for the Allies than on fighting (August 1943).

Thus it came to pass that while many thousands of Japanese were still at large in isolated 'pockets' all over the South-West Pacific, Australia herself was soon full of uniformed men and women 'resting'. Nevertheless, while Australia's active participation in the war gradually slackened, the enlightened Curtin worked hard to lead his countrymen into taking a more effective part in the peaceful affairs of the outer world. He easily induced the Inter-State Conference to resolve that Australia must remain a member of the Commonwealth and at the same time co-operate with other free nations; he next exchanged High Commissioners with New Zealand and, finally, signed the Canberra Agreement with that Dominion (January 1944). Besides prescribing closer official co-operation and consultation, this instrument called for an international authority to control ocean air-routes, and for a Conference of the South-West Pacific Powers to deal with security, post-war development and native affairs, always provided that each of the two Pacific Dominions should continue to control its own immigration policy in which, on New Zealand's insistence, there should be no hint of a colour bar. Curtin won no support at the ensuing Prime Ministers' Conference in London for his proposal that the British Commonwealth be better equipped to resist aggression by endowing it with a permanent Secretariate which should maintain continuity between one Imperial Conference and the next; but, for all that, in spite of failing health, he pegged away to make the two Pacific Dominions at least a twin 'bastion' of British institutions.

During the later stages of the Axis war, Curtin's chief preoccupations were in the domestic field, in short, with the Federal issue and strikes. Abandoning all idea of another hopeless 'reference' to the State legislatures, he carried an Act which gave the Federal authorities wide powers to run for five years after the war, provided for a Convention thereafter to revise the Constitution, and decreed that a referendum should be held forthwith on the proposed extension of wartime powers. In view of the fact that this measure was promulgated in a murky atmosphere of official inquisition and indulgence in plain dishonesty by some of Curtin's more doctrinaire colleagues, it is small wonder the Fadden's Country Party should have won the South Australia State elections and that two-thirds of the States should have gone decisively against the Government at the referendum. Undismayed, the Labour rank-and-file forced Curtin, never master in his own house, to go some way towards breaking his election promise not to seek to achieve Socialism in wartime. In face of this, early in 1945, the two Opposition groups drew together as a Liberal Party under Menzies. If anything were needed to consolidate this new party it was the Government's nerveless handling of the spate of strikes, which, always worst in New South Wales, soon became so widespread that Australians could never be sure of anything from theatres and transport to meat and hot baths, and reached their climax when Communists, doubtless in part revenge for the Labour Party's refusal to allow them to affiliate, held up much of the vital wool-production. Thus it was that Curtin died in the midst of economic chaos leaving his Treasurer, Joseph Chifley, to reign in his stead, and thus it was that when the Axis war ended, Australia's Communist war began.

The reaction of New Zealanders to the tidings of Pearl Harbour was very different from that of so many Australians. The disaster caught them with close on one-tenth of their 2,000,000 folk overseas and with no more assurance than their neighbours that anyone either could or would come to the rescue; nevertheless, they kept their heads, brought home a mere handful of experienced officers and N.C.O.s to train reinforcements, and got on with the job. They had their reward: for instead of the Japanese there came friendly United States soldiers, Lend-Lease and the knowledge that, in spite of the Battle of the Atlantic, masses of their products were still reaching the United Kingdom at prices well calculated to maintain the national income. As witness, however, to the enhanced importance of North America in the Pacific scheme of things, they exchanged Ambassadors with the United States and High Commissioners with Canada. In his desire to avoid party politics in wartime, Peter Fraser, the Labour Prime Minister, wisely invited six members of Holland's National Party to join a National War Cabinet, leaving the regular Cabinet to carry on as usual. The feeble handling of a strike of the North Island coal miners by the Government drove these Opposition members to resign, though to be sure one or two of them resumed their seats as private individuals. Public finances remained good throughout, thanks largely to the heavily burdened United Kingdom's generosity in shouldering the cost of the New Zealand equipment lost in Greece, Crete and North Africa, and in taking the whole of the wool-clip at high prices. The balance of trade, again, continued to be favourable, though the Government had to tax, float loans, and stabilise incomes and, in face of a grave housing-shortage, rents also to check inflation arising from the demand of the distant British for produce and of resident Americans for food and coin. As the threat of a Japanese invasion faded away, New Zealanders found leisure to celebrate the tercentenary of the discovery of their islands by the Dutch voyager, Abel Tasman, and once the tide had turned at Alamein, began to release Regulars at home for service in war factories or the Air Force and relieved Home Guardsmen of many duties on condition that they went farming. This done, they gave Labour a renewed lease of power with a reduced majority and saw their Prime Minister become head of the new Department of External Affairs and of the administration of the dependent Cook Islands, Niue and mandated Western Samoa (September 1943).

New Zealand fully maintained her fighting forces throughout the remainder of the war, including one division in the Pacific and another in the Mediterranean. Of her continued membership of the Commonwealth there could be no doubt, nor of her readiness to work with the rest of the free world. Everyone was pleased with the Canberra Agreement with Australia and the subsequent Mutual Aid Agreement with Canada, and few were perturbed when Fraser secured the repeal of all anti-Chinese laws. On the whole also, Fraser handled the domestic situation well, harassed though he was by the risk of inflation, the rising cost of living and the growing tendency of coal miners, waterfronters and many other urban workers to 'go slow'. Much more serious was widespread discontent because the official policy of wage stabilisation seemed to ignore the fact that export prices fixed 'for the duration' by no means met the rising cost of imports. Coalowners grumbled that by their subservience to truculent trade unionists the authorities were apparently bent on forcing them to agree to the nationalisation of their mines; landlords resented the fact that since 1936 they had had no legal means of getting tenants out of their houses, and, late in 1944, farmers began to talk of forming a party of their own when the Government proposed to devote to the general public, as compensation for the abnormal rise in prices, the whole of the sum forthcoming from the United Kingdom's contract to take New Zealand's agricultural surplus for four years, instead of paying it out to the primary producers on whose industry the country ultimately depended.

As the war drew to a close, public finances remained so steady that more than one war loan was over-subscribed without recourse to the banks and, in spite of the continuing housing-shortage, demobilisation proceeded smoothly enough. On the other hand, growing numbers of citizens became impatient at the swelling stream of strikes and the unblushing determination of the Left Wing to force the Government to go back on its promise not to introduce controversial legislation in wartime. One such measure now gave 'the Minister' wide discriminatory powers in the licensing field, made the cohorts of Government servants eligible for election to local government bodies, and put the rural franchise on the same footing as the urban by giving mere residents the voting power hitherto reserved for ratepayers; another measure nationalised the Bank of New Zealand without even giving its Directors notice; yet another aimed at giving each constituency roughly the same number of voters as the others by directing the Commission which delimited those constituencies after each quinquennial census to base their calculations on the adult European population instead of, as hitherto, on the total such population, and debarring it from giving extensive and thinly-peopled areas the time-honoured favourable percentage allowance. Having thus abolished the so-called country quota, the authorities proposed to hold a census and delimitation before the next general election in the hope that Labour would benefit from the new arrangements at least as much as from its recent abolition of the means test for family allowances and its promise to increase superannuation payments and workmen's compensation. It was on this note of gerrymandering that the Axis war ended for New Zealand.

In South Africa, Smuts, who had backed Russia for all her Communism as soon as Hitler fell upon her, saw to it that war should be declared on German-occupied Finland, Hungary and Roumania as well as on Japan immediately after Pearl Harbour. Recruits poured in so fast that volunteer South Africa had soon raised as many men as conscript New Zealand and, in proportion to the white population available, as many as any Dominion. During the Black Year of 1942, however, Smuts had to face war on the home front. He was first obliged to round up some hundreds of the Police, many of them *Ossewabrandwag* stormtroopers and far too many possessed of illicit bombs; and then, on the morrow of the publication of the draft Constitution of Malan's projected Nationalist

'Kruger Republic', see Nazi-minded saboteurs blow up power-pylons on which the Rand gold mines depended and cut railway and telegraph lines in the Orange Free State and the northern Cape Province. Unabashed, Malan replied to the numerous arrests and the prescription of the death penalty for sabotage by demanding peace at once, because, he insisted, the Germans were bound to win and the blameless Japanese were only seeking for 'living room'. The Prime Minister startled him by retorting that if they sought it in South Africa, he would arm the non-Europeans in defence of their homes, and in due time averted any possible Oriental invasion by joining with the British and Free French in occupying Vichy Madagascar. Thus the Union fought on, suffering at home little more than sinkings off her coasts for many of which local traitors were to blame, shocked by the loss of nearly two divisions when Tobruk fell, and saddened by the death of the rejected Hertzog a few short weeks before Alamein.

Thereafter, South Africa struggled round the corner in the political sense more successfully than in the social and economic. Scarcities and rising prices bred inflation, and such was the wear on rails, roads and rolling-stock that bus and long-distance train services had to be cut down. The growing network of controls, based on the erroneous idea that the Union was a surplus-producing agricultural country, sought to keep up prices for producers in the restricted home-market by obliging growers to export part of each crop at a loss and leaving them to recoup themselves at the expense of the would-be local consumers. So fast had supplies dwindled at the first hint of restrictions that the Bantu had often gone hungry for lack of mealies, orange-growers had only been partially deterred from destroying much of their pick by the bribe of a subsidy, and the larger towns had to endure one meatless day each week. Meanwhile, Smuts essayed to deal specially with two sections of the country's heterogeneous population. In 1939 and again in 1941, Parliament had 'pegged' the *status quo* in the Transvaal where Indians, Moslems for the most part, were debarred from owning land and lived precariously in the gold-mining towns under temporary trading licence. Now, in 1943, Smuts carried yet another 'Pegging Act' covering this time semi-Indian Durban as well as the Transvaal. As touching the Bantu, the Native Affairs Department might still be wedded to the twin ideas of making sure of native labour for the gold mines and developing the inadequate Reserves as the homes of this very mixed people; but many officials and business men and at least one Commission were agreed that more must be done for folk whose services were after all needed by fast-expanding secondary industry. Smuts bade white South Africans rid themselves of the fear that had hitherto dictated their non-European policies, and Hofmeyr, eager as ever to help the underdogs, gave to the Native Trust for the first time the whole of the proceeds of the native tax to be spent on Bantu education.

At the elections of July 1943, the Coalition, already safe in the Senate, gained the biggest majority in the Assembly since Union. In spite of criticism by the compact and well-disciplined Nationalist Opposition, Smuts readily accepted the recommendation of a Commission that the pay of Bantu mine-workers should be raised, but, thanks mainly to the intransigeance of the Natal Provincial Council, failed to settle by mutual agreement the Indian question which was embarrassing his own government and that of the United Kingdom in their anxious dealings with India. Public finances continued to be better than had been expected, largely because the British taxpayers had undertaken to arm and equip the Union's forces overseas in return for a very modest sum; on the other hand, various Nazi-minded organisations joined with the Nationalists in demanding a Republic that should control capitalism, ensure white domination, institute 'unified direction' of economic life, set up a more rigid colour bar and handle the Indian 'menace' more firmly. Behind the Nationalists stood the *Broederbond*, which had been founded in 1918 as a charity but had since become an all-pervasive and largely secret society whose aim was to make the *Boerenasie* the South African *Herrenvolk*. This powerful extra-parliamentary organisation included so many leading Nationalists that Malan, himself a member, could accuse Smuts of persecuting the *Afrikaner Volk* when he stigmatised it as a public danger and prepared to shut its members out of the public services. To make matters worse, anti-native Labour men and the anti-Indian Dominion Party echoed the Nationalists' demand for a strict colour bar, and were as startled as they when Smuts declared not only that traditional native policies were bound to be affected by the rapid urbanisation of the Bantu, but that the Union must ignore colour if it were to make the best use of its man-power, and no less angry than they when Hofmeyr, during his chief's absence at the San Francisco Conference, took steps to finance Bantu education out of the general revenue. On the Prime Minister's return, with the end of the war in sight, the Government began to overhaul its public health organisation, took powers to compel local authorities to do their duty in the matter of housing, checked 'the new despotism' of wartime by resorting less than formerly to the magic incantation 'as the Minister may direct', and in deed as well as in word re-affirmed the democratic supremacy of Parliament.

In India, a group of Hindu Liberals, men of high standing but lacking effective organised political support, assembled at Bombay in March 1941 under the chairmanship of Sapru, to propose a compromise between the demands of Congress and the British Government's recent offer. They asked that India be treated forth-with in all respects as a Dominion, that the Governor-General's Council be manned entirely by unofficial Indians who should be legally responsible to the Crown during the war but deal with important matters on the Cabinet basis of collective responsibility, and that India be promised powers equal to those of a full member of the Commonwealth within a specified time. Later on they asked that the Viceroy, the man on the spot, be empowered to do much that was still being done by the distant Secretary of State on the lines proposed for a Governor-General of East Africa by the Hilton-Young Commission of 1929, for only by the abdication of 'the Great Mogul at Whitehall' could the political centre of gravity be transferred to Delhi.

These non-party proposals were welcomed by Indian Liberals, though with little hope of success since Sapru had failed to convince either Gandhi or Jinnah. Some Congressmen, moreover, who saw that *de jure* responsibility to the Crown must become *de facto* responsibility to the legislature, were inclined to acquiesce, and the orthodox *Mahasabha* also provided Hinduism was given special representation in any executive that did not include Congressmen. The Moslem League, on the other hand, regarded the proposals as a Hindu manoeuvre. It merely repeated its promise to co-operate within the four corners of the Government's existing offer on condition that Moslems were given an equality of power with Hindus or, alternatively, a substantial share of power in any execu-tive from which Congress might exclude itself. The Secretary of State for his part insisted that Indian politicians must compose their differences before H.M. Government could make any further advance; whereupon Congress reiterated its old claim to speak for British India, and the Moslem League demanded independence for 'Pakistan' apparently without the federal links with the rest of the country that it had envisaged hitherto.

In June 1941 the British Government tried to meet Sapru's Liberals halfway by implementing their year-old offer. They enlarged the central Executive Council and, though they retained the four vital portfolios of finance, defence, home affairs and communications in British hands, transformed the character of that body by entrusting the eight remaining portfolios to unofficial Indians. They also set up a National Defence Council of thirty-one members, nine of whom were representatives of the Princely States and all, with one exception, Indians.

These reforms indicated a radical change in the balance and spirit of the constitution; but Congress, prizing the letter above the spirit and distrusting the India Office profoundly, refused to be satisfied. Nehru pleaded that he could not help the British while they denied to him and his the freedom for which they claimed to be fighting, while Jinnah first obliged Moslem Premiers to resign from the Defence Council and then led his followers out of the central legislature for the session to mark his disapproval of the Government's subservience to Hindu dictation.

While Indian politicians thus bickered and stalled, the military leaders, backed by masses of humble folk, carried on so manfully that when the Japanese attack on Pearl Harbour made India the key of the Allied front from Egypt to the Philippines there were 250,000 Indians overseas mixed as ever with British soldiers. Apparently, most Indians preferred the British to jack-booted Nazis, but this did not move the rival seekers after power. They let their country drift into political deadlock. The release of Nehru and most of his fellow anti-war campaigners in December 1941 and Gandhi's resignation of the Presidency of Congress immediately thereafter availed nothing. Congress promised the Mahatma full support in his mission even to the point of civil disobedience, and presently, while the Japanese were pouring down the length of the Malay Peninsula, Nehru explained to Chiang Kai-shek in person that Congress's hands were tied, since collaboration must be directly with the British in India and only indirectly with the gallant Chinese. He did not tell him (perhaps he did not know) that some of his colleagues on the Congress High Command had just resolved secretly to demand immediate power, the withdrawal of the British and American troops from their country and the opening of negotiations with Japan for a free India. The *Mahasabha*, on the other hand, concluded that there was now no choice but to co-operate with the powers that be in defence of India's civilisation, and Sapru's Liberals found much well-informed support in the House of Lords for their programme; but the Secretary of State, calling once more for mutual agreement, asked in passing whether India was to be regarded as the home of one people or of many, and was told by the Moslem League that any British action that prejudiced the prospects of an independent 'Pakistan' would be a breach of faith and the signal for an 'unexampled catastrophe'.

Emboldened by Churchill's leftward reconstruction of his ministry, the Chinese Generalissimo then called upon the British, in the name of wisdom and their own reputation, to give Indians 'real political power', and on Indians to let the morrow take care of the things of the morrow and meanwhile address themselves, 'as in duty bound', to averting catastrophe at the hands of Japan. He was answered by a confused clamour. Moderate Congressmen disclaimed indeed all thoughts of domination, but joined with their fellows in demanding a national government based on the democratic principles which a majority would not forego; the *Mahasabha* insisted that power in such a government be given to Hindus in strict proportion to their numbers, including the millions of Untouchables; Ambedkar, leader of these scheduled classes, conscious of the caste barriers which all Gandhi's efforts had failed to break down, appealed to the British authorities to impose a settlement since their very presence forbade Indians to have recourse to the violence that had solved more than one deadlock in Europe and the Empire. Jinnah muttered of 'revolt' if too much were given to the Hindus.

Some outside force must be used to break the deadlock. This force the British Government sought to exert by sending Sir Stafford Cripps, Lord Privy Seal, with a Declaration that was intended to clear away all doubts of their good faith and hasten the day when India should have *purna swaraj* (March 1942). The stars in their courses fought against Cripps. The Japanese poured through Burma right up to the Indian frontier, and, behind that frontier, none of the politicians, parties and religious sects had yet agreed what they should do when the British were gone, especially as

s

touching such matters as defence, security for public servants, the vast majority of whom had long been Indians, the protection not so much of Minority Parties as of Minority Peoples, and the future of the six hundred Princes who were bound by personal ties to the King-Emperor. The British Declaration dealt with all these problems. It proposed that at the end of the war the Princes should nominate and the Provincial Lower Houses elect an Indian Constitution-making Assembly. This Assembly should then conclude a treaty with the United Kingdom covering essential obligations, while those Provinces that preferred to stand aside might do so and yet be accorded the full Dominion rights that the rest of the country was to have. On these conditions the British Government would implement the Constitution.

Cripps fought hard but without avail to win agreement. Jinnah was pleased that the proposed freedom for dissident Provinces to go their own way virtually conceded his claim to a separate 'Pakistan', but even he would not commit himself till he knew more of the details of the scheme. The Puritan Hindu Sikhs and the ultra-Hindu *Mahasabha*, united for once, would not hear of such a 'Pakistan'; the Mahatma chanted monotonously that the British must not invite 'general disaster' by holding on in face of the imminent Japanese, and, in the end, Congress wrecked the whole debate by clamouring that the central Government be 'popularised' by the immediate surrender of all power by the United Kingdom. Undeterred by the nomination of two Indians respectively to the War Cabinet and Pacific War Council in London and of three more Indians to the Viceroy's Executive Council in Delhi, Gandhi proceeded to blackmail the hard-pressed British. At Wardha, he easily persuaded the Congress Working Committee to insist that the British must 'quit India' forthwith under pain of having to face all forms of resistance short of physical violence. The newly-constituted Executive Council gave fair warning of what must come of Gandhi's frankly avowed 'open rebellion' with the enemy at the gates. This done, it waited till the All-India Congress Committee had enthusiastically adopted the Wardha Resolution at Bombay (August 1942). It then proclaimed Congress Committees unlawful assemblies, detained Gandhi and all others who had attended the Bombay meeting, and left the Provincial Governments free to arrest the vastly more numerous persons whom they might deem dangerous. It was just in time. A few days later,

Sardar Patel, one of Gandhi's leading henchmen, and other lesser Congress lights let loose a revolution unparalleled since the days of the Mutiny. Town mobs committed murder and sabotage whole-sale and for weeks on end cut the communications of Wavell's mixed British and Indian army that was facing the Japanese in the mud of the monsoon rains which, if it helped to avert an invasion, made the restoration of order harder. At last, however, the uproar was quelled at the cost of 3,000 casualties, Gandhi relapsed into silence, and the *Mahasabha* made a characteristic comment on the whole affair by wrecking a Conference which a moderate ex-Congress leader had convened to discuss unspeakable 'Pakistan'.

The real comment on the disastrous 'open rebellion' came a little later in the form of a major breakdown of the food supplies during which countless humble folk died and many presumably responsible Indians behaved so badly that even sympathetic onlookers might well have doubted their fitness for *purna swaraj*. This calamity was not due to the loss of the Burmese 'rice bowl' nor to any shortage of grain in the country as a whole; the real trouble was that the authorities, faced with an utter absence of Provincial and public will to co-operate and a wholesale pilfering of grain in transit, found it well-nigh impossible to get supplies to needy areas through the tangle of Central, Provincial and Princely administrations. Still less did the crash come without warning, for thousands were dying in grossly over-populated Bengal before the Viceroy sought to steady prices by inducing the British to send enough wheat to carry India over to the next harvest. By the time that Wavell had taken over the Viceroyalty from Lord Linlithgow in June 1943, half-starved Bengali country folk were pouring into Calcutta to die in the streets by thousands, while many of the inadequate civilian staffs failed to do their duty and, in that headquarters of the *Mahasabha*, Hindus obstructed everything a Moslem ad-ministration tried to do for them. Some Provinces and States averted disaster by the honest use of such supplies as Delhi managed to send them, but it was only in December 1943 that a fine rice-crop saved hard-hit Bengal and left all concerned to ponder Wavell's soldierly reminder that whereas talk buttered no parsnips, adminis-trative co-operation would make political advance easier.

The Viceroy was answered by the customary uproar, in the midst of which Gandhi, a sick man, tried in vain to convince him that the woes of India were due to the British and in no wise to that Congress which had just broken its boycott of the Central Legislature long enough to help Moslem Leaguers to throw out the Budget by a single vote. 'Dear Friend Wavell' did, however, release the Mahatma who, realising that his 'quit India' prescription stood in the way of talks with his still-interned Working Committee, diluted it to the extent of offering the Allies every facility for the defence of India short of physical help in return for an immediate transfer of power. In the event, defence was furnished, as ever, by the British and India's own admirable fighting men, who, directed by Lord Louis Mountbatten from his new base in Ceylon, thrust deep into Burma. But while the real India was putting forth a war effort almost greater in proportion to her resources than that of any other Allied nation, the country was so short of coal and transport that civil and military needs were in jeopardy. At this stage, Wavell's common-sense suggestion that Indian leaders should set up a 'transitional' Government within the framework of the existing Constitution at least impelled Gandhi, now restored to health, to discuss the forbidden topic of 'Pakistan' face to face with Jinnah for the first time. Lacking authority to conclude a settlement, Gandhi did little more than seek to secure a joint demand for the British withdrawal which he knew Jinnah desired as keenly as he, but Jinnah would not hear of that until 'Pakistan' as defined in the widest sense had been recognised. The Mahatma, therefore, retired into the silence of his Wardha *ashram* under doctor's orders to give up all work *sine die*, whence he presently emerged for a moment to discuss the formation of a Central Coalition Government with the Viceroy, the Deputy Leader of the Moslem League and the Congress Leader in the Central Legislature. That discussion was drowned by quarrelling between those many rank-and-file Congress and League politicians who welcomed the Executive's recent hints at State industrial action and the wealthy Hindu and Parsee masters of Congress who shuddered at the very idea.

Plainly, Indians, as their custom was, were leaving it once more to 'the Great Mogul at Whitehall' with whom, indeed, legal power and responsibility must rest until the actual handover. That distant authority, pressed forward by a growing weight of British, Dominion and American opinion, knew only too well that it could not go on indefinitely washing its hands of the mess and telling the apparently irreconcilable Indian faction-leaders to clear it up themselves. Yet, what was to be done? 'Quit India' at Gandhi's bidding the British would not, and rule India at the point of the bayonet they probably could not even if they would, because their *Raj* had been a mere caretaker Government ever since the grant of self-government to the Provinces had sapped its foundations years ago, their own prestige as Sahibs had been dimmed by defeat at the hands of Asiatics, and the military oath to the King-Emperor might not always hold their composite Indian regiments firm against the pull of rival religious and political loyalties. As it was, not many months back, Mahrattas had gone into battle cheering for Sivaji, the seventeenth-century Hindu hero who had defeated John Company and the Great Mogul. Germany having surrendered, Whitehall tried a third alternative by promising that India should have *swaraj* as soon as Japan had also given in; that, meanwhile, the Finance and Home Members of the Viceroy's Executive Council should be Indians for the first time, and that another Indian Member should presently take over External Affairs from the Viceroy thus leaving only two British members on that Council: the Commander-in-Chief and the Viceroy himself who would, as in the immediate past, use his veto very sparingly (June 1945). Finally, at its bidding, Wavell released the members of the Congress Working Committee and, with great difficulty, convened an All-Party Conference to suggest the names of members of the reconstituted Executive. So fiercely did this Conference quarrel that Wavell had to dismiss it, just as Japan surrendered. Generously taking the blame for this breakdown on himself, Wavell prepared to hold on yet a little longer, at least until the Central and Provincial general elections, the first for many years, might open the way to a settlement acceptable to all.

XIII

THE TWO WORLDS, 1945 ONWARDS

WHEN at last the Axis War ended the world was in a sorry state. War is rarely a good school of morals, and though the loss of life had been less than during the Kaiser's War, the destruction of houses, plant and communications had been much greater and, this time, a rapidly increasing world population must seek means to keep itself alive in face of a grave universal shortage of food and basic materials. Nearly everything depended on how the five Great Powers worked together among themselves and on the new and untried United Nations Organisation. Of those Powers, China counted for little at the moment and shattered France for very little more, while the United Kingdom, for all her deservedly high prestige, had borne so much of the weight of two world wars in a single generation that she no longer had the strength and authority she once possessed. Had the Commonwealth been even a loosely federated State the outlook would have been much more hopeful. As it was, the scattered and independent Dominions must leave the main burden to be carried by the United Kingdom, the senior member of what was little more than a 'Club', a member who had shown in the immediate past that she could not defend her Empire single-handed, and could not now speak on even terms with the two remaining Great Powers: the United States and the U.S.S.R.

The policies of the two federal giants of the East and West were such as to make the Commonwealth anxious. At one extreme, the capitalistic and democratic United States made an abrupt end of her various Lend-Lease agreements, while her businessmen set out to acquire as much as might be of the world's mercantile shipping and airlines, and her farmers clamoured for one-way free trade in the shape of export subsidies and guaranteed home markets. Further, despite the fact that the Atlantic Charter and the Anglo-American Lend-Lease Agreement had safeguarded the imperial preferences on which so many members of the Commonwealth and Empire had based their economies since the Ottawa Conference of 1932, millions of Americans demanded at the very least the reduction of those preferences to mere token figures in the interests of the old multilateral trade that suited them but, apart from the dollar-using Canadians, no single community in the Empire.

At the other extreme was the collectivist U.S.S.R. However little part the Soviets might have taken in the Far Eastern War, there was no denying that they had taken the main strain of the land-fighting in the West, and now held all Eastern Germany and part of divided Berlin. So far from fulfilling Churchill's hopes that they who had been such difficult Allies in war would prove to be good companions in peace, the men of the Kremlin showed at once that they proposed to hasten the 'inevitable' collapse of capitalist society by maintaining heavy armaments, more than hinting at war, honeycombing 'bourgeois' institutions, fomenting strikes, hampering the British in their attempts to stabilise shaky Greece, sabotaging the making of peace treaties with Italy, Austria, Germany and their own satellite States, and using their veto on the Security Council ruthlessly. Not only so, but while the Soviet system was arising in all the dependent countries of the Slav *bloc*, Stalin extended it still farther westward by forcing the Social Democrats of Eastern Germany to combine with the Communists. By thus lowering 'the Iron Curtain' between her European satellites and the West, Russia not only made an end of the hope of One World but ruined all chance of re-creating a united Germany. The leading Allies had recently agreed that this battered and populous heart of Europe should be divided into zones, each of which was to be occupied by the troops of one or the other of them, and should yet be treated as a single economic unit which must pay the occupying Powers for essential supplies with its exports other than those earmarked for reparations. By refusing to carry out this agreement fully and, in especial, by seizing as reparations everything mechanical that took their fancy in agricultural Eastern Germany, the Russians drove swarms of Germans from those parts to seek refuge in predominantly industrialized Western Germany which was thus obliged to look to its principal enemies late in arms for the very means of livelihood. At length, in desperation, the United Kingdom threatened to run her now overcrowded zone as a closed economy, and though France, fearing a revived centralised Germany, hung back, the United States offered to treat her zone likewise. Harry Truman, the new Democrat President of the United States, went even further by proposing to 'contain' militant Communism wherever it might appear, to hold a Japanese peace conference if necessary without the Slav *bloc*, and to promote the economic recovery of Europe in general and of Germany in particular.

The perplexed members of the Commonwealth tried to hold a middle course in this Cold War bred of mutual Russian and American fears and antipathies. Presently, however, they all became conscious of a growing dollar gap, which they sought to fill by cutting down dollar purchases or, in the case of South Africa, making a great deal of gold available to the United Kingdom, the banker of the informal sterling *bloc*. The situation was eased somewhat when they and many others signed at Geneva a general agreement which indeed limited the specific margins of imperial preferences but only on condition that the United States, the universal provider, should lower still further her already dwindling tariff-walls. Hope that it might be yet more eased was then held out by the United States Secretary of State, General George Marshall, who proposed that his country should make free gifts and money grants to such European Governments as should seek closer economic and, maybe, political co-operation among themselves (5 June, 1947).

The eagerness with which sixteen European Governments, led by that of the United Kingdom, jumped at the generous offer of Marshall Aid was a sign of the times. Indeed, both sides in the Cold War were busily closing ranks. The French and British had replied to the Russo-Polish Treaty of April 1945 with their Dunkirk Treaty of Alliance (March 1947), whereupon the U.S.S.R. had lined themselves up politically with their European satellites in the Cominform (September 1947). Early in the following year, Russia backed a *coup d'etat* which saddled democratic Czechoslovakia with a Soviet régime, and then bound the rest of her western dependants to herself by treaty. Such doings, accompanied as they were by persistent Communist agitation within their borders, called forth counter-measures from the United Kingdom and some other members of the Commonwealth, vigorous action by the Fascist-minded Athens authorities against Communist-supported rebels, the creation of the Benelux Union by Belgium, the Netherlands and Luxemburg for many common purposes, the extension of this Union to include France and the United Kingdom, and the adhesion of a score of Western Powers to the newly-formed Organisation for European Economic Recovery (March–April, 1948).

None of these manoeuvres could, however, get to the root of the trouble which was the power possessed by sovereign independent states to breed recurrent wars. Only governance could do that, a fact at which a few leaders in the United Kingdom and South Africa had been more than hinting for some time past. Now, Churchill called for a downright European Federation and, in spite of a jealous Labour Government at home, joined British and foreign delegates at the Hague Conference in proposing the transference to some overriding body of such sovereign powers as might achieve the political and economic integration of Western Europe in the first instance, and the convening forthwith of a European Assembly to consider the next steps (May 1948). Despite her recent conclusion of a trade agreement with the United Kingdom, Russia retorted by sabotaging Marshall Aid and seeking to squeeze the Allies out of Berlin by cutting their communications therewith. She thus drove the United Kingdom to rearm tentatively and, having failed to prevent the Allies from supplying their sections of Berlin by their amazing air-lift, turned away to combine her European satellites with herself in an economic union, the Comecon. Most of the Western Powers thereupon signed the North Atlantic Treaty which aimed at sweeping away economic and passport obstructions and envisaged mutual defence arrangements (April 1949). Better still, Churchill's Council of Europe began to take shape. Its Consultative Assembly, meeting at Strasburg, first gave full weight to the recommendation of the Council of Ministers, its 'Upper House', that a European Economic Union should be formed and that the British pound sterling should be recognised as an international unit of exchange, and then went on to call for a draft Convention of the Rights of Man, breach of which should be reported by a European Commission to a European Court of Human Rights, to debate the admission of Germany to its own membership, and, finally, to leave no doubt that it wished the indispensable United Kingdom to be at once a member of the European Union and of the British Commonwealth (September 1949).

Meanwhile, the Cold War was steadily becoming world-wide. In spite of their dismal failures in the Italian, French, New Zealand, Australian and British general elections, Communists diligently stoked up strikes from the Antipodes by way of Canada to the United Kingdom, while Russia's manufacture of the atom bomb and the treachery of trusted Western scientists in her interests stampeded thousands of ruthless and impressionable United States citizens into demanding the making of the still more devastating hydrogen bomb. Those same Americans also cried out that their country's policy in Asia had failed while that of the U.S.S.R. was going from strength to strength in those parts. It was only too true. Recent Japanese victories had shattered the prestige of the white man in the eyes of Asiatics who all knew of the successes of semi-Asiatic Russia in the East and nothing of her disastrous reverses in the unimagined West, while those millions of them who were poverty-stricken peasants understandably saw in Communism hope of land, an end of 'colonialism', and relief from usurers and corrupt officials. Russia, entrenched in Outer Mongolia, was nibbling at Chinese Turkestan rich in minerals and vital to the Transasiatic air-routes; she virtually controlled Japanese-industrialised Manchuria, had an economic agreement with adjacent North Korea, and hung like a thundercloud over American-occupied South Korea. Now the international and Communist-dominated Federation of Trade Unions resolved at Pekin to spread rebellion in Asia under the direction of a kind of Eastern Cominform (November 1949).

It all began to answer according to plan. Mao Tse's Communist People's Government concluded a treaty with the U.S.S.R., conquered all mainland China and swept the wrecks of Chiang Kai Shek's incompetent administration into island Formosa; other Communists, working on the oppressed peasantry, paralysed the American-sponsored Government of the Philippines; yet others, many of them Chinese, inflamed war or rebellion against the British, Dutch, French and Asiatic rulers of Borneo, Malaya, Siam, Indonesia and, lastly, Indo-China whose rebel Government the U.S.S.R. duly recognised (January 1950). The West prescribed what remedies it could. The Commonwealth authorities at the Colombo Conference proferred economic aid to dull the ears of Asiatics to the siren songs of Moscow and Pekin; in Europe itself, men as diverse as Churchill, Reynaud and Montgomery insisted that some of the weight must be taken off the shoulders of the bored and attenuated Allied occupation forces by the rearming of Germany and the revival of the vast German steelworks of the Ruhr in the service of Western Christendom against the Marxian East. From his capital Adenauer, Chancellor of the recently-recognised West German Republic, accepted membership of the Council of Europe albeit in a secondary role for the time being, and delighted some Frenchmen and terrified others by proposing a Franco-German Union, while the French Foreign Minister, Schumann, propounded a scheme whereunder a joint European authority should control the coal, coke, iron and steel industries of Lorraine, Belgium, Luxemburg, the Ruhr and, preferably, the United Kingdom also.

At this critical juncture, the North Koreans, who had just seen the backs of the Russian troops but who were themselves still firmly under Russian and Chinese influence, suddenly fell upon the South Koreans from whose territory the scanty United States garrison was contemplating withdrawal (June 1940). They soon had their enemies cooped up far to the south, but they had also impelled Churchill to call for a 'European Army' strong enough to cope with the largely mechanised hordes of the new Great Khan of Moscow. What was more, they had galvanised U.N.O. into effective life for the first time. In spite of the inevitable Russian veto, that august body found means to proclaim joint action against the aggressors and was rewarded by the ready response of the United Kingdom, some of the Dominions and many other Powers. Since the main strain must be taken by the unready and unwilling United States, it followed that all these United Nations forces should be put under the American Commander-in-Chief, General Douglas MacArthur. He soon thrust the invaders back to the Chinese frontier, and there, in spite of warnings from Peking, bombed them within sight of massed Chinese divisions. Truman seized this moment of relief to read the blatantly anti-Democratic MacArthur a much-needed lesson on the relative positions of the civil and military powers under the United States Constitution; Russia sought to paralyse her enemies by forming a Peace Front of all those kindly folk who could be induced to sign a Peace Pledge calling for peace on her terms, while the Western Allies appointed the able and genial American, Dwight Eisenhower, Commander-in-Chief of their North Atlantic forces and began to rearm with all speed (January 1951). And then came a setback in Korea. In response to MacArthur's bombing, well organised masses of Chinese 'volunteers' poured into Korea and drove the United Nations' soldiers before them. Reinforcement from many quarters and a General fresh from Washington to take command on the spot soon restored the situation, but some months passed before Truman could venture to recall MacArthur. Thereafter, the dreary and costly Korean campaign dragged on to the accompaniment of interminable negotiations for a cease fire, while the United States guaranteed Chiang Kai Shek's Formosa, signed a treaty with the Philippines and a military agreement with the lawful Government of Indo-China, took the lead in achieving a general peace settlement with Japan, and overcame the objections of Australia and New Zealand to the consequent prospect of a rearmed Japan by joining them in a Pacific Defence Pact from which the Mother Country was excluded (September 1951). The United States hoped thus to safeguard her own interests, but she showed that she was not always careful of the interests of others. After the triumphant election of Eisenhower as President, the first such Republican victory for twenty years, she hinted at a blockade of the Chinese coasts to the alarm of her allies, rearmed Chiang Kai Shek and left him free to 'proceed independently'. This the ruler of Formosa did by despatching a force to co-operate with rebellious tribesmen against their newly-independent Burmese rulers and thus impelling the Rangoon authorities to appeal to the Security Council. At this threatening juncture, Stalin died (March 1953). His death was followed by a welcome change of tone at the Kremlin and Pekin, for not only did Malenkov, his successor, show himself accommodating all along the line, but the North Koreans, with the significant backing of the Chinese Prime Minister, effected a mutual exchange of such prisoners as were willing to go home and resumed the recently abandoned negotiations for an armistice in Korea.

In the West, meanwhile, France, Benelux and Western Germany had accepted a French proposal for a European Defence Community, and all the Powers concerned, with the exception of the United Kingdom, had ratified the Schumann Plan (February–April 1951). All was not so well, however, in the explosive Middle East, where nationalism was rising *crescendo*. True, the withdrawal of Franco-British control from Libya, in accordance with long-standing promises, caused no difficulty beyond anxious questionings by those many Frenchmen who were exercised by the violent agitation for popular government in adjacent Tunisia; but in the Nile valley and the Persian Gulf it was otherwise. The Irani Ministry, amid a skilfully stimulated public clamour against 'colonialism', obliged the Anglo-Iranian Oil Company to vacate its giant oil-refinery at Abadan. At Cairo, the ultra-nationalist Wafd Ministry not only demanded that their country's rescuers should pay their debts for supplies and services furnished at usurious rates during the Axis war, but insisted that the British should accord Egypt a treaty more flattering to her self-esteem than that which their predecessors had been frightened into signing by Mussolini's seizure of Abyssinia. They clamoured for the withdrawal of the British troops, who, in terms of the existing treaty, occupied the internationally vital Suez Canal Zone, successfully badgered the predominantly French company which had cut and still operated that waterway into giving Egyptians more well-paid seats on its Board, and presently exceeded their powers by holding up oil-tankers passing through 'the Ditch' on their way to Israel with whom Egypt was still formally at war. Next, this Ministry claimed control of the whole of the Nile Valley and, therefore, the ending of the Anglo-Egyptian Condominium in the huge territory of the Sudan by no means all of whose inhabitants were even Moslems, let alone Egyptians or Arabs. Its King, Farouk, regardless of the fact that the British had long been helping the Sudanese to develop great irrigation and cotton-growing schemes and training them for self-government, boldly proclaimed himself 'King of the Sudan' and dismissed the British Governor-General at Khartum. At this stage the Cairo mob stepped in. Taking its cue from the Ministry, it first vainly assaulted the British troops on the Canal, and then launched a concerted and most destructive attack on Europeans and, there was reason to believe, on the authorities in the capital. The Egyptian King promptly sent in his troops to quell the uproar and summoned less flamboyant advisers to his counsels, while the British remained to discharge their international functions in the Canal Zone; the 'dismissed' Governor-General stayed on in Khartum, and the British and Egyptian Governments began to negotiate a general settlement. King Farouk then dismissed the Chamber of Deputies, but, a little later, was himself forced to abdicate by Major-General Mohamed Neguib and a group of army officers (23 July, 1952).

After ruling for a time through a civilian Prime Minister, Neguib took his place and secured his rear by retiring some hundreds of officers for dangerous political activities. He then proclaimed a three-year Constitution which gave himself supreme powers, but provided that he should formulate policy with the help of the Committee of the Revolution, that is, the committee of thirteen officers, and the legislative Council of Ministers. In due time, he proclaimed Egypt a republic under his own presidency. Meanwhile, he had demanded that the British should evacuate the Canal zone; but if he himself was ready to admit that evacuation was 'a very distant target', his truculent second-in-command insisted that it must be 'immediate, complete and unconditional' with no room for a possible return thither of British troops even in the event of war. With regard to the Condominium, Neguib agreed that the Sudanese should have speedy self-government and the right of self-determination within three years (12 February, 1943). Even though he was only persuaded with difficulty that they should, if they wished, remain within the Commonwealth and then accused the British, without any good evidence, of trying to upset this accord, he at least showed himself ready, as his predecessors had not been, to let the Sudanese decide their future for themselves. And that was what the British had been aiming at these many years past.

The United Kingdom was affected more directly by all these post-war developments than any other member of the Commonwealth, because apart from the fact that she was the only one to have world-wide commitments, if Russia went east she had much to defend in those regions, and if Russia came west she would have to take much of the initial shock because Germany was in ruins and France in not much better case. She could not well keep out of any major war that might come, because, lying as she did in the middle of the land and sea expanses of the Northern Hemisphere, she was a group of those 'islands in the North Atlantic' on which Roosevelt had set such store, at best a bridgehead from which overseas warriors might leap across to what was still 'the Continent', at worst a mere target and bomber-base.

Attlee's new Labour Government, backed by a good majority in the Commons, faced up to its task. It carried a reasonable Budget, took quietly enough the abrupt termination of Lend-Lease, accepted reluctantly an onerous American loan, and ostentatiously repealed the hated anti-trade union legislation passed after the General Strike of 1926. It also pushed on successfully with demobilisation at the risk of letting loose a flood of unemployed on a country that might well fail to recover economically in any event, wondering the while whether a remedy could be found in an emigration which would cost the Mother Country many of her young and active folk and face such Dominions as might desire newcomers with the difficult problem of finding them jobs and passable houses. Housewives were in a measure consoled for continued rationing and shortages of coal, food, raw materials and houses by the National Insurance Act and, less certainly, by the nationalisation of the Bank of England. Labour men might be cheered by substantial signs of industrial recovery and possibly impressed by the rash boast that inflation was dead and done with, but nearly all of them were irritated by the Communists' white-anting of trade unions, and disappointed when an eagerly demanded inquiry into the evils arising from the capitalist ownership and control of the Press showed that most of their suspicions had been unfounded. What troubled the nation as a whole, however, were the recurrent strikes which, though less frequent than after the Kaiser's War, were sometimes so dangerous that on one occasion troops had to be called in to maintain the very life of the capital. In the background, the isolated miners only agreed most grudgingly to allow a few of the swarming Polish refugees to go down 'their' pits, and by their own slackness hampered industry and their country's foreign policy by denying coal for export. So grave did the lack of fuel become that at the height of the fiercest winter for two generations the authorities had to deprive industry of power and thereby see two million souls thrown out of employment and all but the cheapest newspapers suspend publication. It must have been a relief to the Royal Family to get away from all this into the sunshine of Southern Africa, leaving the Prime Minister to tell their people, 'We either work or want'.

The public welcomed the raising of the school-age, but was less enthusiastic about the guarantee of a five-day week to the coal-miners and the Supplies and Services Act which gave the Government perilously wide powers. Then, one impelling reason for this omnibus measure became apparent as the economic disequilibrium which had existed between the United States and the rest for more then a generation threatened to tilt right over. The post-war sellers' market had been passing away for some time when foreigners began to scramble so furiously on the London market to convert their holdings of sterling into the dominant United States dollars that drastic steps had to be taken if the United Kingdom were to keep any of her rapidly dwindling store of those dollars. The Government, therefore, jumped at the offer of Marshall Aid, cut down imports from, and sought to increase exports to, the dollar area, and suspended the convertibility of sterling (August 1947). Further, Attlee gave Cripps the new office of Minister of Economic Affairs and, in due time, the Chancellorship of the Exchequer also, and was soon encouraged by a Budget which provided a genuine surplus instead of recent imaginings and by Cripps's cautiously expressed belief that accounts might just be squared before Marshall Aid came to an end in 1952.

While the nation was thus pulling out of the slough into which it had slid, domestic quarrels raged over three measures: first, the National Health Act which only came into force after a bitter struggle between many organised doctors and Aneurin Bevan, the truculent Minister of Health; secondly, the British Nationality Act which went far to reduce the once proud title of 'British subject' to an eviscerated boast; and, thirdly, a Bill nationalising iron and steel. To make matters worse, the authorities abolished the special representation of the Universities and the City of London in defiance of inter-party agreements reached by previous Parliaments, and ensured the breakdown of an All-Party Conference which sought to frame a scheme for that reform of the 'Other Place' which was desired by Conservatives, Liberals and many of the Peers themselves. This done, Lords, Iron and Steel and the parlous state of the Forces were all debated in a Special Session during which the Prime Minister indeed secured a three-months' deferment of demobilisation and an intensive recruiting campaign for the Territorials and Reserves, but under Left Wing pressure cut down the period of compulsory National Service from a possibly adequate eighteen months to an assuredly insufficient twelve (September 1948). The Houses met for their next regular Session in a bad temper, for not only had Cripps outraged trade unionists by calling for a pegging of wages, but Bevan had indicated that to him all Tories were 'lower than vermin'. In this electrical atmosphere, the Commons passed a measure which reduced from two years to one the period during which the Upper House could delay Bills, a measure which, in spite of Ministerial denials, was obviously intended to prevent their Lordships' blocking the passage of the Iron and Steel Bill during the life of the current Parliament. The Lords passed the unpalatable measure perforce, but were assured by the Conservatives that they would repeal it and effectively remodel the constitution and powers of their Chamber.

At the close of 1948, Cripps could note a marked improvement in the dollar situation, but he had to ask for huge supplementaries to cover the unexpectedly high cost of National Insurance, and raised a storm in business circles by hinting that the State might even one day engage in 'competitive public enterprises' against private firms. He then raised a storm even greater, first, by telling his own followers that the limit of redistribution of incomes by means of taxation was very near if only because 'the rich' were no longer so numerous nor so rich as they once had been, then by warning them that so far from getting further social services they must work harder to keep those they had, and finally, by fixing a ceiling for the rocketing food subsidies and raising the cost of certain basic foods by fourpence a head each week to meet the cost of what could not be paid for out of the current subsidy of eleven shillings. Six months later came a serious setback. In face of another run on British dollar-holdings by jumpy business men, Cripps repeatedly denied all thought of devaluation, and then, with Cabinet backing, gave scant warning to France and the Dominions and devalued the £ sterling from four dollars to a mere two dollars eighty cents (18 September, 1949). However, after the initial shock, most members of the sterling *bloc* followed the United Kingdom's example, and, while the cost of living was already creeping up, the British Minister of Food could boast unconvincingly that the dollar shortage had been met by a 'massive switch' of food purchases to non-dollar areas.

In February 1950 the Government risked a general election. Partly because it won only by the shortest of heads and partly because so many of its leading members were tired if not ill, it talked no more of nationalisation, but merely gave up the direction of labour, restored recent housing cuts, fixed a ceiling for food subsidies and promised to fix one for National Health also. In response to the summons of the United Nations, it sent to Korea what ships, planes and men it could spare after garrisoning the United Kingdom and her many dependencies, including vulnerable Hong Kong, and providing for the weary war in Malaya; in addition, it extended the period of compulsory National Service. Nevertheless, gold and dollar deficits were wiped out so steadily that the ailing Cripps, before resigning office, could announce that he would take no more Marshall Aid after the end of the year. Thereafter, the Ministry began to go to pieces visibly. Rejecting Churchill's suggestion of

T

a Coalition, it plodded on through a spate of Communist-inspired strikes, shouldering as best it could the heavy cost of rearmament as well as that of social services. Presently, Ernest Bevin, the stalwart Foreign Secretary, died amid almost universal regret, and Aneurin Bevan resigned to lead the anti-Attlee wing of the Labour Party. There was nothing for it but to go to the polls once more (October 1951). This time the Conservatives won narrowly.

In due course, Churchill and Eden, Prime Minister and Foreign Secretary respectively once more, journeyed to Washington and Ottawa to talk over with the President, *inter alia*, the much-discussed exclusion of the United Kingdom from the Pacific Defence Pact which his Government had recently made with Australia and New Zealand (January 1952). Much good came of this renewal of diplomacy by personal contact, but no diplomacy could remedy the grave shortage of rearmament materials or reprieve the British taxpayers from shouldering the biggest deficit in their country's history. Personal sorrows, however, soon outweighed material anxieties. King George VI, long desperately overworked, underwent a serious operation and had to give up all immediate hope of visiting his Pacific Dominions. As he began to pull up, Princess Elizabeth and the Duke of Edinburgh visited the United States and Canada, and then set off for Ceylon, Australia and New Zealand by way of Kenya. At Nairobi, the news reached them that the King was dead (6 February, 1952). Thus it was that for the first time in British history the monarch had to be called home from overseas to take up the burden that awaits a constitutional ruler at Westminster. It was a good augury that the first year of the new reign should have seen an improvement in the country's gold and dollar reserves, and, in the long run, an augury even better that folk of all classes should have rallied manfully to the relief of sufferers and the repair of damage in their own eastern counties and the Netherlands after the dreadful floods that swept both lands early in 1953.

In Dublin, de Valera hailed the end of the Axis war by triumphing that since 1937 his country had occupied a unique constitutional position in that he himself had been the representative of that King who had then been relegated to the chilly office of mere 'Sole Head' of the Irish Free State in external affairs. This trumpet-blast may have warmed the hearts of the *Taioseacht's* supporters, but it did not stop the Channel Islanders, themselves scarcely more closely linked to the United Kingdom than were the Free Staters, from deporting as 'aliens' Irishmen who had worked in Germany during the Nazi occupation of their little archipelago, nor the House of Lords from rejecting the appeal of an Irish murderer on the ground that he too was an alien over whom they had no jurisdiction. It positively stung Sir Basil Brooke, who still ruled Northern Ireland within the United Kingdom, into warning de Valera bluntly that his rhodomontade had made Partition more real and lasting than ever.

Having sent his country's first ambassador to the Vatican, de Valera turned to domestic affairs. Politically, the situation was reassuring, for, however riddled with jobbery and corruption parliamentary life might be, his own *Fianna Fail* party had never been stronger over against its divided adversaries. Economically, however, the scene was not so hopeful. Now that the war was over, the purchasing power of the pound was dwindling, the cost of living rising faster than wages, and the flow back of wartime emigrants from the United Kingdom breeding unemployment. Worse still, the renewal of fixed and working capital had fallen into arrears and the volume of production and exports was far below what it had been in 1939. Worst of all, the fertility of the soil on which Ireland ultimately depended had been sadly diminished by archaic farming methods, the subdivision of holdings and de Valera's persistent neglect of agriculture at a time when her farm produce was especially desired by the United Kingdom, always her chiefest customer, now her only great debtor for war supplies, and as ever the provider of most of the machinery, fertilisers and other goods she needed so desperately. On the other hand, the Free State had neither external debt nor any marked inequalities in income and, mercifully, her relations with the United Kingdom were improving. The hungry British negotiated eagerly for foodstuffs, bought flights of Irish greyhounds for 'the Dogs', rejoiced with all good Irishmen when de Valera reopened the famous Dublin Horse Show, and steadily strove to beat down Russia's resistance to the admission of the Free State to U.N.O. The Free Staters, in return, bought six British corvettes, welcomed uproariously a visiting British naval squadron to Cork, and though de Valera sought to check the wholesale purchase of real property by newcomers by imposing stiff stamp duties, cheerfully fleeced the droves of British income-tax dodgers who braved their atrocious hotels and charges for the sake of square meals. Communications drew the two islands closer together. Their authorities agreed that the headquarters of the company which operated the cross-Channel steamers should be in Dublin, and that British transatlantic planes should touch down at the fine new Shannon air-port, the first free air-port in the world. Dublin entertained an International Conference on North Atlantic air-routes, and de Valera could hope that his new School of Research in Cosmic Physics might further those world interests which he himself had seemed to ignore for so long. He even sought to further some of them himself by sending strong delegations to the London Food Conference, the United Nations Food and Agricultural Organisation and the Paris Conference on European Reconstruction, and by encouraging his people to send as much food and clothing as they could spare to a shattered Continent. But though he and they, as staunch Roman Catholics, hailed Churchill's call for a rally of Western Christendom against the forces of the Communist East, neither he nor they did more.

At one moment, it seemed possible that North and South might draw together when they worked hand in hand to bring to justice an I.R.A. stalwart who had long been wanted for the murder of a Dublin policeman; but these hopes were dashed when the newly-formed *Clann na Poblachta* in the south drove Brooke to import religious passion into Ulster politics by clamouring for an All-Ireland Republic. De Valera, meanwhile, had troubles of his own as the terrible winter of 1946-47 clamped down ruining the harvest and so drenching the turf-beds that he was forced to appeal to the United Kingdom and the United States for well-nigh unprocurable coal, if only to avert the further closing of branch lines and the bankruptcy of the Great Northern Railway which linked Dublin and Belfast in spite of the Border. He met with a poor response when he warned industrialists that they must rely on turning out better goods rather than trust to the tariffs which he himself had constructed so laboriously that the poor could scarcely afford boots and clothes, and was dismayed at the widespread condemnation of his cherished campaign for compulsory 'Irish'. Driven to desperation, de Valera at last joined other leaders in parading 'Partition' in the Dail and the Dublin streets. He would not listen when Brooke suggested that Northerners and Southerners could become good friends in a divided Ireland even if they could not live together in one house, and was wrath when the British Government carried the Northern Ireland Act, which, for all that it sanctioned agreements recently made by the Two Irelands for joint public utility schemes of transport, arterial drainage and hydro-electricity, also gave the Northern Parliament wider powers. Some Northern enthusiasts, who disliked being in tow of a Socialist Government at Westminster, returned thanks by talking of Dominion status for their little enclave; one Southern leader proclaimed that the Free State must come out of the Commonwealth altogether, and de Valera insisted that it lay with the United Kingdom alone to eradicate all age-old Irish hates and suspicions by making of the Two Irelands a single neutral federation ruled from Dublin. Neither this bid for popularity nor yet his disastrously belated promise to rescue Irish agriculture could save the *Taioseacht* from defeat at three bye-elections and the consequent general election (February, 1948). He handed over to John Costello, *Fine Gael* leader of a shaky coalition, and dashed off to convince the already converted Irish of the United States, Australia and New Zealand that Partition was the root of most evils.

Costello was soon in difficulties. Strikes by Dublin butchers and bakers and Southern Railway employees and a continuance of public overspending answered his warning that masters and men must change their ways if the cost of living was to be brought down. Plainly, as one way of restoring his waning prestige, he decided to overcall his predecessor's hand. Sallying forth, he told New York reporters that Partition alone stood in the way of his country's co-operation in the maintenance of the general peace and, though the idea had never been mentioned during the recent election campaign, boasted at Ottawa that he meant to break the last frail link with the Crown. This he did on his return by securing the repeal of the External Relations Act (December, 1948). Henceforward the Free State was to be the Republic of Ireland and its elected President the supreme executive in all spheres external and internal. Thus, by an abrupt confidence trick, thousands of Irishmen in all parts of the Commonwealth and Empire were transformed into aliens and Northern Ireland forced to become a foreign land.

The inauguration of the new Republic on Easter Monday, 1949, was marked by the grim silence of de Valera and Brooke, the refusal of the Dublin and Cork corporations to take part in the celebrations, and the announcement by Costello, in response to the generous good wishes of His Abolished Majesty, that he would not sign the North Atlantic Pact while the 'occupation' of the North by British troops continued to inflame the resentment of 'the Irish people'. The new *Taioseacht* ignored the Northern Prime Minister's suggestion that the Republic and the United Kingdom should conclude a defence agreement; but he came down to earth when Brooke's Unionists gained a clear majority at a general election, and positively sprang to attention when all parties at Westminster combined to pass the Ireland Act. On the one hand, this measure minimised the effect of the recent Irish Declaration of Independence by providing that the Republic was not to be classed as a foreign country for the purposes of any law in force in the United Kingdom or her colonies, and that persons born in its territory before the Treaty of 1921 who had not resided there since could retain their British nationality; on the other, it promised that neither the whole nor any part of Northern Ireland should ever cease to be a portion of the United Kingdom without the consent of its own Parliament. In face of this thunderbolt, Costello and de Valera outbid each other in the Dail and O'Connell (late Sackville) Street, while other highly-placed Irishmen bombinated in the European Assembly at Strasburg. But none of all this could save the Republic from having to follow the United Kingdom into devaluation. The knowledge that this step at least helped Northern Ireland's linen to earn dollars emboldened Brooke to cross over to the United States to put his country's case. There, by dwelling on the perils of Communism, he impelled the House of Representatives to rescind the snatch vote which Irish-Americans had just carried demanding that Marshall Aid be withheld from the United Kingdom till she had sacrificed loyal Belfast to independent Dublin.

This rebuff did not, however, deter the doughty Captain Paeder Cowan from causing the delighted Dublin crowds to grin by parading his private army, the whole fifty of them, pledged to make a forcible end of Partition. But sanity had not altogether deserted Ireland. North and South could still work together to set up a planetarium at Armagh, launch the Erne hydro-electric scheme, acquire the fishing-rights on Lough Foyle and belatedly rescue the bankrupt Great Northern Railway. But this was little enough. The Twenty-six Counties of the Republic of Ireland were now definitely outside the Commonwealth and the Six Counties of the

North more determinedly within it than ever—and the Border still straggled across the map.

At the close of the Axis war, Canada's Liberal Prime Minister, Mackenzie King, gingerly led his fellow-countrymen out into the new world far enough to make the United Kingdom a loan, and then led them back to attend to the domestic problems which interested him and most of them much more than other folk's troubles. How were they to maintain their high standard of living in face of strikes, lack of coal, non-existent domestic servants and the disappearance into the backblocks of swarms of operatives who would not work now that they could no longer command the inflated wages of wartime? And, at a time when politicians and business men were crying out against the continuance of controls for yet another year, would export credits to maintain employment of themselves avert inflation? Of course, one possible long-term cure for inflation was immigration, but that was a sore subject to most of the mere 12,500,000 folk who were strung out in semi-isolated groups along a narrow strip three thousand miles in length between the Undefended Frontier and the Arctic snows and could not decide what the best kind of immigrant was. Apart from the French-Canadians who held that the best kind was the kind that did not come, they were agreed only on three points: firstly, immigrants must come at their own risk and cost and must never fall on the public charges; secondly, they should have capital wherewith to create employment, a kind not easy to find now that Canada was no longer a ready borrower but a heavy investor overseas; thirdly, they must be English-speaking folk or at the very least North Europeans. Room must, naturally, be found for the few thousand Polish refugees and displaced persons whom their Prime Minister was admitting as well as for the many thousands of overseas spouses of ex-Service folk whom he could not very well shut out; but beyond that no organised political group was ready to go as yet.

The domestic battle-scene was confused. Though Labour had no party of its own, Collectivist parties were gathering strength. Communists camouflaged as Labour Progressives pegged away to the glory of Stalin; the Social Credit Party, long entrenched in Alberta, had not ventured to enforce its peculiar economic doctrines, but preferred to display a blatant imperialism and, in its hatred of all internationalism, to accuse 'financiers' of using U.N.O. for their own base ends, while the frankly Socialist C.C.F., was strong on the Prairies even though it had not yet made much impression farther east. Of the two great parties, Bracken's Progressive-Conservatives were making fair headway by attacking the Government for its many sins of commission in the matter of controls and of omission in the wide field of Commonwealth co-operation, while Mackenzie King's Liberals, after emphasising their country's cherished independence and seeking to bring home to Canadians that they were Canadians by drawing a marked distinction between 'Canadian citizen' and 'British subject', jogged along with a promise to fight Socialism as far as they could under the handicap of a Minister of Agriculture who insisted on wide and arbitrary powers for his Canadian Wheat Board. As an earnest of good intentions, the Government began to lift controls and slash Federal expenditure.

At the moment, most Canadians were less concerned with the party fight than with their economic future. Their troubles in that field had been coming on for some time. The strain of the Kaiser's War had twisted the trade triangle within which they had been wont to sell the United Kingdom all the wheat and bacon they could produce and spend the proceeds in the United States. They had indeed run short of United States dollars during the Axis war, but thanks to controls and American purchases of their war material, they had been affluent enough at the end of it to raise their own dollar from ten per cent discount to parity. Now, however, what with the way the world was going and the huge loans and gifts they had made to keep needy but necessary overseas customers on their feet, the familiar triangle was being warped out of all recognition. Most of their disbursements had come home in the form of purchases of Canadian products and, for lack of non-American supplies to square the account, had been spent so whole-heartedly in the United States that by mid-1947 Canadians saw their store of United States dollars draining away fast. Then, in the nick of time, came Marshall Aid. The Canadian Government made another large loan to the United Kingdom, strove to check the extravagance of their own people, and bullied the harassed Mother Country into taking bacon she did not want as the only means of getting at high prices something of the wheat she must have, and that on terms that would give her people less bread for a year to come and leave Canada free to 'reconsider' the financial arrangements at the end of the first three months. Canada also signed a favourable Reciprocal Trade Agreement with the United States, learned that the dreaded Geneva I.T.O. Agreements had preserved to her most of her cherished imperial preferences besides giving her reasonable access to the United States market for the first time these many years, and was assured that the products she was to contribute to the European Recovery Programme would be bought in her country.

In these cheering circumstances, the Progressive-Conservatives sounded the electoral war-cry and trained their batteries on a Government that was losing popularity by reimposing controls to check fast-rising prices and horrifying Provinces which, unlike Ontario and Quebec, had no alternative waterways by raising railway rates. Again, the Socialist C.C.F. had not only lost its foothold in Quebec but had alienated many of its individualistic Prairie supporters by its very successes in Ontario and distant British Columbia. But it did not augur well for the new-found progressivism of the ailing Bracken's party that it should have had to accept his resignation and elect in his stead George Drew, a keen Ontario imperialist and spokesman of Toronto big business. The Liberals, for their part, demanded free enterprise and an ending of Mackenzie King's dictatorial methods, and elected as Deputy Leader, St. Laurent, the Prime Minister's chief *Quebecquois* henchman. Having thus received its marching orders, the Government accepted the North Atlantic Treaty and embarked on the election campaign. This was a confused affair turning almost entirely on questions of bread and butter. What, many Canadians asked, were their bacon and egg producers to do now that the sterling *bloc* would take little more than wheat, cheese, base metals and other raw materials? What was the use of secondary industries if these were to make Canadians less ready to take United Kingdom manufactures and, to that extent, reduce the United Kingdom's ability to pay for Canada's basic exports, and what should be Canada's retort to the alleged attempts by the United Kingdom to squeeze her out of the West Indian and other sterling markets? Progressive-Conservatives had long been lamenting that the recent Anglo-Canadian Wheat Agreement would rob farmers of high world prices and that the contracts for the supply of meat and other farm-produce to the United Kingdom would drain the I.T.O. Agreement of all substance. Now they complained that the ratification of this latter Agreement held out small hope of release from dollar difficulties,

because it forbade the increase of existing preferences and the granting of new ones unless these were intended to promote development
and reconstruction. And where, Canadians asked, could they look
for new preferences unless they entered into a customs union with
the United States, an economic merger that could hardly stop short
of that political union which few of them were ready to face as yet?
So they went to the polls.

The result of the general election was a surprise. The C.C.F.
was routed even in Saskatchewan, the Progressive-Conservatives
did badly, and the Liberals, who already had a five to one majority
in the Senate, won an unparalleled majority in the Lower House,
though on a minority of the votes cast. The Federal Parliament
was now far too Roman Catholic to please Protestant Canadians,
but they could take comfort from the thought that St. Laurent,
the new Prime Minister, was no bigot and, withal, much less
dictatorial than his predecessor. St. Laurent began tolerably well by
controlling rents and giving further help to farmers, but he had to
face strong official and parliamentary criticism of the laxity with
which the Estimates were passed and, when the United Kingdom
proposed to buy Danish bacon, listen to many Canadians asking what
was the value of the British connection. Nevertheless, he followed
Cripps into devaluation readily enough, because that, after all,
brought the dollar and sterling *blocs* closer together and thus might
enable Canada to balance precariously between them. Then, the ageing Mackenzie King died in July 1950, but his isolationist spirit
remained to inspire the abolition of appeals to the Judicial Committee of the Privy Council. Had he lived, he would have been
pleased to see reluctant Newfoundland come in as the tenth Province
and little-considered Alberta strike oil, but he would have been
less pleased to see British Columbia threaten to block the projected
pipe-line to the United States unless it ran through her territory.
Long before oil was ready to oust coal, Canada was smitten by a
railway strike, just as the Korean bombshell burst. The isolationist
Ministry, which had always insisted that U.N.O. was an organisation far superior to any mere British Commonwealth, rallied so
poorly to the summons for co-operation that it could announce
that it had no men to spare for Korea because it must keep all the
47,000 Regulars in its three services at home to defend Canada
in the Third World War that was surely coming. At long last,
however, under pressure of the English-speaking Provinces, St.

Laurent held a special Session during which the railway strike was settled, the Canadian dollar set free to find its own level and thus enable Ottawa to buy American arms and equipment, and provision made for the raising of an expeditionary force of 9,000 men, some few of whom were duly packed off to Korea.

St. Laurent's reaction to the more deadly situation in Europe was hardly more inspiring. Harking back to Canada's attitude at the outbreak of the Axis war, he opined that his country could help more effectively by selling food and arms to her allies than by sending men, and tartly dismissed Churchill's suggestion that he should send a division to Europe as an unwarranted attempt to dictate Canada's foreign policy. Once more, however, pressure by his opponents forced him to agree that Canada should henceforth maintain an expeditionary force ready to go anywhere to fulfil her obligations under the U.N. Charter and the Atlantic Pact. Long accustomed to seeing defence agreements and joint manoeuvres with the United States, he began to buy equipment in that country for his three armed services which slowly doubled their numbers. But he had to carry an intensely unpopular Minister of National Defence, listen to complaints by his own *Quebecquois* that far too few French-Canadians were promoted and, presently, see numbers of military men and civilians arrested for wholesale thefts of military stores. Disappointment and disgust at this sorry performance went far to explain why his Liberal Party lost several Federal bye-elections and, during the ensuing Provincial elections, saw the C.C.F. carry Saskatchewan once more and run a close second to the victorious Social Credit Party in British Columbia and found itself ruling far less than half of Canada's 14,000,000 inhabitants from Provincial capitals.

Be that as it might, St. Laurent, in keeping with his 'national' policy, advocated the dropping of the honoured name of 'Dominion', made the admirable choice of Sir Vincent Massey as Canada's first home-born Governor-General, and bestowed his blessing on an ambitious scheme for a St. Lawrence Seaway which would not only give Ontario the hydro-electric power she needed but bring the Great Lakes nearer to the Atlantic. He and President Truman agreed that this seaway should preferably be a joint Canadian-United States undertaking, if only because without the co-operation of Washington the hydro-electric power would not be forthcoming and, without that, the truncated scheme could not pay. Attempts to overcome opposition in Congress having failed, St. Laurent decided to go forward alone and was soon encouraged by Eisenhower, Truman's Republican successor, to hope that the seaway might after all be a joint venture of their two countries.

If Canada was a bourgeois Paradise, the two Pacific Dominions were a Red Valhalla. Once the war was over, Communists and fellow-travellers let themselves go, and in Australia, which probably fared worse in this respect than even New Zealand, tried for a start to dictate their country's foreign policy. When Indonesian seamen refused to take Dutch ships from Sydney to the rebellious East Indies, Dutch soldiers got one away by loading it themselves. At this, Communists easily induced the Waterfront Federation to ban all vessels suspected of carrying arms. Chifley, the new Labour Prime Minister, indeed deported the recalcitrant Indonesians, but promised that only ships loaded with food and medicines should be despatched. Even so, the Communists held up Dutch ships and soldiers for another week, and, thereafter, sought to destroy the elaborate system of Arbitration Courts and secure a forty-hour week by staging strikes by seamen and iron, steel, and base metal workers. Having worn these trouble-makers down for a time, Chifley faced his more normal preoccupations. He failed to persuade fundamentally isolationist Labour to sanction conscription for the maintenance of the 84,000 troops he had undertaken to find as garrisons in scattered posts in the Pacific, but he fared better with his advocacy of a scheme for a South-West Pacific Regional Council to shoulder defence and other responsibilities jointly, and hopefully projected a Federal University at Canberra. He then faced a general election and referenda on his demand for powers to regulate conditions of work, collective marketing of primary products and social services. He gained only a narrow victory at the polls and was merely given power to deal with the social services that everyone desired (September 1946).

Thus barely confirmed in power, Chifley managed to find a sympathetic locally-born but otherwise not entirely satisfactory Governor-General, induced Australia to subscribe to the International Monetary Fund, welcomed the British Commonwealth Conference to Canberra, and then turned away wearily to cope with renewed labour troubles and the rising power of the States. A growing number of voters who were sick of labour totalitarianism were rallying to the States with whom it lay, far more than with the Centre, to say how much or how little effective collectivisation there should be. Victoria and Tasmania had already defied the Federal authorities and now the Victorian Upper House had, for the first time, precipitated a State election on a Federal issue by refusing supply. It was not surprising that successive public opinion polls should have recorded a marked swing against further nationalization, because the Labour rank-and-file were getting well-nigh out of hand. Strikes spread like a plague in the four eastern States, and worst of all in Victoria, not this time strikes by extremists but by steady-going trade unionists who demanded the forty-hour week, protested against wage-pegging and too often defied the Arbitration Courts. In the end, the Federal Arbitration Court itself conceded the forty-hour week and, by so doing, hampered many official undertakings and obliged the railways to raise fares because Canberra would not meet their consequent deficits.

The meaning of deficits was brought home to Chifley when the United Kingdom suspended the convertibility of sterling (September 1947). He promptly restricted dollar purchases, but when, lacking an electoral mandate, he nationalised the fourteen privately-owned Banks, he was told by the Judicial Committee that the Act was invalid (August 1948). Meanwhile, his demand for permanent control of rents and prices had been decisively rejected at a referendum, and he was fain to promise that he would give up these controls and control over land sales also. After attempting in vain to interest his followers in the fate of the distant Western Democracies and more successfully directing their attention to the economic stabilisation of South-East Asia, Chifley had to watch domestic strife moving to a climax. On the one hand, rapidly increasing masses of voters demanded a limit to public ownership, a check to the multiplication of expensive social services, and a reduction of the taxation which swelled State deficits and, thereby, strained the relations of the States with the Centre. On the other hand, Labour as a whole, regardless of soaring prices, was going straight ahead towards its sectional objectives, while the Communists were clamouring for yet more of those 'concessions' which were already causing shortages in coal, electricity and oil and a sadly reduced output per man-hour, and constructing bottle-necks so ingeniously that the outraged Governments of Queensland and Victoria were driven to take drastic and effective action.

When Chifley called for more production, the Reds not only put forward an impudent demand for a great increase in pay and a thirty-hour week, but set themselves to smash the hated arbitration machinery by stoking up gratuitous strikes. They found the water-fronters and coal miners such ready tools that they soon had the mines flooded and the larger industries idle in the key State of New South Wales. And then the kangaroo kicked. Security Police collected much useful information by raiding the Communists' Sydney headquarters, Federal troops began to mine open-cast coal, and any number of trade unionists defied their Red leaders. When the Prime Minister, the Arbitration Court and the Australian Council of Trade Unions went into action seriously, the whole movement collapsed (August 1949). The Australian Labour Party expelled prominent Communists and the reddest party branches in New South Wales prudently committed *felo de se*.

The end soon came. Chifley was obliged to follow Cripps into devaluation and was presently defeated at a general election by Menzies' Liberal and Fadden's Country Parties (December 1949). These two allies could not shake the carefully nursed Labour majority in the Senate, but they gained a substantial joint majority in the House of Representatives. Menzies, the new Prime Minister, increased the pay of public servants, and then essayed to uproot the Communist upas tree by fighting through a measure which would have exposed the extreme Left and possibly others to 'conviction by Parliament' and other departures from the British idea of the Rule of Law. This drastic Act was, in the end, declared invalid by the High Court. In spite of this rebuff, Menzies worked as well as he could with the United States, sent representatives to the Colombo Conference which discussed the political and economic problems of South-East Asia, and rushed off to Korea such forces as he could scrape together in a country which had rigidly limited the sphere of action of its garrison in Japan, and had let its Home Army fall so far below establishment and disperse itself in such a maze of non-operational units that it could not even reinforce its single air squadron in Malaya. But when he started an intensive recruiting campaign, Chifley, a sick man, sullenly refused to co-operate.

After a second electoral victory, which was followed speedily by the death of Chifley, Menzies returned to the charge. This time his anti-Communist plans were defeated at a referendum, a setback from which he scarcely recovered when he accepted an un-popular Japanese peace treaty in return for the signature by the United States of a Pacific Defence Pact with his country and New Zealand (September 1951). His prestige was damaged still further six months later, when he sought to rectify the adverse balance of payments by slashing imports so wildly, and without warning, that he dealt a heavy blow to the already shaken Lancashire textile industry and compelled many of his own business-men to cancel overseas contracts. It may, however, have consoled Australians somewhat for this loss of public credit that they had registered a net gain of nearly 470,000 immigrants during the past five years, fully one-third from the United Kingdom.

In New Zealand, once Japan was down and out, Fraser's Labour Government watched the American flood ebb away and was soon welcoming home its own soldiers, other than the 4,000 on garrison duty in Japan, and hailing as Governor-General its fellow-country-man, Sir Bernard Freyburg, v.c. New Zealanders continued to play their invaluable part in the international sphere. Their Prime Minister served as chairman of the Social, Humanitarian and Cul-tural Committee of U.N.O.; their representatives agreed with those of Australia and the United Kingdom to form a joint agency to run the Commonwealth airlines, and their Finance Minister, Walter Nash, presently attended the Commonwealth Prime Ministers' Conference in London cheered by the knowledge that the United States and his own country had written off such small differences as existed in their mutual Lease-Lend accounts. At home, men of all parties welcomed their first two women Legisla-tive Councillors and then prepared for a general election. Labour, shaken though it was by the comment of the retiring Chief Justice that it was far too ready to deny citizens access to the Courts, stood on its usual collectivist platform; the Farmers' Union made ready to attack an urban-minded administration which, in their opinion, had done far too little for countryfolk, and Holland's National Party came out for lighter taxation, free enterprise and free trade. The somewhat half-hearted campaign was fought in an atmosphere of national 'go slow'. House-building languished for lack of materials and hands, mothers of families were infuriated by the closing of shops on Saturdays, and the Left Wing was staggered when the authorities intimated that they would have to work much harder if they wanted more social services. The result was that Labour scraped home so narrowly that it had to rely on the four Maori members for its majority in the Lower House.

Fraser's restored Government appointed New Zealand's first woman Minister, gave the United Kingdom £12,500,000, reduced its garrison in Japan by arrangement with Whitehall, and joined with the Western Pacific High Commission Territories and Fiji in a public health scheme. Then, realising that its isolated group of islands bore a white population that was too scanty for the work that had to be done, and that was, moreover, growing 'older' and failing to reproduce itself, it offered to take a few immigrants from the Old Country each year according to the shipping available. Meanwhile, large numbers of its Labour followers were scrambling for 'concessions' so blindly that they threatened to tear down the whole social and economic structure. Partly to check the dairy-workers, who were in the van of this dangerous campaign, and partly to give their employers a fair chance, Fraser sought to organise this all-important industry by setting up a partially official Dairy Industry Commission, which was indeed bound to follow the directions of 'the Minister' but was also bidden to take into account the burden imposed on producers by the weekly wage allowance on which prices were based. In spite of this attempt to stop the rot, the war on the industrial front became more heated. Employers bid against one another in a limited labour market where too many trade unionists showed an increasing disinclination to abide by conciliation awards and demanded such wages and pay for overtime as would hold their total takings at the inflated wartime level: those workers who could not do their forty hours of work in five days bickered with those who could, and the more extreme attacked the conciliation courts and the railway tribunal for peddling with such petty details as wages, conditions of work and finance instead of seeking to 'preserve industrial peace'. And sometimes the authorities played into the hands of the malcontents: for instance, one official 'compromise' was entirely in favour of the truculent waterfronters who had now displaced the dairy-workers as chiefest of those who troubled Israel, and the Prime Minister himself gave the Arbitration Court an effective hint to bear in mind the coming withdrawal of stabilisation subsidies when fixing wages.

Non-Labour voters may have been worried when Fraser talked of making price controls permanent, and positively alarmed when he nationalised the coal mines and gave a monopoly of quoting for employers' liability to a State Fire and Accident Board and another monopoly to the National Airways Corporation; but few of them cavilled when, faced by a shortage of dollars, he followed Cripps's lead and suspended the convertibility of sterling. Noting Russia's behaviour on the Security Council, New Zealanders recalled how right he had been to resist the granting of the much-abused veto at San Francisco; they were proud and pleased when he took the chair at the committee which drafted the Trusteeship clauses of the U.N. Charter and then gave Western Samoa a liberal measure of autonomy; they approved, on the whole, when the Finance Minister, in negotiations with various European and Asiatic Powers, stood up successfully for imperial preferences, the recognition of his country's contracts with the United Kingdom for bulk sales and purchase, and the governmental 'patterning' of production and distribution. Nor were there many regrets when New Zealand fell into line with the other Dominions by taking full advantage of the half-forgotten Statute of Westminster so that she might be free to deal with her unsatisfactory Legislative Council. Having thus reached full 'legal age', New Zealanders recalled their early days by celebrating the centenary of the foundation of Otago by emigrant Scots of the Established Kirk.

There was widespread satisfaction when the United Kingdom agreed to take nearly all New Zealand's exportable surplus of butter and cheese for seven years to come, again when Nash produced a Budget surplus and restored the New Zealand pound to parity with Australian and British pounds, and yet again when Fraser check-mated the attempts of the isolationist Left to hamper recruiting for the Army by asking for and getting an overwhelming vote in favour of compulsory military service (June 1948). Such a resolute stand suggested that matters were moving to a crisis. The public demand for legislation to check Communist activities in the public services and trade unions grew apace, especially such activities as impelled the 'Wharfies' to threaten to strike unless the police, who had been sent to stop wholesale pilfering of cargo, were withdrawn from the docks, and, by their inveterate slackness, to deter some London firms from sending ships to be held up by such as they. At last, the disillusioned Federation of Labour replaced militants on its own Executive by men who recognised the rights of the nation, and the

U

Minister of Labour, finding that the rank-and-file Auckland carpenters were sick and tired of a grossly uncalled-for strike engineered by Reds, 'deregistered' the Auckland crusaders and 'registered' a rival union on their campaigning ground. Holland, leader of the National Party, went further by promising that he would proclaim the Communist Party a subversive organisation and see to it that none of its members were ever again in a position to serve their Moscow masters. On that cry he won the general election (November 1949). It was hard on such fine men as Fraser and Nash, but a salutary lesson to very many of their followers.

The new Ministry took office in a land whose headlong over-spending had been masked by the thick drifts of unbacked paper money poured forth by the state-controlled Reserve Bank. It raised railway rates, but though it had to face a rise in official expenditure and a big deficit on social services, it left taxes much as they were. Nevertheless, countless small investors celebrated their release from the monstrous regiment of the Left by over-subscribing a development loan. They were rewarded when the authorities increased social service benefits, cancelled or reduced costly subsidies, began to overhaul import controls and denationalised vigorously. Parliament restored coal mines to their owners, allowed private firms to quote once more for employers' liability, dropped the $33\frac{1}{3}$ per cent surcharge which had long been demanded of those who paid tax on unearned income, and took steps to break the monopoly held by the National Airways Corporation. Further, it went back to the traditional practise of taking the total European population as the basis for the delimitation of constituencies, gave speculators too free a hand by reckoning at current values the price of land available for purchase by ex-servicemen, rendered the Army and Air Force liable for service the world over, and reimposed that capital punishment which had been discontinued by the recent Government. Finally, Parliament realised one of the Prime Minister's dreams by abolishing the Legislative Council, an ineffective body each of whose members was appointed for seven years and the whole of which had long been threatened with being made elective. Thus, at the close of 1950, New Zealand had become the only member of the Commonwealth to have a single-chamber legislature and was like to remain so till the duly appointed committee had devised a new Upper House.

On the outbreak of the Korean war, Holland, with Fraser's warm support, at once sent off a couple of frigates, but could not send the special K land force for some six months or so. Meanwhile, stock-piling as a result of that war, together with rocketing prices for wool, made it so hard to bring down the cost of living that the United Kingdom was called upon to pay more for New Zealand meat and dairy products and the authorities had to prescribe a marked increase of wages. Even so, Auckland railway workers struck on the eve of Christmas just as Fraser died and Nash took his place as leader of the Labour Party. Then the waterfronters went into action by starting the worst series of strikes the country had had to endure for a generation. Before long they had caused such losses that overseas shipowners were driven to charging penal rates for freight and, before the end, had obliged Holland to proclaim a state of emergency and call out the troops. So impossible did the 'Wharfies' become that at last the Federation of Labour expelled them in a body. Thereupon they announced that they had broken away, rallied thousands of other trade unionists to their red banner and formed a separate Trade Union Congress. Only then did they consent to return to the docks. The Prime Minister seized the opportunity to go to the polls, whence he was returned with a largely increased majority (1 September, 1951).

Thus confirmed in power, Holland carried measures designed to ensure that control of trade unions should rest with the rank-and-file and not with handfuls of militants, and, in face of hot criticism, to give the Police dangerously wide powers to suppress intimidation and sedition. He then joined Australia and the United States in a Pacific Defence Pact and sent his Minister of Industries to lay the foundation-stone of an All India Medical Institute at Delhi, first-fruits of his country's participation in the Colombo Plan. He was, however, unable to construct a new Legislative Council chiefly because Labour insisted that a referendum on the question had been promised, and before the year was out, had had to cut imports drastically in line with his fellow Commonwealth Finance Ministers. On the other hand, he was able to give Western Samoa an Executive Council and rejoice in an unexpected Budget surplus, thanks mainly to the duties collected on the flood of imports that had rushed in after the 'Wharfies' hold-up had been lifted. It was thus a reasonably hopeful community of which Sir Willoughby Norris became Governor-General in December, 1952.

In South Africa, the Coalition ended with the war. The Labour and Dominion parties crossed the floor of the House, leaving Smuts, still with a comfortable majority, to cope with an agriculture that was hampered by soil erosion, unscientific methods, low efficiency and the misguided official help which had tempted farmers to plough huge areas of unsuitable land for wheat, and a secondary industry that was too often carried on in small and indifferent factories scattered about the countryside. Both problems raised the issue of the colour bar on whose retention Nationalists and Labour men were set and the United Party deeply divided, and both led back to the system of migratory labour whereunder natives went away to work for longer or shorter periods and left their families to live as best they could. Though the powerful gold mines attracted less than half the Union's migratory labour, they were its chief advocates and could not complain if an increasing number of industrialists and farmers were asking how much longer they, working a wasting asset, were to set the pace and even stand in the way of development in other directions. Many Europeans began to realise that the migratory system was bad in that, combined with the colour bar, it forbade masses of Bantu from ever becoming either competent farmers or skilled workers, and destroyed family life, tribal cohesion and social morals by taking away far too many of the able-bodied males at one time from a given area. They, therefore, argued that permanent dwellers in the reserves must be helped to find homes and employment there; that family accommodation must be provided on the mines, and that they themselves must face the fact that the Bantu in the towns were no mere 'foreigners' but folk entitled to homes, freehold rights and advancement therein. It was at least a beginning when a Lancashire calico firm built a factory in the Ciskei, and the Board of Trade, condemning repressive measures, pointed out that fuller use of natives in skilled jobs would benefit even the dominant white folk. Meanwhile, unemployment had not been increased appreciably by the closing of the weaker wartime factories, and the new slant to native policy was confirmed by the splitting of the Labour Party, the larger half of which continued to support Smuts while the remnant went over to the Nationalists.

During the 1946 Session, the Government carried much valuable social legislation affecting all classes and, by welcoming immigrants of 'the right type' and smoothing the path of private organisations that brought out skilled workers, encouraged an immigration larger than South Africa had known for many years. It then found itself involved in difficulties with the Indians, the Bantu, South-West Africa and the United Nations. As regards the first, Smuts's recent Asiatic Land Tenure and Indian Representation Act was much more liberal than any preceding 'pegging' measure. True, it did not give the Natal Indians the much-desired right to move freely throughout the Union in which the vast majority of them had been born, nor confer on those in the Transvaal the right to own real property; but it did go a long way towards relieving Natal Indians of the checks imposed on their social and economic advancement by their legal inability to own land and houses. The Act extended the Durban landholding regulations to the whole of Natal by empowering Europeans and Indians to deal freely with one another in generously defined 'exempted areas', forbade them to do so elsewhere without Ministerial leave, and relied on a European-Indian Land Tenure Board to see that no real injustice was done. Further, it restored much of what the Natal Indians had been robbed a generation back by giving them and the Transvaal Indians a communal franchise, whereunder they could elect one European Senator to sit beside another appointed by the Governor-General, and the Natal Indians alone could elect two Provincial Councillors who might be Indians. This half-loaf might have been acceptable to the mass of the folk concerned; but it was not to the Natal Indian Congress which organised passive resistance, nor to supporters in India who stigmatised it as 'hellish', nor yet to the Delhi Government which broke off all relations with the Union and thus prevented her farmers getting the jute-bags of which India was by far the largest source of supply.

If the Indians were the smallest, the Bantu were by far the largest groups of those 'wards' for whom the white minority claimed to exercise trusteeship. The Government did indeed find white volunteers to train Bantu to build cheap houses for their needy urbanised kinsfolk in spite of resistance by white trade unionists, but they spoiled the effect of this gesture by their mishandling of native trouble on the Rand. There, 50,000 Bantu, whose European colleagues had long been demanding higher wages, themselves struck for more pay. Since their trade union had no official recognition, thousands of them marched into Johannesburg, where the Police drove them back with the loss of five killed and many injured (August 1946). The authorities then indicted, without any proof, Communists and other agitators for having incited the strike and had to be content with imprisoning some of them for having merely abetted it after it had started. Undismayed, Smuts foreshadowed a fairer deal for Bantu trade unions and the handing over of the administration of the reserves to the partially-elective native Representative Council. Unfortunately, at that very moment, this Council, dissatisfied with its existing powers, suspended its sittings *sine die* and, presently, boycotted the election of a so-called 'native' parliamentary representative.

Finally, there was the problem of South-West Africa and the United Nations. The Union had ruled 'South-West' as far as possible as part of itself in terms of its C mandate either directly or through a local Legislative Council elected by the handful of male European residents. During the Axis war, the Germans had been deprived of naturalisation and the vote, but now they pressed for a restoration of both; the Windhoek legislature asked unanimously for incorporation in the Union, and at a not altogether satisfactory referendum, the mass of the natives were said to have agreed thereto. Hence, Smuts promised that the territory should soon have representation in the Union Parliament and himself went overseas to ask the United Nations to smile upon the proposal for incorporation. In the event, South-West Africa was scarcely mentioned in the prolonged and acrimonious debates of the General Assembly; rather did the representatives of India, the U.S.S.R. and many Latin American republics seize the opportunity to attack South Africa for her obscurantist non-European policies and, in especial, for her 'oppression' of her Indians. Setting aside Smuts's plea that, in terms of the U.N. Charter, 'South-West' was a purely domestic matter exempt from outside interference, and his reasonable suggestion that the issue be referred to the International Court of Justice at the Hague, a large majority of the General Assembly demanded that the Governments of India and the Union should report to it at its next meeting what steps they had taken to relieve the 'oppressed' Indians. Not one of the critics so much as mentioned the new Indian franchise. Angered though they were by this flood of odium, much of it unjustified, poured on their country by outsiders, the majority of the House of Assembly accepted Smuts's promise to continue to administer South-West Africa as heretofore and to submit reports to the Mandates Commission.

Little of this strain was visible when the King and Queen and their two daughters toured Southern Africa during the early months of 1947 to be given the warmest of welcomes by folk of all colours and classes, from hundreds of ex-republican *oustryers* in commando to the thousands of Natal Indians at Durban who defied the orders of their handful of Congress enthusiasts to boycott the whole affair. The Royal visit could not change the course of local politics nor prevent Havenga from working ever more closely with Malan, but, be that as it might, the Union made the United Kingdom a large gold loan to help her out of her difficulties and also to avoid having to cut down her own excessive dollar-spending, accepted the Geneva Agreement on imperial preferences and tariffs, and saw her Prime Minister sail for England to talk with certain other Commonwealth Prime Ministers on the occasion of the marriage of Princess Elizabeth to the Duke of Edinburgh. On his return, Smuts found awaiting him the admirable report of the Fagan Commission advocating the gradual abandonment of the migratory labour system, the simplification of the pass laws and the better treatment of urbanised Bantu. He had no time, however, to act upon that Report, even if he would, because the statutory life of Parliament was ending and he must face a general election. That contest was not racial in the sense of being Afrikander *versus* British, but it was most certainly racial in that the non-European question was the main issue. Malan stood for *apartheid*, that is, the separation of each racial group in the Union from the others lest the white minority be swallowed up in 'a coffee-coloured sea' and thus lose all hope of maintaining its rule, racial purity and civilisation. He taught, perhaps less fervidly, that this sorting out would be best for all concerned in that many causes of inter-racial friction would be removed. In the unexpected event, the Dominion and other splinter parties were wiped out, and Malan achieved a dead-heat with the United Party in the Senate, and, on a minority of the votes cast, a majority of five in the Assembly which he owed to Havenga's Afrikaner Party (May 1948).

Malan had won over many English-speaking voters by promising not to press for a republic and to abandon neutrality if ever Russia became aggressive; now, while thanking them for their support, he assured them of equal rights and of his desire to maintain the Union's 'uniquely friendly relations' with all the members of the Commonwealth. His next steps were, however, much more disquieting, for not only did he speedily cease to encourage immigration, but allowed public servants to once more join the *Broederbond* and *Ossewabrandwag*. Presently, Havenga, his Minister of Finance, who had inherited a large surplus and a hopeful revenue, was dismayed to find that lavish buying in North America was draining the Union's dollar reserves fast. He, therefore, imposed import controls, first on dollar imports and then on such sterling imports as did not originate in Southern Rhodesia and the High Commission Territories. Next, he raised the relative price of gold by devaluing the long-overvalued South African pound, and was encouraged to learn that huge quartz reefs had been discovered in the northern Orange Free State which promised a prolonged life to mining provided always that water and native labour were forthcoming.

Early in 1949, substantial successes in the Provincial elections and the untimely death of the liberal Hofmeyr emboldened Malan to press on with his policy of *apartheid*, and thus set each of the chief racial groups free to 'develop along its own lines' in its respective areas, even at the cost of asking his own followers to do more of their own work than hitherto and face unwelcome immigration. As far as the Bantu were concerned, he was definite enough. Setting aside, on the one hand, demands by some Cape and Transvaal Nationalists that land already purchased for native use should be bought back for the use of *Christenmense* and, on the other, the impracticable suggestion of some Afrikander Professors and Dutch Reformed Church ministers that there should be a 'Bantustan', virtually a large subordinate Bantu state, he reaffirmed the old dictum that 'redundant' Bantu must go to the already overcrowded reserves which might one day cover one-eighth of the surface of South Africa. He then warned the recalcitrant Native Representative Council of its impending dissolution and, if he did give larger appropriations to native education, cut down the feeding of native school-children, the youngsters who needed it most. He dealt with the Indians shortly by withdrawing their recent franchise, and harassed the Coloured folk in the comparatively civilised Cape Peninsula by appointing, for the first time, separate post and booking office counters, waiting rooms and railway carriages. Further, he urged the Universities of Cape Town, the Witwatersrand, Natal and Rhodes (Grahamstown) to fall into line with the officially pure white Afrikaans-speaking seats of higher learning by setting up colour bars. He then introduced *apartheid*, up to a point, among the dominant white folk. This he did by virtually repealing the clauses in his own Nationality and Flag Act of 1927 which safeguarded the position of 'Union nationals' as 'British subjects'. Inspired by the distinction recently drawn between similar capacities by Canada, the United Kingdom, New Zealand, Australia and Ceylon, and arguing that the still more recent retention by republican India of her membership of 'the Club' had destroyed the very idea of a common Commonwealth status, he waited till Smuts was safely embarked for London and Cambridge, of which University he had been elected Chancellor at the very moment of his fall from power, and then unexpectedly prolonged the Session and crashed through an utterly unforeseen Nationality Bill. Henceforward, Union nationals were to be merely 'South African citizens' with no mention of British subjecthood, a status that could be attained either by birth in the country, descent from a Union national or cumbrous registration which left much to 'the Minister's' discretion. To ensure that few newcomers should be able to vote at the next general election, the Act decreed that immigrant British subjects, even those recent arrivals who had come in the belief that they would get the franchise after the time-honoured wait of two years, would have to wait five years and genuine aliens six.

At this stage, Malan was checked in mid-career. His indispensable Minister of Finance would not hear of further tampering with Bantu representation without 'an adequate majority', and, recalling promises by Hertzog and other prominent men that the political rights of the Coloured folk should remain inviolate, held that it would be a breach of faith to put Coloured voters on a separate roll. Deaf to Malan's anxious expostulations that, unless those voters were segregated, ministerialists could hardly hope to carry the sixteen Cape seats in which they were numerous, Havenga obliged him to shelve his projected franchise legislation. In other directions, however, *apartheid* marched on. The Bantu were relieved of all responsibilities, but also denied all benefits, under the Unemployment Insurance Act; such few members of the white and non-European communities as might indulge in illicit intercourse with one another, or even marry one another, were subjected to criminal penalties, and every adult was bidden carry an identity card inscribed with his or her racial origin.

Welcome breaks in this official organisation of envy, malice and

all uncharitableness were afforded by the dedication of the Voor-
trekker Monument near Pretoria whose excellent historical bas-
reliefs were innocent of political or racial rancour, by the presenta-
tion of a Budget which reflected the steady financial improvement
effected by the recent controls, and by the relaxation of some of
those controls after the conclusion of an Agreement with the
United Kingdom and the United States. Six months later, Smuts
died (11 September, 1950), leaving his successor, Jacobus Strauss, and
a sadly divided Party to make what opposition they could to Malan's
apartheid. The United Party did not object to the abolition of the
appeal to the Judicial Committee, a dead-letter these fifteen years,
nor to the Suppression of Communism Act which was more or
less in line with measures passed by the United States and several
Commonwealth countries, while its resistance to the prescription
of compulsory residential segregation on a colour basis by the Group
Areas Bill was weakened by the refusal of some of its anti-Indian
members to vote either way. It cannot have been surprised that
India's retort to this last measure should have been a refusal to take
part in a round table conference on the Indian question. And then
came the South-West Africa elections to revolutionise the situation.
A few months back, the Union had given her mandated territory
financial autonomy, offered its German residents the citizenship
and votes they had lost during the Axis war, and provided for the
gross over-representation of its 40,000 Europeans by four Senators
and six Assembly members in the Capetown Parliament. In the
event, the 3,000 recently enfranchised Germans swayed the balance
and gave the Nationalists all the new seats in both Houses. Thus
did Malan gain the prospect of a long lease of power and a majority
of his own regardless of Havenga's Afrikaner Party.

Need's must when the Devil drives. Almost at once, Havenga
agreed with the Prime Minister that the Coloured Folk in the Cape
and Natal should have a partially elective Coloured Affairs Board
which few of them desired, be represented by one European
nominee in the Senate, and, segregated on a separate voters' roll,
elect four Europeans to the Assembly. In addition, those in the
Cape were to elect two Provincial Councillors who might be
Coloured men. Legally the situation was governed by one of the
few 'entrenched' clauses in the South Africa Act which had brought
the Union into being. That clause laid down that no law should
disqualify anyone from being a voter by reason merely of race or

colour unless it were passed by a majority of both Houses sitting together and, on the third reading, by a two-thirds majority of the total strength of both Houses. Knowing that he could not get such a majority, Malan proposed to rely on bare majorities throughout on the plea that by making the Union truly sovereign the Statute of Westminster and the consequent Status Act had cancelled the entrenched procedure. Legality apart, the Opposition resisted this claim as immoral, the Natal Provincial Council condemned a precedent that would endanger the entrenched official languages clause, the Coloured folk protested respectfully and large numbers of ex-Service men and women formed the Union-wide and non-party Torch Commando to defend against a totalitarian-minded administration at home the liberties they had defended against Nazis in the field. Nevertheless, the Bill went through by bare majorities and, just as white South Africans were celebrating the tercentenary of the foundation of Capetown, the Appellate Division pronounced the measure invalid because it had been passed in defiance of the still operative entrenched clause. Malan hotly refused to accept the verdict, threatened legislation to debar Judges from 'testing' Acts of a sovereign Parliament and, thereby, inspired the Opposition, the Labour Party and the Torch Commando to proclaim a joint crusade to rid the Union of his administration.

True to his word, Malan carried a measure constituting Parliament a High Court empowered to overturn any judgement of the Appellate Division which invalidated an Act. This High Court, reduced by the absence of other Parties to the level of the Nationalist caucus, overthrew the recent verdict of the Appellate Division. When, however, that Division invalidated the Act constituting the High Court, Malan accepted its verdict but promised to make Courts *versus* Parliament an election issue. Meanwhile, the African National Council and the South African Indian Congress had organised meetings here and there to protest against discriminatory laws, and, after the Government had failed to stop them by naming five of their leaders under the Suppression of Communism Act, let loose a passive resistance campaign (26 June, 1952). In spite of the Minister of Justice's strong hint to the Police to go 'slightly beyond their powers in isolated cases', only 800 people had been arrested by the end of the first month, and only a score had been convicted of technical or 'statutory Communism'. The authorities were then answered by groups of Liberals led by an Anglican Bishop, an ex-Judge, four Senators and 'native' members of the Assembly who demanded equal opportunities for all and a return to the old Cape civilisation franchise. The Government then made it a serious offence to hold meetings for Africans or to incite Africans to break the law; thereupon, white volunteers joined the resistance movement, one of whom, Patrick Duncan, son of a late Governor-General of the Union, together with Manilal Gandhi, son of the Mahatma, were duly fined. Much harm was done to the cause by serious rioting at Port Elizabeth, East London, Kimberley and on the Rand, and though elsewhere all the demonstrations were peaceful, fully 8,000 arrests had been made by the end of the year. The authorities replied with drastic laws which made incitement to break the law a grave crime and, in the event of a serious threat to the public safety, empowered them to suspend almost any common or statutory law and, thereafter, proceed by regulations which would lapse unless they were approved by Parliament though without prejudice to anything that might have been done under them. So, the Union drove on towards a general election in which the supremacy of Parliament and 'People' over the Courts was indeed an issue, and in which Malan might expect much support from English-speaking voters in the parts affected by the recent 'resistance' riots.[1] It was pure gain to him that, at that very moment, two British battalions should have had to be flown to Kenya to cope with the Mau Mau atrocities committed by some of the Kikuyu against Europeans and, even more, their fellow-tribesmen, and that, nearer home, Bantu should have shown signs of planning organised resistance to the white folk's proposal to federate the Two Rhodesias and Nyasaland against the wishes of the vast majority of their inhabitants.

The ending of the Axis war brought India no relief from internal strife. The communal disintegration which had set in long before that war reached its climax at the turn of 1945-46 in the election campaigns for the Central Legislative Assembly, the first since 1934, and for the Provincial legislatures, the first since 1937. All were fought under a threat of famine so dire that Delhi had to beg the United States for grain, and with a ferocity for which the chief blame must rest on the newly-released members of the Congress

---

[1] Malan's Nationalists won the general election of April 1953 by an increased majority, though again by a minority of the votes cast.

Working Committee. That body clamoured for a 'National' Government at once and refused even to discuss the 'Pakistan' which Sardar Patel, its most forceful member, insisted must mean civil war. As it was, the killings in Bombay, Calcutta and other large centres were so desperate that Gandhi, in terror and in vain, begged his bloodthirsty fellow-countrymen to desist and was answered by a mutiny of part of the Indian Navy and signs of unsteadiness in other Services. In the event, at the Centre, the *Mahasabha* failed to win any seats, the bitterly anti-Moslem Sikhs elected among others two members of the ultra-communal Akali Party, and the Moslem League more than held its own; but Congress gained comfortable majorities both in the Central Assembly and in the Provincial legislatures by winning some of the seats reserved for special groups as well as all the general or Hindu sects.

As usual, the next push forward came from overseas. Backed by an assurance that Indians could have independence even before they had framed a Constitution, Cripps and two of his colleagues arrived with a federal scheme. This plan met one of Congress's chief demands by providing for a strong Centre, but its essential effect was to give the Moslem League its way by laying it down that Provinces were to be free to form themselves into groups each of which should decide which powers were to be retained by themselves and which handed over to the central authority. It warned the Princes, the smaller of whom were worried because the six hundred States had already been reduced by 'grouping' to some two hundred and fifty, that paramountcy must go with the British, but that none of them should be simply 'transferred' willy-nilly to any Indian Government. Finally, it empowered the Viceroy to set up an *interim* Government in which all portfolios, even that of War Minister, should be held by Indians possessed of 'the full confidence of the people'. Gandhi, Jinnah, the Working Committees of Congress and the League and even the All-India Congress Committee approved in principle, and then the trouble began, for no single one of India's rival leaders would negotiate with any other unless his views were accepted in advance. Of all the troublemakers Nehru was the worst. He induced Congress to go back on its Committee by alleging that the rights of the minorities were matters for Indians alone and not for the British, to torpedo 'Pakistan' by denying the right of Provinces to 'opt' out at the start, and to support his threat that, on entering the projected Constituent Assembly, it would not hold itself bound by any conditions whatsoever. Inevitably, the Moslem League in its turn repudiated its Working Committee's acceptance of the plan and gave fair warning that it would not suffer Congressmen alone to enter the Constituent Assembly and there devise a Constitution that took no stock of the Cabinet Mission's vital recommendations.

The elections for the Constituent Assembly were held with the customary results (July 1946), but such had been the accompanying bloodshed in Bombay, Calcutta and Bihar, and such the now endemic famine in swarming and mainly Moslem East Bengal, that however doggedly they might boycott the Assembly, the Leaguers were frightened into taking their seats alongside Congressmen in the new *interim* Government. The coming of that Government marked the real going of the British, because, though power *de jure* might still lie with the Secretary of State and the Viceroy who could overrule the legislature if it endangered the peace and welfare of India, power *de facto* now lay with Indian Ministers strong in the support of the elected representatives of the two great parties. Under the chairmanship of the dictatorial Nehru, the fourteen politicially inexperienced men who composed this Government welcomed a High Commissioner to look after purely British interests and exchanged Ambassadors with the United States. They then indicated plainly that the overburdened British taxpayers and not they must find pensions for those British members of the I.C.S. who might wish to go when India became legally autonomous, watched the civilian Services become demoralised as effective British authority faded away, and fended off famine by importing grain from whence they could. Meanwhile, the exclusively Congress Constituent Assembly carried enthusiastically Nehru's motion that India was to be a sovereign independent Republic.

Attlee now made up his mind that it was time that the British did indeed 'quit India'. He therefore gave the divided sub-continent the final thrust that carried it into *purna swaraj* and partition by telling the astonished politicians that if they had not made shift to rule themselves by making their own Constitution before the end of June 1948, the United Kingdom authorities would have to decide between handing over the powers of the Central Government to some sort of Government for British India as a whole, or in some areas to existing Provincial Governments, or in others to such an administration as it might deem suitable. Having thus indicated that even British patience had limits, he proved that British intentions were good by sending out Lord Mountbatten as Viceroy to wind up what was left of the British *Raj* within the appointed time. Hailed by the delighted Mahatma as representative of the first people in history to give up dominion of its own free will, the new Viceroy was sworn in at Delhi amid general acclamation (24 March, 1947). He at once gained the confidence of the leading politicians by tactfully quieting the alarm expressed by Congress's big businessmen at the taxation imposed on such as they by the Moslem Minister of Finance, and, in a land trembling on the brink of civil war, persuaded Gandhi and Jinnah to issue a joint appeal against the rampant communal killings and displacement. But neither he nor they could stop Hindus and Sikhs from bristling against each other, the Punjab Sikhs from threatening mass disobedience, the Congress Working Committee from resolving that there must be a most unsuitable partition of the Punjab, or the *Mahasabha* from condemning all 'vivisection' of Mother India and then proposing to raise a private army to 'vivisect' predominantly Hindu Western Bengal from the overwhelmingly Moslem half of that unwieldy Province. Still less could they stop Nehru from frightening the Princes by telling them that those who did not send representatives forthwith to the Constituent Assembly would be treated as foreigners and must take the consequences. The Viceroy, therefore, arranged a reasonable procedure for the election of State representatives, flew to London for discussions, and came back resolved to anticipate the date fixed for the transfer of power.

Mountbatten induced Hindu, Moslem and Sikh leaders to accept an agreement providing for the creation of Pakistan and the subsequent granting of Dominion Powers and status to it and to truncated 'India' (2 June, 1947). Thus was Jinnah victorious at last. Probably for that very reason the agreement had a mixed reception. The inevitable mob outbreaks in Delhi, Lahore and Calcutta soon subsided; but, however pleased Hindus might be that the bulk of the Indian Empire was to be ruled by men of their faith, they resented the 'vivisection' of that Empire and the prospective loss of the Pakistani granary from which the Moslems of Sind were already refusing to send them grain, while, if the Moslem Leaguers could take comfort from the thought that Western Pakistan would at least preserve to them the earliest conquests by Moslem invaders of Hindustan and might hope to become the leading Moslem State in the world, they knew that they must in all probability lose much of the Punjab and Bengal and cope with enemies who were demanding that a 'Pathanistan' be carved out of the flank of their main block of territory. As for the minorities, the Indian Christians were satisfied and the multitudinous Untouchables were ready to accept Congress leadership in return for access to Hindu temples and the dropping of all talk of 'caste Hindus' and so forth; but the mixed-breed Anglo-Indians dreaded lest Nationalists should deprive them of their wonted employments, while the Princes, the most notable minority of all, viewed the future with justifiable anxiety. However, these potentates knew that the Crown could not shelter them much longer and believed that by acceding to one or other of the two future Dominions they would be simply carrying on under a system of control to which they were accustomed. Hence, though the majestic Nizam of Hyderabad reserved the right to become independent after the going of the British, nearly all the rest yielded to the arguments and occasional discreet pressure of the Viceroy and of Patel, Member for the States Department, and signed instruments providing for the transfer to the future Dominions of those responsibilities for defence, communications and external affairs that had always been reserved to the Imperial authorities. They were assured that by so doing they had not bound themselves in any way to accept the Constitution of either Dominion. Thus was the final plan accepted. In due time, Assam 'opted' for India, while Sind, the North-West Frontier Province and Baluchistan 'opted' for Pakistan. The Boundary Commission got to work as soon as the Sikhs had voted for the partition of the Punjab and the Bengal Legislative Assembly for the 'vivisection' of its immense Province. Mountbatten announced that the splendid Indian Army would have to be 'vivisected' also, and that he himself was to be Governor-General of India as well as chairman of a Joint Defence Council. Jinnah, deservedly, was to rule Pakistan as Governor-General from its newly-chosen capital of Karachi.

The Day of Independence, 15 August, 1947, was hailed with enthusiasm and an accentuation of communal killings in Delhi and Calcutta. And then came disaster. Hordes of Hindus trekked from East Bengal into West Bengal and from Western Pakistan into the United Provinces to the accompaniment of widespread violence which reached its climax in Delhi, where the murder and expulsion of Moslems and the inrush of Hindus were such that the old capital of the Moguls lost its Islamic character. In Western Pakistan there was more panic than killing, though Pathans invaded the North-West Frontier Province whose incompetent Congress Ministry Jinnah dismissed. A far worse story had to be recorded of the partitioned Punjab in either half of which governance and the divided police force had broken down even before the Day of Independence. There, some 4,000,000 folk fled in opposite directions from they knew not what, choking the roads and railways and too often meeting their deaths on the way from starvation, cholera, drowning, or at each other's hands. The one redeeming feature of the catastrophe was that Nehru and the Prime Minister of Pakistan, Liaqat Ali Khan, dashed off to the scene together and, failing to check the Great Treks, set their respective troops to directing the human torrents much of which flowed as far east as Hindu Bihar, or into neighbouring Princely States whence the survivors presently flowed back because killing was going on there also.

In spite of the Punjab horror, both Governments kept their feet, maintained undivided India's embargo on South African goods, and assailed the peccant Union in the General Assembly of U.N.O. On the other hand, neither Government had been able to get forward with day-to-day tasks. India had indeed published her draft Constitution, but Pakistan had hardly touched hers and neither had found leisure to tackle the rampant Provincialism, the corruption and callous disregard for the underdogs displayed by many Provincial administrations, or the grave falling-off in the quantity and quality of production induced by the demands of employers for higher profits and of hands for higher pay. Small wonder that many folk, desiring a strong Centre, should have talked of going back to the British Cabinet Mission's projected federation. Nehru elected rather to extend his power by drawing in the Princely States, nearly all of which were either embedded in, or adjacent to, his India. The vast majority had been drawn in thus even before the Day of Independence, more than half of them to be incorporated with neighbouring Provinces, many others to be grouped in *Saurastra*, and all to be subjected to 'a perfect welter of democracy'. Nearly all of the thirty that survived as separate entities had 'acceeded'

x

to India, but three were proving difficult. Nehru and Patel, therefore, proceeded to show them that no State was to be allowed to defy their 'purposive policy'; in short, they compelled them to come in.

The first of these three States was Junagadh, a tiny principality with a Hindu population not far from Sind. Its Moslem Nawab had acceded to Pakistan, but was not forced to change his mind at the point of the bayonet. The second was Hyderabad, the largest of all the States, again with a predominantly Hindu population. Its Moslem Nizam, trusting to the promises of Mountbatten and Patel, had chosen an independence which was recognised by the rest of the world. But not by Nehru. Fearing probably that the Communist ideas, which were carrying all before them in China, might take root in semi-feudal Hyderabad and spread thence to India, he began to bring pressure on the Nizam by stopping Moslems from entering his territory on the ground that they were recruits for the Razakars, the militant wing of the Moslem minority, a danger to Hindus and the real masters of Hyderabad. Presently both parties subscribed to a one year stand-still agreement, and Nehru found his hands free to deal with the third of the recalcitrant States, Kashmir-Jammu. This principality was a very different proposition, because it formed part of the dangerous North-West Frontier and was bordered on the far side by the Pakistani North-West Frontier Province in whose inflammable Pathans neighbouring and independent Afghanistan took a keen stepfatherly interest, and on the inner side by India herself along the difficult frontier of East Punjab. Her Maharajah was a Dogra Hindu, but, save in Hindu Jammu, the vast majority of her peoples were Moslems. The majority religion, trade, communications and the flow of the Indus and her tributaries, the Five Rivers on which so much of the life of the Punjab and Pakistan depended, all drew her towards Karachi, but, failing inclusion in Pakistan, she was a good case for partition. Nehru would have neither one solution nor the other. Himself a Kashmir-born Brahman who hated the very idea of Pakistan, a frequent visitor to the disputed State in the interests of Congress democracy, the warm friend of the leader of the local Moslem Congress, Sheikh Abdullah, who was at the moment in gaol by order of his sovereign, he meant to have the whole of his native country for India.

The Maharajah dithered while both sides courted him and, as he afterwards alleged, Pakistan applied economic pressure. Liaqat, on the contrary, declared presently that he had resolved to accede to India even before Hindu mobs had sent Moslems flying to Peshawar and Lahore and committed outrages in Pakistan itself. At news of these wild doings, Moslem Pathan tribesmen from the ungarrisoned marches of the North-West Frontier Province forced the Maharajah into the open by rushing to the rescue of their coreligionists and sweeping up to the very gates of Srinagar, the capital (October 1947). The Maharajah, thereupon, released Sheikh Abdullah, wired to Delhi for help, interviewed Nehru and then, leaving him to collogue with the Sheikh, hurried off to the comparative safety of Jammu whence he appointed his newly-liberated prisoner head of a 'popular' government. Meanwhile, pleading that it would be a 'betrayal of trust' to desert a ruler in distress who had called for help, Nehru flew in troops. These chased the invaders away from the capital, but failed to clear them out altogether before winter stabilised the front.

Nehru raised the Kashmir issue in the Security Council accusing Pakistan of having allowed 50,000 Pakistanis to raid the State and of maintaining 100,000 more on its borders. Possibly because he saw that the British and Americans took an unkind view of his imperialism, he secured the adjournment of the debate and went home to deal with the economic war that was embittering the mutual relations of the two new Dominions to the usual accompaniment of communal killings that were only stayed when Gandhi fasted, for the last time. Nehru found Sind stopping refugee Hindus from taking with them goods which, it held, were essential to Pakistan, unofficial Indians retaliating by withholding from Pakistan much-needed machinery, vehicles and coal, and his own colleagues keeping back millions of rupees which were due to Pakistan under a recent agreement on the division of assets and liabilities between the two countries. He had scarcely agreed to hand over these rupees in exchange for Pakistani rice when the Indian Empire came to an end suddenly. On 30 January, 1948, a Hindu fanatic shot the Mahatma dead; on 28 February, the last British battalion marched down to its ships through the Gate of India at Bombay to the strains of *Auld Lang Syne*, and, on 1 March, India and Pakistan proclaimed each other foreign territory. It was the end of a long and notable story.

India, now legally a full Dominion, carried on under her elderly Ministry and Parliament ignorant of world affairs. The Delhi authorities concluded a sterling balance agreement with the United Kingdom, launched a sorely-needed ten-year plan of industrial and agricultural development, and warned Provincial enthusiasts that they would not meet deficits arising from their varied and often fantastic schemes of betterment. They were then faced with full-dress war in Kashmir. There, invading Pakistan troops fought the Indians in occupation, while Afghanistan openly supported local troublemakers, one of whom was a great friend of Congress, by demanding an independent 'Pathanistan' which should include half the North-West Frontier Province. Jinnah, however, brought Kabul to a better frame of mind by taking swift action against the local malcontents, and then went near to partitioning Kashmir by setting up the Azad Government in the part that Karachi controlled over against Sheikh Abdullah's administration in the part the Indians held. It was thus a land at war of which Mountbatten took a cordial farewell (June 1948), a land anxious also lest Nehru's imperialism might face it with yet another war, this time over Hyderabad into which, after months of futile bickering, Nehru sent his troops on their 'mission of mercy'. In face of this 'police action', the bewildered Nizam promptly acceded to India.

The bellicose Nehru now went to London and was assured by his colleagues in the Prime Ministers' Conference that room could be found in 'the Club' even for his Republic (October 1948). He returned home to work for an early election, which might give Congress a compact majority in the Central Legislature thanks to the new adult suffrage uncomplicated by communal electorates. To clear the ground for this contest, he induced the existing legislature to complete the Constitution *inter alia* by adopting English as the official language for the next fifteen years and, thereafter, Hindi, while, in the economic field, he cut hard currency imports, pushed on with schemes for producing more food, and meanwhile bought in the sterling area the food India must have. At this stage the Kashmir scandal passed into another phase. A Commission sent out by the anxious Security Council induced both sides to agree to a cease fire, but could in no wise persuade Nehru to agree to a plebiscite on the future of the country. Rather did the Indian Prime Minister proclaim publicly that Kashmir was part of India which no power on earth could take away, and have the satisfaction of seeing the Maharajah set off on his travels leaving one of his sons and Sheikh Abdullah to act for him. The departing monarch also left the rival armies glaring at one another across the cease fire line while their Governments quarrelled about the precise location of that line and the disbanding of the Azad Government's forces.

In such circumstances, Honourable Members at Delhi were dismayed to learn that far from Dominion status giving them the promised cheap government, expenditure had actually risen largely because of their Prime Minister's warlike adventures. Conceiving that the limit of direct taxation had been reached, they fell back wholeheartedly on that indirect taxation which hits the masses hardest of all, and then listened ruefully to ministerial comments on the strained condition of the finances of most of the Provinces, laments by leading Congressmen that many of these great areas were in the hands of men who had no idea of leadership or traditions of parliamentary rule, and protests from more than one Prince that the 'democratisation' of their States had put authority into the hands of inferior understudies of Congress who made the rulers' lives a burden. Unabashed, Nehru hurried overseas to refurbish the tarnished Congress legend in the United States and came home to share in the rejoicings at the proclamation of his Republic (January 1950). An elected President took the place of the Governor-General and, now that appeals to the Judicial Committee had been abolished, the Indian Supreme Court became the final legal authority. Thus uplifted, Nehru expressed his wish to see Communist China represented on U.N.O.; but when the United Nations called for help in Korea, he could only offer suave advice. Troops he could not send, even if he would, because most of his were locked up in Kashmir.

Relations with Pakistan grew steadily worse. The erection of customs barriers had not led to the expected end of all trade with that country because humble folk on either side of the new line had organised a barter traffic at which the rival authorities prudently winked; but when Pakistan refused to follow India in devaluing her currency, trade did come to a stand. Even when the two Governments agreed to exchange a few goods for three months, Nehru withheld Pakistani assets and refugee property, wrecked a conference on the control of the headwaters of the Five Rivers, and, over Kashmir, showed himself as obstinate as only a Brahman could be. He refused to go with Liaqat in accepting the Security

Council's United States nominee as arbitrator, or in adopting the informal suggestions of his Canadian and Australian successors that there should be a mutual and simultaneous withdrawal of troops followed by plebiscites and partition, because, in his eyes, the Pakistani 'aggressors' would be 'appeased' if the Maharajah, *videlicet* Sheikh Abdullah, were denied full control of the country during those plebiscites. Nor would he listen to yet more informal advice from some of the members of the Commonwealth Prime Ministers' Conference (January 1951). Dwelling on the undesirability of settling inter-Dominion disputes by force, he held on to his part of Kashmir by that very means, and forgetful that religion had given him his chief excuse for seizing overwhelmingly Hindu Hyderabad, insisted that the future of predominantly Moslem Kashmir must be settled on purely political and economic grounds without the distractions of religious 'propaganda'. Possibly to show what he meant, he began to lend increasing unofficial support to Moslem Afghanistan's renewed demand for a 'Pathanistan', which was now to be extended right up to the Indus at the expense of loathed Pakistan. Then came the elections for the Lower House of the Indian Central Legislature and the Provincial legislatures (October 1951-January 1952). The results held out little hope of a change for the better, for though the *Mahasabha* and other sectarian parties fared ill, Congress dominated most of the Provinces and got home again at the Centre. On the other hand, it had only done so with a healthily reduced majority, and must face a fairly solid Communist Opposition which had not only gained the upper hand in several Provinces, especially in the Untouchable South, but had won many seats at the Centre.

Nehru must now bear a heavier burden than ever because Patel, the devoted sharer of his multiple ministerial burdens, had just died (December 1950). Distressed by the falling off in quality of university aspirants for public office, he had to face increasing difficulties with Provinces which, even when the rice ration was cut drastically, showed no readiness to co-operate in the distribution of such supplies as there were. On the heels of this depressing display came the census returns, which showed that the population had risen by 108,730,000 during the past generation and that the average span of life was twenty-seven years and the average income less than £20 a year. Plainly, there was need for the Five Year Plan of development which Nehru now launched.

Equally plainly there was need for a settlement in Kashmir, but this he postponed by wrecking the most recent attempt of the Security Council to mediate. Then, while the rival armies concentrated on either side of the cease fire line, he went a long way towards integrating the disputed State with his Dominion by agreeing with Sheikh Abdullah that, *inter alia*, the Dogra dynasty should make way for a 'Head of the State' recommended by the Kashmir legislature, a Head who soon proved to be a son of the ex-Maharajah, and that Kashmir should have a Constituent Assembly to which, in due course, all the Sheikh's nominees were returned unopposed. Ill content with the rule of a Moslem Prime Minister, the Hindus of Jammu, backed by the extremist Akali Sikhs and the *Mahasabha*, started a furious agitation for the incorporation of their section of Kashmir with Hindu India. And then the expected happened. Pakistan, scourged by drought, accused India of taking more than her fair share of the vital headwaters of the Indus basin, and was not placated by Nehru's bland denial that she was doing anything of the sort. As if to atone for thus accentuating the strain with the Government of a sister Dominion, Indian delegates made statesmanlike proposals which in due time led to a check on the fighting in Korea, while Nehru himself agreed with some reluctance to give free transit to such Gurkhas as the British might recruit in landlocked Nepal, and praised the Commonwealth connection so warmly that the House of the People at Delhi overwhelmingly rejected a motion that India should withdraw from an association whose great virtue, in its Prime Minister's opinion, was that it bound none of its members.

Pakistan's principal problems were religious, constitutional and economic. Jinnah, as a modernist, first successfully resisted the efforts of Islamic enthusiasts to clamp the new Dominion into the mould of a theocratic State and then turned to wrestle with the Provincial hydra. He admitted that distant East Bengal must have its own Provincial authority and, though the main mass of Pakistan in the west was not too large to be ruled from a single centre, resisted the temptation to make himself a second Ataturk. Nevertheless, he took a strong line in those parts by dismissing the Premier of Sind and arraigning him in the courts for gross corruption, and by clapping other leaders into gaol for plotting a 'Pathanistan' in collaboration with the hostile Afghans and proposing to turn the whole of

Pakistan into a Union of Free Socialist Republics. To hold the Pathans yet more firmly in check, he took powers to deal sternly with frontier trouble-makers, especially such as were egged on by foreigners. In the economic field, he convinced of their error those many Pakistanis who accused the British of fearing competition when they did not give them all the capital equipment they demanded overnight, and reassured hesitant British investors by showing that he wished his country to remain within the Commonwealth and, presently, by revealing a fairly marked preference for free enterprise. He began to shed controls, called in British and Scandinavian industrial experts, set up a State Bank to make his Dominion autonomous in currency and finance, and smiled upon the new Research Organisation that was to reconcile Allah and Mammon. So might Pakistan, reasonably self-sufficient in the matter of food-supplies, hope to earn plentiful foreign exchange by the sale of her wool, hides, cotton and, above all, the jute of which East Bengal produced some three-quarters of the world supply, and hope also to supplement her scanty coal with hydro-electric power once she had loosened Nehru's hold on the headwaters of her Five Rivers. Meanwhile, in the external sphere, Jinnah was so angry at the feeble way in which U.N.O. handled the Junagadh and Kashmir disputes, and so furious at Truman's interference in predominantly Moslem Palestine, that he exchanged Ambassadors with Russia. Again, from the moment that he suspected Mountbatten of favouring India unduly, his relations with Delhi had become more and more strained and nearly reached breaking-point when Nehru snatched Hyderabad (September 1948). Twenty-four hours later, Jinnah died.

The new Governor-General and his Prime Minister, Liaqat Ali Khan, were happy to escape war over Hyderabad and readily accepted a cease fire in Kashmir. They then agreed with India on financial problems arising out of the partition of the Punjab and Bengal, but, facing the fact that only one of their Provinces showed a surplus, instituted an inquiry into the corrupt practices of the ex-Premier of Sind and entrusted the administration of West Punjab entirely to its Governor. During a short Session, Liaqat effected a compromise between Moderates and Moslem die-hards and made some progress towards drafting a Constitution. He could do little to relieve the housing shortage, but he did carry a Budget which, like the first, showed a surplus and left the main weight of direct taxation on the shoulders of the well-to-do where he himself had placed it in his famous Budget for undivided India. Disappointed by his experiences at a Commonwealth Conference (May 1949) and doubting the value to his country of membership of a 'Club' which did not give her the security she craved nor do anything definite about Kashmir, he showed signs of departing from Jinnah's prudent policy in two respects: first, in face of Afghan jeers and threats of highly-placed enemies in Sind and West Punjab to split the Moslem League, he got rid of two British Governors and filled their places with Pathans, and then flirted with Stalin to the point of securing, first of Dominion Prime Ministers, an invitation to Moscow. Though such a visit would have been an effective counterblast to Nehru's recent visit to Washington, Liaqat did not go. Rather did he swing back towards the Commonwealth camp, realising that the British were sending Pakistan all the capital goods and defence equipment they could spare and that some of their newspapers were saying many of the things he thought about Nehru. He did, indeed, cut off appeals to the Judicial Committee, but he helped the United Kingdom by reducing dollar expenditure and agreed with India that she should send Pakistan more coal and other goods and receive in exchange less jute and cotton than formerly. So far, so good; but there was still trouble in many Provinces over the wide powers held by the Centre, and, in the east, Patel, the *Mahasabha* and an irresponsible Hindu Press partly caused and partly inflamed the rioting and bloodshed that spread rapidly from Calcutta over the whole of the Two Bengals. At last, however, the tumult died down and Liaqat was free to visit the United States. Next, after a first refusal to go unless Kashmir was discussed, he took his seat once more at a Commonwealth Conference, whence he returned home disappointed of any result arising from informal talks on that wearisome topic for the now invariable reason (January 1951). Be that as it might, he doggedly induced his people to look westward where the United States, encouraged by the United Kingdom, was seeking to ease the strain between Pakistan and Afghanistan, and both great Powers were projecting a welcome peace settlement with Japan. If Hindus chose the moment at which the Kashmir crisis had become almost unbearable to panic out of East Bengal, it was reassuring that they should have been checked speedily by their own leaders, a sign that their Province was indeed a part of Pakistan and no mere colonial appendage. Nearer home, moreover, Liaqat was able to deal decisively with a group of army officers who conspired with Communists to overthrow his administration. At this anxious juncture, he was shot dead by a young Pathan, a refugee from Afghanistan (16 October, 1951). But he and Jinnah had done their work. Pakistan was no longer merely one man's imagining, but an established State rejoicing in hopeful finances and a trade boom.

Liaqat's successor first tried to calm India's agitation by giving a plain hint that however much he might sympathise with Moslem Egypt in her dispute with the United Kingdom over the Suez Canal zone and the Sudan, he would not join any Middle East Defence Organisation unless that quarrel was ended and Egypt herself joined. He then released his Provinces from their crippling dependence on the Centre by accepting the Raisman Award which recommended the transfer to them of important sources of revenue (December 1951), a wise measure which he hoped might raise the standard of public life in East Bengal and some other Provinces, and encourage West Punjab to carry much-needed land reforms still further. The Government was rewarded by a resounding Moslem League electoral victory in the North-West Frontier Province, a victory which was by no means entirely due to the new adult suffrage. Then good luck deserted Pakistan. While the authorities were devising a long-term scheme of education, the slump came suddenly. A bumper cotton crop, stiffer United States restrictions and revived cut-throat Japanese competition brought prices down with a run at the very moment that Pakistanis found far more jute on their hands than overseas buyers, the Calcutta weavers and their own three pioneer mills could possibly take. To make matters worse, drought forced the Government to risk losing popularity by maintaining import restrictions. Nor were troubles merely economic. Educational grievances inspired students, vigorously supported by roughs, to riot in Karachi to such effect that the troops had to turn out and gain the authorities time in which to remedy those grievances. Sectarian differences were fundamentally far more serious. The *mullahs* and their numerous rural followers started a campaign to have the somewhat heterodox Ahmedis treated as a non-Moslem minority, and thereby attacked the Foreign Minister who was a zealous member of that sect. Before the end, martial law had to be proclaimed in Lahore. Similarly, religious antipathies showed themselves in a measure in the Hindu exodus from East

Bengal set on foot by the proposed institution of a full system of passports and visas; but this movement was once more stopped by local leaders and the belated institution of that system.

It was against this stormy background that the Constituent Assembly debated the Constitution (December 1952). It had before it the report of a committee, which, without indicating whether or no the country should remain within the Commonwealth, recommended that Pakistan should become a federation of Provinces and acceding States. At the Centre, Provinces and States were to be represented by the 120 members of the House of Units and the public by the 400 members of the House of the People elected by adult suffrage. In order to hold the balance true between West and East Pakistan, the committee risked offending the proud Punjabis by proposing that these two halves of the Federation should have equal representation in both Houses, for, after all, East Bengal contained a very high proportion of the total population. Again, to placate the *mullahs*, it proposed that boards of men well-versed in Islamic law should advise the authorities at the Centre and in each Unit on the possible repugnancy of legislation to that law, and thus laid itself open to the charges of being undemocratic by giving such wide powers to extra-parliamentary bodies and, worse still, of being un-Islamic by virtually recognising the existence of a priesthood. No final conclusions were reached yet awhile. It was possibly with relief that the Assembly turned away to accept a Budget which was by no means as terrifying as had been anticipated. Meanwhile, the Kashmir scandal dragged on exacerbated by a quarrel with India over the use of the headwaters of the vital Five Rivers (February 1953). Such was their indignation that many Pakistanis held that war was the only way out.

The British had not forgotten their dependencies even during the Axis war. At first they had not been able to do much for them under the Colonial Welfare and Development Act of 1940, but as shipping became less scarce, they did more and more, offering to pay for such schemes put forward by them as did not demand staff or imported materials and, in the constitutional sphere, giving Jamaica adult suffrage and a strong thrust in the direction of self-government. Early in 1945, they amended the Act of 1940 by raising to £120,000,000 the original sum of £50,000,000 that was to be spent on welfare, development and research during the coming ten years.

The British were not left free to effect colonial reforms without criticism and obstruction. Beside demanding the Falkland Islands, the Argentine, and neighbouring Chile also, claimed footings in British Antarctica farther south mainly on the strength of a meteorological and a whaling station which they had acquired respectively at British invitation. In 1947, a bevy of Argentine Admirals and the Chilean President in person superintended the foundation of further meteorological stations of their own in that region. Thus emboldened, Guatemala pressed her claim to the whole or part of British Honduras so vehemently that the British had to send troops and a cruiser to the colony's capital (1948). These disputes were then transferred to Bogota, the chief city of Colombia, where, in spite of the chilly reminder that other folk's colonies were no business of theirs, the purely consultative Pan-American Conference accepted Brazil's claims to British Guiana and similar territories, and resolutions by Chile and the Argentine against British 'colonialism'. It even offered the inhabitants of the said possessions the choice between independence and incorporation with some neighbouring republic, and, finally, condemned the retention by Europeans of any colonies whatsoever in the Americas.

At the time of writing, the Union Jack still flies at the accustomed places in those Americas and, above all, in the Caribbean area. So far were West Indians from accepting either of the alternatives proferred by the Pan-American Congress that they contemplated some form of that federation which the Imperial authorities had proposed from time to time. This was a solution which had many attractions in spite of the obvious difficulties of wide dispersion, poor communications, the poverty and backwardness of the masses, lack of educated folk of whatever colour, and inter-island jealousies. At Whitehall's suggestion, representatives from all the Caribbean colonies met in 1947 at Montego Bay, where they appointed a drafting committee. Encouraged by the grant of near self-government to Barbados and Jamaica and the foundation of the West Indian University at Kingston, they met again three years later. 'Continental' British Guiana and the distant Bahamas and Bermuda hung back, but the rest, disregarding Guatemala's protest, accepted federation in principle.

In Asia, the British let three dependencies go, held on to a fourth with difficulty and promoted yet another to the rank of Dominion. The first to be let go was mandated Transjordan which became the independent State of 'Jordan'. The second was Palestine. Here, to end the quarrelling, if that might be, of political Zionists and the resident Arab majority, the United States and the U.S.S.R. drafted a scheme of partition and secured the appointment by U.N.O. of a Commission which was soon at work arranging for the transfer of Jews and Arabs to their respective areas. This Commission relied on the patient British Tommies to enforce its recommendations, but the British, sick of the whole infuriating business, gave up their mandate, and, after due notice, marched out leaving it nominally in charge. The unhappy Swedish head of the Commission was soon murdered; some of the states of the Arab League, led by Egypt, attacked now-independent 'Israel' and got the worst of it, and, amid the uproar, the Zionists drove out swarms of Arabs to make room for an unlimited number of Jewish immigrants to the Much Promised Land. They left the refugees to be saved from starvation by the harassed United Nations.

Burma, the third of the British dependencies to be jettisoned, this time reluctantly, was much more imposing than either of these little Middle Eastern territories. The vast majority of its 17,000,000 inhabitants were Burmese Buddhists who were worried by the presence of hill tribesmen, perhaps one million unassimilable South Indian Tamils, inveterate usurers, forestallers and regraters, and a quarter of a million Chinese, Communists for the most part. Burmans were also irritated by the fact that nearly all the major activities of their country were in the hands of the much more vigorous British, Indians and Chinese. When Burma had at last been cut off from alien India in 1937, it had been endowed with a most liberal Constitution which gave its people control over everything except defence, external affairs and the hillmen, few of whom had ever been controlled by Burmese kings. Communism had already been spreading even before the Japanese invasion. During that invasion, the able and unscrupulous Burman, U San, and his supporters massacred in the wake of the Japanese so energetically and backed every 'popular' cause so vehemently that they spread Communist doctrines widely and, when the British returned, continued to massacre with such zeal that most Burmans believed they were the real liberators of their country. The British proposed that there should be progress by easy stages from official rule to full Dominion status, a proposal that probably satisfied most of the inhabitants, except the Hillmen who loathed the Burmese. Not so U San. Having been appointed Head of the Home Department in the prematurely-created Executive Council, he recruited enough of his country's swarming dacoits to man a large People's Volunteer Army and then, by dint of gerrymandering and terror, had himself returned to the prematurely-created Legislative Council by an overwhelming majority. His speedy assassination by rivals did not stay the march of events. Having exacted a mild treaty which bound Burma in a special relationship to the Commonwealth, the British left her in January 1948 in sovereign independence to spread her version of Communism to adjacent Siam, Indo-China, Malaya, India and China herself.

Frequent casualty lists still show that the British did not likewise abandon the jumble of Provinces and States that men call 'Malaya'. Outside the three Straits Settlements of Penang, Malacca and Singapore, Sultans and their British Resident ruled a very mixed population, the majority of them excitable Malays with whom were interspersed locally-born Eurasians, Tamils and Chinese. Prior to the Japanese invasion, there had been but little racialism other than the resentment of the racial minorities that all administrative posts should go to British or Malays. The coming of the Japanese changed all that. Not only did Chinese-born Communists scatter themselves over the countryside, but the Malayan Communist Party made their Malayan People's Anti-Japanese Army the spearhead of the Resistance. Once the war was over, the leaders of that army proceeded to fight for a Communist State, recruiting their forces almost entirely from Chinese newcomers and relying on terror and killing to produce supplies, silence tongues and get rid of owners, managers and staffs from the mines and plantations that were dotted about a country which was eighty-five per cent jungle, a veritable Thugs' Paradise.

The insurgents failed. In spite of heavy loss of life, rubber and tin flowed out to earn dollars for Malaya and the United Kingdom, and the British pushed on with constitutional and other reforms. They made Singapore a separate Crown colony and, after an initial false start by a dictatorially-minded Fabian Colonial Secretary, induced the nine Sultans to combine in a Malayan Union under a Governor and Executive and Legislative Councils, which could look forward to bringing in Singapore and Brunei, British North Borneo whose administration the Chartered Company now surrendered, and Sarawak from which the Brooke dynasty presently withdrew. But the jungle war went on.

Ceylon was destined to a happier fate than either Burma or Malaya. Like theirs, her population was very mixed. The vast majority were strict Buddhist Sinhalese, poor businessmen but numerous enough to swamp the minorities at the polls or, if that failed, to secure the seats on the Executive Board for their own folk by gerrymandering and family politics that would have done credit to eighteenth-century Whig magnates. The minorities were Moslems, handfuls of British and of half-caste Burghers who recalled the old Dutch days, and a floating population of imported Tamils who for the most part worked on the tea and rubber plantations and shared the political views of the Indian Congress Party. These unassimilable South Indians had only a limited franchise in place of the adult suffrage enjoyed by the other racial groups, and were a source of furious altercation between India and Ceylon because the Colombo authorities had more than once tried to get rid of them.

As they watched India surging forward to *swaraj* during the Axis war, the Sinhalese majority in the Legislature demanded like powers and status. Whitehall, however, merely asked them to draft a constitution conferring self-government in purely domestic matters only and promised that, if this constitution was approved by a three-fourths majority of the Legislature, it would send a Commission to examine it after the war. The Executive Board duly complied, but then tried to rush the position by declaring that the Secretary of State had promised to take the draft constitution as it stood, withdrew the draft and resolved to boycott the expected Soulbury Commission. When, after all, leaders of the minorities and the ambitious Don Stephen Senanayake, their own leader in the House and Vice-Chairman of the Executive Board, collogued with the distinguished visitors, one of the Ministers pushed through the Legislature a measure giving Ceylon the very fullest measure of Dominion powers. The Royal assent was withheld.

The Soulbury Report recommended that there should be a

Senate half nominated by the Governor and half elected by the Lower House, adult suffrage for all other than the Tamils of whose franchise it said nothing, and a generally desired Public Service Commission to check the customary official jobbery. It suggested, moreover, that Ceylon should not become a full Dominion until she had shown she could work the proffered constitution. The overwhelming majority of the Legislature accepted this offer amid the lamentations of the minorities-about-to-be-abandoned. Parties took shape, notably Senanayake's United Party which attracted the mass of the Sinhalese, many Moslems and even some Tamils, while the Imperial authorities warned all concerned that they must expect no further powers until they had signed a treaty covering the position of public servants, external affairs and defence. In the event, a good many Tamils and a few Communists got home, as well as a scattering of Independents on some of whom the United Party had to rely for its majority in the vital House of Representatives. Undismayed, Senanayake formed his Cabinet which included the leader of the Tamils as Minister of Agriculture. Despite the fact that Nehru now wrecked the most recent attempt to settle the Tamil problem, the Westminster Parliament passed the Independence Act just as Russia vetoed Ceylon's admission to U.N.O. A two-thirds majority of the Colombo Legislature accepted the new Act. The Prime Minister, mindful of the proximity of teeming China and India, announced that his country should remain within the Commonwealth despite opposition jeers of a 'false independence', and, determined as he was to see it become a Dominion, signed the necessary Defence Treaty with the United Kingdom. A week later, the Duke of Gloucester opened Ceylon's first Dominion Parliament (February 1948).

The Dominion Cabinet was little more than a loose coalition held together by the strong personality and skilful leadership of the Prime Minister, who was sure of the support of the United Party's rank-and-file however much some of his ministerial colleagues might bicker in public. Shepherded thus, Parliament created two types of citizen: the first by descent, and the second by the registration each year of the handful of folk who could prove that they had been already naturalised and had rendered special service to their adopted land; it also went some way to meeting the Tamils on the score of their comings and goings and sanctioned the raising of a national Army, Navy and Air Force. The Prime Minister then presided over the Conference of Commonwealth Foreign Ministers which outlined the Colombo Plan and himself created a Central Bank. Taken together, these two measures made it easier for him to reach a temporary settlement of sterling balances with the United Kingdom and to carry an unspectacular Budget (1950). Revenue promised to remain high and, given peace, economic prospects were hopeful, for though population and the cost of living were both soaring, prices for rubber and tea were abnormally good, while British and Indian firms showed no signs of withdrawing capital and had, moreover, long been anticipating the popular cry for the 'ceylonisation' of business by training young Sinhalese for executive posts. Thus encouraged, the authorities took steps to improve the harbour at Colombo and the electricity supply, arranged for the settlement of industrial disputes and, by carrying a hotly-debated Land Acquisition Act, sought to relieve congestion in the land-hungry villages. Further, they set on foot a six year development plan for the production above all of much-needed food. Thereafter, having seen the first of his country's hydro-electric plants in operation, the Prime Minister set a good example, as a keen farmer should, by repairing ancient 'tanks' and, generally, advancing agriculture. He was, however, soon faced with a regular Parliamentary Opposition when an eloquent, mildly Socialist and always difficult Minister crossed the floor of the House and formed his own Sri Lanka Freedom Party. Nevertheless, Parliament passed Ceylon's biggest Budget yet, sanctioned the formation of a state-aided airline in conjunction with an Australian concern, gave local authorities greater freedom from central control, legislated for soil erosion and public health and extended the term of the recent development plan from six years to ten. This done, the nation advertised its abounding prosperity by holding a highly successful Colombo Plan Exhibition at the capital (February–March 1952).

At the close of that Exhibition, the Prime Minister was killed untimely by a fall from his horse and, in response to popular demand, was succeeded by Dudley Senanayake, his able forty-year old, Cambridge-trained son. The new Prime Minister was confirmed in power at the ensuing general election all the more easily since the Opposition Parties were united only by their desire to leave the Commonwealth, his own Party had latterly been organising in the constituencies and, to the accompaniment of stubborn passive resistance, most of the swarming and pro-Indian Congress

Tamils had been disfranchised. On the other hand, he was soon in trouble. In face of a sudden financial crisis, he had to risk loss of popularity by restricting imports from non-sterling areas and heavily increasing taxation, and had to seek means of buying food by offering rubber to the United States in exchange for sorely-needed rice. The Great Republic proposed to dole out a little rice at high prices in dollars, which Ceylon lacked, and to pay a poor enough price for rubber. When, however, Senanayake made a trade agreement with the Communist Chinese and began to send them rubber in return for adequate rice supplies, Washington protested vigorously, and was hardly placated when he made a similar trade agreement with Western Germany.

The United Kingdom's colonial ventures were not solely in the constitutional sphere. True to the policy of 'philanthropy and five per cent', she resolved to finance productive schemes in various colonies similar to those which had been undertaken latterly on a small scale in tropical Africa and Malaya (1947). Faced with a grievous shortage of fats and ignoring the piled pyramids of Northern Nigerian groundnuts that only asked for a few comparatively cheap lines of railway to make them available, Parliament created a complicated machinery of interlocking public and private organisations, all of them in the last resort dependent on the Exchequer, to grow groundnuts and sunflowers in Tanganyika. Off clattered experts and bull-dozers to rip up vast tracts of untried East Africa, and to pray that the Lord would send rain in due season. When He did not, the Imperial authorities abandoned the scheme, substituted another of more modest dimensions under the presumably cautious Colonial Office, made the most of the new harbour, road and railway which were all they had to show for the bill of £36,000,000 that had to be footed by the still fatless British taxpayers, and then called upon those same milch kine to foot another little account for a costly though less grandiose project that had failed to produce eggs and poultry on the Gambia.

As if to atone for these miscarriages, H.M. Government ensured Africans fuller representation in the legislatures of Kenya, Tanganyika, Nyasaland and Northern Rhodesia. She also gave the Gold Coast something very like self-government, a bold step which led to complications in far-away South Africa. Holding the views he did on the proper relations of White and Black, the Union

Prime Minister, Dr. Malan, could not restrain his indignation that the United Kingdom should have gone so near to making the Negro Gold Coast autonomous and, still more, should have talked of making it a Dominion without consulting its prospective colleagues. Malan then embarrassed the British Government by asking them to transfer to the Union the governance of the three High Commission Territories of Basutoland, Swaziland and the Bechuanaland Protectorate, the procedure for which had been laid down in the South Africa Act.

Further complications arose for the British Government immediately to the north of the Union. Shortly before the Axis war, that Government had shelved the most recent of the many schemes for the federation of Southern and Northern Rhodesia, but at the end of it, it had constituted the Governors of those territories and of Nyasaland also a Central African Council with a permanent Secretariate at Salisbury. For all that this executive federal authority had begun to concentrate various common services at the Southern Rhodesian capital, it could scarcely be the end of the story, especially as politicians on either side of the Zambesi did little to help it to become effective. It was doubtful, however, whether the British Labour Government would look at any form of closer legislative union of which the immense African majority did not approve. Native policy had always been the rub. Each of the three territories concerned had its own native policy, but whereas in colour bar Southern Rhodesia, where effective power lay with the local Europeans, the British Government had little say, in the two Northern provinces, where elective Europeans had to share power with Africans and Imperial officials, it could and did enforce its policy of trusteeship. The British had seen in Natal, the Union and in Southern Rhodesia something of what might come of defying Lord Lugard's warning that native masses must never be put at the mercy of an immigrant minority. Were they now to risk something similar by sanctioning a federation which would inevitably be dominated by white Southern Rhodesians reinforced by Northern Rhodesians who, being for the most part highly-paid white trade unionists in a black man's country, were even less liberal than they? On the other hand, the arguments for closer union were cogent. Federation might not be cheap nor easy to man, but the British could not deny that it would give a sense of security to isolated Europeans, some 200,000 all told, who were scattered among fully 6,000,000 Bantu and perched precariously on the frontier of a Union which most of them disliked and many of them feared. Still less could they deny the economic advantages that would accrue to these landlocked and mutually complementary provinces which were only linked to one another and to distant 'foreign' ports by single-track three-foot-six railways and indifferent roads, and which now believed that nothing but political closer union would improve their overseas credit sufficiently to enable them to finance the development of coal, steel, railways, and hydro-electric power.

Events were to prove that the economic advantage of closer union was the argument that really mattered. Inspired by a Northern Rhodesian copper boom in a rearming world, delegates from all three provinces decided at the Victoria Falls Conference to press for a federation on Australian lines that would ensure the new State's speedily becoming a Dominion (February 1949). Checked for the moment by Whitehall, Huggins gave an unhappy foretaste of what many folk feared would be the outcome of federation by raising the qualifications for the Southern Rhodesian 'civilisation' franchise so high that fewer Africans than ever could get the vote, while the same Colonial Secretary who had handled the federation issue in Malaya so ineptly saw to it that Roy Welensky, leader of the dominant white trade unionists and also of the elected Members in the Executive and Legislative Councils of Northern Rhodesia, should be virtually 'Prime Minister' of a British Protectorate. Thus encouraged, Central African politicians met in conference once more (September 1951). This time they heard the not altogether unfavourable comments of the visiting Labour Secretaries of State for the Colonies and Commonwealth Relations, and though some of the few African representatives opposed federation, Huggins on his subsequent visit to London found that Oliver Lyttelton, Colonial Secretary in Churchill's new Conservative Government, was almost as keen as he himself to press the scheme forward. In spite of the dissent of its two African nominee members, a further Conference in London approved a scheme which, among other changes, proposed that the impossible independent Minister who had originally been suggested as a safeguard for African interests should make way for a non-parliamentary and somewhat impotent African Affairs Board. The background for the final Conference, in London again, was provided by a strike of the African Mineworkers

Union on the Northern Rhodesian copper mines, a strike that was only ended by their acceptance of the award of an impartial British arbitrator (January 1953). This Conference, which such Africans as were invited refused to attend, adopted a scheme under which the 6,000,000 Africans were to be represented in a Federal Assembly of thirty-six by three specially elected Europeans and six elected Africans with no hope of any more unless that were agreed to by a two-thirds majority, a mere standing committee of that Assembly was to take the place of the hated African Affairs Board, and most matters affecting Africans, especially land questions, were left to the territorial administrations which it was optimistically stated would maintain their Protectorate character north of the Zambesi. Protests by visiting Nyasaland chiefs and well-informed British sympathisers were rudely brushed aside and, driven on by the full weight of the Government and most of the national Press, a great majority of the Commons approved of the scheme after a poor debate. And already transplanted Africans were waxing wrath in the West Indies, and rueful Africans in more than one part of their own great Continent were excusing the British for this policy of 'scuttle' by presuming that they were finished and knew it.

There was one conceivable scheme of federation that would have put any mere local colonial federations into the shade. This was the federation, not of the heterogeneous Empire as a whole, but of the United Kingdom and the Dominions which had drawn so completely out of that Empire that they were separate political entities capable of taking their own line. The prevalent conception of this British Commonwealth was that it was an organisation whose nature, functions, methods of procedure and mutual relations had been laid down for all time by the Balfour Declaration of 1926 and whose several independencies had been ensured by the Statute of Westminster of 1931 so effectively that separation had got the better of cohesion. Here were Dominions basking in the glory of sovereign independence not so much by virtue of their own strength as by reason of their voluntary association with each other and, above all, with the Mother Country of whose help they were sure, if only for old time's sake, but with whom, as the Balfour Declaration itself had stressed, they were in no way bound

Y*

to share the burdens of foreign policy and defence between the wars and to whose aid they were not bound to go when wars came. The truth was that the Commonwealth was little more than a 'Club' whose members by no means always spoke or acted with unanimity. Recent occurrences had confirmed late eighteenth-century Anglo-Irish and early twentieth-century South African experience that separate States and colonies under the same Monarch were apt to go their several ways, even to the point of war. An increasing number of observers were persuaded that the Commonwealth must set its house in order if it were to continue to function at all.

Of course, there were still Commonwealth links such as conference by arrangement, sometimes at ministerial level, a quasi-diplomatic network of High Commissioners and lesser lights, the common use of diplomatic and consular services in the absence of national functionaries, preferential tariffs, various forms of military co-operation and imperial postal charges lower than foreign. But the more formal links were either gone or wearing thin. The Judicial Committee of the Privy Council, since 1897 the one truly federal imperial institution, had been robbed of much of its influence as the final Court of Appeal for the Empire overseas by the recent cutting off of many Dominion appeals; the traditional and regular Imperial Conferences had been wellnigh superseded latterly by casual and not always full meetings of Commonwealth Prime Ministers; the very Crown was no longer the golden link it had been from the beginning since republican India had been allowed to retain her membership of the 'Club'; finally, the common status of 'British subject' had been destroyed. That common status had always bound each British subject of whatever origin to the others and the Crown by a common allegiance; the nationality laws of all countries which derived from the English Common Law and imperial statute had been based on that idea; those Dominions who had defined their own 'nationals' had been careful to make it plain that these local citizenships were derived from the basic and original British nationality and subjecthood. That care had been thrown to the winds by Canada in 1946, and the whole idea of British subjecthood had been cast overboard by the United Kingdom herself two years later. In terms of the British Nationality Act, all those within the Empire and Commonwealth who were not aliens must either be subjects and, in the most formal manner, citizens of one or other of the Dominions, or else, and this meant the vast majority, new-fangled 'citizens of the United Kingdom and Colonies'. Thus were British subjects deprived of the cherished distinction they had enjoyed hitherto of forming a group privileged above all others by virtue of their British nationality and subject-hood. Such an example from Westminster inevitably inspired South Africa and some other Dominions to imitate or even surpass it.

Various prescriptions were offered for the cure of this amorphous Commonwealth. One such was 'more of the same', the policy of letting it drift on as a discordant cacophony trusting that (God and the United States willing) common traditions, ideas, hopes, beliefs and fears would make it all right on the Day. Another, less negative, envisaged the conduct of a joint policy of defence in this area or that by the Powers directly concerned or even a more general carrying over of wartime co-operation into times of peace. The third policy was that of federating, for a start, all or some of the members of the Commonwealth under a real Government for certain purposes in the hope that, later on, the United States and European parlia-mentary democracies might rally to this centre of stability. Such a federation would put the Commonwealth on something more of an equality with the giant federal United States and the U.S.S.R. by permitting it to maintain a Navy and allied services comparable to those which the United Kingdom had maintained alone between 1805 and 1914 and, by so doing, averted all world wars. If a federated Commonwealth could avert such wars, it would have done much more than merely winning them, and if it could not, it would stand a far better chance of winning them than any one of its members could do by itself alone.

The majority of the peoples of the Commonwealth lived in federations or unions which, having been so long recognised as separate political entities, could surely draw together voluntarily without loss of face, especially as the federal capital need not be Westminster. Nevertheless, the cry went up from all of them that no political leader would suffer any abatement of sovereign powers for the common good nor electorate hear of federation even if it knew what it meant. And yet, the union of England and Scotland and the still more amazing federation of the Old Thirteen had been achieved, both of them at times when distances were far more

formidable than they were when British and South African statesmen could fly thousands of miles in a few days or even hours to
spend week-ends with a United States President on the Potomac
or exercise the functions of a University Chancellor on the banks of
the Cam. Meanwhile, no outstanding public man or woman had
yet put the issue of Commonwealth federation to a single one of the
electorates directly concerned.

Most federalists were agreed that if anything were to be done, the
lead must come from peoples of the English speech. Peoples of that
speech have been great political amalgamators. Political unity had
been imposed on the English themselves first of all the considerable
nations of Western Christendom; they had learned to value it early,
and, if they had failed to achieve a working arrangement with the
Irish, had succeeded tolerably well with the Welsh and Scots. Now,
overseas, the federal United States, federal or unitary Dominions,
the Federated Malay States, and schemes for closer union in the
West Indies and various parts of Africa bore witness to the constructive powers of men of British stock or predominantly British
training and tradition. *Tria juncta in uno—E pluribus unum—Ex
unitate vires*—might not at least the English-speaking peoples,
with their ready acceptance of unity in diversity, find a way to
surpass their earlier achievements now that the need and the opportunity were so great?

The spirit at all events was one. Hear the voices down the years
declaring the custom and expressing the ideals that the mass of
English-speaking folk everywhere have known they ought to live
up to. For a long time the voices are 'mere English'; King Alfred
warning all 'who reck of God's mercy as of ours' that henceforward
the lives of his Wessex men and Guthrum's Danes were to be held
equally dear—at eight half marks of pure gold apiece; Ethelred's
Witan decreeing that punishments in general be mild, 'and let not,
for a little, God's handy work and His own purchase be destroyed,'
and then the Barons and a Mayor of London guaranteeing the
Charter they had extorted from the King. 'No freeman shall be
arrested, imprisoned, disseised, outlawed, exiled or in any way
destroyed . . . save by the lawful judgement of his peers or the law
of the land; to none will we sell, deny or delay right and justice; no
scutage or aid shall be levied in our realm save by the Common
Council; we will forthwith remove from the kingdom all foreign
soldiery, both horse and foot. . . .' So runs Magna Carta, Latin in

word but thoroughly English in spirit with its tough insistence on personal liberty, at all events for free men, and respect for tradition and prescriptive right. A copy sealed with John's seal, bridging the centuries, was long cherished at Washington side by side with the original of the Declaration of Independence whose authors informed their 'Brittish brethren' and the rest of mankind that they would no longer yield obedience to a King who had obstructed the administration of justice, deprived certain Americans of trial by jury, imposed taxes on all of them without their consent and was at that very moment sending 'large Armies of foreign Mercenaries to compleat the works of death'.

The Abbey, scarred now by barbarian bombs, had been new when elected knights of the shire and burgesses came up together from all parts of Edward the Lawgiver's England 'with full and sufficient powers for themselves and their community' to carry out whatever might be ordained by the Parliament at Westminster, and, by the same token, a somewhat similar Assembly was meeting at Dublin in England's first colony of the Irish Pale. There were, and long had been, Welshmen as well as Englishmen in the House of Commons that told its Scottish King, one year after the Pilgrim Fathers had landed at Plymouth Rock, that 'the liberties, franchises, privileges and jurisdictions of parliament are the ancient and undoubted birthright and inheritance of the subjects of England'. The City of London had rebuilt itself after the Great Fire, and its lovely churches, many of them now blackened ruins, witnessed freshly to the genius that was Wren's, when another Parliament pursued its fleeing sovereign to France with the reminder that 'the Pretended power' of suspending or dispensing laws without consent of Parliament was illegal, and the novel assertion that 'the raising or keeping a standing Army within the Kingdom in time of peace unless it be with the consent of Parliament is against law'. And what held good for the Mother Country held for the Colonies also. Men in the Old England of William and Mary could take it for granted that New England had 'all English privileges and liberties, and can be touched by no law and by no tax but of their own making'.

There were Scots as well as Englishmen and Welshmen in the Houses that heard Burke pleading for conciliation with the American colonists on this very matter of taxation since 'a great Empire and little minds go ill together', and Chatham, the man who had driven the Bourbon despots out of North America, exulting in that 'glorious spirit of Whiggism' which had moved 'three millions of Americans . . . a mighty continental nation' to resist a Tory Patriot King. A continental nation in truth! In due time 'We, the people of the United States', made them a constitution 'to secure the blessings of Liberty' to themselves and their posterity, and in the making of it eschewed theory and consulted their experience of the liberties that were the birthright of Englishmen.

The voices ring out now all round the seven seas. Irishmen were sitting beside the rest in that House of Commons, which 'conceiving the African Slave Trade to be contrary to the principles of justice, humanity and sound policy' relinquished the Empire's share of the traffic in human flesh. 'The meaning of the enactment we take to be' —it is John Company commenting on the Charter Act of 1833— 'that there shall be no governing caste in India; that whatever other tests of qualification may be adopted, distinctions of race and religion shall not be of their number'; while Gladstone, separated by a hundred years from Sir William Johnson of New York on the one hand and Lord Lugard on the other, could, like them, 'conceive it to be an undoubted maxim that the Crown should stand in all matters between the colonists and the natives' and thus secure the greatest happiness of the greatest number. Writing in the very year in which the Commons first occupied their new chamber that was destined to be destroyed in our own day by Goering's bombs, the Scottish Governor-General who made colonial self-government a reality in Canada could avow himself 'possessed with the idea' that British institutions, given 'freely and trustingly', were the best safeguard of the British connection. 'Faith,' Lord Elgin affirmed, 'when it is sincere, is always catching.' Abraham Lincoln knew that well, and held fast also to hope, when he called upon his fellow-countrymen across the Federal and Confederate graves at Gettysburg to 'highly resolve that these dead shall not have died in vain— that this nation, under God, shall have a new birth of freedom— and that government of the people, by the people, for the people, shall not perish from the earth'. And Joseph Chamberlain was surely not untouched by the third great Christian virtue when he appealed to 'the Boers, our former foes', to shake hands and co-operate with the British 'under a flag, which, whatever may be said of us, has at all events protected differences of race, differences of religion, differences of languages'.

Faith, hope and charity were justified in the long run. The free and trusting gift of British institutions was repaid with respect, even affection, and repeated help in time of trouble; the United States, 'conceived in Liberty and dedicated to the proposition that all men are created equal,' remained united and 'neither slavery nor involuntary servitude' survived within her borders; Boers, more truly Afrikander than ever, did shake hands with the British in numbers sufficient to make the Union for a time an inspiration instead of a source of weakness to the Commonwealth. And so the voices rise in a clamorous appeal to liberty: from Imperial Conferences—'autonomous communities within the British Empire, equal in status, in no way subordinate, united in a common allegiance, freely associated'; from Royal Commissions—'more, and not less, participation by the people in the work of government is a real necessity for lasting social advancement'; from Franklin Roosevelt, President of the United States—'We choose human freedom, which is the Christian ideal, . . . we assert our abiding faith in the vitality of our Constitutional Republic as the perpetual home of freedom and tolerance and devotion to the word of God'.

Hear the conclusion of the whole matter from an Afrikander quoting Thucydides to a Scottish University audience—and who have fought for liberty harder than Athenians, Scots and Afrikanders? 'In freedom lies happiness,' said General Smuts at St. Andrews, 'and in courage lies freedom. Freedom is the most ineradicable craving of human nature; without it peace, contentment and happiness, even manhood itself, are not possible.'

INDEX

Z

B/7/58